THE SEVERED SNAKE

DATE DUE

Carolina Academic Press
Ritual Studies Monographs

Pamela J. Stewart
and
Andrew Strathern
Series Editors

THE SEVERED SNAKE

*Matrilineages, Making Place, and
a Melanesian Christianity
in Southeast Solomon Islands*

Michael W. Scott

CAROLINA ACADEMIC PRESS
Durham, North Carolina

Library of Congress Cataloging-in-Publication Data

Scott, Michael W.

  The severed snake : matrilineages, making place, and a Melanesian Christianity in southeast Solomon Islands / by Michael W. Scott.
    p. cm.
  Includes bibliographical references and index.
  ISBN 13: 978-1-59460-153-8 ISBN 10: 1-59460-153-4
  1. Arosi (Solomon Islands people)--Kinship. 2. Arosi (Solomon Islands people)--Land tenure. 3. Arosi (Solomon Islands people)--Religion. 4. Matrilineal kinship--Solomon Islands--Makira and Ulawa. 5. Land tenure--Solomon Islands--Makira and Ulawa. 6. Christianity and culture--Solomon Islands--Makira and Ulawa. 7. Makira and Ulawa (Solomon Islands)--Social life and customs. 8. Makira and Ulawa (Solomon Islands)--Religious life and customs. I. Title.

DU850.S36 2007
305.89'95--dc22

                    2006005146

Carolina Academic Press
700 Kent Street
Durham, North Carolina 27701
Telephone (919) 489-7486
Fax (919) 493-5668
www.cap-press.com

CONTENTS

LIST OF ILLUSTRATIONS

Series Editors' Preface

Andrew Strathern and Pamela J. Stewart

We are pleased to add Michael Scott's book, *The Severed Snake: Matrilineages, Making Place, and a Melanesian Christianity in Southeast Solomon Islands*, to those in the Ritual Studies Monograph Series.[1] Dr. Scott's study of the dialectics of continuity and change on Makira in the Solomon Islands makes a series of fundamental contributions to anthropological thinking: in the context of Solomons ethnography, in relation to wider debates about social structures in the South-West Pacific, and in terms of the historical anthropology of Christianity in colonial and postcolonial circumstances. This series of contributions is linked together by a single consistent theme: the transformations of a basic way of conceptualizing and acting in the world which Dr. Scott defines as one of poly-ontology. By this he means that groups among the Arosi people of Makira have an irreducible notion of their separate origins as ancestrally established groups, each with its own story of its beginnings. Such a notion, we may comment, is a concomitant of a widespread principle among Austronesian-language speakers, identified by anthropologists as the principle of precedence: seniority of claims upon land depends on being recognized as the first comers to the land or as autochthonous to it. Dr. Scott recognizes that the idea of autochthony, combined with poly-ontology, may be modified at different times in a people's ethnohistorical views of themselves. It is nevertheless, he argues, deepseated and tenacious and informs periods of historical change, including for the Arosi the history of colonization, movements of protest, and missionization.

Along with this conceptualization goes another, also found widespread in the Pacific and South-East Asia, that ancestors are as much a part of the group as are its living members. The custom of burying group members inside the houses lived in by their descendants is one testimony to such an idea. Another is to be found in the construction of special tombs that house all the members of a particular group, as described for the Merina of Madagascar by Maurice Bloch (Bloch 1971). The general idea is not, of course, confined to Austronesian speakers, for it is basically found throughout the central highlands of New Guinea and also in the lineage-based acephalous societies discussed long ago by anthropologists such as Meyer Fortes (Fortes 1969). The corporate group of people includes their ancestors. While the ancestors may in some senses be thought of as different from, or outside of, the daily lives of their descendants, they are still seen as essentially linked to them in terms of influence, and as custodians of a range of social norms and guarantors of privileges. This point, then, is also basic to Dr. Scott's argument, in contrast to those who have argued, or have appeared to argue, that the dead are "outside of society." Of course, these matters are contextual and perspectival; but at the heart of the argument is the observation that ancestors are often seen as continuing "powerful presences" in the land, as Dr. Scott remarks on for the Arosi.

In developing his argument, Dr. Scott is giving an original, and surprising, twist to a long-standing debate in anthropology about the character of social life and social groupings in the South-West Pacific. These debates, starting in the early 1960s, have centered on issues of fluidity and fixity. Are social groups fluid or fixed? By picking on certain aspects, one can argue for both viewpoints in any given case. Arguments for fluidity basically derive from observations of the vicissitudes and contingencies of practice and experience; for fixity, from discourses of continuity and ideological bases which inform the character of groups over longer runs of time. In a variant of this debate arguments for fluidity have also focused on ideology, suggesting that the basic ideology is itself one of fluidity, deriving from an idea of persons as themselves the sites of multiple relationships. While this view has some empirical support, Dr. Scott argues that it ignores the other side of ideology, i.e., the idea of the fixity of origins for groups and their separate existence in the world. At the same time he acknowledges that this ideology of the primordial has to be brought into practical connection with the need for groups to make alliances and come to terms with one another in the social world. Dr. Scott's conceptualization, here, is close to that of many New Guinea groups themselves, for example those in the Hagen and Duna areas of the Highlands (Strauss and Tischner 1962; A. Strathern 1972; Strathern and Stewart 2004), whose origin stories often tell of a unique and special source of their vitality derived from a transcendant world of spirits, coupled with a narrative of how each group has also entered into alliances by marriage with others. The opposite conceptualization, made by some anthropologists, reverses this order of primordialities, seeing groups as only contingently and contextually elicited out of a wider, undifferentiated, mono-ontic universe of "relationships." While this model might appear to draw its persuasiveness from the suggestion that groups can in fact be observed to emerge in this way over periods of historical time, it remains the case that there is often a more resilient core of continuity that is persistent over time as well as a constant adaptive flux of changes. The wider reality perhaps encompasses both kinds of process, but Dr. Scott's formulation is certainly one that fits most clearly the indigenous or folk-models that we are aware of from our own field areas (Hagen, Pangia, and the Aluni Valley Duna) in the Papua New Guinea Highlands (see, e.g., Strathern and Stewart 2000a, 2004; and A. Strathern 1984). In any case, his argument should serve to revitalize debates on issues of this sort which for some time now have been muted by the dominance of the elicitation model. By re-formulating the discussion at the deep level of poly-ontologies versus mono-ontological models Dr. Scott has brought a fresh and compelling voice into these debates.

Before leaving this aspect of his work, we should note that Dr. Scott makes it clear that he does not wish to resurrect "descent theory" in its entirety. He means that he does not wish to explain his data simply in terms of "descent." Manifestly, this could not be done, because of the immense changes Arosi society has undergone. But the debates, on both New Guinea and Africa, regarding descent as a principle of social structure, were often confused in the past because of a failure to see how notions of descent operate in domains different from those of filiation or of affiliative residence and co-operation. If we see that the Arosi concept of *auhenua* is essentially a concept about ancestrality and therefore descent in a broad sense, we can understand that it operates as a basic philosophy of personal emplacement in the landscape, and therefore as the sheet-anchor of people's senses of embodiment, place, and identity. Because of the immense changes, including dislocations (or "dis-emplacements"), that have occurred, the Arosi at first told Dr. Scott that there were no *auhenua* groups among them, only "incomers" (*sae boboi*). This was partly because of residential shifts that had occurred from bush areas to coastal areas. Yet later, in private, people reversed this narrative and gave multiple and conflicting stories attributing *auhenua* status to their own matrilineal descent categories, in effect granting precedence to themselves in relation to the areas they had lived in. These covert claims were in turn obscured or overlain by statements that in the new Christian world of community relations, everyone was equal and all were joined together in Christian amity: a religious axiom replacing the axioms of kinship, resulting in complex and ambivalent senses of identity, which, via their inscriptions in place, constitute a heterotopia, in the terms of Foucault as Dr. Scott deploys the concept. It may seem surprising to find Foucault's concept, developed by him for a different context, applied here; but Arjun Appadurai's notion of "ethnoscape," which he invented as a part of his ideas on globalization and transnational flows (Appadurai 1996), can also be applied in micro to the passages of different categories of people through the landscape in New Guinea; so there is no reason why "heterotopia" should not be applied in the case of the Arosi, reminding us that so-called simple contexts may actually be just as complex as any others, with the un-making and re-making of places occurring over time. As with ethnoscapes, so with heterotopias: these notions can be applied comparatively as well as among the Arosi.

Dr. Scott's main focus is on the Arosi themselves, of course. But he briefly notes that aspects of his analysis may apply elsewhere, citing our work among the Duna people. The comparison is a good one, in several ways. It shows that basic ideas may be comparable across different kinds of descent and residence arrangements. The Duna recognize cognatic as well as agnatic descent, and their *rindi*, or traditionally conceived local groups, are seen as linked to their land through an unbroken line of agnatic descent from a founding spirit entity. The representatives of this line of descent, the *anoagaro* or "man-standing" members, are like the *auhenua* members of Arosi groups. The Duna *rindi* had also been severely disrupted and subject to population loss through epidemics of introduced diseases that hit them soon after the arrival of colonial outsiders in their world. Notions of cosmic entropy, or in their terms, "the ground finishing" (*rindi itaraiya*), may have been exacerbated by this experience of illnesses and deaths, although they are in principle focused on myth-narratives of greater antiquity. With the Duna, the epidemics came in the 1960s; with the Arosi they were much earlier, and were followed by massive land alienation in the Solomons generally, a process that did not occur at all with the Duna. However, this loss of people among the Duna may have led to a greater renewed stress on the agnatic genealogies protecting people's ultimate spiritual and practical links to the land. In Hagen, also, among one group, the Kawelka, a massive precolonial migration of the group to a different area, occasioned by a catastrophic defeat in warfare, was followed in early colonial times after initial "pacification," by a return to the previous territory, and this was validated in part with reference to the genealogies of a few men who had clung on to their residence in the territory after others had all left it (see for example Strathern and Stewart 1998 and n.d.). Among the Duna origin stories, or *malu*, recount the pathways from original places traversed by some groups, and in the late 1990s these stories were renewed and brought out more into the public domain when an oil company set up a drilling rig near to the Strickland River which marks the western end of the Duna speaking groups. What was uncovered in this process was like a mild version of heterotopia. Conflict was avoided partly by all the groups making potential claims to royalties, and partly by the fact that at this time the drilling for oil was unsuccessful (see Stewart and Strathern 2002 for a full discussion).

Among the Arosi the Administration had ordered the early consolidation of residences into census villages, where people could readily be assessed for head tax purposes. Later, after the aura of further disruptions occasioned by World War II and the impact of American troops in the Solomons, Maasina Rule emerged as a concerted attempt to improve people's perceived economic and political standing. Americans were seen as returning descendants of abducted ancestors, who might also, however, supersede local people's claims to their land. Indigenous practices were revived and codified in a "school of custom," as happened also with the Kwaio and others in the Solomons (Keesing 1992). Rumors spread widely, as they are apt to do in circumstances of uncertainty (see Stewart and Strathern 2004). And "custom" was set up in opposition to "kolonia," British rule. In the midst of this, the Arosi themselves decided to leave their bush territories and colonize the coastal areas. Dr. Scott points out two things here: one is that the move to the coast was a response to the perceived threat of land alienation, and that it paradoxically acted also to cut off the people from their old territories. In this regard, *auhenua* claims were made more problematic, contributing to the later situation of heterotopia. Dilemmas and complexities resulting from this move perhaps included alterations in the meanings of the ritual of cutting the umbilical cord of childhood and planting it along with a coconut palm as a mark of local emplacement and coeval growth. In the old territories this may possibly (although Dr. Scott was not able to establish this point) have marked a direct matrilineal tie to the land; but, if so, in the new ones this meaning could not be sustained. However the act still signifies a link to the land of Makira in general, paralleled by further acts to consolidate that link. Overall, the Maasina Rule movement, Dr. Scott suggests, should be seen partly as a kind of civil rights movement, a formulation that could also be applied comparatively.

When he comes to discuss the influences of Christianity, Dr. Scott weaves together Arosi cosmogonic myth relating to the snake grandmother Hatoibwari and crucial events of change. "Hatoibwari" can stand for a particular lineage or be expanded as a trope to stand for the whole island of Makira (on cross-cultural ideas regarding pythons, see Strathern and Stewart 2000b). In the same way Christianity stands for the whole community, linking the various covertly recognized *auhenua* groups together. Christianity, through the idea of one universal human origin, provides a new mono-ontology which may, incidentally, have contributed to the process of making earlier origin traditions, with their poly-ontological implications, secret. Individuals struggle with the implications of this new transformation, and tentative "ethno-theologies" are produced. Christianity in some ways implies a rejection of the past. Yet in other ways, it may be used to reaffirm certain values, as in the local idea that God would sympathize with the claims of the *auhenua* groups to their land. Arosi ethno-theologies therefore consist of both "past-renouncing and past-affirming" reflexive elements (see Strathern and Stewart 2004 for comparable discussion of New Guinea highlands cases, including the Pangia case as analyzed by Jeffrey Clark, Clark 2000, and compare also Burt 1994). The emphasis here on the efforts by individuals to think their way through the problems of change as a new kind of "onto-praxis" is valuable, and is mirrored in many ways both by the earlier literature on the phenomena labeled as "cargo cults" (e.g., Burridge 1961; Lawrence 1964; A. Strathern 1979–80; A. Strathern et al. 2002: 66–71), and by more recent studies of turmoils associated with the advent of the millennium (Stewart and Strathern, eds. 1997, 2000; Robbins, Stewart and Strathern, eds. 2001, including the paper by Stritecky 2001) and studies of how people have grappled with Christianity in other parts of the Pacific (e.g., for Papua New Guinea, Barker 1992; Jebens 2005; Robbins 2004). In the Pangia area, already in 1967, less than ten years after effective administration and missionization in one group area, indigenous members of the community would get up in Lutheran church services as semi-formally recognized "committees" of the church, and give their own lengthy and elaborate interpretations of scriptures, weaving mythopoeic ideas around the notion of Christ as "the lamb" (an animal that had never been seen in the area and was therefore a mystery in itself to themselves and their listeners). Throughout New Guinea and the South-West Pacific this mythopoeic faculty has been at work since colonial times (as it undoubtedly was before then), as people have been trying to come to terms with and make use of introduced ideas by "domesticating" them within their own landscapes of cosmological emplacement.

Dr. Scott's book contributes broadly and effectively to these various spheres of the revitalization of anthropological analysis. Like the creators of ethno-theologies, he weaves together old and new strands of analysis into a colorful and rich tapestry, revealing continuity and change, conflict and co-operation, and personal and collective efforts by people to re-shape their senses of being in the world.

Notes

1. Other titles in the Ritual Studies Monograph Series include: *Fragments from Forests and Libraries* (Valerio Valeri), edited by Janet Hoskins, 2001; *The Third Bagre: A Myth Revisited*, by Jack Goody and Kum Gandah, 2003; *Contesting Rituals: Islam and Practices of Identity-Making*, edited by Pamela J. Stewart and Andrew Strathern, 2005; *Ritual and World Change in a Balinese Princedom*, by Lene Pedersen, 2005; *Xhosa Beer Drinking Rituals: Power, Practice and Performance in the South African Rural Periphery*, by Patrick A. McAllister, 2005; *Asian Ritual Systems: Syncretisms and Ruptures*, edited by Pamela J. Stewart and Andrew Strathern, 2006.

References

Appadurai, Arjun 1996. *Modernity at Large: Cultural Dimensions of Globalization*. Minneapolis: University of Minnesota Press.

Barker, John 1992. Christianity in Western Melanesian Ethnography. In James G. Carrier ed. *History and Tradition in Melanesian Anthropology*, pp. 144–73. Berkeley, CA and Oxford: University of California Press.

Bloch, Maurice 1971. *Placing the Dead: Tombs, Ancestral Villages, and Kinship Organisation in Madagascar*. London: Seminar Press.

Burridge, Kenelm O. 1961. *Mambu: A Melanesian Millennium*. London: Methuen and Co.

Burt, Ben 1994. *Tradition and Christianity: The Colonial Transformation of a Solomon Islands Society*. Amsterdam: Harwood.

Clark, Jeffrey 2000. *Steel to Stone: A Chronicle of Colonialism in the Southern Highlands of Papua New Guinea*, ed. by Chris Ballard and Michael Nihill. Oxford: Oxford University Press.

Fortes, Meyer 1969. *Kinship and the Social Order: The Legacy of Lewis Henry Morgan*. Chicago: Aldine.

Jebens, Holger 2005. *Pathways to Heaven: Contesting Mainline and Fundamentalist Christianity in Papua New Guinea*. New York and Oxford: Berghahn.

Keesing, Roger M. 1992. *Custom and Confrontation: The Kwaio Struggle for Cultural Autonomy*. Chicago and London: The University of Chicago Press.

Lawrence, Peter 1964. *Road Belong Cargo. A Study of the Cargo Movement in the Southern Madang District, New Guinea*. Manchester: Manchester University Press.

Robbins, Joel, Pamela J. Stewart, and Andrew Strathern eds. 2001. Charismatic and Pentecostal Christianity in Oceania. *Journal of Ritual Studies* 15 (2).

Robbins, Joel 2004. *Becoming Sinners: Christianity and Moral Torment in a Papua New Guinea Society.* Berkeley, CA: University of California Press.

Stewart, Pamela J. and Andrew Strathern eds. 1997. *Millennial Markers.* Townsville, Australia: James Cook University, Centre for Pacific Studies.

Stewart, Pamela J. and Andrew Strathern eds. 2000. *Millennial Countdown in New Guinea. Ethnohistory* special issue, 47 (1), Duke University Press.

Stewart, Pamela J. and Andrew Strathern 2002. *Remaking the World: Myth, Mining, and Ritual Change among the Duna of Papua New Guinea.* Washington D.C.: Smithsonian Institution Press.

Stewart, Pamela J. and Andrew Strathern 2004. *Witchcraft, Sorcery, Rumors, and Gossip.* Cambridge: Cambridge University Press.

Strathern, Andrew 1972. *One Father, One Blood. Descent and Group Structure among the Melpa People.* Canberra: Australian National University Press.

Strathern, Andrew 1979–80. The red box money cult in Mount Hagen 1968–71, parts 1 and 2. *Oceania* 50: 88–102, and 161–175.

Strathern, Andrew 1984. *A Line of Power.* London: Tavistock.

Strathern, Andrew and Pamela J. Stewart eds. 1998. *Kuk Heritage: Issues and Debates in Papua New Guinea.* University of Pittsburgh: Okari Research Group.

Strathern, Andrew and Pamela J. Stewart 2000a. *Arrow Talk: Transaction, Transition, and Contradiction in a New Guinea Highlands Society.* Kent, OH: The Kent State University Press.

Strathern, Andrew and Pamela J. Stewart 2000b. *The Python's Back: Pathways of Comparison between Indonesia and Melanesia.* Westport, CT and London: Bergin and Garvey.

Strathern, Andrew and Pamela J. Stewart 2004. *Empowering the Past, Confronting the Future: The Duna of Papua New Guinea.* New York: Palgrave Macmillan.

Strathern, Andrew and Pamela J. Stewart n.d. Hagen Settlement Histories: Dispersals and Consolidations. In P. Swadling, J. Golson, and J. Muke eds. *Nine Thousand Years of Gardening: Kuk and the Archaeology of Agriculture in Papua New Guinea.* Bathhurst, Australia: Crawford House Publishing.

Strathern, Andrew, Pamela J. Stewart, Laurence M. Carucci, Lin Poyer, Richard Feinberg, and Cluny Macpherson 2002. *Oceania: An Introduction to the Cultures and Identities of Pacific Islanders.* Durham, NC: Carolina Academic Press.

Strauss, Hermann and Herbert Tischner 1962. *Die Mi-Kultur der Hagenberg—Stämme im Östlichen-Zentral Neuguinea.* Hamburg: Kommissions Verlag Cram, de Gruyter and Co.

Stritecky, Jolene Marie 2001. Israel, America, and the ancestors: narratives of spiritual warfare in a Pentecostal denomination in the Solomon Islands. *Journal of Ritual Studies* 15(2), special issue on "Charismatic and Pentecostal Christianity in Oceania" guest editors Joel Robbins, Pamela J. Stewart and Andrew Strathern, pp. 62–78.

ACKNOWLEDGMENTS

My greatest debt is to the people of Arosi, who in sharing their lives with me and educating me about their ways of being and knowing showed much kindness and generosity. All of the people of Tawatana village with whom I lived for extended periods between February 1992 and December 1993 deserve my special thanks. I must thank first Mr. Benjamin Mononga'i and his wife, Sera Gedetanara, for supporting my research from its inception. I cannot imagine how this work would have been completed without Mr. Ben's trusting response to my initial inquiries as a graduate student in anthropology, his family's loving support throughout my field research, and their unending material care. Casper Kaukeni, a frequent companion and thoughtful teacher, made much of my study possible through his challenging questions and keen insights into Arosi today. I am most grateful for his friendship and the laughter we came to share. I deeply appreciate the many people who taught me the Arosi language, especially Billy Raruimae for his patient and persistent instruction. As I recount in chapter 1, I am grateful to Ben Aharo for orchestrating the construction of my house and for his energetic enthusiasm in all our ventures; to Sebiulan Rodomoi for teaching me to cultivate a garden and accompanying me on a memorable walk to Kirakira; to Lemek Taro for taking me pig hunting; and to George Ta'aiwape and Esther Bwairageni, my closest neighbors once I moved to the Tawatana hamlet.

I am indebted to the many people who extended their hospitality to me as I mapped their hamlets, recorded narratives, and visited gardens. Arosi sat with me for countless hours generously sharing stories, answering questions, engaging me in their daily activities, and sharing gifts of food or betel nut. They include, among others: Harry 'Abu, Keme Amaeo, Henry Awaihaka, Alan 'Awaimae, the late Barnabas Bo'osae, Basil Bunaone, Ishmael Dingi, the late Paul Dururongo, Samuel Ha'aheuru, Elizabeth Ha'ai, Haruta, Hauni, Irene and Gordon Hidawawa, Don Ho'asi, Hoahoura'imae, Eunice Huna, George Huruani, Sakias Kahoa, Clement Keremumu, Sandra Kerimaeoha, the late Elson Kimanioha, Madehu, Rosemary Magewa, Joselyn Manureirei, Dorothy Mononga'imae, Wilfred Muriani, Douglas Mwaru, Michael Ngaraediri, Agnes 'O'oniha'a, Mabel Orakeni, Selwyn Orisiha'a, Lisa Orimae,

Reginald Peri, Ellen Rabu, June Rahe, Harry Ramo, Frank Rautaiha'amwane, the late Eunice Mary Rebiraha, Tomas Rehu'a, John Steel Ri'itau, Shadrack Ruaho'asi, Julianne Ruasau, Martha Saumore, the late Clement Saunigao, Winifred Sauruhi, Hezron Sinaha'a, Soianiha'a, Timoti Sura'au, Batha Surohu, Rosalynn Ta'ai, Christopher Tahaani, Mama Abel Ta'aimaesiburu, Eleanor Tarogoroniha'atei, Michael Taroheia, the late John Christian Tarorodo, Alan Tarosubani, Jim Taroura, Janet Tarugeni, Mama Augustine Taukerei, Abel Tawai, Martin Toku, John Selwyn Toraai, Anges Mary Ubwasiaro, Wilsman Warioha, and Rose Weteau.

I thank all those who hosted me on trips away from Tawatana, especially Graves Waokahi and Mesi at Waarau; Margaret and Johnson Bwaurari at Hauwaibora; Mama Fred Ta'aru and Mary Ta'aru at Taraaharau; Lillian Bebe, Alfred Saromaesimao, Rose and David Raha, Moffat Maetara at 'Ubuna; Peter Itamwaeraha and Nesta Nunu'au at Hagaura; Michael Saikei at Tadahadi; Walter Ramo, Angela Si'oha'a, and Patteson Maetawa and Judy Rahageni at Honiara.

Many other people in Arosi helped make it possible for me to carry out this study. I regret that limited space prevents me from mentioning everyone here by name. In order to acknowledge particular individual's insights and contributions to this study, throughout this ethnography I have changed Arosi personal names only when providing confidential or sensitive information.

Among the many people who provided advice, practical assistance, sustenance, and support in various stages of my work, I am particularly indebted to David Akin, Margaret Atkin, Robert Bera, Bishop Terry Brown, Peter and Mary Bürgi, Ben Burt, Murray Chapman, the late William Davenport, William Donner, Father John Espagne, Richard Feinberg, Lawrence Foanaota, Benson Ha'amori, George Hagaru, Rex Horoi, the late Roger Keesing, John Keopo, Redley Lapo, David and Lillie Makarana, Paul and Elaine Motion, Jens Pinholt, Alec Rukia, Audrey Rusa, Peter Tahaani, Gabriel Taloikwai, Esau Tuza, Moffat Wasuka, and Giles and Elspeth West. I thank Hugh Laracy and his family for graciously providing direction and friendship while I conducted pre-field archival research in Auckland. Geoffrey White kindly provided me with generous post-field hospitality and an institutional home while I stayed in Honolulu.

The field and archival periods of my research were both made possible by a grant from the Wenner-Gren Foundation. The Foundation's assistance is gratefully acknowledged. All research carried out in Solomon Islands was conducted with the permission of the Arosi I Area Council, the Provincial Government of Makira/Ulawa Province, and the National Government of Solomon Islands.

Intellectually, this project has a long trajectory originating in the teaching and mentorship of Simon Mitchell at the University of Glasgow and the guidance and friendship of William E. Mitchell, who first sparked my interest in Oceania when I spent a formative undergraduate year as an international exchange student at the University of Vermont. I respectfully acknowledge the diverse influences and perspectives of the members of my dissertation committee at the University of Chicago: Marshall Sahlins, Raymond Fogelson, and Nancy Munn. As teachers, interlocutors, and critics they have enlightened, complexified, deconstructed and then re-edified my approach to anthropology, modeling for me an always-evolving, re-thinking, open-ended engagement with ethnographic particularity and theoretical debate. Although the late Valerio Valeri did not see this project to completion, it owes much to his early direction of my interests and scholarly example.

A number of people have read and commented on early drafts of various chapters. I thank David Akin, J. Bernard Bate, Judith Boruchoff, David Dinwoodie, Ilana Gershon, Christopher Kirby, Bruce Lincoln, Debra McDougall, Suzanne Oakdale, Michael Puett, and Rob van Veggel. I especially recognize the constructive critical comments of Christine Dureau, Christine Jourdan, Pamela J. Stewart, and Andrew Strathern, all of whom read the manuscript in its entirety.

For their unflagging financial and moral support, I thank my parents, Elizabeth and Cyril Scott, and my brother Peter and his family. Finally, it is difficult to express the debt of gratitude I owe to my wife Krista Ovist. She has given unstinting support, intellectual and otherwise, during the post-field phase of this project. The final form of this book benefits from her interpretive insights, expertise as a historian of religions, and diplomatic editorial and aesthetic suggestions.

I am grateful to the librarians and archivists of Regenstein Library, University of Chicago; the Melanesian Archive, University of California at San Diego; the Auckland Institute and Museum Library; the Auckland Public Library; the Kinder Library, St. John's College, Auckland; the Alexander Turnbull Library, Wellington; the Solomon Islands National Library, Honiara; the Solomon Islands National Archives, Honiara; the Hamilton Library, University of Hawai'i; UCL Library Services, University College London; and the School of Oriental and African Studies (SOAS) Library Archive, London.

I thank Bob Conrow and Tim Colton of Carolina Academic Press and especially Karen Clayton who remained cheerfully obliging and constructively engaged throughout the production process. Credit is due also to Mina Moshkeri of the Design Unit, London School of Economics, who worked patiently with me to design and generate the maps and figures. All photographs from the Beattie Collection were provided by the British Museum and are used with the Museum's permission. On behalf of the Melanesian Mission UK, Canon Desmond Probets granted permission to publish the photograph of Charles E. Fox.

Brief passages from the Prologue and chapters 5 and 6 originally appeared in variant or highly condensed form in "Hybridity, Vacuity, and Blockage: Visions of Chaos from Anthropological Theory, Island Melanesia, and Central Africa," *Comparative Studies in Society and History* 47(1): 190–216 (2005). They are reprinted with the permission of the Society for the Comparative Study of Society and History and Cambridge University Press. Brief passages from the Introduction and chapters 2 and 6 originally appeared in variant form in "Ignorance is Cosmos; Knowledge is Chaos: Articulating a Cosmological Polarity in the Solomon Islands," *Social Analysis* 44(2): 56–83 (2000). They are reprinted with the permission of the University of Adelaide and Berghahn Books. Brief passages in chapter 9 originally appeared in variant form in " 'I was Like Abraham': Notes on the Anthropology of Christianity from the Solomon Islands," *Ethnos* 70(1): 101–125 (2005). They are reprinted with the permission of the National Museum of Ethnography, Stockholm, Sweden, and Taylor and Francis (http://www.tandf.co.uk).

~

All royalties from this book are returned to the people of Arosi for purposes of community support and development.

PROLOGUE

In early 1993, about midway into a nineteen-month period of doctoral research among the Arosi of Makira in the southeast Solomon Islands, I inadvertently stirred up a latent land dispute. The incident that gave offence was my visit, in the company of two men from the coastal village of Tawatana, to an old pre-Christian ossuary situated on a rocky outcrop above the fringing reef. Our visit to the ossuary was the suggestion of one of my escorts, Andru Ba'ewa, whose childhood adventures had included investigating the human skulls and bones still visible at such funerary sites, known in Arosi as *hera*.[1] Andru rightly supposed that, like my anthropological predecessors in the area, Charles Fox, Roger Green, and Daniel Miller, I might be interested in the types of relics he had spied out as a boy. Accordingly, one Sunday afternoon following the regular Anglican church service at Tawatana, Andru and I set off to meet Henry Angisihaka at the gravesite known as Hausi'esi'e.

Because the ossuary is situated about six meters above the beach on top of an hourglass-shaped limestone outcrop, we had to construct and scale a rough pole ladder to reach our goal. Henry went up first into the tangle of palm trees and bushes that, from a distance, gives this top-heavy natural monolith the look of a floating desert island run aground. From below, I heard him mutter something I could not fully hear as he pushed into the thicket. "He is asking, getting permission," Andru explained. "He is saying, 'We know you; we don't come to spoil you, just to visit.' No one from the church has gone up there yet to bless the place, so we must still speak like this. You don't just go up without asking permission."

We climbed up behind Henry, and in the dense undergrowth we eventually located four human skulls along with several long bones set inside a low circle of stones. Apparently undisturbed for many years, some of the bones had become entangled in the roots of a tree that had sprung up and destroyed a por-

---

1. In order to avoid stirring up this controversy again, I use pseudonyms for all personal names in this account.

tion of the stone enclosure. To my surprise, Andru and Henry gingerly but freely handled these relics, holding them up individually and arranging them together so that I might photograph them at what they considered to be the best advantage. While we were thus engaged, three young boys from the neighboring village passed by and, noticing our ladder, clambered up to see what we were doing. They soon seemed to lose interest, however, and moved off as independently as they had arrived, leaving the three of us to relax in a rock shelter below the ossuary. There it emerged in conversation that, despite having greeted the deceased with the salutation, "We know you!" neither Henry nor Andru had any idea whose bones we had been inspecting, nor did they know any lineage narratives that told who had built the grave in the pre-Christian past. That evening I asked John Duruhoro, another of my closest Arosi consultants, what he knew about the place, and he averred that he had never in all his fifty-some-year life heard anything regarding the identity of the dead at Hausi'esi'e.

The following evening I was sitting with Duruhoro when Shem Maeronga, a son of Duruhoro's father's brother, came to warn me that two men from the neighboring village had been in Tawatana that day grumbling to Robert Gupuna about our excursion to Hausi'esi'e. The boys who had briefly joined us had obviously been talking about what they had seen, and now these two men—Taraiburi and his sister's son, Warakori—were disgruntled that they had not been consulted before we visited the *hera*. They had told Gupuna that we should have asked their permission to go up and they wanted him to convey their complaint to the Chairman of the Tawatana Village Committee.

If Taraiburi and Warakori were indignant at what they interpreted as a disrespectful liberty taken against them, Duruhoro and Shem were indignant at their indignation. This complaint, according to Shem, was tantamount to a land claim. By ascribing to themselves authority to grant access to Hausi'esi'e, Taraiburi and Warakori were insinuating that their matrilineage enjoyed ancestral precedence at Hausi'esi'e as the *auhenua*—the original autochthonous matrilineage—of the coastal land surrounding the *hera*. But Duruhoro and Shem found this suggestion preposterous. They knew, they said, that Taraiburi's grandmother was not even Arosi, but had been brought to Makira from a neighboring island; her matrilineage could not possibly be *auhenua* at Hausi'esi'e. Dismissing their grievance as ridiculous, Shem admonished me: "If those people come and ask you for compensation money, don't give it to them—wait first!"

Although he made no reference to it that evening, I suspected that Shem took this strong position on account of his own interest in the land. Unlike Taraiburi and Warakori, however, who seem to identify their matrilineage as the *auhenua* of the place, Shem and his siblings argue that the true original landholders at Hausi'esi'e have long been extinct. They say that control of the land was allocated to Shem's paternal grandfather, Paul Korekore, by a non-matrilineal kinsman of the deceased *auhenua*. In the absence of a recognized autochthonous matrilineage in this area, Shem thus understands a putative bequest to his grandfather and the subsequent history of occupation by three generations of Korekore's descendants to be the only valid criteria for determining who has authority in the environs of Hausi'esi'e.

As I reflected on Shem's motives for intervening on my behalf in this light, I also considered that Duruhoro represented yet a third construction of who rightly maintains oversight of this land. Himself a grandson of Korekore on his father's side, Duruhoro had told me on several previous occasions that he gave his general endorsement to Shem's interpretation of the current disposition of the land. But I was also aware that, at the same time, he tacitly understands his own—still very much alive—matrilineage to be the authentic *auhenua* of the land in question. While Duruhoro does not deny that Korekore had been invited to settle on the land, he quietly holds that the man who extended this invitation was not a non-lineage representative of the late *auhenua* but an ancestor from within his own matrilineage. Thus, from Duruhoro's point of view, his matrilineage's interest in the land is prior to and encompasses that of "the children of Korekore."

On the following morning the picture became even more complex.

I went down to the main hamlet of the village to continue work on the construction of a guesthouse that I would soon occupy. As we sat assembling thatch sections out of sago palm leaves, I learned from Andru Ba'ewa, one of my accomplices in alleged trespass, that he had heard directly from Robert Gupuna about the complaint against us. But he seemed unperturbed at the possibility of an escalating dispute. "Let them bring it up," he said, "and we'll have Shem's youngest brother speak about it. He will speak to show that even the young people know that Taraiburi's group came here from elsewhere ... but if they want to talk about the *hera*, our fathers will speak."

Like Shem and Duruhoro, Andru inferred that Taraiburi and Warakori brought their complaint on the grounds that they represent the *auhenua* matrilineage of the land at Hausi'esi'e. He was suggesting that even Shem's youngest brother could refute their claim by his knowledge of their alien origins. It was also possible, however, that Taraiburi and Warakori would try to counter this evidence with a narrative of their own that attributed both the construction of the *hera* and the human remains there to their matrilineal ancestors. This was to be expected because, although Arosi no longer openly make sacrifices at *hera* or at the spirit-shark shrines known as *birubiru*, these

Figure 0.1. Hausi'esi'e: "That is a very old *hera*, so there's a chance that no one knows who was placed in it."

sacred sites, collectively called *dora maea*, remain active as indices of unique *auhenua* identities in the land and as the loci of enduring ancestral powers. Arosi agree that only one matrilineage can be *auhenua* at any place, and members of such a matrilineage should be able to narrate a genealogy that tells how their ancestors alone first occupied their land, made ossuaries, created tabu places, formed shrines to the spirits of their dead, and left personal names associated with areas of habitation. Andru anticipated that, should Taraiburi and Warakori reference Hausi'esi'e in this way, he would have to call on village seniors who might know different stories about the *hera* that would challenge such an account. But he also admitted, "That is a very old *hera*, so there's a chance that no one knows who was placed in it."

Then, after a pause, Andru offered an entirely new perspective on the matter—one that involved yet a third possible *auhenua* matrilineage at the site. Perhaps, he volunteered, Hausi'esi'e is a *hera* belonging to his father's matrilineage. Before her marriage, his father's maternal grandmother had lived in a hamlet near Hausi'esi'e. This fact made it likely, Andru reasoned, that her matrilineage was *auhenua* there. To this speculation he added, almost as an afterthought, "On Sunday night I had a dream after visiting that *hera*. I didn't sleep well. I dreamed that someone was coming toward me with a strong light like a flashlight. Then I woke up."

* * *

At first impression, Arosi—like many people in postcolonial contexts—seem to inhabit what some analysts would characterize as a culturally fragmented, ruptured, heterogeneous, and hybridized world. A recent colonial and postcolonial history of broadening and proliferating interconnection has intensified the normal processes of borrowing and hybridization, travel and exchange, that have always characterized Makira as part of the Oceanic "sea of islands" (Hauʻofa 1994, 2000; cf. Gupta and Ferguson 1997; Thomas 1997). Makira, also known as San Cristoval, first entered European awareness in 1568 with the arrival of the Spanish explorer Álvaro de Mendaña. Following whalers and traders, Anglican missionaries arrived in the mid nineteenth century, regularly taking island youths back to their school in New Zealand. Labor recruitment to Queensland and Fiji between 1870 and 1911 also placed Arosi people in unfamiliar Pacific settings from which they brought back a variety of foreign goods and new ideas about their relationships to other parts of the world. In 1893 Britain declared the Solomon Islands a Protectorate, and colonial administrators, together with Christian missionaries, introduced sweeping changes that included pacification, socio-spatial reorganization, and the appointment of village headmen in lieu of ritually anointed chiefs. These changes helped to localize "the Arosi" as a category of people regulated in a place called Arosi. Today the electoral districts of Arosi I and II at the northwest end of Makira are nested within the larger provincial and central political order of a nation-state independent since 1978 and known simply as Solomon Islands.[2] Virtually every aspect of Arosi life has undergone exceptionally rapid and extensive reconfiguration: Arosi no longer speak, worship, dress, construct houses, cultivate gardens, cook food, or organize communal work in the ways they used to do. Moreover, as reflected in the multiple perspectives elicited by my visit to Hausiʻesiʻe, the changes of the last two centuries have dislocated and transformed a land tenure and village polity system predicated on *auhenua* matrilineages anchored in their ancestral territories.

Three principal historical processes—depopulation, local deterritorialization, and the acceptance of Christianity—have especially problematized the reproduction of coastal *auhenua* identities in Arosi. From the mid nineteenth century, introduced diseases decimated many Arosi villages, and assertions like Shem's that the *auhenua* matrilineage of a given place is extinct are now

---

2. Although some readers will find it ungrammatical, I omit the definite article with the proper name of the nation-state of Solomon Islands in accordance with Solomon Islands usage since 1975 (Saemala 1983).

common. Partly in response to the crisis of disease and depopulation, missionaries and Protectorate officials encouraged the resettlement of bush-dwelling Arosi to the coast in the early twentieth century. References to this period of relocation inform a current Arosi discourse through which many people on the coast describe themselves—but more frequently their neighbors—as *sae boboi*, "people who have come from elsewhere." Arosi understandings of Christianity have furthermore rendered attitudes toward the physical markers of matrilineal connection to land highly ambivalent. Most Arosi assume that the spirits of the dead, called *adaro*, are still present and potentially dangerous at several types of sacred sites, regardless of whether Christian exorcisms have been performed at them. Several of my consultants vividly likened the spirits resident at *hera* and other such sites to a radar system: *adaro* observe everyone in the vicinity and protect those whom they recognize as their descendents but punish unknown interlopers. Owing to differing ideas regarding the relationship between the Christian God and the agency of *adaro*, however, the degree and manner in which *adaro* continue to influence events is subject to differing Arosi interpretations. There are even a few people who condemn the reckoning of relationship to land through *dora maea* as "arguing from the time of darkness," the time before Christianity.

These interdependent influences have fostered a general uncertainty among Arosi regarding the history of the coastal land where nearly everyone is now concentrated. Just as Andru and Duruhoro expressed ignorance about Hausi'esi'e, many Arosi similarly lack specific knowledge, or are skeptical of claims they have heard, regarding which matrilineages founded other local *dora maea*. Duruhoro's covert self-understanding as *auhenua* in the environs of Hausi'esi'e shows that it is not impossible to hold an *auhenua* identity at a particular place without such knowledge, but Andru's concern that the *hera* may be too old for anyone to know anything about it reveals how difficult it is for Arosi to enact discursively and experience a connection to a place without a lineage narrative that contextualizes it. Andru's dream is, I suggest, parabolic of the way many Arosi feel about their relationship to certain places. They endow the land on which they live with keen eyes that scrutinize them, as if under an intense beam of light, but they may not know who it is that sees them and whether they have been seen as a relative or as a stranger.

Yet, if the fallout from my visit to Hausi'esi'e seems to demonstrate the ruptured nature of Arosi socio-spatial order, it also reveals that there is simultaneously a more elusive side of Arosi life in which people are striving to reproduce what they regard as their customary land tenure system. This less accessible side of local life is one in which, through a variety of discursive and non-discursive techniques analyzed throughout this book, members of competing matrilineages are quietly emplacing themselves as the *auhenua* of their littoral villages in contradictory ways. For reasons explained in the Introduction, this enterprise is not a cooperative one, however. Rather, as Duruhoro's tacit self-understanding as an *auhenua* person in the environs of Hausi'esi'e exemplifies, members of different matrilineages may covertly see themselves as representatives of the true *auhenua* of the coast even while paying lip service to the general consensus that such matrilineages are extinct. This covert but pervasive construction of incompatible *auhenua* identities has produced an intangible and invisible spatial phenomenon that is aptly comprehended by Michel Foucault's (1986: 25) notion of a heterotopia—a physical context "capable of juxtaposing in a single real place several spaces, several sites that are in themselves incompatible." Constituted by diverse matrilineal points of view on the same terrain, this heterotopia is the inadvertent result of Arosi attempts to fill a socially and morally depleted landscape through the formation of mutually generative relationships among matrilineages, places, and the ancestral subjectivities said to inhabit them.

Why and how do Arosi negotiate "the special problems that beset the production of locality" (Appadurai 1996: 188) in postcolonial contexts in ways that produce heterotopia? It is the integrating thesis of this book that anthropological understanding of Arosi heterotopia depends on analysis of Arosi ideas about ontology and cosmology. More precisely, such understanding requires recognition and theorization of the largely overlooked model of being and relatedness I term poly-ontology and its practical manifestations. Not unique to Arosi, this model of ontology—as an ethnographically precipitated datum rather than an anthropologically applied philosophical premise—is here formulated and contrasted with mono-ontology as an important category for the comparative study of ontologies and their embeddedness in the social and spatial organization of experience and practice. Both in and beyond Solomon Islands, moreover, such comparative study of ontologies and their materialization in local modes of making place is increasingly relevant to state and international projects of political, legal, and developmental engagement with a variety of lived heterotopias as sites of actual and potential conflict.

For a period beginning in the late 1990s, Solomon Islands as a nation-state became administratively disabled and socially fractured by internal strife, peaking between 2000–03 in incidents of murder and civil combat between armed factions, primarily on Guadalcanal, the seat of national government. Multiple problems and grievances contributed to this situation, including loss of export revenue owing to the Asian financial crisis of the 1990s, mismanagement of natural resource extraction and foreign investment, lack of employment opportunities coupled with increased fee-based education, and the widespread perception of government as compromised by corruption. Among these causes of tension, disputes between those who understand themselves to be customary land owners on Guadalcanal and those they see as usurpers—economic migrants from other islands; purchasers of improperly alienated land; and the government itself—have been especially volatile and intractable (Dinnen 2002; Fraenkel 2004; Moore 2004).

Accordingly, in late July 2003, when the deployment of over 2000 military personnel as part of the Australia-led Regional Assistance Mission to Solomon Islands (RAMSI) occasioned a rush of communication on ASAOnet, an email list-serve for Oceanist studies hosted by the Association for Social Anthropology in Oceania, one issue immediately surfaced by this intervention was the question of whether it is possible or desirable to implement customary land registration in Solomon Islands as a preventative against future outbreaks of violence over land. In West Kwara'ae (Malaita), it emerged, a successful initiative to write down genealogies and sort out customary land tenure had been cut short by the coup that ended the government of Bartholomew Ulufa'alu in 2000. But the suggestion that this program ought to be resuscitated with the aid of RAMSI and generalized in some form throughout Solomons Islands prompted a number of skeptical responses. People familiar with a variety of Solomon Islands and other Melanesian contexts were quick to point out that land tenure custom exhibits enormous local variation; there could be no one-size-fits-all system of government-implemented land registration. Moreover, the example of West Kwara'ae notwithstanding, several contributors expressed doubt whether the requisite consensus on matters such as genealogies and territorial boundaries could ever be achieved in the regions they knew. Even highly devolved local projects of land registration, they suggested, might therefore prove impractical in some places.

This book does not pretend to offer a solution to the vexing and, for the citizens of Pacific nation-states, vitally pressing dilemmas of land tenure. Rather, what it contributes is a detailed explanation of one among many specific Solomon Islands land tenure systems that seeks to lay bare—to its ontological foundations—the dynamic workings of that system: its fundamental assumptions about the nature of being, the practical consequences of those assumptions, and what ultimately is at stake for Arosi, existentially and materially, in the current possibilities for postcolonial and Christian transformations of those assumptions.

ABBREVIATIONS

Note: Most abbreviations pertain to the description of items in the records of the British Solomon Islands Protectorate. Others refer to institutions and archival collections listed in the bibliography.

ABM	Australian Board of Missions
ADO	Acting District Officer
AR	Eastern District Annual Report (and successor titles)
ARC	Acting Resident Commissioner
ATR	Arosi Sub-District Tour Report (title varies)
BC	British Consul
BSIP	British Solomon Islands Protectorate
DCCS	District Commissioner, Central Solomons
DO	District Officer
DOSD	District Officer, Southern Division
IMA	Inspection of Mining Area
MM	Melanesian Mission
MR	Eastern District Monthly Report (and successor titles)
PIM	*Pacific Islands Monthly*
PMB	Pacific Manuscripts Bureau Microfilms, Australian National University and subscription libraries
QR	Eastern District Quarterly Report (and successor titles)
RC	Resident Commissioner
RCCNSI	Roman Catholic Church, North Solomon Islands
SG	Secretary of Government
SSEM	South Sea Evangelical Mission
TBCP	Tahiti British Consulate Papers
WPHC	Western Pacific High Commission

THE SEVERED SNAKE

COMPARATIVE ONTOLOGY

Getting Our Ontological Assumptions Right

Twenty years ago, Fredrik Barth observed that in the anthropological investigation of cultural variation "we must always struggle to *get our ontological assumptions right*: to ascribe to our object of study only those properties and capabilities that we have reasonable ground to believe it to possess" (1987: 8, italics in original). For Barth, this meant grounding structural analyses of ritual in local histories and social processes so that such analyses arise from and reference, not putatively universal logics and their permutations, but empirical events—lived realities, interactions, perceptions, dilemmas, and innovations. In my doctoral dissertation (Scott 2001; cf. 2000), from which the present ethnography evolved, I sought seriously and systematically to apply Barth's injunction and to develop it into a general methodology for the study of the historical transformation and reproduction of cultural processes. In so doing, I interpreted Barth's rejection of ahistorical structuralist comparisons on the grounds that they generalize a particular (implicitly Western) ontological outlook as a call to investigate indigenous ontologies and their relationships to processes of cultural and historical change. Informed also by Gregory Schrempp's (1992) work on comparative cosmology, I argued that such an anthropology of ontology must inquire first and foremost of the historical or social context under study: What are the root assumptions operative here concerning the essential nature of things and their relationships within multiplex, and at times even contradictory, cosmological schemes? By paying primary attention to these ontological questions, anthropological analysis avoids, not only the unmotivated global comparisons of early structuralism that Barth (1987: 8) critiqued, but also the similarly artificial production of rubrics (power, knowledge, identity, hybridity, etc.) or recourse to isolated socio-cultural phenomena (land tenure, land disputes, leadership, violence, etc.) as the topical foci for local and cross-cultural study. The ontology-centered method I began to formulate asks how these concepts and phenomena manifest contextually specific mappings of the number, nature, and interconnections among fundamental categories of being.

Within the past decade, a number of other anthropologists have independently begun to promote the ethnography and theorization of indigenous ontologies as an intentional focus. With an emphasis on how indigenous people engage with "alien ontologies," especially in Fourth World contexts, John Clammer, Sylvie Poirier, and Eric Schwimmer (2004; cf. Poirier 2005; Povinelli 2002) are demonstrating that it is practically as well as hermeneutically necessary to identify different theories of being and the ways in which they may be implicated in intercultural conflicts. Working in the structuralist tradition, Philippe Descola (2005; cf. 1996; Pedersen 2001) is proposing a comparative typology of ontological schemes based on ethnography from diverse regions and analyzed in terms of abstract logical as well as concrete social relationships. Other ethnographers have pointed to the work of Bruce Kapferer (1988) as a model for an ontology-sensitive approach to thought and practice (e.g., Lattas 1998; Taylor 1999), and still others have noted that the study of what has often been labeled indigenous epistemology is inseparable from questions of ontology (Bird-David 1999: S87; Viveiros de Castro 1999: S79; cf. Poirier 2005: 10). This book represents a contribution, therefore, to a non-unified but growing literature that explores the ways in which human imagination and agency reference and reveal different configurations of the essential nature of things.

As well as picking up a lead from Barth, the particular turn to ontology proposed here also draws on and seeks to elaborate Marshall Sahlins's comparative work on the intersection among ontology, cosmology, and praxis. Sahlins (1985: xv; cf. 1981: 13) points out that cosmology, especially as laid out in cosmogonic myth, often provides the "most abstract representation" of the categories of being posited in a given cultural context. This is because cosmogonic myths not only offer accounts of the origin of all things, they also often explicitly formulate the relations and distinctions thought to exist in the cosmos. These relations and distinctions, in turn, can inform human actions and thus entail historical consequences. In a now classic example, Sahlins (1985: Chapter 1) develops this correlation among cosmogony, ontology, and praxis in the context of his analysis of the "Aphrodisian" pattern of Hawaiian culture. Recounting the primordial unions between male and female principles that characterize both Hawaiian and Maori cosmogonic processes, he elucidates the way in which the Hawaiian ontological system of "commonalities and differentiations of substance" (1985: 14) is generated. The ontological relations and distinctions in Hawaiian culture—between men and women, chiefs and people, gods and humans, etc.—and "the paradigms of their historical actions" (1985: 14) are, Sahlins argues, represented in their cosmogonic mythology. Thus, every Hawaiian sexual union is part of "a total cosmological project of sexual reproduction" that "recapitulates the original congress of male heavens and female earth ..." (1985: 13, 14).[1]

In the study of Arosi, however, the analytical turn to ontology cannot begin with recourse to an ancient corpus of cosmogonic myth. Like many Melanesians, Arosi do not tell all-encompassing cosmogonic myths that condense the relations among the categories of being they recognize. Consequently, there is no single shared narrative that lays out the ontological premises of Arosi cosmology. Rather, Arosi hold a number of unintegrated and often closely guarded lineage narratives, each of which describes the formation of a single discrete ontological category.

Oceanists, responding to similarly non-totalizing narrative traditions elsewhere in Melanesia, have frequently sought to elucidate cosmologies through the examination of ritual symbolism (e.g., Barth 1975; Gell 1975; Schieffelin 1976). Today, however, Arosi no longer perform any large-scale rituals that might provide a means of access to the dynamics of their cosmology. But the absence of comprehensive myths and rituals does not mean that Arosi cosmology and ontology are inaccessible or unintelligible. As Christopher Healey notes, "cosmologies are not figured exclusively in the religious or ritual domain" (1988: 106). Rather, cosmologies "emerge contextually and partially" in actual social situations (Healey 1988: 107; cf. Mimica 1981, 1988; Silverman 1996). For the Maring of Papua New Guinea among whom Healey studied, such situations include warfare, witchcraft accusations, and encounters with wild animals. Similarly, while Arosi generally do not discuss their ideas about the nature of being in a direct and systematic fashion, one can come to understand Arosi ontology and cosmology through the close observation and analysis of everyday problems and practices. Arosi ontological assumptions become apparent when one explores such varied and frequently mundane fieldwork data as marriage, childbirth, planting an infant's umbilical cord, dream reports, illness, gardening practices, treatment of ancestral shrines, and village meetings. These and other aspects of Arosi thought and practice furthermore suggest that Arosi cosmology and ontology are most fully condensed in the multivalent conjuncture of discourse and practice to which Arosi, from one direction or another, regularly return: the way of being and becoming they call *auhenua*.

---

1. For a critical response to the claim that such appeals to cosmology in the anthropological analysis of practice imply cultural determinism, see Scott 2005a: especially 190–197.

"There Are Many Thoughts in the Idea of *Auhenua*"

The word *auhenua* is a compound of *au*, meaning "person" or "thing," and *henua*, which, along with its local variant *hanua*, is the Arosi exemplar of a widespread group of Austronesian cognates for "land" (e.g., de Coppet 1985; Davenport 1986: 104; Fox 1978; Hviding 1996: 137–141; Keesing 1993: 94; Ravuvu 1983: 70–84; Saura 2002; Williksen-Bakker 1990). Although Arosi offered me the definitions "village," "area of land," or "island" when I queried them about the term *henua*, I never heard people use this word to indicate these referents in everyday speech. In fact, Arosi today do not commonly use the word *henua* on its own. Instead, they generally use this word only in a few compounds and names, as in the words *auhenua* and *hoahenua* (a village divided by disputes), or in the names Henuaasi (the name of a matrilineage and of a submerged island) and Hanuato'o, the Arosi name for Makira that means "The Strong Island."[2]

Over time, I learned to appreciate the truth of one man's observation that "there are many thoughts in the idea of *auhenua*." Arosi use the compound *auhenua* to refer to any living thing, object, or any intrinsic quality of the island of Makira. Rocks, birds, mythical beings, spirits, ethical norms, and human matrilineages can all be said to be *auhenua*. To be *auhenua* is to be essentially and irrevocably autochthonous to the island. The Arosi men and women to whom I was initially directed on the grounds that they were people well versed in Arosi custom (Arosi: *ringeringe*; Solomon Islands Pijin: *kastom*) all agreed in presenting proper Arosi socio-spatial order as constituted by exogamous landholding matrilineages.[3] They frequently employed the lo-

---

2. This name for Makira is also used on the neighboring islands of Ulawa and Small Malaita (Fox 1978: 197; Ivens 1929: 90) and by the Church of Melanesia, which has designated Makira, Ulawa, and their smaller neighboring islands as the Diocese of Hanuato'o since 1991. In the sixteenth century, Spanish explorers named the island San Cristoval (also written San Cristobal, San Christoval, St. Christoval), and this label endures in Euro-American cartography and anthropological literature. In conversation today, however, Arosi typically refer to their island as Makira, an indigenous name originally pertaining to a locale along the shore of what is now known as Makira Harbour (Verguet 1854: 113–115).

3. There has been much scholarly debate concerning the objectification, politicization, and emotional force of custom in Melanesia, especially with reference to Melanesian discourses that deploy the Pijin forms *kastom*, *kastomu*, or *kastam* (e.g., Akin 2004; Foster 1995; Keesing 1982b, 1992; Thomas 1997: Chapter 8; J. Turner 1997; White 1993). Because most of my consultants communicated with me in the Arosi language, however, I have chosen to use the English word "custom" in most instances throughout this book, both in my own voice and to represent my consultants' use of the Arosi term *ringeringe*. By this usage

cution *burunga i auhenua* to designate an Arosi matrilineage that is said to be autochthonous to the island of Makira and that, furthermore, resides in a substantial lineage territory over which it exercises control by virtue of a long history of ancestral habitation.

Thus, in addition to signifying a given condition of simply being of the island, the term *auhenua* also refers to an achieved condition of connection between a particular matrilineage and its territory established in the past through the deeds and deaths of ancestors. Lineage narratives recount how autochthonous ancestors were the first to enter an open uninhabited area of land. By planting trees, building shrines, and entombing their dead, they gave the land form and character and anchored their matrilineages in terrain. Arosi state that the spirits of their deceased ancestors continue to reside in the territory they first inhabited and to hold it through their protective power for their descendants.

When describing to me the relationship between *auhenua* matrilineages and their lands, Peter Itamwaeraha of Hagaura village resorted to graphic representation. He picked up a stick and drew a row of contiguous rectangles in the sand. Each rectangle, he explained, depicted a matrilineage in its land as a spatially discrete unit. This diagram nicely concretizes what I found to be the prevalent conceptualization of an *auhenua* matrilineage: it is the unique combination of a matrilineage in its ancestral territory such that no other matrilineage can be the *auhenua* in that space.

Applied in this way to matrilineages, it becomes apparent that the concept *auhenua* does not exist in isolation; rather, its semantic value is defined by its semiotic relations with the Arosi concepts *'awataa, mahuara,* and *boboi*. The *'awataa* are those who are not *auhenua* where they live but reside as guests on the land of the *auhenua*. These guests include people (usually but not exclusively women) who have married a member of the *auhenua* lineage and live with their in-laws on the latter's land, and other people whom the *auhenua* have allowed to settle in their land. As one man explained to me by answering his own rhetorical question: "Am I *'awataa* [here] because I only stay here due to a woman, [and because] I live with my in-laws here? That's *'awataa!* I

I do not intend either to accept Arosi representations of indigenous traditions uncritically at face value or to imply that *ringeringe* cannot entail the types of self-conscious objectifications of tradition associated with the Pijin word *kastom*. Rather, my aims are, first, to avoid creating the impression that Arosi consistently use the word *kastom* when speaking of their ancestral ways and thus, second, to avoid reifying *kastom* more than they do (cf. Akin 2004: 302). Accordingly, I use the word *kastom* only with respect to contexts in which my interlocutors made use of this term.

just stay here, I don't have betel nut trees, I don't have coconut palms, [and] I don't have nut trees. [The *'awataa*] only has a woman here with those people of her lineage. I live as an *'awataa*." Because the *'awataa* do not come from the land on which they live, people state that the *'awataa* and their descendants will someday return to the places where their own lineages are *auhenua*. In contrast both to the lineage of the land and to their long-term guests, *mahuara* are strangers who are traveling through the land. *Mahuara* include doctors, nurses, priests, education officials, government employees, and anthropologists who briefly visit a village before continuing on their journey. Finally, the word *boboi* might be glossed as "from elsewhere" or "foreign to the land." Collapsing the distinction between the categories *'awataa* and *mahuara*, *boboi* is the generic term for any non-*auhenua* person or lineage. The term *boboi*, which is used more frequently than either *'awataa* or *mahuara*, has the net effect of reducing these categories to a fundamental opposition between *auhenua* and non-*auhenua*. According to this opposition a person and his or her lineage either is or is not *auhenua* in any particular area.

For Arosi, the term *auhenua* also connotes a set of social and moral practices, or a mode of conduct that a lineage or person ideally ought to embody.[4] People often refer to these practices as constituting the *ringeringe auhenua*, an expression they occasionally translate into the Pijin locution *kastom lo*, or even the equivalent English phrase "custom law." This *ringeringe* includes prohibitions such as: "don't chase people away [from your place]," "don't be selfish," "don't cause fights," "don't gossip," "don't be jealous," "don't steal," and "young men! don't play around [with girls]." These prohibitions tend to take the formal structure of the biblical Ten Commandments, and some people make the parallel quite explicit, stating that the "*ringeringe auhenua* follows the commandments." Many Arosi echoed, in their own terms, one man's formulation: "The Church (*haisoi*) came, but it was not at cross purposes with the *auhenua*; things that *kastom* forbids, the Church also forbids."[5]

The *ringeringe auhenua* also includes positive exhortations. People should "show love," "share with others," have "good thoughts," demonstrate "perseverance," "be gentle," and always "truthful." Once again, Arosi explicitly relate

---

4. Some of the Austronesian cognates of *auhenua* also refer to particular cultural values and social practices (e.g., Ravuvu 1983: 76–84; Williksen-Bakker 1990).

5. The Ten Commandments appear to have been published in the Arosi language for the first time in 1886 and remain a central part of Arosi catechism today (Church of Melanesia 1982: 229–230; MM 1886: 19–20). More or less explicit adaptations of the Ten Commandments as representing pre-Christian practices are also evident elsewhere in Solomon Islands (e.g., Burt and Kwa'ioloa 2001: 15; de Coppet 1985: 81).

these truly Makiran exhortations to Christianity: "The Church's way (*ringeringe haisoi*) of goodness hasn't just newly come … it was already here in the island." Arosi usually stress the continuities—not a contrast—between the pre-Christian *ringeringe auhenua* and ideals of Christian morality. Casper Kaukeni, for example, without any hint of irony, could explain to me in English that "*auhenua* means righteous living pleasing to the devils [i.e., the ancestral spirits] and now [pleasing] to God."[6]

Arosi use the locution *ringeringe auhenua* to refer both to the ways of Makirans in general and to those of their own matrilineages in particular. Adults admonish their children: "Don't follow the ways of people who have merely come [to Makira, because theirs is a] way belonging to a different island." They instruct their children to act, instead, in accordance with "our *ringeringe* belonging to our island." At the same time, Arosi use the expression *ringeringe auhenua* to refer to the customary ways of the original matrilineage of a particular area. These are, they say, "the ways of the lineage of the land." As discussed in chapter 2, when pertaining to the ethical precepts thought to be upheld by an *auhenua* matrilineage in its land, the *ringeringe auhenua* can play a subtle but important role in inhibiting Arosi from engaging openly in land disputes. This is because judgments regarding a person's behavior can be used to question or confirm whether that person is genuinely *auhenua* where he or she resides. It is widely held that people who are truly *auhenua* in a given area of land should not embarrass those who are *sae boboi* (people from elsewhere) in their midst by reminding them of their dependent position in the land. Anxious to avoid displaying delegitimating un-*auhenua*-like qualities, Arosi are careful not to offend others by openly and directly voicing claims to *auhenua* identity. The aftermath of my visit to Hausi'esi'e offers a case in point. Rather than approach the Village Committee directly, Taraiburi and Warakori complained informally to Robert Gupuna, a neutral party known by all to originate from the other end of the island, who could mediate their claim and enable them to avoid the unbecoming act of voicing it themselves. It was due, ultimately, to this general desire to escape criticism for behavior unworthy of the *auhenua* that none of the parties to the conflict surfaced by my visit to the *hera* chose to pursue the matter. As for *sae boboi*, Arosi also expect them to maintain a certain mode of correct conduct. Ideally, they should live quietly on the land of the *auhenua* and follow the latter's lead in all things without provoking them to unseemly assertions of authority.

---

6. The accent on continuities between pre-Christian and Christian morality reflects an important difference between Arosi Anglicanism and Anglicanism on Santa Isabel where, according to White (1991: 127), Cheke Holo speakers emphasize "contrasts with the past."

A central aim of this book is to elucidate how, as well as being the basic units of the present widely-shared Arosi model of customary socio-spatial order, *auhenua* matrilineages are lived and imagined as the bearers of a plurality of originally disjunctive categories of being that remain the presumptive underpinnings of the present postcolonial situation of heterotopia (see Prologue). As described in chapter 4, Arosi represent these elementary categories of being in terms of autonomously arising primordial proto-human beings who became the progenitors of fully human matrilineages through connections that prefigured lineage exogamy. Despite the ongoing processes of lineage exogamy that necessarily enmesh Arosi persons in broad kin networks, the antecedent ontological independence of these categories endures in the unique matrilineal identities of the *auhenua*, who understand themselves to be permanently anchored in their exclusive ancestral territories. The original plurality of these most elementary ontological categories may be described in two ways. First, original plurality implies that the processes of Arosi cosmogony are necessarily poly-genetic; that is, they are processes of aggregation through which an original multiplicity becomes a constructed totality. Second, original plurality implies that Arosi cosmology is fundamentally poly-ontological; that is, it posits a cosmos in which the parts precede the whole. Below, I define these terms more fully and develop a model of Arosi poly-ontology by situating it comparatively vis-à-vis the more familiar cosmogonic and ontological models of mono-genesis and mono-ontology. Having identified the distinguishing features of poly- and mono-ontology, I suggest ways in which an ontology-centered analysis, cognizant of these distinguishing features, can be employed productively alongside the so-called "Melanesian model of sociality."

Accessing Ontologies through Cosmology and Praxis

Mono-ontology

Considerable research has explored the mythologies of mono-genetic cosmologies and their attendant natural philosophies (e.g., Eliade 1965; Fienup-Riordan 1994; Lincoln 1986; B. Smith 1989; Traube 1986; Valeri 1995). Mono-genetic cosmologies assume the consubstantiality of all things as a result of their common origin. Myths of mono-genesis represent processes of internal differentiation and separation within an original unity. These processes can be modeled through a variety of narrative starting points, including sexual generation following the separation of an androgynous monad, self-sacrificial dismemberment, auto-eroticism, or emanation. Regardless of the particular model of original unity employed, or the degree of differentiation imagined, the definitive feature of a mono-genetic cosmology is its underlying monism, or mono-ontology.

Although most familiar from the contexts of religions such as Hinduism or Daoism, or in the form of Neoplatonic philosophical and mystical systems, mono-ontological cosmologies have also been documented in the anthropological study of Melanesia. Among the Iqwaye (Yagwoia) of Morobe Province, Papua New Guinea, Jadran Mimica (1981, 1988) deduces a mono-ontology from a combination of esoteric cosmogonic myth and the indigenous number system. According to Mimica, the Iqwaye inhabit a cosmos that originated from the substance of the primordial anthropomorphic being, Omalyce. Owing to their common source in the body of Omalyce, all the diverse components of the universe share in a single unity of being. "The unity of the primary elements of the cosmos can be understood as meaning that the primordial world, the totality, is a homogeneous extension. Every region of the cosmic being is the same. There is, thus, sameness throughout the primordial whole. All its parts evince a single self-identity" (Mimica 1988: 78). As an original totality, Omalyce comprised all that was to come into being, "but as yet only as the non-differentiated possibilities" (1988: 78, italics omitted). Separation arises from a self-induced cut that bifurcates Omalyce into the binary principles of sky and earth, male and female, sun and moon, day and night. This initial bifurcation, in turn, establishes "the relationship between the one and the two, the basic numerals operative in the Iqwaye counting system whereby all other numbers are generated" (1988: 79).

Without appealing to an all-encompassing cosmogonic myth, James Weiner (1988) ascribes to the Foi of the southern edge of the New Guinea Highlands what may be characterized as a deep mono-ontology. Distilling this outlook from a variety of social practices and myth-based metaphoric relations, Weiner asserts that "[t]he Foi live in … a world of immanent continuity.... The resemblances between—indeed, the essential unity of—all the different human, animal, vegetable, meteorological, and other vitalities is for them 'given' or part of the innate nature of things" (J. Weiner 1988: 9). Again, as in any originally "undifferentiated cosmos" (1988: 14), distinctions are secondary and must be continually reintroduced in order to be maintained. For the Foi the agent of separation is the human actor; thus, "[t]he moral foundation of human action, that contrastive realm that they view in opposition to this given cosmic flow, is to halt, channel, or make distinctions in it for socially important purposes" (1988: 9). Respecting their neighbors, the Daribi, Roy Wagner (1967) argues similarly that the premise of society is a system of given interconnections. Daribi social groups must therefore be formed in opposition to an underlying unity that continually threatens to dissolve the differences and boundaries between these groups. Likewise, each person must "defend and define himself" against the diffuse but dangerous forces in the world in order "to keep the freedom and mobility of his soul" and ultimately his distinct "identity" (1967: 62). In such an apparently mono-ontological universe "man's obligation and moral duty is to differentiate, and differentiate properly" (Wagner 1977: 623).

Arosi Poly-ontology and Totemism

Other than Valerio Valeri (1995; 2001: Chapter 11), few anthropologists or historians of religions have begun explicitly to isolate examples of, and to theorize the nature of poly-genetic cosmologies.[7] Briefly defined, a poly-ontology is any cosmology that posits two or more fundamental and independently arising categories of being. Thus, theoretically, the simplest form that such a cosmology could take is that of a dualism that envisions all things in the universe as belonging to one of two ontological elements. Other poly-ontologies, such as that of Arosi, may understand the universe as the sum of multiple spontaneously generated and essentially different categories of being.

In Arosi, poly-ontology is most unambiguously expressed in narratives of independent autochthonous origins and in spatial representations of the theoretically unique territorial situations of each matrilineage. Made up of multiple matrilineages, understood as carrying forward separate ontological categories, Arosi society depends on forces that construct productive inter-lineage relations through practices that include exogamous marriages, the sharing of access to land, and mutual hospitality. These practices constitute Arosi cosmogony. In such a poly-ontological condition, the achievement of a social polity is the achievement of cosmic order as poly-genesis: the coming together of the many to construct the one.

---

7. Tony Swain's (1993: Chapter 1) reconstruction of precolonial Australian Aboriginal ontology exhibits features of what I am terming a poly-ontology. I approach with caution, however, his claim that the whole of precolonial Australia fits this paradigm. He includes, for example, data pertaining to Yarralin (Northern Territory) in support of his thesis, but Deborah Bird Rose (1986; 1992: 209, 224) gives a Yarralin cosmogonic myth that could be read as indicative of a mono-ontology.

This type of cosmology is not unique to Arosi. Valeri too identified an example of what I refer to as a poly-ontological cosmology among the Huaulu of Seram, Indonesia. According to Valeri, the Huaulu cosmogonic myth

> depicts a society formed by the consensual confederation of originally separate and autonomous groups. In contrast to myths which account for the parts by the breaking apart of an originally undifferentiated whole, the origin myth of Huaulu society puts the parts ontologically before the whole and views the latter as a reversible result, not as a primary, and therefore unchallengeable, condition. (Valeri 2001: 293, references omitted)

Valeri recognized that when a society is formed as an aggregate of ontologically prior units, the resulting community is tentative and vulnerable because it is not envisioned as the original and fundamental premise of order. Rather, the primordial condition of originally separate and autonomous groups is understood to be the permanent foundational ontology on which a secondary structure of relations among disparate groups has been socially constructed. This layering of achieved—and therefore reversible—relationships over an a priori—and therefore immutable—disjuncture exemplifies what philosopher Roy Bhaskar (1994) describes as "ontological stratification." Although each level of reality in a stratified ontology entails practical tendencies, these emerge from, and are influenced by, the deepest level of being.

The deepest level of reality in Arosi is one of poly-ontology represented by diverse, not yet fully human, proto-lineages emerging in social and physical isolation as pure ontological types. This poly-ontological condition is discernable in two main media: one narrative and one spatial. First, individual lineage origin stories depict ontological uniqueness by recounting ultimate origins in the island. Some lineages claim that their ancestors were animate rocks formed with the island; others say they originated from snakes that gave birth to human daughters; another narrates its descent from an anomalously-born female whose mother was killed when her daughter was still in her womb; and two lineages trace themselves to different instances of congress between two species of mythological quasi-human island beings. Members of each lineage may know the origin story of their lineage and may have some knowledge of other lineages' origin stories; unlike Huaulu, however, Arosi share no mythological narrative that encompasses the originally separate and autonomous proto-lineages. The lineages neither own parts of a larger mythological cycle that enfolds the entire island, as has been described elsewhere in island Melanesia (Bonnemaison 1994: 114), nor do they perform a collective ritual in which they symbolically represent themselves as a cosmological totality (Harrison 1988: 330).

Second, the diversity of Arosi categories of being is expressed in terms of the pre-existing nature of the boundaries between different matrilineages' territories. All of my consultants pointed to rivers, the water courses of streams, ridges, and stones as demarcating an unchanging or "natural"—as one man said in English—partitioning of the island. These relatively large lineage territories are supposedly permanent and are thought to have been fixed prior to human activities on the land. Thus, one of my interlocutors listed the rivers on the north coast of Arosi that he believes serve as lineage territory boundaries today. A second person, having described similar boundaries, succinctly characterized how the forerunners of each lineage originated in their own already bounded domains on the island: "The spirit of God placed the lineages on the land; it split the land for us. These divisions in the land already existed."

Figured in their original condition as discrete and, as yet, unrelated categories of being, Arosi proto-lineages appear to be a collection of micro mono-ontologies. When viewed from this "close-up" perspective, each ontological category initially lacks any meaningful or enduring internal differentiations. Arosi narratives depict these isolated primordial entities—whether envisioned in terms of a pre-human agent, an ancestral animal, or a group of proto-people—as existing without the separations and distinctions, personal identities and relationships that define the life of a truly human matrilineage. To introduce a key example analyzed in chapter 4, Arosi accounts highlight that some proto-people are unable to separate a newborn from his or her mother: the mother must be killed in order to deliver the baby. This inability to reproduce rather than replace is symptomatic of a primordial predicament in which proto-lineages are cast as homogeneous groups comprising anonymous and interchangeable actors. Moreover, these proto-lineages inhabit contexts that are seen to be spatially and temporally indeterminate. Land is not yet formed and reformed by the activities of successive generations of human inhabitants, and it is not possible to order events chronologically. In all these respects, no principle of relativity is discernible. Analogous to many mono-genetic macrocosms, which are represented as coming into being through processes of internal division, these monadic proto-lineages give rise to human matrilineages through events that fracture their wholeness without negating their unique ontological unities. Emblematic of these paradoxically broken but integral wholes is the recurring image of the severed snake, a common and multi-form Arosi representation of matrilineal continuity that, even when cut in two, spontaneously rejoins its parts together again as one.

Elsewhere, other poly-ontological systems express ontological diversity through markedly different social forms and natural phenomena. Simon Harrison's (1987, 1988, 1989, 1990, 2001) analysis of the Manambu living at

Avatip, a Sepik River community in Papua New Guinea, presents an example of a cosmology comprising a large number of ontological categories.[8] The numerous Manambu descent groups are not "simply social categories"; rather, they are "the basic intrinsic categories of the world order" (1989: 3). Each group has "its own distinctive origin-myths, land, totems, techniques of magic and sorcery, special hereditary functions in the male initiatory cult, and initiatory sacra such as flutes and slit-drums" (1989: 2). Furthermore, each group claims control over aspects of the natural environment—"the fertility of land, crops and game, the rise and fall of the rivers, and so on" (1989: 2)—so that "virtually everything in the world" (1990: 2) is encompassed by these claims. Bringing their cosmological powers and attendant ceremonial functions to ritual contexts, these descent groups collaborate "to maintain the total world order" (1990: 3). In so doing, these ontologically diverse groups ("'speciated' ritually," in Harrison's phrasing), collectively "represent themselves in ritual and cosmology as an 'organically' indivisible totality and maximally indispensable to each other" (1988: 330). In the context of the "interlocking of cosmological functions" (1987: 500) within these rituals, each group contributes the resources it claims to control and makes them available "for one another's sustenance" (1988: 330).

Harrison's ethnography also bears out the principle that the several categories of being in a poly-ontological system are, at the same time, small-scale mono-ontologies in need of internal differentiation as a prerequisite for the establishment of socio-cosmic order. Theoretically limitless in their geographical extent, the original heterogeneous Manambu clans must undergo internal segmentation through the introduction of "artfully contrived barriers" (2001: 271). These barriers are indispensable to the formation of village polities, each of which is a nexus of multiple clans and subclans that microcosmically replicates a macrocosmic poly-genetic totality. Village cohesion, which Harrison (1993: 64) characterizes as "inherently uncertain and provisional," is predicated on denial of the consubstantiality that binds fellow clan and subclan members across village boundaries. Thus, the very means to achieving inter-category relationships is the suppression, even to the point of violation, of intra-category relationships (Harrison 2001: 269–270). Yet pre-

---

8. Responding to an earlier formulation of this appeal to his ethnography, Simon Harrison (letter to author, March 27, 2002) has registered his general assent that Manambu cosmology is fundamentally poly-ontological. At the same time, he has prompted me to theorize more fully the mono-ontological character of each category of being within a poly-ontology and to take into account the practical consequences that this entails. Without holding him accountable for my use of them, I am grateful for his insights.

cisely because the "categories are immanent in the structure of the world order and cannot be destroyed" (Harrison 1993: 44), these disowned and negated intra-category relationships do not die. At the end of life, the permanent absolute integrity of each category reasserts itself as Manambu anticipate reintegration within their pre-social ontological units in "ghost villages ... compartmentalized among the various descent groups" (Harrison 2001: 263–264).

It is likely, I suggest, that it was the poly-ontological and poly-genetic nature of Arosi social order that the Anglican missionary ethnographer Charles E. Fox was observing when he described what he identified as Arosi totemism.[9] Based on his residence on Makira between 1911 and 1924, Fox's writings constitute the only sustained ethnographic discussion of Makira to date.[10] Fox (1919a, 1924) depicted Arosi as a locus of the "true" or classical form of totemism. In making this judgment, he relied on W. H. R. Rivers's definition of totemism, according to which a diagnostic criterion was "[t]he connexion of a species of animal or plant ... with a definite social group of the community, and typically an exogamous group or clan" (Fox 1924: 350, paraphrasing Rivers 1914, 2: 75). "[T]he totems are birds;" Fox reported, "the people think the clans are descended from them; the birds must not be killed by their clans, and sacrifices are made to them" (1924: 350). He viewed the totems, however, not as differentiating the various exogamous matrilineages, but rather as serving to unify, through a shared cultural form, what he believed were racially and culturally heterogeneous groups of Islanders. Following Rivers's (1914) theory that the Pacific had been peopled by successive waves of immigrants, Fox used racial and evolutionary classifications to argue that totemism was a recent development on Makira. He concluded that the totemism he discovered in Arosi was not "a primitive institution" but was "an introduced and later state of so-

---

9. Colin Allan's (1957: 85, 91) observations that "in Arosi it was stated that lines are completely autonomous" and "older men 'think' of the clans ... as 'different people,'" likewise seem to point to the ethnographic situation that constitutes what I term Arosi poly-ontology.

10. Fox was headmaster (1911–14) of St. Michael's, the Melanesian Mission school at Pamua on Makira, before serving as the "San Cristoval and Ulawa District" missionary from 1915 to 1924. Although the Mission's District Headquarters were at Raubero in Bauro, Fox was often itinerant throughout the island and stayed at Heuru and Wango in Arosi for extended periods—especially between 1920 and 1924 after the district was made into three separate districts with Fox assigned to Arosi and the Melanesian priests Joseph Gilvelte (Bauro) and Martin Marau (Ulawa and Ugi) assigned to the other two districts (Fox 1985: Chapters 7–8; MM SCL, November 16, 1911: 254–255; July 1, 1914: 370–372; March 1, 1916: 673; June 1, 1918: 3–4; May 2, 1921: 7–10; September 1, 1922: 5). For an earlier account of Arosi by a Roman Catholic missionary, see Verguet 1854, 1885.

ciety" (Fox 1924: 276) that overlaid and thus obscured the real racial and social diversity he thought existed on the island.[11]

At first sight, Fox's analysis seems of little relevance to the latent conflicting claims to *auhenua* identities that I found in Arosi, and his work, informed by long outdated diffusionist theories, might appear to be of interest solely to an intellectual historian. Nevertheless, a reconsideration of what Fox called the "fully developed totemism" (1924: 276) of Arosi provides support for an analysis of Arosi matrilineages as the bearers of distinct categories of being and, ultimately, for understanding the nature of present-day Arosi heterotopia. This claim is perhaps surprising given that, even during Fox's (1924: 12) time, totemistic tabus seemed to be on the wane and today the Arosi—who are all Christian—no longer sacrifice to bird totems. Yet despite the decline of "genuine" (Fox 1924: 350) totemistic practices, Arosi ontology continues to posit the independent origins, or poly-genesis, of different matrilineages presupposed in the form of totemism that Fox described.

As noted, Fox depicted Arosi totemism as functioning to create a common set of beliefs and practices that served to conceal the diverse origins of different Makiran peoples. By contrast, Claude Lévi-Strauss, in a generally overlooked passage, observes that "a totemism in which the clans are considered as originating from different species must be, by this fact, polygenetic...." (1963: 31). In Lévi-Strauss's terms, "so-called totemism" is by definition based on the disparate origins of "categories [i.e., species] which are mutually exclusive" (1963: 30). Based on this characterization of the nature of totemism, it appears that Fox, unwittingly sensitive to the diversity of Arosi categories of being, transposed this diversity into a discourse about waves of immigrants as hypothesized by the diffusionist theories of his time. To borrow Lévi-Strauss's (1963: 15) turn of phrase, Fox "vaguely perceived that certain phenomena, arbitrarily grouped and ill analyzed though they may have been, were nevertheless worthy of interest." That is to say, Fox discerned the characteristics of—but misinterpreted—a poly-genetic logic in Arosi.

---

11. Fox and Rivers first met at Norfolk Island and traveled together on board the mission vessel *Southern Cross* in 1908 while Rivers was conducting the Percy Sladen Trust Expedition to Melanesia (on which his *History of Melanesian Society* [1914] was based) and Fox was on his way to Arosi for the first time. An active intellectual dialogue and correspondence followed, which, according to Fox, intensified after he visited Rivers at Cambridge in 1915 (Fox to Smith, in Smith 1924: vi–vii). Although some of this correspondence appears to have been lost (Durrad n.d.: n. 1), I have recently discovered that the Perry Papers at the University College London (UCL) Library, Department of Special Collections, contain the typescripts of eighteen letters from Fox to Rivers (and two from Fox to Grafton Elliot Smith) dated 1915–20.

Onto-praxis

The foregoing examples of mono-ontological and poly-ontological cosmologies suggest that a cosmology can be weighted in favor of a primary deep stratum of ontology. Both sets of cosmological assumptions pertain to the ways in which social actors seek to mediate the tension between unity and distinction, and in neither system is one of these conditions valued to the exclusion of the other. Actors informed by the logic of either system attempt to reach what Lévi-Strauss characterizes as "the threshold, undoubtedly the most profitable to human societies, of a just equilibrium between their unity and diversity" (1983: 255; cf. Valeri 1995: 94–95). Yet, as Wagner's characterization of Daribi "moral duty" (1977: 623) suggests, the first-order problematic for actors engaged with mono-ontological assumptions is to separate substances in a universe that is—in Sahlins's (1985: 13) phrase respecting the Hawaiian cosmos— "charged with immense forces of semantic attraction." Because mono-ontological cosmologies posit the primordial oneness of all things, the relationship between oneness and multiplicity is asymmetrically encoded into a cosmos weighted in favor of unity. Therefore, the primary burden on praxis is to achieve and maintain differentiation. A second-order burden, however, becomes the need to establish productive relations between the categories achieved through separation without undoing the processes of differentiation and reverting to primordial unity. In contrast, poly-ontological cosmologies that posit an original state of plurality present an inversely asymmetrical relationship between unity and diversity. As a first-order burden on praxis, actors engaged with poly-ontological assumptions must create unifying relations among multiple pre-existing categories of being. In so doing, as a second-order burden, they must also find ways to preserve their distinctive identities without rupturing the ties they have formed and reverting to primordial disjunction.

The case of the Manambu as documented by Harrison offers a particularly fascinating example of how the mono-ontological quality of each of the multiple categories within a poly-ontology can seem to equalize the need to promote intra-category separations with the need to promote local communities as instances of inter-category cohesion. By Harrison's account (1993: 49; cf. 2001), the "conceptual substructure" of Manambu clans is an obstacle to the stability of multi-clan village polities such that, in order to create and maintain the latter, the former must be negated. Ironically, then, in this particular situation of deep poly-ontology, the first-order burden on praxis to construct viable unities yields the practical tendency to carve distinctions. Accordingly—at the microcosmic level of their individual descent groups— Manambu appear amenable to comparison with the Iqwaye, Foi, and Daribi as analyzed by Mimica, Weiner, and Wagner, respectively: all appear to give primary attention to projects of partitioning. Yet to allow this comparison to assimilate the Manambu to these other Melanesian peoples as inhabiting a cosmos that is—at its most comprehensive level—"a world of immanent continuity" (J. Weiner 1988: 9) would be seriously to misread the nature of the effects achieved through the carving of Manambu intra-clan distinctions.[12] If, for Foi, to "halt" the "cosmic flow" of certain pre-existent relationships is to "precipitate" other similarly pre-existent relationships out from an otherwise "undifferentiated cosmos" (J. Weiner 1988: 9), for Manambu, to resist the pre-existent "underlying clan structure" (Harrison 1993: 49) is to create the conditions of the possibility for the production of otherwise non-existent cross-clan connections. When viewed from the macrocosmic level of a world constituted as a plurality of multi-clan villages, Manambu acts of differentiation become chiefly, if simultaneously, the means to an inverse end: the forging of the cross-clan links that are the *sine qua non* of socio-cosmic order.

My proposal here—that anthropological interpretations must situate praxis relative to the deepest level of ontology operative within a given cosmological framework—builds on Sahlins's identification of a relationship between cosmologically embedded ontology and historical action. In distinguishing Polynesian cosmological systems from Lévi-Strauss's (1963) "so-called totemism," Sahlins (1985: 13–14, 53) suggests that Polynesian mythologies that represent cosmogony as a "total cosmological project of sexual reproduction" encode a "veritable ontology" with a corresponding "mythopraxis."

> Because this [i.e., Polynesian cosmogonic myth] is a system of common descent, the semantic relations between the several planes of cosmos and society are not metaphoric only, or merely metonymic in the sense of a physical contiguity. Descent in Polynesian thought is a logic of formal classes: the ancestor is to his descendants as a general class is to its particular instances. The offspring are tokens of the

---

12. In her analytical equation of the suppositions underlying the Iqwaye number system and the Manambu system of personal names, Marilyn Strathern (1999: 241–244) appears to suggest such a problematic assimilation. An essential corrective to this mismatching of ontological strata is to recognize that when Harrison (2001: 270) writes, "[t]o Avatip people what is irreducibly given is … an underlying substructure of relatedness, a sociality of which their [village] society therefore represents the partial negation or curtailment," the substructure of relatedness to which he refers pertains only to each discrete descent group and not to the universe as a whole.

parental type. The system, then, is a veritable ontology, having to do with commonalities and differentiations of substance. Relations logically constructed from it—e.g., heavens are to earth as chiefs are to people—are expressions of the essence of things. Hence the relations and deeds of primordial concepts as represented in myth become, for the persons descended of such concepts, the paradigms of their own historical actions. Every Hawaiian union recapitulates the original congress of male heavens and female earth, and what is born of chiefly parents is another god. The genealogical scheme thus serves the *pensée étatique* as "totemism" functions in the *pensée sauvage*. (Sahlins 1985: 14)

Recognizing that "historical actions" that are "expressions of the essence of things" also prevail in cultural contexts where no totalizing cosmogonic myths clearly delineate those essences, Sahlins compares, and at the same time differentiates between, his concept of "mythopraxis" and Pierre Bourdieu's (1977) concept of "habitus." Mythopraxis he defines as the organization of historical action "as the projection of mythical relations," while habitus is structure "practiced primarily through the individual subconscious" (Sahlins 1985: 53–54).

Without necessarily endorsing Sahlins's, arguably reductive, characterization of habitus, I suggest that both mythopraxis and habitus, as models of what mediates between structure and practice, may be refined into a model of what might be termed onto-praxis: that is, the organization of praxis as the situational engagement of social agents with ontological categories—even to the point of sometimes transforming the terms of the deepest stratum of ontology. What I mean by onto-praxis is thus at once as broad as habitus but more specific than either mythopraxis or habitus. It encompasses the mutually transforming relationships, not only between myth and history, but also between the received and internalized dispositions, or practice-generative schemes, of a given socio-cultural context and people's everyday activities therein. At the same time, however, it specifies that the contextually possible and selected answers to questions such as, Which came first, the many or the one? and, Are the categories negotiated in a given situation essentially different or the same? are what is most fundamental to the structuring of practices and their meanings.

In proposing the model of onto-praxis I acknowledge Mimica's (1981, 1988) parallel project of developing the idea of "mythopoeia." Mimica's project seeks to trace the connection between forms of thought and practice and their underlying ontological assumptions by expanding the concept of myth to comprehend more than narrative elaborations of those assumptions. Accordingly, myth-making among the Iqwaye comes to include all modes of articulation of "the Iqwaye way of being in the world" (Mimica 1988: 5), especially their system of enumeration. Sahlins too appears to gesture toward a need to destabilize and reappraise the category of myth. In referring to the traditional narratives of Melanesians as "so-called myths," Sahlins (1995: 180) may mean to suggest that myth, like Lévi-Strauss's (1963) "so-called totemism," is an illusion that is better understood as the representation of a particular conceptual tool applied to the general problem of "being and the world." Although sympathetic with these initiatives to rethink the relationship between myth and ontology, I prefer here to offer the idea of onto-praxis as a more immediate way of describing the nexus between agency and models of being that requires no preliminary re-theorizing of myth and focuses analysis instead on seemingly non-cosmological concepts and speculations and concrete quotidian practices as additional and crucial sources that can render ontology accessible.

Moreover, the study of onto-praxis is the attempt to identify the deepest level of ontology operative in a given time and place, and to situate particular ideas, practices, and institutions with respect to the proper strata of ontology to which they give expression and on which they may impinge in transforming ways. The bivalent nature of precolonial Arosi leadership briefly described in chapter 2 provides a case study. Historically, local Arosi chiefs were given authority and responsibility to fulfill a uniting and stabilizing function. But the forces and processes that promoted stable relations could also erode the primary underlying and necessary integrity of matrilineage identities. Whenever the interests of social cohesion were seen to impinge excessively on the prerogatives of the *auhenua* of a particular place, a remedial anti-social and even violent response could erupt in the form of a warrior or defender of the local lineage and its land. The complementary activities of chief and warrior may be analyzed in terms of the first- and second-order burdens that the poly-ontology of Arosi cosmology can be experienced as placing on human social action.

In the *auhenua*-based polities of precolonial Arosi, the cosmologically delineated first-order burden to create and sustain relations among diverse matrilineages rested on an anointed chief. At the same time, although this chief also shouldered the second-order burden to safeguard and renew the unique identity and privileges of the *auhenua* matrilineage on whose land he built his polity, this burden often also rested on a second personal agent, the warrior. Chief and warrior worked in tandem to achieve and maintain cosmos in the form of a social polity comprising representatives of multiple ontologically distinct matrilineages. Failure to hold these matrilineages together in a balanced compromise between their achieved unity and their a priori diversity could result in two opposing forms of chaos. If a priori diversity gained an excessive upper hand in social relations, the polity could fragment and its lineal constituents scatter back into primordial isolation. Conversely, if achieved unity gained an excessive upper hand, the polity could implode upon itself in a chaos of decentered non-differentiation (cf. Guidieri 1975: 135–136).

Viewed strictly in terms of kinship and social organization, this form of political leadership may appear inevitable and, hence, unremarkable. The descent and land tenure system that Arosi represent as customary—exogamous landholding matrilineages with patri-virilocal residence patterns—resembles several of the social arrangements A. I. Richards (1950) identified as conducive to what she named the "matrilineal puzzle." As in some of the African contexts analyzed by Richards, in Arosi, descent through women provides the primary means of access to land, yet because women usually go to reside where their husbands live, they often reproduce and raise children for their matrilineages away from their own land. Accordingly, the tension between inter-lineage community and matrilineal integrity in any particular place could be analyzed simply as a function of the classic problem of how the matrilineages maintain their numbers and political authority in their territories. When viewed in terms of the ontological stratification implicit in Arosi cosmology, however, this particular chief-warrior paradigm emerges as also a distinctively Arosi articulation of a more fundamental deep ontological problematic (cf. Scott 2007).

Similarly, if regarded strictly as a political phenomenon, the relationship between chief and warrior, especially when instantiated by a set of brothers as it often was, resembles the diarchic kingship shared between sacred seniors and juniors documented for some Polynesian contexts (Valeri 1990; cf. 1982, 1985, 1989). Although beyond the scope of the present analysis, future comparative study of the chief-warrior symbiosis in Arosi and diarchic kingship in precolonial Polynesia may also demonstrate the importance of giving consideration to the influence of deep ontology. *Prima facie*, these two forms of Pacific leadership look deceptively alike. Both map the same polarity of stability and destruction; as in the southeast Solomon Islands, in Polynesia this polarity could be expressed temporally in the life of a chief who moved from violent warrior to sedate leader (Barraud et al. 1994: 44–45; de Coppet 1995: 269; Keesing 1985; Sahlins 1985: Chapter 3; Valeri 1982: 10). If, however, these apparent similarities are contextualized in their respective models of cosmic and social formation, the chief-warrior dyad in Arosi emerges as a systematic inversion of the examples found in Polynesia. Only when the premises of the deepest level of ontology are taken into account can the differences between such phenomenologically similar patterns of action be perceived and recognized for the differences they make.[13]

In ways especially germane to the present study, the otherwise ethnographically rich and analytically productive Comparative Austronesian Project led by James Fox further illustrates the incompleteness of comparative work conducted without a model of ontological stratification. Although attentive to diverse Austronesian "origin structures," contributions to this project omit to interrogate the ontologies implicit in these structures, focusing instead on identifying regional reflexes of an impressively consistent set of metaphors of ancestry and precedence (J. Fox 1988, 1995, 1996). This method has tended to yield imprecise characterizations of the sometimes diverse models of being and relatedness mapped by these metaphors in a given context. E. Douglas Lewis, for example, describes Ata Tana 'Ai (eastern Flores, Indonesia) conceptualizations of clan origins in a manner that seems, at first glance, to point to an instance of poly-ontology: "at the heart of the domain's constitution is the idea that the domain's clans are fundamentally social entities of independent and diverse origins, even though in contemporary times they are closely bound together by both ritual and affinal relations" (1996: 156; cf. 1988: 32, 48, 118). In a subsequent passage, however, Lewis appears to contextualize this assertion within a larger Ata Tana 'Ai theory of mono-genesis: "In the myths of origin of the Ata Tana 'Ai, the time before the creation of the social order was a time in which the major categories of later creation were monadically whole" (1996: 170; cf. 1988: 51). This ad hoc presentation of different images or stages of origin and their corresponding visions of human relatedness raises many questions relevant to the interpretation of Ata Tana 'Ai socio-spatial order. Is it the case that Ata Tana 'Ai maintain more than one view of human origins and ontology? If so, do they coexist in a tensive relationship with practical consequences, or are they separated through patterns of selective attention? Alternatively, is it the case that Ata Tana 'Ai models of human divergence are encompassed by assertions of human unity? If so, what

---

13. As the subtitle to Sahlins's (1985: Chapter 3) essay "The Stranger-King; or, Dumézil Among the Fijians" makes plain, the diarchic patterns here in question are not even confined to the Pacific, but have been discerned in the records of ancient Indo-European societies as well. In his theory of Indo-European tripartite socio-religious ideology, Georges Dumézil argued that the first function, that of sovereignty, comprised two distinct aspects: the *gravitas*, or peaceful modality and the *celeritas*, or violent modality. Such broad attestation of seemingly analogous concepts and practices further reinforces the need to attend to ontological stratification in comparative endeavors.

practical burdens, emerging from which phase of coming into being, do various rituals and everyday activities primarily address?

Poly-ontology and the Limits of the "Melanesian Model of Sociality"

Contemporary ethnography of Papua New Guinea shares a broad, if not wholly uncritical, commitment to the particular model of Melanesian sociality routinely attributed to Marilyn Strathern (1988), but also largely indebted to the data and insights of Roy Wagner, among others (e.g., Clay 1977, 1986; Mosko 1983, 1985; Munn 1983, 1986; Wagner 1977, 1986; J. Weiner 1988).[14] Historically, this model is traceable to critiques of Africanist descent theory as inadequate to the task of accounting for social formations in the New Guinea Highlands (e.g., Barnes 1962; de Lepervanche 1967–68; Langness 1964; Wagner 1974). Although Strathern and those who find her model analytically productive have not explicitly claimed that it is equally applicable in all Melanesian contexts, the apparent dominance of Papua New Guinea-based anthropological research in defining both what is Melanesia and typically Melanesian (e.g., Sillitoe 1998) and the fact that the model is known as "Melanesian sociality" have combined to privilege this model within anthropological discussions of Melanesia. On the basis of my work in Solomon Islands, however, I find two interrelated problems with this model that, I submit, might be redressed by supplementing the model with attention to the question of deep ontology. First, owing to its intellectual and contextual origins, Strathern's model may be used prescriptively to preclude the possibility of identifying any indigenously recognized singular or stable entities — whether conceptual or empirical — in Melanesian contexts. Second, as a direct consequence of such a prejudicial ban on fixed or given entities — that is to say, on parts in relation to wholes (M. Strathern 1992: Chapter 5) — Strathern's model inevitably constructs the ethnographic situation to which it is applied as the analytical equivalent of a mono-ontology.

---

14. Some recent Melanesianist literature that reflects this broad commitment includes: Bamford 1998; Battaglia 1990; Foster 1995; Harrison 1993; Hirsch 2001; Leach 2003; Mallett 2003; Mosko 1992; Reed 2003; J. Weiner 1995. That the model is becoming taken-for-granted orthodoxy by some Melanesianists is evident in general discourse about the Melanesian person as "relational" (e.g., Foster 2002: 75; Robbins 2002) and in corrective appeals to the model as a standard by which to evaluate Melanesianist ethnography (e.g., Mosko 2000; M. Strathern 1992: 115 n. 6).

The presumption against the existence of indigenously naturalized unique constituent categories, persons, or groups in Melanesia has its roots in the deconstruction of Africanist descent theory in the early ethnography of Highland New Guinea. Almost from its inception in the 1950s, the anthropology of the Highlands yielded an ostensible paradox: diverse Highlands peoples represented themselves in ways that anthropologists described as patrilineal, yet in practice these same peoples did not consistently privilege patrilineal descent as a criterion of recruitment to social groups. Despite often strong indigenous discourses of what ethnographers termed patrilineality, a host of potential criteria and contingent variables—including relationship through women, histories of co-residence, adoption into agnatic lines, territorial contiguity, the personalities of individual leaders, population density, and economic conditions—appeared to organize Highlands societies in ways that resisted classification in terms of rules or regular correlations between variables. Faced with this apparent mis-match between indigenous discourse and practice, anthropologists attempted to model Highlands societies as exceptions to the rule of unilineal descent by developing the tropes of structural looseness, fluidity, plasticity, and flexibility to describe a wide variety of extra-descent-based social relationships and collectivities (e.g., Kaberry 1967; Pouwer 1960; Watson 1965). These tropes, although initially designed to extend the capacity of descent theory to explain patterns of social practice, highlighted phenomena that challenged the structural-functionalist teleology of stable solidarity and prompted some anthropologists to ask: "are there social groups in the New Guinea Highlands?" (Wagner 1974).

Moreover, debates regarding the perceived incongruity between indigenous ideology and practice contributed to a pluralization of theoretical approaches in Melanesianist anthropology that has tended to eclipse both the concept of descent and the notion of stable social groups. For influential writers such as Harold Scheffler (1965) and Roger Keesing (1971), the observed fluidity and flexibility of many Melanesian social configurations meant that models of descent—whether indigenous or anthropological—are subordinate to contingency and individual choice in the shaping of social action. In contrast, Wagner (1967, 1974, 1977; cf. Schneider 1965) argued that the same fluidity and flexibility means, not that ideology is secondary or unimportant in social action, but that the notion of descent cannot account for Melanesian social practices because it is exogenous and incommensurable with the "analogic" ideology of relatedness culturally particular to Melanesia (cf. Carrier and Carrier 1991: 18–19). Subsequent Highlands ethnographers concluded that the initial emphasis on patrilineal descent as the core principle of Highlands social organization was exaggerated and turned, along with other Melanesianists, to the

study of exchange and reciprocity for insight into the logic of Melanesian social forms (e.g., Feil 1984; Forge 1972; Schwimmer 1973; Wagner 1967; A.
Weiner 1976). As indicated below, there have been dissenting voices in these
debates that have called for continued anthropological investigation of indigenous idioms of descent and their relationships to practice. Nevertheless, these
broad theoretical and ethnographic developments have combined to deflect interest and analysis away from descent, either as a concept comparable to at least
some Melanesian tropes of relatedness, or as the rationale behind some
Melanesian social formations. This has been especially true in the literature informed by the work of Marilyn Strathern, which largely elides discussion of descent and social formations into analyses of personhood and sociality.

Appropriating McKim Marriott's (1976) idea of the "dividual," Strathern
argues that Melanesians regard a person, not as a unique individual, but as a
composite and partible being produced through a plurality of relationships.
Similarly, a group, in the eyes of Melanesians, is not a given whole but is manifested only when a number of persons elicit one another's potential affinities
and capacities. According to this model, Melanesians see one another as inherently replicating the multiple relationships and substances that produced
them. It is taken for granted that a person is thus born fully integrated within
a pre-existing continuum of those social relationships and substances, and no
mode of relationship takes automatic priority over, or is foundational to, the
others in defining who a person is. There is no baseline person; a person is a
wholly relative or "relational" construct.

It is only in the context of particular lived relationships that a person "de-
pluralizes," or selectively activates some relational aspects of his or her personhood while suppressing others (M. Strathern 1988: 13–14). This process
of de-pluralization can be either the outcome of action initiated by the person or the effect of another person's agency. Furthermore, no person is ever
fully or permanently committed to the activation of only one aspect of personhood; rather, multiple aspects of personhood may be concurrently activated in different relational spheres. The person in this conceptual scheme, although not an integer, is nonetheless a microcosm of all relationality—a
synecdochic or fractal ingredient in a boundless, always already realized field
of sociality (M. Strathern 1988: 176). Nowhere is there an identifiable a priori unit; in every context, human action serves to individuate persons and collectivities by means of processes variously described as "fraction," "partition,"
"de-conception," and "decomposition" (Mosko 1992; M. Strathern 1988; Wagner 1991).

Without seeking to deny that Strathern's model may be descriptively accurate for some Melanesian contexts, I caution that it should not be generalized

as an analytical tool applicable to all parts of Melanesia (and, increasingly, beyond) without serious qualification and counterbalancing attention to indigenous ontologies.[15] It may be said, for example, that Arosi understand themselves to be the sites of multiple relationships. Like the Melanesians of Strathern's model, Arosi too recognize that they are the composite products of the social relationships that went into the processes of their generation and that consequently flow through them in their embodied situations. Certain circumstances and events, such as the arrangement of bride-price payments, or practices, such as midwifery and naming, can activate or construct particular subsets of relationships that define persons socially. At the same time, however, it would be inaccurate to say that Arosi persons and collectivities see themselves as entirely relationally determined. From an Arosi point of view, at the core of each Arosi person stands an unchanging matrilineal essence concretely imaged as an unbroken umbilical cord. Whereas an ethnographer looking at Arosi through the lens of Strathern's model might be inclined to conclude that matrilineal connections are elicited only situationally when issues of landholding emerge (cf. Foster 1995: 67), I hope to show, to the contrary, that Arosi grant priority to a map of social, spatial, and, ultimately, cosmic order made up of ontologically unique categories embodied by matrilineages anchored in their mutually exclusive territories. If my interpretation is correct, it suggests that ethnographers ought not to approach all Melanesian social settings with the assumption that there are no integers to be found there. Such assumption may function as a blinder inhibiting the ethnographer from perceiving both empirical and conceptual social, and perhaps ontological, indigenous categories that may, after all, be present in some parts of Melanesia. If persuaded that such categories do not exist, the ethnographer may overlook, minimize, exclude, or otherwise struggle to explain away evidence to the contrary.

This problem is particularly evident in attempts to apply the Melanesian model of sociality to contexts where mortuary rituals appear to reference processes of return to primordial or pre-social root categories that are also often correlated with indigenous models of descent. As documented by ethnographers working in diverse areas of Papua New Guinea (e.g., Fortune 1932; Foster 1995; Harrison 2001; Macintyre 1987, 1989; Munn 1986; Thune 1989;

---

15. With greater and lesser degrees of attention to indigenous ontologies, anthropologists have begun to apply the model of so-called Melanesian sociality developed by Strathern and others to geographical and conceptual contexts beyond Melanesia, including West Africa (Piot 1999), Native Alaska (Fienup-Riordan 1994), the whole of Austronesia (especially Polynesia, Mosko 1992), and the anthropology of art (Gell 1998).

A. Weiner 1978, 1980, 1988), many Melanesians see death as a process that disarticulates putatively autonomous categories, figured as descent lines, from the network of relationships that make up lived sociality. Strathern (1992: 114–115 n. 4) herself even recognizes that, in what she terms "the so-called lineal systems," it is these categories that are regarded as most "complete" in themselves, such that sociality renders them "incomplete" and death restores them to an original integrity. Yet despite this footnoted awareness of Melanesian models of multiple primary essences, Strathern unaccountably asserts that Melanesians "make an assumption of particularism but not essentialism" (1992: 74); that is, they acknowledge no core essences within persons. What is it, then, that "de-composition" gets back to in this type of mortuary distillation of unilineal entities? The possibility of paring back or sloughing off social relations in this way implies the existence of underlying realities, multiple disparate remainders.

In order to prevent such data from undermining her claim that the Melanesian "vision of the world" has "no problem with how parts fit together" (1992: 114), Strathern pushes them outside the frame of her model. She implies that, because a person cut out from social relations at death is no longer a person (1992: 98, 100), ideas about what a dead person becomes are irrelevant to her model, which seeks to describe only how Melanesians understand living persons and fully constituted human sociality. Melanesian visions of primordial, "pre-procreation" (M. Strathern 1992: 115 n. 4), or postmortem conditions are thus not only pre- or post-social, but anti-social—antithetical to the way things really are and therefore corroborative of, rather than challenging to, her representation of the Melanesian vision of the way the world actually is. But to bracket out what amounts to a large measure of myth and religion in this way is to cast these representations of alternative realities as purely negative and negated by the conditions of lived reality and to deny that such representations may entail indigenous assumptions about the necessary and ongoing premises on which lived reality depends. It is to dismiss from the beginning the possibility that, for some Melanesians, such premises may be more real than the way things appear right now.

Representations of conditions prior, contrary, or ultimate to the present are not semantically empty or without practical consequences, however; a fact that can lead those who attempt to apply Strathern's model to such data into instructive difficulties. Robert Foster, for example, develops a persuasive analysis of how Tangan (New Ireland Province, Papua New Guinea) mortuary feasting enables host matrilineages to assert their instantiation of the primordial condition of a mythically imagined autonomous and auto-reproducing matrilineage (Foster 1995: 141–144, 215). But because he accepts that

Strathern's model of integer-less relationality describes what Tangans take to be given and primary, he is compelled to identify a second ancillary form of Tangan sociality, one that "privileges autonomy and self-sufficiency" (1995: 194), in order to account for his own counterindicative findings. This second form of sociality, he argues, is innovated in the rituals themselves when the host matrilineages presume to act autonomously and thereby temporarily eclipse the relational foundations of "conventional" sociality (1995: 218). These latter are never irreversibly negated or totally destroyed, however. The bifurcation of Tangan sociality that mortuary practices induce is a brief rupture in reality, "even a mirage" (1995: 218; cf. 1990: 435, 444), that posits the transient and morally ambiguous possibility of a complementary opposite in which the matrilineages, as "collective individuals," can claim to pre-exist and stand outside their quotidian interdependence (1995: 215–216).

But something is not quite right with this picture if the aim is to apprehend Tangan understandings. The problem is not that Foster interprets Tangan rituals as the sites of symbolic inversions of what Tangans regard as the conditions of normal human sociality. The problem lies rather in the way Foster appears to allow the Melanesian model of sociality to trump Tangan representations of an underlying pre-social condition in his own representations of what Tangans take to be most fundamentally real. This is to invert the import of what Tangans seem to be saying through their myths and mortuary practices: namely, that what Foster subordinates as a secondary form of sociality is what Tangans in fact assume as given, while something resembling the form of sociality described by Strathern's model (but not radically integer-less) is what they see as the constructed outcome of cosmogonic transformations and continuous human strategies for interconnection via exchange. These strategies are required precisely because it is the form of sociality that privileges autonomy and self-sufficiency that Tangans both value and fear as the condition that is never irreversibly negated or totally destroyed. Accordingly, there is a discernible slippage between Foster's (1995: especially 215–216) argument that autonomous matrilineal identities are produced *de novo* in the mortuary context and his acknowledgment that Tangans operate with a general and constant distinction between matrilineal identity as "natural" or "given axiomatically" and paternal relations as "optional," "created" (Foster 1995: 155, 263 n. 20, cf. 68). Furthermore, Foster's own convincing symbolic interpretations of Tangan mortuary practices with reference to Tangan myth suggest that the alternative realities figured in these cultural forms are—not belied by—but

constitutive of what Tangans think they know about the true essential underpinnings of lived sociality and personhood.[16]

As an abstract semiotic critique of Tangan myth and ritual, Foster's analysis is unassailable. And from a social scientific point of view, fully relationally
constituted human beings come first; myth and ritual are epiphenomenal
transformations of otherness. Where Foster may be making one consequen-
tial misstep, I suggest, is in ascribing a functionally equivalent point of view,
under the name of the Melanesian model of sociality, to Tangans themselves
as their most comprehensive outlook. This, ironically, may be to mistake a
cropped view of their model of lived sociality for the whole of their mythic
imagination, the baseline of their understanding of reality relative to which
all other configurations are ultimately ephemeral. But if the most comprehensive Tangan vision of the nature of things is one according to which there
are no entities-in-themselves, only the fluid shaping and reshaping of completed relationship, why do Tangans periodically tell themselves that their matrilineages comprise and can sometimes perfectly embody such self-defined
terms? Their aspirations for permanence and "transcendence" (Foster 1995:
216, 224) might rather be expected to index return, not to multiple matrilineally defined categories, but to the pleroma of relatedness out of which their
lived shifting relational alignments have all been equally passingly precipitated.

Put another way, despite Strathern's (1988: 6) disclaimer that her model
does not describe indigenous Melanesian ontology, but is rather "a kind of
convenient or controlled fiction" for analytical purposes only, the imputation
to genericized Melanesians of a perspective that prioritizes relatedness as
given—with no preconstituted entities or starting points other than the full-
ness of sociality itself—effectively inserts a virtual mono-ontology behind
the conceptual object termed "Melanesian sociality." This is hardly surprising
in light of Marriott's (1976: 109) clear qualification that his concept of the
"dividual" derives from and describes a context of "systematic monism," that
is to say, Hindu cosmology. Characterized as "the whole cloth of universal

---

16. Foster (1990; 1995: 141–142, 215) appears to present the main myth that informs
his analysis as though it refers to the origin of death and sociality at a universal scale only,
implying a mono-genetic origin for the multiple Tangan matrilineages as the products of an
original division within a single primordially self-replicating matrilineage. Thus, Tangan ontology may well be monistic. According to Thune (1989: 156), however, regional variants
of this myth on Normanby Island (Milne Bay Province, Papua New Guinea) also function
at a microcosmic scale to account for the transition of multiple primordial categories from
parthenogenetic wholeness to endogamously constituted human matrilineages (see chapter
8 below). The ambiguity of scale inherent in these myths leaves the question of Tangan ontology open and illustrates the need for closer attention to ontology in such analyses.

congruence" (Wagner 1991: 166), "an open-ended, infinite world" (M. Strathern 1999: 258), or a condition of "universal states or flows" (Goldman, Duffield, and Ballard 1998: 6), Melanesian sociality is conceptualized as a boundless plane of unified being that must be cut at multiple levels in multiple ways to release recognizable entities: societies, villages, groups, and persons (M. Strathern 1992: 113). What is implied in such language is far more than an indigenous view of empirical human society disassociated from mythic, pre- or post-human alternatives; what is implied is a whole indigenous cosmology and ontology. Myth and the non-human have never really been bracketed out, only barred from contradicting. It may well be that the indigenous ontologies of many of the New Guinea peoples whose practices form the empirical foundation on which the model is based are monisms. But once it is recognized that the model entails and imposes a virtual mono-ontology, one has to ask: Why construct an analytical tool that functions in lieu of an indigenous ontology rather than inquire into the nature of actual indigenous ontologies?

In seeking to temper the nascent orthodoxy of Strathern's model with these observations and the counterexample of Arosi, I connect with that strand of Melanesianist anthropology that has continued to explore what Melanesian idioms of descent mean to the people who hold them and what else, if not the strict principles of recruitment to groups, they might be about (e.g., Lederman 1986; de Lepervanche 1967–68: 173; A. Strathern 1972, 1979). This means resisting the injunction written into the Melanesian model of sociality to place Melanesian representations of unilineal descent under erasure on the grounds that "everywhere in this part of the world the composite person is a cognatic system, to be undone or otherwise depluralised, transformed into a unitary entity at particular moments in time" (M. Strathern 1992: 99). In recent ethnography, for example, Andrew Strathern and Pamela Stewart's (2004; Stewart and A. Strathern 2002a) studies of the Aluni Valley Duna of Highland Papua New Guinea take seriously Duna prioritizations of their agnatic lines as the emplaced centers of larger cognatic and otherwise compositionally negotiable residential groups, even where agnates constitute a minority of those settled in their ancestral territories. Members of these agnatic lines furthermore represent and ritually coordinate the multiple land areas, spirit beings, and resources that make up the wider social and ecological world the Duna experience as their cosmos. Working with a similar respect for the possible conceptual salience and practical relevance of unilineal descent discourses in Melanesia, I seek to show how the model of descent through women inherent in the Arosi concept of *auhenua* and the diverse practices with which it is dynamically engaged are ultimately about Arosi cosmology and thus about the categories and transformations of Arosi ontology.

It is not my intention, however, on the basis of this conclusion about Arosi descent idioms, to resurrect classic descent theory disguised as a theory, either of ontology in general, or of poly-ontology in particular. The specific integers composing a poly-ontology need not be descent categories. Theoretically, ontological units could be defined by other criteria, including gender; ritual, political, or other social functions; identity with natural phenomena; control over geo-physical regions or territories; and any other form or practice that can represent identities as grounded in deep ontology.

Moreover, although it may often be productive to interrogate descent idioms for what they reveal about ontology, strong unilineal descent categories alone cannot be taken as diagnostic of poly-ontology—even where people envision the dead as organized according to such categories. It is always possible that what appear to be multiple unrelated descent categories in one social context may be represented in another as the results of processes of cosmogonically achieved separations within an original unity. Correspondingly, death may be viewed as a multiphase return to original unity via graduated funerary processes. In such a scheme, an initial funeral that returns the deceased to a pure unilineal category might index de-conception from social relations (understood as an achieved tertiary stratum rather than a given primary one), back to a secondary stratum of achieved differentiation, prior to further decomposition to a primary monistic stratum by means of further specialized mortuary practices. To discern what levels of ontology are indexed by different ancestral categories or postmortem states requires the analytical juxtapositioning of such categories and states with mutually informing representations of ultimate origins and cosmogonic transformations. In all this the ethnographer must be sensitive to the ease with which variant versions or positioned interpretations of origin myths, different scales of origin, or differing claims about an apical originary being that may or may not unite several or even all descent lines, can invert ontological implications or signal the coexistence of competing, or exoteric versus esoteric, ontologies. Rather than formulating strict rules for correlating descent idioms with ontologies, therefore, this ethnography aims to model an anthropology of ontology, ontological stratification, and ontological pluralism that begins to attend more systematically to the possible interrelations among these and other types of potentially repercussive data.

Constant Cosmogony

In chapters 1–3 I describe and situate historically the current bifurcation of Arosi socio-spatial organization into a surface level based on consensus that the *auhenua* matrilineages of the coast are dead and a hidden level involving competing *auhenua* identities. Traceable in part to such factors as the demise of ritually anointed chiefs of the *auhenua*, disease-induced depopulation, and colonial regimes of reorganization, the surface level is one at which Arosi understand their social polities to be constituted solely through a recent history of mutually "entangling" inter-lineage connections. These connections include exogamous marriages, namesake relationships, obligations of reciprocity perpetuated through cooperation in amassing bride-price, foodstuffs, or other items of exchange, and the putative history of their ancestors' relocation under the auspices of "the people of old." The Melanesian model of sociality would seem adequate for the analysis of such entanglements were it not for the fact that Arosi themselves act and speak in ways that reveal that they regard sociality in this mode to be deficient. If, as Marilyn Strathern (1992: 115 n. 6, following Chowning 1989: 99) implies, studies of the Massim (Papua New Guinea) have distortively emphasized "unilineal groups as though maintaining them were the central concern of their members," by reflecting precisely such a concern, the hidden level of Arosi socio-spatial organization suggests that such a skeptical reading of Melanesian ethnography may, in some cases, be unwarranted. Nor is there evidence that the Arosi concern to maintain unilineal landholding groups is strictly a product of recent colonial and postcolonial history. Presenting Arosi perspectives on the post-World War II political movement known as Maasina Rule, I explore how fears of land loss inculcated before and during the movement have contributed to the present-day Arosi preoccupation with securing *auhenua* identities in the land. I seek, however, in so doing, to show that Maasina Rule has heightened rather than created this preoccupation. The preoccupation itself inheres in Arosi commitment to a poly-ontological socio-cosmic order as an ideal that requires the presence of *auhenua* matrilineages anchored in their lands as the centers around which inter-lineage entanglements can coalesce into coherent and stable polities. It is the shared, but ironically divisive, aspiration on the part of Arosi to re-emplace foundational *auhenua* identities below the surface of their entanglements that is the primary stimulus to the production of heterotopia.

In chapters 4–6 I analyze the ontological underpinnings and socio-cosmogonic processes that inform the production of Arosi heterotopia. By cross-referencing diverse elements of Arosi life, including metaphors of relatedness, midwifery, child-rearing, lineage narratives, and ancestral sites, I identify practices and imagery through which Arosi represent and effect coming into being as an ongoing transition from one mode of primordiality to another. The first mode, which I term utopic primordiality, is a static mode figured by mythic primordial people and proto-lineages dwelling in asocial purity in indeterminate pre-social spaces. These mythic images express Arosi deep poly-ontology as a state of primordial chaos characterized by excessive isolation among originally multiple categories of being. The second mode, which I term topogonic primordiality, is a dynamic mode figured by the exogamous generation of truly human ancestors who fuse matrilineages with socialized territories through the production of ancestral spirits in the land. The transition from the first to the second mode is mediated by the establishment of mutually constituting relationships among the diverse categories of being and achieves the construction of a poly-genetic socio-cosmic totality.

If, however, by definition, the "primary characteristic of a cosmos is its claim to wholeness" (de Coppet and Iteanu 1995: 1), how do Arosi hold together this socially achieved condition of productive relationship among inherently distinct categories of being? The formation of the Arosi cosmological whole is to be found, not in a single foundational past event, but in present primordialities: in the everyday practices that continuously revisit the transition from utopic to topogonic primordiality to bring isolated ontological categories into ordered relations. Constant renewal of connections among Arosi matrilineages is imperative because, as Valeri (2001: 293) observes with respect to Huaulu society, the aggregation of constituent components is "a reversible result, not ... a primary, and therefore unchallengeable, condition." The possibility of return to the primary condition of asocial isolation is always present. Furthermore, particular circumstances and historical events can promote the course of regression to the given mode of static atomism.

In chapter 7 I suggest that colonial transformations in Arosi have fostered just such a functional return to utopic primordiality, a condition in which land is conceptualized as empty, open, and available for transformation into newly formed lineage territories. In this context of virtual reversion to utopic primordiality, the normally constant cosmogonic processes of transition from utopic to topogonic primordiality have become intensive. Experiencing the postcolonial moral and social vacuity of their coastal land as both an obstacle and an incentive to the reproduction of their locality, Arosi today are creatively engaged in advancing this transition through a variety of neo-topogonic activities. By surreptitiously manipulating pre-existing shrines and burial sites, constructing lineage narratives that incorporate these markers of ancestral presence, and retrieving lineage personal names, Arosi are reframing and revaluing the topogonic activities of their lineage ancestors in order to anchor themselves in the coastal land. At the same time, however, by struggling to establish and preserve their respective matrilineal identities as the necessary precondition for productive and harmonious inter-lineage relations, the diverse Arosi matrilineages are generating a coastal topography comprising overlapping and incompatible configurations formed by multiple lineage points of view.

Beginning in chapter 7 and continuing through chapter 9, I examine evidence that heterotopia is not the only possible outcome of Arosi attempts to achieve order in the face of a colonially induced return to an Arosi form of chaos. While many Arosi are unintentionally producing heterotopia, others are struggling to reconcile Arosi poly-ontology with the fundamentally incompatible ontological premises of Christianity in ways that have the potential to transform Arosi ontology and sociality in the image of one lineage united under God and the Church. In this book as a whole, it is not my aim to provide a comprehensive ethnography of all aspects of Arosi Christianity. Treating Christianity as embedded in virtually every aspect of Arosi people's lives, my analyses engage with Christian discourses and practices where they emerge spontaneously as part of people's understandings of the nature of their matrilineages and their relationship to place. In the final two chapters, in particular, I seek to contribute to the anthropological study of what I term ethnotheologies—the constructive theological speculations of indigenous Christians. Like Arosi techniques of *auhenua* identity reproduction, Arosi ethno-theological projects of rapprochement between custom and Christianity are varied and innovative; some are personal and idiosyncratic. One man tells an anomalous version of the myth of the severed snake, Hatoibwari, that makes this indigenous being into an agent of God who placed an original couple on Makira from whom all people are endogamously descended. As an apparent synthesis of Christian and Arosi models of origins, his account furthermore highlights the capacity of this myth to index more than one scale of origin—universal, insular, matrilineal—either uniquely or simultaneously. Another man wants everyone to acknowledge that the old matrilineal system of landholding is defunct and to adopt father to son inheritance as de facto Arosi custom. This "plan," he says, will overcome the divisiveness of suppressed land disputes and unite all Arosi "in the likeness of God." Still others are quietly thinking through the implications of the common conviction that the rule of God has always worked through the *ringeringe* of the *auhenua* in their land. Like many other gentile Christians, they are working out systematic ethno-theologies that locate them and their past in a universal divine plan.

With these alternatives to heterotopia, the present ontology-based investigation confronts the fact that, in any given social context, more than one cosmological system—and therefore more than one deep ontology—may coexist in tension. In his analysis of Maori cosmogonic myths, Schrempp (1992: 68–70, 90, 96, 137) coins the label "dual formulation" to describe the coexistence of two competing answers to the question: What is the number and na-

ture of the ontologically distinct elements in the universe? The dual formulation evident in Arosi today is one conditioned by the recent history of conjuncture between Arosi cosmology and Anglican Christian models of
monotheism and human mono-genesis. It remains to be seen whether Arosi
will continue to live indefinitely with the ontological dissonance between these
two cosmologies or whether they are in the process of transforming and inverting their model of distinct matrilineally embodied categories of being into
a model of radical human unity vis-à-vis the biblical universal creator God.

This open question points, furthermore, to the need to reconcile Barth's
injunction to ground structural analyses in empirical events and historical dynamics with an admission of the value of universal abstract logics in the analysis and speculative contemplation of such data. Allowing that contingency and
culturally situated innovative human agency will always be the ultimate de-
terminants of how structures transform over time, it is nevertheless possible
and useful to see, in broadest terms, what the logically related alternatives are
when it comes to the question of deep ontology. Mono-ontology and poly-
ontology are, after all, but logical inversions of one another. As such, the possibility that—even the processes whereby—one might be turned over into the
other may be imagined apart from history. Such imaginings cannot reconstruct the precolonial history of Arosi ontology or predict its postcolonial future, yet the inherently destabilizing proximity in opposition between these
two prioritizations of unity and diversity—not to mention the wealth of comparative data from the wider region of island Melanesia, especially—underscores that we are always *in medias res* in the study of particular historically
conditioned ontologies.

CHAPTER 1

THE APPEARANCE OF
AN AROSI VILLAGE

Makira is located at the southeast end of the Solomon Islands archipelago, south of Malaita and southeast of Guadalcanal. The island is about one hundred and forty kilometers long and up to forty kilometers wide. Together with the smaller islands of Ulawa, Ugi, Bio, and the Three Sisters to the north, and Santa Catalina and Santa Ana to the east, Makira has been designated Makira/Ulawa Province, one of nine provinces in the independent nation of Solomon Islands.[1] The area known as Arosi is situated at the northwest end of the island and is divided into the electoral districts of Arosi I and Arosi II. The people of Arosi speak an Austronesian language, also called Arosi, that has been classified as a descendant of Proto-Eastern Oceanic (Tryon and Hackman 1983). Most Arosi also speak the national language, Solomon Islands Pijin, and many have a basic understanding of English. The 1995/96 Village Resources Survey enumerated just under 5,800 people in the whole of Arosi (Statistics Office 1997). During my period of field research I lived and worked at Tawatana village on the coast of Arosi I and made occasional research visits to other coastal villages throughout this district.

Arosi I extends along a section of the north coast of Makira for approximately thirty kilometers from Mwaniwaro village in the east to Tawabara settlement in the west. This portion of the north coast of Arosi is striated by a number of small rivers that flow north out of the bush to the coast. Some of these rivers debouch into the sea at expansive sandy beaches; most, however, force narrow passages through the coral reef platform that fringes much of the coastline. These passages provide access to land for ships' tenders and canoes. The narrow coastal plain, which varies from approximately ten to one hundred meters in depth, soon gives way to gentle rolling hills. Behind these hills,

---

1. A British protectorate from 1893, Solomon Islands gained independence on July 7, 1978.

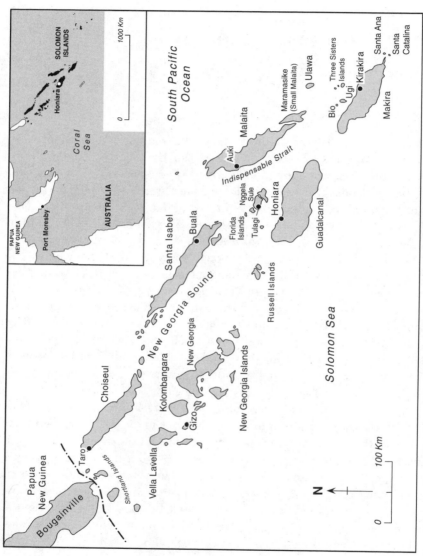

Map 1.1. West, central, and southeast Solomon Islands

the bush interior, cut by many small streams, is extremely rugged and broken. The coastal plain has been intensively planted with coconut palms; the undeveloped bush is densely covered by primary and secondary-growth tropical rain forest. A rough unpaved road follows the coast from Kirakira, the provincial center, down to Maro'u Bay at the northwest tip of the island. In parts of Arosi this road is overgrown and gets very little motorized traffic.

All of the villages in Arosi I are situated on the coast, and most are located at the mouth of a fresh water stream. The main villages, moving east to west, or "down" in Arosi terms, along the bending coastline, are Mwaniwaro, Borodao, Wainari'i, Tadahadi, Maniora, Asimaanioha, Hagaura, Haurango, Tawania'u, Heuru, Heraniauu, Maranu'u, Tawatana, and 'Ubuna. These villages are all similar in their basic configuration. Each is made up of a central settlement area with open meeting ground and church surrounded by several satellite hamlets, each with its own name.[2] Scattered between these villages are occasional smaller isolated settlements.

Tawatana Village in the 1990s

Changes on the Coast: Hamlets, Houses, Copra Driers, and Chicken Coops

Tawatana, where I was based, is centered on a passage in the reef formed by the stream Wai Tawatana. This stream seeps through a pebbly embankment into the sea, except during the particularly rainy months of January, February, and March, when it can burst open the sandbar and flow swiftly out into the surf. As there are no plumbing facilities of any kind in the village, villagers rely on this stream for all of their fresh water needs.[3] Drinking water is obtained well upstream from areas where people bathe. Although the residents of Tawatana are Anglican, men continue to follow the pre-Christian practice of avoiding what Arosi call "women's dirt" ('aharau).[4] Men, therefore, bathe

---

2. Arosi do not verbally distinguish between villages and the smaller hamlets which they comprise, but use the same word, 'omaa, to refer to both. For them, the larger villages gain their coherence as settlements that share a common orientation around the nearest church.

3. Installation of a system of communal fresh water taps had begun at the time of my departure in late 1993.

4. "Women's dirt" includes menstrual blood, women's odor, and clothing. As one man explained, however, a woman's children—male and female—can walk under her clothes if they are hanging up, and a brother can walk under his sister's clothes because "they are one blood" (see chapter 4). It should be noted that, in contrast to what has been well doc-

upstream from women, and women bathe in the pools of water nearer the mouth of the stream. It is generally the women who also use the largest pool for washing cooking utensils and doing laundry. Designated parts of the reef serve as a toilet area with separate sections for men and women.

According to my 1992 village census, the total population of Tawatana is 387, making it the second largest village, after 'Ubuna, in Arosi I (Statistics Office 1997: 122). The central hamlets of the village, 'A'agi, Tawatana, and 'Omaaraha, are located on the flat sandy land near the mouth of the stream. By the early 1990s, Tawatana, the hamlet from which the entire constellation of twenty neighboring hamlets takes its name, had become more a meeting area than a residential hamlet. A large leaf and timber Anglican church dedicated to St. Mary, which was in the final stages of construction during my stay, stands imposingly on a gravel foundation abutting a steep incline. The nearby temporary church, where almost all the services I attended were conducted, has been dismantled. The land beside the new church had previously been leveled to provide an area for village meetings, feasts, and for casual conversations under the shade of a large tree. 'Omaaraha hamlet, immediately to the west of Tawatana hamlet, has two residential houses. 'A'agi hamlet lies across the stream to the east of Tawatana hamlet. It has six residential houses, four separate buildings for cooking, and a small store, owned and operated by George "Kapu" Ta'aiwape, where such basic items as rice, tinned tuna fish, and blocks of soap are available for cash purchase.

The largest hamlet in the village, Mwanihau, is located at the top of a bluff behind Tawatana and 'Omaaraha. A large flat open area used for football and netball marks the center of Mwanihau. Spaced around this playing field are sixteen residential houses accommodating one hundred and ten people, eleven kitchens, two small stores, an oven that is occasionally used to bake bread, a copra drier, and two chicken coops. There are nine other hamlets to the west, strung along the road as it runs behind Mwanihau down to the next large river

---

umented among some Malaitans (e.g., Akin 2003; Keesing 1982a; Maranda 2001), there is no evidence that Arosi formerly treated menstruation and parturition as processes that had to be marked by periods of seclusion (for similar situations in Small Malaita and Ulawa, see Ivens 1927: 76–77, 88–89). Nevertheless, it is clear that pre-Christian Arosi practice entailed a situationally dynamic semiotics of gendered powers and substances in which menstrual blood and other secretions could be harmful or beneficial in different contexts. Although insufficient to reconstruct this semiotics in detail, the data I was able to collect support the work of theorists who have problematized the notion of "pollution" and suggested that the analysis of such powers and substances must be informed by "the cosmological ideas that in the past formed the encompassing backdrop to social practices" (Stewart and A. Strathern 2002b: 36; cf. Hoskins 2002; Valeri 2001: Chapter 8).

Map 1.2. Arosi

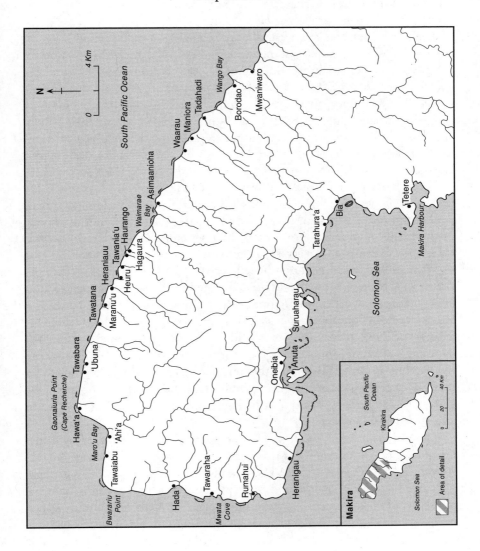

at Haurahu—about three quarters of a kilometer away. Maraunigau is representative of these small hamlets positioned up toward the gardening area on the slopes above the beach. It is set back from the road on the cleared top of a wooded knoll and contains two residential houses accommodating twelve people, two kitchens, and one chicken coop.

The hamlets of Ena and Tagarodo are located on a bluff behind ʻAʻagi on the eastern side of the Tawatana stream. Beyond them is Ena School at Mwaniʻege. This primary school serves day pupils from Tawatana and the neighboring village of Maranuʻu.[5] All of the teachers are residents of Tawatana village. The four remaining hamlets are further to the east, the farthest away being about half a kilometer's distance from Tawatana hamlet. Two of them are close to the beach, and two are on the slopes above the road as it runs east to the neighboring village of Maranuʻu. An occasional copra drier stands among the coconut groves that stretch between the coastal hamlets.

When I arrived in Tawatana I lived temporarily in Tagarodo hamlet. My first domicile was the "modern" house of the local school headmaster, Benjamin Monongaʻi. Mr. Ben, as he is known in the village, was not occupying the house at the time because it was still under construction, and he and his wife, Sera Gedetanara, had access to alternative housing at the school. Because Mr. Ben and his wife are schoolteachers receiving cash incomes from the government, they have been able to build a large house made of imported timber, iron, cement, glass, and masonite. The house is of a rectangular design and is elevated about three meters off the ground on cement piles. Despite the luxuries of louvered windows on all sides, relative spaciousness, and wood-paneled interior, this house, like the others in the village—and throughout Arosi—has no electricity, and at the time, had no plumbing. Only one other house in the village was of similar manufacture, and it was occupied by the chief, George Huruani. This house had been built by the chief's son, who was also a schoolteacher.

I soon transferred my residence to the home of Casper Kaukeni, a bachelor in his mid-fifties, who was living with and looking after Selwyn, his sister's young son. Casper's house was the only other besides Mr. Ben's in Tagarodo hamlet. This house was a more typical example of a present-day Arosi house. It was made entirely of local wood and leaf materials. It too was elevated, like most houses in the village, but only by about one meter on wooden stilts. The floor plan was a basic rectangle divided into two rooms on one side and a long, partially walled sitting area on the other. The raised floor was

---

5. A junior high school was started at this site in 1997–98.

Figure 1.1. Casper Kaukeni's house, Tagarodo, Tawatana.

made of long strips of betel palm wood bound to a row of supports. The most distinctive feature of this house, however, was a carved wooden house post of Casper's own design and execution. The image depicted is of an ithyphallic canine-like creature rearing on its hind legs, its mouth open in a ferocious grimace, its eyes and teeth painted livid white. For many years Casper has worked painstakingly to cultivate a well-manicured clover cover in the expansive level clearing surrounding his house and has planted flowering shrubs in among the scattered coconut palms.

When I left Tagarodo hamlet it was to move into my own house. Under the direction of Ben Aharo, the village men and I built a house for me adjacent to the new church site in Tawatana hamlet.[6] When it was finished, this structure also occasionally served as a visitors' house. Like Casper's house and most such structures in the village, this residence was a four-sided rectilinear structure with a gable roof. After the women helped us to clear the site, we began

---

6. For the most part, both men and women participate in the work projects described in this chapter. Any act, however, that would require a woman physically to pass over a man or to step over anything that will be lifted above a man's head is avoided. This means that women should not climb scaffolds to assist with house building, climb trees in the presence of men, step over house building materials, or hang their laundry in a place under which a man might pass.

construction by driving six heavy logs into the ground to serve as the main weight-bearing house posts. Across the tops of these posts we placed a series of horizontal beams and three vertical posts down the center length of the house to support the ridgepole and the rafters. These rafters consisted of slender poles, some of wood and some of bamboo. We tied these poles to the support beams using vines and bark strips,. positioning the poles parallel to one another at intervals so as to form two frames joined along the top ridge of the house. The building team then reinforced these rafters by undergirding them with perpendicular poles, creating a latticework effect. When this roof structure was in place we covered it with layers of closely bound sago palm thatch sections that the women had helped us to prepare. To complete the walls, we added vertical strips of bamboo between the main house posts and reinforced these with horizontal bamboo poles. We finished the outside face of this latticework with a covering of sago palm thatch held in place by long thin sections of wild betel palm trunk. My house was one of a few village houses built directly on the ground, and for the floor, we spread a layer of coral chips. Outside, beyond the main entrance, we also constructed a separate cooking hut with a circle of stones to form an oven. This separation of cooking and living quarters was a typical design originally instituted under colonial rule as a safety and hygiene measure.

Like the separate cooking huts, many aspects of the present-day Arosi house design are recent innovations. People stated that in precolonial Arosi all houses had been built directly on the ground with strong walls made solely from betel palm strips (cf. Fox 1924: 330; Verguet 1854: 133–134; 1885: 221–226). The current design, they said, had been brought to Makira by a group of indigenous Anglican teachers from Santa Isabel in the 1920s. George Huruani, born in 1911, remembered: "The old houses were on the ground, but the government had them raised.... The old houses were much stronger than today's ones. They sat on the ground and had low doors that people would have to bend down to enter, and [if they were enemies] they'd be killed. Today's houses are Bugotu [Santa Isabel] style, which are easier to make. The old style wasn't needed when the government and Church stopped killings."

As part of my induction into Arosi life, I also learned how to make a garden. Gardening in Arosi is a multi-stage enterprise that can be pursued successfully only through persistent application over several months. Sebiulan "Sibo" Rodomoi and Harry 'Abu helped me to find an appropriate site up in the gardening area located in the rolling hills immediately above the village. This area is relatively deforested, being covered in a patchwork of gardens currently under cultivation and abandoned former garden sites. Husbands and wives will generally make separate but adjacent gardens, which they tend somewhat independently of one another. Some people have constructed small huts close to their gardens to provide shelter during the heat of the day or inclement weather; these are sometimes equipped with oven stones so that a gardener may bake a small meal while working. We selected a site, not far from Harry's garden hut, that had been under cultivation long before but had become thickly overgrown. The first step was to clear this site by cutting away the secondary growth. We then left the cleared area to let the cut vegetation begin to die and dry out.[7]

After a week, Sibo and I returned to the site a number of times to burn off the drying vegetal debris and attempt to burn down the larger trees we had not been able to fell with an axe. Again a lapse of time was required to allow for the rain to wash the charred residue into the ground. Once we had cleared away everything that had not burned completely, our next task was to mark out the boundaries of the garden with logs. Arosi compare a garden to a bed for sleeping. Like a bed for sleeping, a garden has a pillow end and a foot end and is generally oblong in shape. It is usually the case that a garden is made on an incline with the foot at the low end and the pillow at the high end. The work of making and planting always begins at the foot and works toward the pillow. Logs are used to mark the perimeter and to partition the interior into small squares. Some people said they make these squares in order to keep different varieties of tubers separated; others suggested that the segments might be reserved for different members of a family.

With the outline of the garden in place we began to hoe mounds in preparation for planting the tips of sweet potato vines. We obtained the vine tips from a nearby garden belonging to Elisabet Ha‘ai, one of Harry's close relatives. Over a period of several days we filled the mounds with three vines each. We also planted maize along the edges of the garden, green onions, and long beans. To seed tomato we took a mash of mature fruits and smeared it over the soil and turned it under. Three months later the maize was tall and ripe and I had a crop of long beans hanging from a trellis Sibo had constructed. It took another month for the sweet potatoes to be ready for harvesting. Like other Arosi, however, we lost some of our produce to the predations of loose domestic or wild pigs and rats.

The items I chose to plant represent the staple items of the Arosi diet. Other villagers grew various types of green cabbage, pineapple, chili peppers, melon, and tapioca. Nearly all of these agricultural items are not native to Makira,

---

7. With the exception of tree felling, women as well as men perform all of the gardening tasks described here.

however. In the pre- and early colonial periods, Arosi cultivated yams and taro in an intensive and highly ritualized preparation and growing season (Fox 1924; Verguet 1854: 135–136, 141; 1885: 226–227). Over the past one hundred years the higher yielding and easier to grow sweet potato has displaced these indigenous tubers as the mainstay of the Arosi diet, and today only a few people grow small amounts of the old varieties of tubers. The labor involved in gardening is no longer governed by ritual and seasonal cycles, but can begin, as did my own, at the discretion and initiative of each gardener. Thus, as with the building of houses, the making of gardens reflects the substantial transformations that Arosi culture has sustained in the past century and a half (cf. MM *AR*, 1913: 5–6). This applies equally to cooking methods. Whereas, in the past, the main methods of cooking were baking and roasting, today people most frequently use aluminum pans to boil food over an open fire.

Changes in Community: Elected Chiefs, Church Committees, and Communal Labor

Today, village politics are nested within the larger structure of Solomon Islands political order. Since Solomon Islands independence in 1978, the men and women of each village have elected a Village Committee to look after general village affairs and organize subcommittees for the coordination and regulation of specific aspects of village life, such as sport and social activities, education, health, cultural affairs, communal work, commercial enterprises, and religious activities. In the election that I observed at Tawatana in early 1993, Willie Muriani, the village representative on the Area Council for Arosi I, convened the villagers and announced that they must nominate people to stand for election to a Village Committee of more than six but not more than twelve members. Eleven people were quickly nominated.[8] One week later ten men were elected to the Committee by a show of hands, or a shout of "yes" or "no" at a village meeting held after the Sunday church service. Although the term of office of a Village Committee member is supposed to be two years, in practice there is no fixed term; people serve as long as they care to and continue to receive popular support. Vacancies are filled as needed. The Committee members elect a Chairman from among their number. Above the level of village administration there are representative councils at the area, provincial, and national levels. At the time of my research, Tawatana had one represen-

---

8. Although five of the eleven nominators were women and six of the eleven seconders were women, no women were nominated for election, and I was not aware of women serving on the Village Committees at other Arosi villages.

Figure 1.2. Eddie Gopa and Ben Aharo, Tawatana.

tative on the Arosi I Area Council; one villager, Harry Ramo, represented the electoral ward in the Provincial Assembly; and another, Rex Horoi, represented Solomon Islands at the United Nations in New York.[9]

Villages also elect chiefs who ostensibly work with the Village Committee; in fact, however, these chiefs tend to be senior men who, in most cases, choose not to take an active role in village politics. George Huruani and Basil Bunaone were elected "first" and "second" chief for Tawatana in the mid 1970s. Initially, these chiefs had assumed a position of moral leadership. They worked with the villagers, told stories to young children, instructed young people about marriage, forbade theft, and inculcated respect for elders and the ethical precepts comprehended by the increasingly objectified notion of Arosi custom. Today, however, their positions appear to be largely honorary. Some peo-

---

9. The late Solomon Mamaloni (1943–2000), a man from Arosi II, served as the national Prime Minister during part of the period of my research.

ple are dissatisfied with the present inertia of chiefs and assert that the first chief ought also to be the Chairman of the Village Committee. One man in particular roundly criticized the political organization of a number of neighboring villages as well, pointing out that "at Maranuʻu [the two chiefs] feel that the Chairmanship of the Committee is the work of the government and Europeans and they feel they cannot do it. It is the same at Heuru as well." I was told that, at yet another village, a falling out between the first chief and segments of the village had made it impossible for the chief to work together with the Village Committee.

At the village level the other important focus of activity is the church, both as a ritual space and as an overarching institution within which many auxiliary social organizations intersect. Even the few villagers who are not active in any of these organizations agree that the church building and the power of faith that it represents provide protection against inimical spirits and the work of Satan. As elsewhere in Solomon Islands, many people explicitly compare the church structure to pre-Christian ancestral shrines and burial places as a place simultaneously dangerous and prophylactic (see chapter 5; cf. White 1991: 106–107). In church, as at the old ancestral sites, one must temper one's language and comportment or risk falling ill. Conversely, for the faithful, the physical presence of the church is understood to shelter those in its orbit from harm. One man, for example, commented that ever since the villagers of Tawatana had begun construction on the present church building, their village had escaped the ravages of cyclones that had struck elsewhere in the Pacific. Accordingly, when exhorting fellow villagers to join in taking responsibility for the church and its activities, people often express the idea that lack of participation is a sign of weak faith and that weak faith will cause God to "turn his back" on the village and withdraw his guardianship. "If the church is weak," they warn, "nothing [in the village] will stand."

Father Taukerei, the ordained Anglican priest who serves the church of St. Mary at Tawatana, is a man of the neighboring village of ʻUbuna. Because he also serves all the other churches in the western part of Arosi I, the majority of worship services, as well as the day-to-day administration of church life, are conducted under lay leadership. In theory, there are two main types of lay leaders: catechists and readers. Catechists are men who have received several years of prescribed training at a church school and are authorized to preach and teach; readers receive little or no training, and their main function is to read the liturgy during worship. In Tawatana practice, however, the roles of catechist and reader tend to become conflated, and the two terms are used interchangeably, along with that of teacher. At the time of my stay in Tawatana, lay leadership of the church had devolved upon two men, Frank Rau and Harry 'Abu, who shared responsibility for daily morning and evening worship, Bible study, Sunday school, and confirmation classes.

In March of 1993 Frank Rau initiated the reconstitution of the vestry, or church committee, the ruling body of the church polity in the village. Membership in this committee had been allowed to lapse so that, since 1990, only Frank and the local school headmaster, Mr. Ben, had remained active. One Sunday morning at the end of a church service that he had conducted, Frank announced his concern that the desultory state of the committee was detrimental to the work of the church and was permitting people to grow lax in their commitment to Christianity. In much the same way that Willie Muriani had called a meeting to elect Village Committee members, Frank retained the congregation after church and asked for nominations to the vestry committee. He had definite ideas as to who should serve on the committee. He recommended that the nominees include a village woman who was a member of the Mothers' Union, a Companion of the Melanesian Brothers, a member of the Society of Saint Francis, and any other people in the village.[10] Nominations were forthcoming but few were seconded, and Frank decided that the election would have to be abandoned for the time being.

At this point, Ben Aharo suggested that people were reluctant to engage in the election "because they do not know the work of the vestry committee." Frank answered that the committee attends to all the business of the church and the physical upkeep of the church building. In short, he concluded, "It decides what's important." Another villager, who occasionally acted as a catechist, added: "The job of the vestry committee is to change things if the church is weak. Also, if a catechist wants to take a break, the committee should meet to arrange this." This list of responsibilities could be supplemented to include appointing a secretary, budgeting for communion wine and kerosene, maintaining an emergency public fund, forming a subcommittee of "church-keepers," and supervising the women who serve as church cleaners. Elaboration of these duties failed to move the election

---

10. Members of the Mothers' Union, of whom there were about twenty at Tawatana in the early 1990s, strive to apply the teachings of Christ in their marriages and family lives, attend occasional meetings, and use "bring and buy" sales to raise money for their activities. The Companions of the Brotherhood are laymen and women throughout the Solomons who commit to pray for and support an Anglican community called the Melanesian Brotherhood (for a history of the Brotherhood and related organizations, see Macdonald-Milne 2003). The Society of Saint Francis is also an Anglican religious order for men with various grades of initiation entailing levels of commitment ranging from lay disciplines of prayer and occasional fasting to full vows as a Brother.

forward, however, and ultimately, Father Taukerei suggested that Frank and Harry appoint a committee themselves, which he then ritually commissioned. Afterwards, some villagers disapproved of this procedure, saying that, like the Village Committee, the vestry committee ought to be democratically elected.

As in other Melanesian societies, a prominent feature in Arosi life is the orchestration and execution of communal work projects that engage kinship networks. Events such as house building and marriages mobilize kin groups to contribute labor, materials, money, food for feasts, and shell valuables for bride-price payments. Increasingly, however, the Village Committee and lay congregational leaders are taking on the function of facilitating these and other forms of collective labor and making them village-wide endeavors. Village Committeemen designate work days, announce specific projects, and delegate tasks, while the period following Sunday church services provides a convenient context for communication of these plans and for lay leaders to exhort villagers to work together in the spirit of Christian charity and fellowship. With respect to marriages, the banns are announced in church, and the Chairman of the Village Committee alerts villagers to offer assistance to the families of the bride or groom. In response, villagers may harvest a garden, carry sweet potatoes to collection points, gather coconuts, prepare puddings, dive for fish, help build a feasting table, or arrange after-feast entertainments. A more frequent chore, regulated by the village health subcommittee, is the cleaning or brushing of the village. This involves cutting back high grasses and bushes, lifting old coconut shells, and removing other objects in which water might collect; these efforts maintain a tidy village and discourage malaria-carrying mosquitoes from breeding.

A large proportion of communal activities center on events and feast days in the Christian calendar. "The day of the church" of Tawatana, which is the feast day of St. Mary (March 25) for whom the church is named, may serve as an example of an important festival in the village.[11] In 1993 preparations

---

11. Speculating that matriliny may correlate with the religious and political elevation of women, some anthropological colleagues have asked me whether the veneration of the Virgin Mary is particularly marked in Arosi. I found no evidence of this, however. The fact that the church at Tawatana is dedicated to Mary is purely an artifact of mission history. Churches in other Arosi villages are named for a variety of saints and Christian concepts, including St. Peter ('Ubuna), St. Paul (Heuru), St. Barnabas (Tawania'u), and Corpus Christi (Hagaura). One indication that the people of Tawatana are not devotionally attached to Mary is the desire of some villagers to change the church's name to that of another saint. Because March 25 (Lady Day) is a special observance of the Anglican Mothers' Union world-wide, the church's feast day draws many local members of the Mothers'

Figure 1.3. Wild pig hunt in preparation for the feast day of the Church of St. Mary, Tawatana. Photo by Ben Aharo.

began on March 7 following the Sunday service. Abel Tawai, a member of the Village Committee, reminded everyone of the upcoming festival and allotted particular tasks to different groups of people. To the women and children he assigned the job of beautifying the church; to a group of able-bodied men (including myself) he gave a commission to hunt wild pigs in the bush; to another group he mandated spear-fishing along the reef; to the old people and women he entrusted the task of refurbishing a long feasting table in Tawatana hamlet; and on the young unmarried men he laid the chore of collecting firewood for cooking. Others were later recruited to collect sweet potatoes, and the women worked to make starch puddings from sweet potatoes and tapioca.[12] Cooperative labor in preparation for the day of the church also reached beyond the village to include the efforts of some guests from neighboring villages who contributed food items and joined in celebrations as a form of trans-

---

Union to Tawatana, an influx that the villagers as hosts can find burdensome and detracting from what they see as the primary focus of celebration, namely, their church.

12. Fox (1924: 314–315) and Verguet (1854: 136; 1885: 196–198) give brief accounts of the traditional pudding called *taumwa*. Because it is left to ferment for a number of weeks before it is consumed, this baked pudding is sometimes referred to as *sikis mans puding* (six-month pudding) in Pijin. Among Solomon Islanders today, *sikis mans puding* immediately connotes Makira.

Figure 1.4. The new "plan of action": work set two builds a house.

village Christian fellowship. Even more extensive planning goes into the production of the village's unique "Christmas programme," or "laugh-laugh night," which entails seven days of lectures, singing, sports, and theatrical performances, as well as a feast.

It happened that while I was in Tawatana the Chairman of the Village Committee, Michael Ngaraediri, instituted a new "plan of action" for communal work. In the typical post-Sunday service setting, he described a new scheme involving five "sets" of men who, headed by different members of the Village Committee, would be detailed to perform required tasks in five separate areas of the village. Wives were assigned to the same sets as their husbands so that couples could take turns working with their set and looking after their own homes and children. The women of the sets could also join together to cook and bring food to their husbands' work crews. Every Tuesday was to be the day that members of the sets should report to their areas of the village. People who wanted to be excused from the work for a day, for any reason other than ill health, could "buy the day," that is, contribute three Solomon Islands dollars to the village coffer.[13] Ngaraediri explained that the purpose of this new scheme was to "help everyone, to help people with anything: houses, coconuts, gardens, fences for pigs or chickens." He urged people not to be embarrassed about coming forward with their needs and made clear that the sets would not expect direct reciprocity from the people they assisted. "If you receive help you shouldn't think that you must feed the people, because then if people think that they have to feed the workers perhaps they won't ask for help, but if you do feed the people that's okay."

Villagers understood the work of the Village Committee, not only in the imposition of this set system, but in the general organization of group labor, to be simultaneously a continuation of the work of precolonial chiefs and a departure from customary forms of cooperation. On the one hand, they saw the Village Committee as carrying on the unifying and coordinating function of the chief who, in the precolonial period, had held the authority to deploy people for communal labor and exact compensation from wrongdoers. On the other hand, villagers were also aware that the primary model behind the activities of the Committee was the work of the village headman under colonial administration. Inaugurated at the time of independence, the Village Committee was, in fact, the direct successor to the old village "boss," who had been elected, in large measure, to carry out the colonial agenda of compulsory government work projects within the village. On the whole, therefore, villagers looked on Committee-mandated village-wide labor as a new thing rooted in the colonial past and Christian ideals rather than in Arosi custom.

The influence of church leaders in promoting the new model of cooperative labor was especially evident when it came time to make arrangements for a wedding in the village. In this particular case the Village Committee failed to broadcast news of the upcoming festivities. Nevertheless, as word of the marriage plans circulated, people began to wonder why everyone was not working together. I asked a relative of the groom, who had clearly taken charge of the preparations, why all of the villagers had not been told how they might help. This man responded: "The idea that everyone should all work together is a relatively new one. Before, only those people related to the person being married would help. The work did not fall on everyone in the village. The idea that we should all work together, everyone in the village, is a new custom (*ringeringe haoru*)—probably encouraged by our working together on the church. But we are wary about jumping to ask peo-

---

13. In actual fact, following the institution of the sets, many villagers worked up to three or four days a week over the course of the next month.

ple to help, since they'll think that we're lazy and will talk about us." Despite the reluctance of the kin group involved to make open requests for assistance, the villagers all wanted to help. As one man put it: "It is a Christian marriage, so we should all be involved in it, not just those who are related." In the end, the villagers' desire to participate was not disappointed. In church on the Sunday before the wedding, the reader announced that the whole village was to be involved in preparing the wedding feast. Having divided the village into six areas, he explained that each area was to make arrangements for collecting food contributions and baking them to bring to the wedding.

This example points to a tension between Arosi practice that emphasizes cooperation within kin groups and a "new custom" that emphasizes total village cooperation across kinship lines. It also highlights the role of social values perceived to be specifically Christian in promoting the latter over the former. As the man who had originally taken on the brunt of the work involved in organizing the wedding acknowledged, the new custom has been encouraged not only by Christian values but by prolonged communal projects such as the construction of a new church building. My stay in Tawatana overlapped with the final phase of this project, which was the single most intensive focus of communal labor. Construction had been in progress already for several years, but a last push was on to complete the structure in time for a hoped-for visit in late 1993 by the then Bishop James Mason of the Diocese of Hanuato'o. This push mobilized the participation of people from neighboring villages as well who brought leaf materials for use in building the church. In the run-up to the Bishop's visit, some villagers were working on the church as many as six days a week, and the unifying influence of this project has clearly generalized into other areas of collective endeavor. When greeted with some resistance to the implementation of the set system, the Chairman of the Village Committee justified the system with reference to the church project, suggesting that the set system would help the villagers to complete other work that prevented them from making the church their top priority. In this way, he modeled the work of the sets in the image of the work of the church as work that belongs equally to everyone.

> Collectively we'll work for good houses—each house is all of ours. We are all concerned about the state of each house, since we go visiting each other and also shelter from the rain in each other's houses. We should all work together for good gardens—hoe mounds together, and plant together—because we all eat each other's food. All these things belong to us all. The Committee wants all of us to develop.

Figure 1.5. Sibo Rodomoi and Shadrack Ruahoʻasi use coral chips to level the precinct around the new church, Tawatana.

This is only the most obvious way in which the church as community has emerged as a village-wide, and sometimes even trans-village, social identity that encompasses older kinship identities. In chapters 8 and 9 I explore more

Figure 1.6. A wedding procession approaches the new church, Tawatana.

fully the less evident ways in which Arosi understandings of Christianity have the potential to transform Arosi ontology at the deepest level.

A Day in the Life of Tawatana

On a typical day in Tawatana, the rhythm of life is loosely structured by the tolling of the church bell. This bell is made from the sawn-off top end of a natural gas canister hung outside the church, and is "rung" by being struck repeatedly with a metal rod. A church reader sounds the bell at about 5 A.M., rousing the nearest hamlets, except on Sundays when the day begins half an hour later. Those who choose to attend prayers rise and perform their morning toilet. A second sounding of the bell then summons them to morning prayer, which begins at about 6 A.M. On a weekday these morning services tend to be sparsely attended with only between five and fifteen people. Others rise at their own pace, and women begin preparing a morning meal. Breakfast usually consists of reheated sweet potato or tapioca from the previous evening, or if no leftovers are available, women begin a fresh soup made of assorted vegetables in a boiled sweet potato base. Young children who attend the Ena School leave their homes for classes until the mid afternoon. There is a paucity of older children in the village because many are boarding away at secondary schools elsewhere throughout the country until the Christmas and other holidays.

Apart from the one or two days per fortnight when the Village Committee declares a communal workday, adults are now free to pursue their normal routines. Both men and women tend to disperse up to the gardening area where they spend the greater part of the day developing the progress of their gardens. Depending on the particular stages that a person's garden has reached, he or she may be found performing any combination of clearing, burning, hoeing, planting, weeding, or harvesting. People who are ready to harvest their produce may collect more than they will use to feed their households, retaining the surplus to sell for cash at the "bring and buy" that often follows the Sunday worship. In addition to these gardening chores, other tasks include foraging for firewood, betel pepper leaf, and fallen coconuts for cooking. Men will climb betel nut palms and coconut palms to gather refreshments and gather canarium nuts in season. Often a snack of roasted sweet potato or maize is prepared and consumed in the garden area; another favorite and easily obtained food throughout the unforested area is wild papaya. Work on the gardens is constant but leisurely, and gardeners frequently rest to chew betel nut and visit with other people in the vicinity. Small children often accompany their parents while they pursue the course of their day's work. Although care for infants and toddlers is primarily the responsibility of women, fathers do share in this work and frequently provide relief for mothers. Sometimes, older women and men who no longer garden as intensively as younger adults will look after very young children while their parents work.

Besides gardening, adults fill their day with a wide variety of activities, chores, and obligations as need arises. In addition to the communal work projects in progress, many people or groups are engaged in long-term projects to which they regularly turn their attentions. Casper Kaukeni, for example, spends many hours weeding his hamlet and leveling the ground to create a lush and attractive open lawn where children and families come together. Martin Toku has single-handedly constructed a stepped path up the steep hillside that leads to his garden area. Others are intermittently engaged in home maintenance and improvement projects that send them up into the bush in search of the raw materials needed for building and repairs.

Some people or kin groups sporadically pursue activities aimed at earning a cash income, or supplementing subsistence gardening. Four kin-based groups, for example, have established small cocoa plantations on land in the gardening area. These "farms" generate sufficient profit to enable the operators to pay back small start-up loans, pay casual labor, cover school fees and supplies for their children, buy rice, cloth, kerosene, and soap, and pay taxes. Because many people find it very difficult to obtain the money required to pay the latter sort of general expenses, occasionally a man will scour an often overgrown old beachfront coconut plantation for nuts with which to make a batch of copra for shipment to and sale in Honiara. The practice of scavenging for fallen coconuts for daily cooking needs in groves close to the village, however, means little copra is produced in these plantations. Other men of the village enjoy and are known for their skill at diving for bêche-de-mer, which can also be taken to Honiara for sale. These same skilled divers can also be found spearfishing, but no one devotes all of his time to fishing. Only during a few months in mid-year, when certain species of fish come to feed on a seasonal seaweed that grows on the edge of the fringing reef, do some men build platforms on the reef from which they fish during the night. A few men have gun licenses, and if any bullets are available they may walk up into the bush to shoot wood pigeons to eat.

Unplanned and regular special activities can sometimes interrupt or postpone the normal course of the day. Often parents must spend a portion of their day taking sick children, or toddlers needing immunization shots, to the nearest health clinic located about one and a half kilometers west at 'Ubuna village. One activity especially popular among young and middle-aged women is the women's Arosi language literacy class. Initiated during the period of my research, this class, led by Eunice Huna, was designed to meet the literacy needs of women who had been able to attend school for only a short period of time as children.

In the late afternoon those who have been working in their gardens slowly filter back down to the village. The reader sounds the church bell a number of times to signal that it is time to bathe before the service of evening prayer. This service, which begins at about 6 P.M., tends to draw a slightly larger congregation than the morning service. An evening meal, usually prepared by women and young girls, is likely to comprise fresh soup, perhaps with a little tinned tuna fish mixed in; occasionally the fare is varied to rice with tinned tuna fish and greens, or baked sweet potato or tapioca pudding. Particularly on well lit full-moon nights, an evening may consist of visiting among relatives and discussing events in the village or stories heard on one of the few battery operated radios owned and shared by villagers. While groups of youths might meet along the beach, strong singers gather in the church for choir practice under the direction of Sibo Rodomoi, and a few people take a late bath. Villagers tend to go to sleep early if there is a shortage of kerosene in the village and on nights with little moonlight.

As this description of village life indicates, most villagers lead geographically circumscribed lives. Some unmarried men live and work in Honiara or elsewhere throughout the country, but upon marriage, many return to live in Tawatana. Only a handful of men have traveled internationally. Michael

Ngaraediri, the Chairman of the Village Committee, visited England and Australia in the course of his police training; Benjamin Mononga'i has been to Australia to study education; George Atkin has likewise traveled as a news reporter based in Honiara; and the U.N. representative, Rex Horoi, was resident in New York for a number of years. While most men have been to Honiara, the national capital on Guadalcanal, some of the older women have never left Makira, and for most residents of Tawatana the trip to Kirakira, whether by foot or motorized canoe, is an infrequent journey. Nevertheless, many Arosi with little or no direct experience of life beyond their villages are deeply interested in distant people and places and global phenomena about which they have heard. Favorite topics of conversation, for example, included the aftermath of the Gulf War of 1991, HIV/AIDS, the problem of homelessness in Europe and America, and the feared consequences of global warming. As explored in chapter 9, on an individual and somewhat idiosyncratic basis, some Arosi are creatively reconceptualizing and theologizing the position of their island in global and divine history.

"We All Eat through the Father"

Within their physically circumscribed and settled way of life, the villagers of Tawatana generally say that they live and garden according to where their fathers and paternal grandfathers have lived and gardened before them. As I began to map the village, Willie Muriani pointed out a residential pattern common to most of the hamlets: a group of brothers cluster around their father. For example, in the beachside hamlet of Tawau at the eastern end of the village, two brothers, Abel Tawai and Philip Damuiasi, have established households in the hamlet where they grew up with their parents, Tomas Rehu'a and Dorothy Mononga'imae. They have brought their wives to live and raise their children there. Before Abel and Philip, their father Rehu'a and his brother Marosugagari had done the same, bringing their wives to make their homes with their father, 'Aridariu. Today, Marosugagari's widow, Mabel 'Orekeni, remains in the hamlet, but two of her sons, together with another of Rehu'a's sons, have established a small annex of Tawau directly inland at a place called Manuri'i. This inland extension of the hamlet came about as a result of a cyclone in the 1970s that damaged many of the village houses close to the sea. Similarly, at Ena hamlet on the plateau above the Tawatana stream, five brothers have remained in the orbit of their father, the "first chief" George Huruani, a widower. They share the hamlet with George's deceased brother's son, Sakias Kahoa and his wife and children. The many smaller hamlets of the village represent even smaller sets of brothers and male cousins, while the largest hamlet, Mwanihau, comprises five distinct fraternal sets. In sum, apart from the occasional in-marrying man who has come to reside among his wife's brothers, Tawatana, like Arosi as a whole, exhibits patri-virilocal residence.[14]

As with residence, the location of gardening land tends to follow a father to son succession of land use. Harry Ramo explained his own practice in these terms:

> I work [my gardens] along the side of [a path that leads straight up from my hamlet through the gardening area and into the bush]. I work where my father worked his garden. He worked his garden up and down a strip beside [this path]. We start at the lower end of this area and work our way up to the top before coming down to the bottom and working our way up again. In the thirty years since coming back from Honiara, I've worked my way up to the top twice and am just starting at the bottom the third time. If you don't go back [to garden there] and the place where you started gets overgrown, someone else will move in there. I clear the land and plant sweet potato, eat it all, and then plant sweet potato again in the same place before moving on up. I might then plant tapioca behind me as I move up the slope. This area is called a path of old gardens and you don't garden in the path of a different person.... This area was forest when [my father] started to garden here.

Harry describes the typical relationship between residential and gardening land when he describes following a path straight up from his house to his garden. Such a swathe of land is called an *odo*. The residents of other hamlets as well make their gardens in the stretches of land, or *odo*, that rise inland up toward the bush in continuous lines from their hamlets. It is counterproductive, however, to garden too high above the hamlet, owing to the predations of wild pigs that inhabit the forest. Consequently, these strips of gardening land are finite, and it can happen that a larger hamlet will not have sufficient contiguous gardening area to support all its residents. The gardening arrangements of Sibo Rodomoi, one of the sons of George Huruani, living at Ena represents such a case.

> I garden at Gohuraha because I had no place, so I asked Toraai about Gohuraha because they make gardens throughout that area. I asked,

---

14. Throughout Arosi a small number of children, both male and female, do not live with their parents but reside in their mothers' natal villages because they have been given names that belong to their mothers' kin groups (see chapter 5). It is often the case that, on marriage, such males will continue to reside in the villages in which they grew up.

"Can I garden with all of you here?" and he said, "Yes." [My father] used to make gardens at Mwarore and Abora'isau but [my brothers and some other villagers] garden in these places. I couldn't make my garden in the bush because a wild pig would eat it. So I garden at Go-huraha because they make gardens throughout all of my father's path of old gardens.

In approaching John Selwyn Toraai, the senior man of Areare hamlet, for permission to garden alongside him and his sons' families, Sibo was respecting the precedence of Toraai's kin group on that *odo* of land as granting them authority to control its use.

When Arosi explain how they are related to the places where they live, garden, or collect naturally occurring foods, they regularly employ the concrete image of eating. To characterize their access to an area and its resources, Arosi will often say that they either "eat through the father" (*ngau suri ama*) or "eat through the mother" (*ngau suri ina*) at that area. To eat through the father is to enjoy the privilege of residing in and taking sustenance from land previously held and worked by one's patrikin: the apparent norm in Arosi today. To eat through the mother is to share prerogatives of land use where one's matrilineage is *auhenua*. Corroborating the picture of brothers gathered around their fathers presented in the above descriptions, many Arosi are ready to acknowledge that today everyone eats through the father. The prevalence of eating through the father to the exclusion of eating through the mother, they say, is a reflection of the fact that the matrilineages that once were *auhenua* in the villages have all died out. When one elderly man pointed out to me where he gardened in the land above the village, I asked him whether he had asked permission to garden there. "No," he replied, "whom would I ask? The *auhenua* lineage is dead. In Tawatana we are all people who have come (*sae boboi*); there are no people of old (*sae bwani*)."

Despite the fact that villagers say "we all eat through the father," at the same time, many are anxious to graft the recent history of their paternal forebears into a longer, more encompassing history that links them indirectly to the *auhenua* lineage of the land where they now live and garden. In seeking to justify their present situation in the land, not on the strength of recent paternal precedence alone, but through affinal and other connections to the *auhenua* of the past, the villagers of Tawatana implicitly acknowledge that the father to son land inheritance practiced today is a weak substitute for firmly anchored matrilineages in their lands. Accordingly, they seek to embed the former in the latter. This compensatory strategy is most clearly illustrated in the reasons villagers offer for why they developed particular areas of village land into coconut plantations during the mid 1950s and early 1960s. Examination of some of the rationales given shows how some Arosi invoke both a simple model of father to son inheritance and a more complex model of mediated connection to the *auhenua* to secure their positions vis-à-vis various areas of land.

Although a few Arosi had planted small stretches of beachfront with co-conuts in the first half of the twentieth century, it was not until the mid 1950s that representatives from the Agriculture Department of the British Protec-torate visited Arosi villages to promote intensive and systematic coconut plant-ing for copra production. Johnson Bwaurari of Hauwaibora village, who had served as an Agriculture Field Assistant at that time, recalled that he was trained and sent around Makira to teach Islanders how best to clear the land and how to space new plantings for optimum yield. The Makira Council newsletter exhorted everyone to "plant ten coconuts every week." Another man emphasized that the government had motivated people to take up these ini-tiatives by suggesting that the resulting copra production would be highly profitable.

> They said we should plant coconuts to get possessions and so that our
> country will be rich. They taught that the coconuts in a plantation
> should be spaced, and that every other tree that grew on the land
> there should be cut down so there would be no shade and the co-
> conuts would produce good fruit. As a result, we cut down *ngari*,
> *'otora*, *'aai*, *uri*, *ao*, *awa*, *ora*, *'etabi*, *'ure'ure* [i.e., various types of
> trees that either produce edible nuts and fruit, or are used to build
> houses and canoes] … cut them all down. Cutting down these trees
> would, the agriculture people taught, stop rats from climbing up and
> spoiling the coconuts. When we plant coconuts we'll be able to buy
> an iron house, pay school fees, get clothes; soon there'll be a road and
> a truck and we'll be able to live like Europeans. Further, they said that
> we'd be able to measure our income in thousands not just hundreds
> of pounds [sterling].

Ironically, after all of this promotion and the loss of many locally valuable trees, low copra prices, poor shipping connections, concentration of labor on communal work projects, and daily coconut scavenging for consumption con-spire to prevent villagers from making much copra today.

As with house building and garden making, people could not simply begin clearing land and planting coconuts indiscriminately anywhere they chose. Rather, people began to develop areas of coastal land with which they under-stood themselves to have an especially privileged connection. Tracing these connections, as mapped out for me by those involved in this coconut plantation drive, readily demonstrates that the developers appealed not only to brief histories of father to son inheritance, but also to their supposed ties to an earlier group of landholders often described as "the people of old" (*sae bwani*), or alternatively, to people interpreted as representatives of their authority over the land. Take, for example, the case of one man who decided to plant coconuts at a certain place where his father had previously made gardens and where his father's father had previously planted a small grove of coconuts. As it happens, however, this man's father's father, whom I will call Ariburu, was a man through whom many of the present-day villagers of Tawatana trace the history of their land occupation and use. Ariburu serves as a nexus among many kin groups and areas within and around Tawatana because it is commonly asserted that he was authorized by a remnant of the now extinct *auhenua* matrilineage of the land to oversee their territory after them. A few people hold that he was even part of such a remnant. These last of the *auhenua*, or alternatively those deputized by them, are often designated "the people of old," or the former "senior men" (*sae maua*). Thus, Ariburu is seen, in one way or another, to have acted with the authority of the *auhenua* to bring people to live with him on the land. He placed people at particular areas and later designated land where they might build a school. Although he was never formally anointed as their chief, the people of Tawatana viewed him as the leader in the village. Today the descendants of the generation settled by Ariburu look back on him as the mediator of a land charter laid down by the original people of the land who chose him as their agent. Thus, his grandson can construe his access to the land where he planted coconuts as doubly secured: first through father to son transmission over three generations, and second through Ariburu's link to the people of old.

An analogous pattern of double connection to place emerges in another man's testimony regarding a coconut plantation he made in the late 1950s. This particular man assumed access to the area he planted because his father had collected fruits and nuts there and his father's father had actually lived there. At the same time, he, along with his father's brothers and their sons, insist that, in reciprocity for a gift of shell valuables, the last representative of the *auhenua* matrilineage had permanently settled his father's father on that land. In the same vein, it should be noted that this man implicates his father's father in yet another double connection to another location where he formerly resided in the village. With respect to the latter location, this man justified his earlier residence there on the basis of a connection to Ariburu. His father's father, it turns out, had married Ariburu's daughter, and Ariburu had placed their son, the father of the man in question, at this particular location. Once again, therefore, this man could comfortably suppose he was free to live there himself both on account of paternal precedence and in accordance with the dictates of Ariburu, the presumed agent of the *auhenua*.

What this last example suggests, not surprisingly, is that the same practice that underlies access to land for coconut plantation projects also underlies access to land for nearly every purpose. The practice of embedding a relatively shallow history of father to son inheritance within the deeper history of a defunct *auhenua* matrilineage is discernible at the base of most people's accounts of why they live, garden, or gather fruit and nuts where they do. Moreover, it is often, although not universally, the case that these accounts intersect in the figure of Ariburu (b. before 1871–d. before 1947), the spokesman for the dead *auhenua*. Especially among the residents of the core hamlets of Tawatana, it is commonly asserted that "we live through [or following] Ariburu"; he is understood to have made the central hamlets a "place for living" and gardening for the whole village that no single person can appropriate for his or her limited use.[15]

In addition to having brought the paternal grandfathers of the current generation to live on the land, Ariburu is said also to have named many men of the current generation, both his own and other people's grandchildren. The names that he bestowed are widely supposed to have been names belonging to the extinct *auhenua* matrilineage that had left him in charge of their land. By distributing these names, Ariburu gave the people he named a stake in the land at Tawatana. Although these names do not grant their bearers *auhenua* status, nevertheless, because they are recognized to be names irrevocably attached to Tawatana through the old *auhenua*, they do serve to distinguish their present holders as people who unequivocally belong at Tawatana. They can even, according to some, allow their present holders to have influence over the spirit-sharks formerly controlled by their pre-Christian *auhenua* namesakes.

This, in sum, is what Tawatana looked like in the 1990s. The village is a constellation of hamlets inhabited by patrikin who justify their use of land where they live, garden, forage, and develop plantations by tracing their fathers and fathers' fathers to links to an extinct *auhenua* matrilineage. In formulae that succinctly and concretely express their relationship to village land they say, "we all eat through the father," or "we all follow Ariburu," or "we are all people who have come from elsewhere." These formulae are all roughly syn-

---

15. Ian Frazer (1973: 1–2, 15) describes a parallel situation in To'ambaita, north Malaita. Here, however, the death of original patrilines with "primary [land] rights," known as *ainifasia*, has fostered the construction of connections to land through women. See also Scheffler (1971: 288) for the general pattern of "friendly or related big-men" settling bush dwellers on coastal land with consequent potential for dispute.

onymous and all presuppose that the matrilineage that once was *auhenua* at Tawatana is now dead.

But at the same time that I was becoming familiar with this presentation of Tawatana, I was also becoming aware of another Tawatana in which it is possible to detect that some people believe that they additionally, and more importantly, "eat through the mother." From their point of view, the Tawatana in which "everyone" eats through the father is a false appearance masking the fact that they and their matrilineal relations are the true *auhenua* who graciously permit everyone else to share their land and good things. This perspective emerged on one occasion when I queried a man who had been confidentially elucidating to me how his matrilineage was the authentic surviving *auhenua* matrilineage at Tawatana. "You told me that you eat through the mother," I said, "but I don't see anyone eating through the mother here; it looks as though everyone eats through the father." To this he replied:

> It is true what you see. It's true, that's how it looks. It is because of the love that resides with the matrilineage [of the place] that allows that group [i.e., this man's sons and brothers' sons and their grandchildren] to reside here. That group should be "patient," as you say it, and just observe the real lineage [of the land]. There are lots of things they shouldn't do on their own. [They should be quiet and patient] because they are just sprouted from the father, they aren't from the mother in blood. If they want blood they should go to the place from which their mothers came. That's the thing that you've seen. It looks as if they all only eat through the father, it looks like this. But it's because of their father—who is inside the lineage and who bought them here [i.e., paid bride-price for their mothers]—that they stay. Good enough, good enough, just stay. But it isn't as if—in staying here—[they] stand beyond the person of the lineage that brought [them] here, it's not like that. But after a time they go and do things on their own and you can look and see; they eat through the father, the people here, they don't eat through the mother, but it only looks like that here.

In this circumlocutory way, this man was asserting that indeed his children and grandchildren, along with those of his brothers, all eat through their fathers, but that he and his brothers are members of the true lineage of the land who have retained their descendants around them by virtue of their ability to eat through the mother where they reside.

If interrogated even further, the rationales that lie behind some people's coconut plantation endeavors reveal, not just mediated links to the dead *auhenua*, but implicit claims to be *auhenua* at the sites chosen for development. Likewise, the fact that some villagers identify particular lineages as the living *auhenua* is also legible in a more recent cocoa plantation initiative of the 1980s. In 1980 the National Agriculture Department encouraged Arosi to develop small cocoa plantations. In Tawatana, initial proposals conceived of a single village-wide community project, but villagers rejected this plan.

> At the very first we held a general meeting in the village to ask if we wanted to make one [cocoa] project, or do many. We decided against the community-wide project since there were too many questions raised and people were concerned that only some people would do the work and others would try to get out of doing the work. So we asked who wants [to start a project]?

Four men stood forward with the intention of initiating four separate cocoa plantations. Of these four, three later established cocoa plantations on land, the use of which they understood to be under their jurisdiction through their fathers, paternal grandfathers, or even great grandfathers. Along with their brothers and father's brother's sons, these three formed core groups that recruited affines and neighbors as "members" to assist with the work of their projects. The fourth man, in contrast, understood himself to be acting on behalf of his sons, who had access to the land in question through their mother's brother. That is to say, the fourth man understands his sons' connection to the developed land to be a matrilineal connection to land where they are *auhenua*.

The villagers of Tawatana are not the only Arosi who suggested to me that the idea, prevalent throughout Arosi I, that everyone eats through the father is only an appearance overlaying a very different reality in which genuine *auhenua* matrilineages are quietly, even secretly, alive and well. The people who put themselves forward as representatives of such matrilineages seemed to regard their existence as an indispensable fact. After we had discussed the various manifestations of eating through the father evident in a village east of Tawatana, another man observed: "You've described to me the way a lot of people have say over one piece of land [in the village], but it is important to remember that [only] one lineage has the land in any particular place [in Arosi] and that all sorts of people appear to have power there because they were all made to sit there by the representatives of [that] lineage."

As more and more Arosi, serially and often in seclusion, presented themselves to me as the living *auhenua*, I began to discern that there are, in fact, two different socio-spatial models coexisting in Arosi. One model—the one already described in this chapter—operates at the surface and is premised on an overt consensus that the *auhenua* matrilineages of the coastal land are dead and that the villagers have all come from somewhere else. This is the model, evident to the naive gaze, according to which hamlets of various sizes, headed by senior men surrounded by their sons and their sons' families, constitute a village with a church at its ritual and social center. The other model—the one that is the primary focus of this study—operates at a hidden level where the ultimate foundation of any collective social polity is an *auhenua* matrilineage anchored in its territory. This second model became evident to me progressively as people tentatively and one-by-one chose to share with me their claims to be the *auhenua* at their villages—claims that they would not normally divulge to members of other lineages. The coexistence of these two models of socio-spatial order in the villages bifurcated my experience of entry into Arosi as an ethnographic field site, creating two parallel trajectories of discovery. Having here traced the trajectory that led toward the surface model, in the following chapter I begin again by delving beneath the appearance of Tawatana to trace the trajectory that led me toward the hidden model of village order. Instead of presenting Arosi land tenure as a simple matter of sons continuing to live and garden where their fathers and grandfathers had done so before them, this latter entry into the field revealed a composite Arosi landscape comprising multiple overlapping and mutually displacing *auhenua* identities.

CHAPTER 2

MOVING TOWARD HETEROTOPIA

When I arrived in Tawatana village in 1992, many people told me that the true owners of the coastal land on which Arosi now live had all died in the epidemics that had swept the island a number of generations ago. "The people of the beach have all died, first from dysentery, then from tuberculosis and malaria," I was informed. "The matrilineage of the land is now finished." Others freely explained: "In Tawatana we're all people who have come from elsewhere (*sae boboi*). The people of the original matrilineage of the land are dead." Villagers frequently used the locution *burunga i auhenua* to describe the matrilineage (*burunga*) that had enjoyed autochthonous ancestral entitlement to the land where the village is located; by virtue of having been first to inhabit the land, this lineage alone had been *auhenua* in the village. Members of such a lineage would have been able to point to graveyards, shrines dedicated to ancestors, tabu sites, and old nut trees as marks of their ancestors' ancient and formative presence in the land. They would have welcomed and settled members of other lineages on their land, granted them permission to build houses, clear gardens, and enjoy the produce of local nut trees. Because Arosi matrilineages are exogamous, these relations of support would have entailed lineage intermarriage, contributing to the formation of a multilineal polity under the "ruling shadow" (*marungi*) of the *burunga i auhenua*.

When I visited people in other villages along the coast, they too informed me that the last representatives of the autochthonous lineages in their villages were also long dead. In some places people openly admitted that they were unsure which lineage had established the local shrines, and confessed that they did not know the names of the people who had been placed in the old burial grounds dotting the coastal landscape. Furthermore, in villages all along the coast, people seemed unconcerned about lineage territories when they chose where to live and garden on the slopes behind their villages. As at Tawatana, at other villages, Arosi explained that they all lived in their villages thanks to their diverse connections to former "senior men" or "people of old." Often unnamed by current villagers, these "people of old" are said to have been either the last remnants of the no longer extant *auhenua* matrilineages, or people

69

who had been settled on and given oversight of coastal village land by such lineages. During a transitional period I can best reconstruct as having occurred between the mid to late nineteenth century, the "people of old," such as Ariburu at Tawatana, presided over localized allocations of village land to diverse groups of settlers whom they had recruited from elsewhere.[1] In the absence of any known or agreed upon *auhenua* lineages to whom they owe their present socio-spatial condition, Arosi reckon their present relationships to one another and to land from this period of reorganization. Rather than situate themselves with respect to large matrilineal territories, they tend instead to mention that a male ancestor—generally a long-dead father or paternal grandfather—first resided and cleared gardens in the narrow *odo* where they currently live and garden. They appeal to their history of ongoing marital and other social connections since the days of the "people of old" as the basis of their village polities, and appear to privilege these relationships over their separate lineage identities in their day-to-day lives.[2]

It appears at first sight, therefore, that customary land tenure is defunct, and that land in Arosi today is unencumbered by ancestral lineage markers and lineage claims. Ostensibly, Arosi is a deterritorialized postcolonial context in which land—to borrow the words of David Harvey (1989: 264)—has been "stripped of [its] preceding significations." But even while empty of *auhenua*, Arosi is, paradoxically, full of *auhenua*. I soon discovered that, despite the overt consensus that the original people of the coast are deceased and the implementation of a remedial land tenure system by the "people of old," many different matrilineages covertly claim to be *auhenua* in the same coastal terrain.

These conflicting identity and land claims came to my attention when I began to collect the kind of unilineal genealogically-based knowledge conveyed in autochthonous histories (*mamaani auhenua*). As in many Austronesian contexts, among Arosi, narrative genealogies tell how the ancestors of a lineage first occupied an area of land, made graveyards, created tabu places, formed shrines where they gave offerings to the spirits of their dead, and left

---

1. I take former Special Lands Commissioner Colin Allan (1990: 126; cf. Fox 1924: 9) to be documenting the same type of discourse when he writes: "the 'former people' consistently emerged in the tangle of previous land transactions when I was on Makira in 1956. Nowhere else in the Solomons did this theme obtrude itself so consistently as on Makira."

2. O'Connor (1973: 77–79) describes a similar situation on the south coast of Guadalcanal in the mid 1960s. As will be discussed in chapter 7, these innovations in Arosi landholding and use are implicated in the designs of some people who are now advocating an explicit and systematic shift to father to son land inheritance.

personal names associated with areas of habitation (cf. J. Fox 1997). Although the majority of Arosi learn about their lineage and its land in piecemeal fashion, in most lineages there is a man or a woman who is recognized as knowing the full extent of his or her matrilineage's genealogy, its shrines and ancestral spirits, and the extent of its land. Sometimes referred to within their lineages as *sae aidangi*, "knowledgeable" or "instructed people," such men and women can often trace their lineage's history for twelve generations. Such holders of lineage knowledge are not formally invested with the rights and duties of a recognized office. Rather, they are typically people who have seldom left their villages for long periods of time to attend secondary school, work, or live in the natal villages of their spouses; they have acquired their special familiarity with their matrilineages because they happen to have resided continuously with their mothers, maternal grandmothers, or mothers' brothers. The extent of one person's knowledge tends, therefore, to be more a function of his or her biography than his or her age. Once they gain reputations as relatively well informed people, they will be consulted to answer questions that less knowledgeable members of their lineages may have; they teach the children of their lineages about their relatives, about whom they can and cannot marry, and about their ancestral land. Potentially, they could also speak on behalf of their lineages in court, should a land dispute escalate to that level. In some lineages with large territories there is an informal division of labor between two people, each deferring to the other as more knowledgeable about his or her own side of the territory.

At first, the *sae aidangi* would often decline to tell me their lineage histories or would stop themselves after only a few sentences. To justify his self-censorship, one man stated that if others heard his narrative it would cause a "big fight or split" in his village. Over time, however, lineage representatives grew more confiding, even eager to share their lineage stories with me. Whenever such knowledgeable people decided to tell me their lineage's history—and many eventually became keen to do so—they preferred to narrate their account only in secluded garden huts. In these settings, the *sae aidangi* recounted genealogical narratives indicating that the land in their particular villages belonged exclusively to their respective matrilineages. They all divulged, each on behalf of his or her own lineage, that they were the true *auhenua*, the only authentic descendants of the original people of the various coastal villages where they resided.

Because of these quiet contradictions, Arosi are at once eager and fearful to discover the contents of each other's lineage narratives. When one man said of a hand-written notebook—what in Pijin is called a *kastom buk*—detailing his lineage's genealogical history, "No one wants to hear about this book," he was not speaking literally. He meant that no one wants to learn information that would challenge his or her lineage narrative and cause disputes. Tacitly aware that other lineages tell competing narratives, but ignorant of the details in their rivals' accounts, lineage representatives closely guard the contents of their own narratives against theft and preemptory falsification.[3] Unwillingness to disclose lineage narratives not only protects the basis of one's own claim, but also avoids denying the merits of another's, thereby avoiding open conflict over land.[4] This secrecy creates multiple latent and overlapping lineage territories, unseen but inscribed on land that is said to be devoid of *auhenua*. It emerges, therefore, that present-day Arosi is not a land stripped of its preceding significations, but displays characteristics of what Foucault (1986: 25) terms a heterotopia: an environment "capable of juxtaposing in a single real place several spaces, several sites that are in themselves incompatible." Nevertheless, in the name of what one friend characterized as "love, peace, and unity," many Arosi collude in forming a general consensus that the coastal *auhenua* are extinct.

Through my conversations with lineage representatives I learned that competing *auhenua* identities and overlapping land claims are not the only factors that inhibit Arosi from freely permitting access to their lineage narratives. Arosi demure to reveal their lineage histories, and the prerogatives to land that they confer, because of a strong conviction that an overt presumption of *auhenua* status and land control is compromisingly inappropriate for those who are truly *auhenua*. As previously discussed, for Arosi, being *auhenua* has an ethical dimension. The *ringeringe auhenua* deters the *auhenua* from being inhospitable and ungenerous. It instructs them, "don't chase people away

---

3. Anthropologists working elsewhere in Melanesia have discerned similar narrative practices in situations where access to high-value resources, such as logging and mining revenues, are at stake (e.g., Stewart and A. Strathern 2002a: especially Chapter 7; Rumsey and Weiner 2001). Throughout the twentieth century, there was no high-value resource extraction in Arosi I. Moreover, in the 1990s, narrative constructions of competing *auhenua* identities did not impinge significantly on people's ability to obtain the use of land for the satisfaction of everyday needs, as there are numerous non-matrilineal modes of access to land for living and gardening purposes. That said, Arosi engage in these types of discursive strategies with a view to protecting their interests in anticipation of future development projects.

4. This attitude indicates that the collective activities reported for the neighboring island of Malaita, where "various leaders" meet "to record genealogies for all the clans of the district" (Burt 1994a: 213; cf. Akin 1993: 540; Naitoro 1993) are virtually inconceivable in Arosi. But see also Burt's (2001: 6) recent discussion of secrecy and genealogical knowledge among Kwara'ae.

[from your place]," "don't be selfish," "don't cause fights," "don't gossip," "don't be jealous," and exhorts them to show "love," "share with others," have "good thoughts," demonstrate "perseverance," be "gentle" and "truthful." For a lineage to insist on its own privileges as *auhenua*, and demand recognition as the rightful landowners on whose open-handedness everyone else depends, is regarded as self-aggrandizing arrogance intended to keep others in a deferential position, if not drive them away altogether. Because such behavior is regarded as clearly antithetical to the precepts of the *ringeringe auhenua*, those who indulge in it are said to demonstrate that they are pretenders. Lineages consequently hesitate to stake their own claims as *auhenua*; to do so would be to risk negating their claim through actions alien to the ethic that shows a lineage to be *auhenua*. Thus, the *ringeringe auhenua*, as well as fear of unknown counter-indicative narratives, functions to silence lineage narratives.

Initially, I was inclined to recognize Arosi secrecy and silence regarding lineage narratives as "discursive control practices" (Lindstrom 1990a: 64) similar to those documented in other parts of Melanesia. Such practices have been depicted as "competitive" strategies that enable disputants "to reveal crucial pieces of knowledge at a strategic moment" in court testimonies (Neumann 1992: 149; cf. A. L. Epstein 1969: 128; Foale and Macintyre 2000: 33; White 1991: 35–36). Gradually, however, I realized that this characterization, when applied to Arosi reticence concerning lineage narratives, is insufficient. Arosi say that few disputes are taken to court by original lineages (cf. Maenu'u 1992: 68). Moreover, there appears to be little desire to perform the types of strategic revelation found elsewhere in Melanesia.[5] Even in what Arosi consider to be the current disputatious atmosphere, lineage representatives remain reluctant to make the narrative disclosures that a court hearing might demand (cf. McDougall 2005).[6]

Recent anthropological literature on land disputes in Melanesia tends to portray forms of "knowledge" such as lineage narratives as tokens of political power that can be skillfully constructed and manipulated in the context of

---

5. For a marked contrast to Arosi, see White's (1993: 485) analysis of the overtly "performative" nature of argumentation in land courts on Santa Isabel. At points, however, White's (1988: 20; 1991: 74) ethnography suggests that in the amalgamated villages of Santa Isabel "regional groups" maintain "submerged" distinctive identities.

6. Due to logistical difficulties, I was unable to consult the local court records and compile exact statistics with respect to the number of times the local court met to hear land cases. The number of disputes that, according to my informants, went to court appears to have been few, however, when compared with other parts of Melanesia (e.g., Burt 1994b; Foale and Macintyre 2000; Hutchins 1980; Maenu'u 1992; Rodman 1987, 1995; G. Schneider 1998; Tiffany 1983; Westermark 1997). During my research residence in Arosi, I was not aware of any contemporaneous court hearings regarding land.

court cases (e.g., Hutchins 1990; Lindstrom 1990b). From such a perspective, the narratives themselves appear—like those White documents for Santa Isabel—to have "little relevance for other dimensions of social life" (White 1991: 35; cf. Frazer 1973: 16–17). Arosi narratives, however, are not merely forms of disembodied knowledge that a lineage might possess and use in court as pieces of evidence to support a land claim. Rather, these narratives are the sources as well as the proofs of highly valued *auhenua* identities. A lineage narrative describes the very ontological nature of a matrilineage as an entity inseparably fused with its ancestral land (cf. Abramson 2000; de Coppet 1985). When lineage representatives narrate their lineage histories they not only trace their matrilineal ancestors' movements over the land, they tell how their ancestors actually gave shape to the landscape. They tell how the spirits of these ancestors continue to inhabit the land and watch protectively over their descendants. A lineage, its narrative, and its land together form a unique organic unity. For Arosi, these unities are the distinct but interconnected constituents that make up their lived world.

Given the existence of competing lineage-cum-land identities, one lineage's revelation of its narrative about a particular stretch of land is not only viewed as an attempt to deny the validity of another lineage's narrative and attendant land claim, it is nothing less than a challenge to the fundamental nature and possibility of the other lineage's existence. For Arosi, the choice to disclose lineage narratives entails not only practical but existential consequences. The revelation of one's lineage narrative is neither merely a property claim nor an offensive insinuation that others are interlopers; it is the divisive assertion of a unique identity that simultaneously violates the ethical norms of that identity. This fact, despite material concerns for control of land and resources, further explains lineage representatives' reluctance to reveal the "true" nature of their identities and their willingness to submerge their claims to land and identity under a fragile consensus that no one is *auhenua* in the coastal villages. Their reticence is, I suggest, a silent articulation of the tension between social relations that foster peaceful coexistence among diverse orders of being and potentially divisive assertions of distinctive identities.

In this chapter and the next, I examine the colonial history that forms the immediate background to the present social construction of the Arosi coast as a world both empty and full of mutually exclusive *auhenua* lineages and their silent claims to land. Because detailed narrative histories of the Solomons in general, and of Arosi in particular, already exist (e.g., Bennett 1987; Byer 1996, 1997; K. Green 1976; Laracy, ed. 1989; Sayes 1976), I give an abbreviated history intended to highlight those interrelated and often concurrent factors that are most relevant to the development of Arosi heterotopia. Accordingly, in the present chapter I focus on the demise of pre-colonial forms of Arosi leadership; the crisis of disease and depopulation from the mid 1800s to the 1920s; the efforts of the British Solomon Islands Protectorate government to curtail epidemics and establish administrative control by relocating Makirans from the bush interior to the coast; the allied role of Christian missions in this spatial reorganization; and the ongoing consequences of colonial land policies. In the following chapter, I examine the Maasina Rule movement as it developed in Arosi, documenting the impetus it gave to completing the evacuation of the bush and the renewal and reification of Arosi custom. To trace the influence of these major factors is to follow a movement toward the configuration of Arosi heterotopia today.[7]

Precolonial Arosi Leadership

As will be discussed in chapter 6, it may well be the case that heterotopia is not a condition entirely original to the present. Yet from the contemporary Arosi point of view, the current situation in which different lineages quietly nurture their identities as *auhenua* contrasts markedly with a previous era in which each territory is said to have been ruled by a clearly identified and accepted *auhenua* matrilineage. Echoing what many Arosi told me, one woman juxtaposed the muted conflicts of the present day with a period of lost transparency during which, "the people who came here [i.e., to her lineage's land] knew we were *auhenua*." "In olden times everyone knew who had the land and so there was no conflict," an old man of east Arosi observed. Arosi readily identify the absence of customary chiefs as a primary cause of what they see as the contemporary state of disorder regarding lineage identities. When there had been chiefs, "the chief [was] the chief in the land of the lineage and those who [were] brought [into the land came] under the ruling shadow of the chief of the lineage that had the land." Today Arosi lament the lack of a true chief who, as a representative of the interests of the *auhenua* matrilineage in its territory, would establish and maintain an unequivocal distinction and just balance between the *auhenua* and those who had come to the land.

---

7. For studies that implicate some of these factors in the creation of land tenure ambiguities conducive to dispute in coastal areas elsewhere in Solomon Islands, see Bathgate 1985: 99–101; Cochrane 1969: 333; Frazer 1981: Chapter 3; Herlihy 1981: 110, 124–125; Scheffler 1965: 27; 1971: 288–289.

Any attempt to determine the nature and characteristics of Arosi leadership in the precolonial period is necessarily a reconstructive undertaking. This is true even for Arosi themselves as they theorize that the passing of their indigenous leadership institutions has undermined their ability to live together in clearly grounded and cohesive polities. The traditions described by my consultants and the earliest ethnographic accounts together suggest that precolonial Makiran political order entailed two types of chief, a "reigning chief" and a "war-chief" or "head-hunter" (Guppy 1887: 19, 20; cf. Fox 1924: 299, 306–307; Verguet 1885: 211–212). These sources also support an analysis of the relationship between the two types of chief in Arosi as a relationship of complementarity between forces of stability and cohesion and forces of destruction and dissolution (cf. de Coppet 1973, 1995; Keesing 1985).[8] Although seemingly oppositional, these counterbalancing forces were both equally essential to reproducing a polity centered on an uncompromised *auhenua* lineage.

The distinction between the roles of the chief and the warrior was not always clear-cut, however. The chief (*mwaeraha* or *araha*), in fact, performed two separate functions: one at odds with, and one parallel to the function of the warrior (*wa'animae* or *ramo*). One major role of the chief was to draw the multiple exogamous Arosi lineages together into an amicable and mutually beneficial social collectivity, a role that could be in tension with that of the "professional fighter" (Fox 1924: 306) whose activities created fear and suspicion among social groups. At the same time, the chief was also responsible for preserving the integrity and residence of the *auhenua* on their ancestral land, even as his hospitality and benevolence made that land accessible to people who were not *auhenua*. In this latter respect, the function of the chief was compatible with that of the warrior whose activities might intensify to assist in policing the rights of the *auhenua* and driving away potential usurpers if the chief himself failed to limit their encroachments. Building on mutually "entangling" (*haia'ia'i* or *haikawikawi*) inter-lineage relationships, chiefs maintained lateral relationships among members of diverse descent groups, reinforcing harmonious coexistence within extended social polities. In contrast, indexing relationships based on matrilineal descent, warriors could articulate exclusive unilineal identities and prerogatives that provoked schisms within these polities (cf. Barraud et al. 1994: 64; de Coppet 1981: 176–177; 1985: 80; 1995: 239–240; Keesing 1985: 248).

A precolonial Arosi chief was not simply an exemplar of the anthropological "big-man" who endeavors to situate himself at the nexus of exchange relations

---

8. For a fuller analysis of this complementary relationship between chief and warrior in Arosi and its cosmological underpinnings, see Scott 2000.

(Sahlins 1963). Rather, he was chosen from birth, or at a very young age, to serve as initiator and sustainer of a social network converging on the territory of an *auhenua* lineage. It is important to note that this child could be a member of a matrilineage other than the one he served, owing to a frequent father to son pattern in chiefly succession. Nevertheless, he became the authoritative representative of the matrilineage that chose him. Oral traditions recount that the *auhenua* of the land would raise a male child to become their chief. At birth, the chosen child was ceremonially bathed on top of shell valuables, a ritual that inaugurated a series of feasts foreshadowing the forging of social relations he would pursue as chief (cf. Fox 1924: 181–190). Once installed, an Arosi chief, like the 'Are'are "peace-master" described by Daniel de Coppet (1995: 236), worked to form a broader-based community than might otherwise have existed. He accomplished this through a variety of diplomatic and judicial activities. He served as leader when the people of his village traveled to be guests at feasts held by neighboring villages and served as host when his village received guests and strangers. As the representative of the autochthonous lineage of the village, the chief would bring people of other lineages to live on the land and encouraged them to intermarry with the *auhenua*. Although the convergence of diverse people on the land of the *auhenua* was a positive goal, no strangers could settle there without the chief's permission. The chief supervised all collective labor in the village and arbitrated disputes. He was at liberty to use the shell valuables of the *auhenua* to mediate antagonisms that threatened the cohesion he had established among diverse people. In short, the chief was the agent and overseer of inter-lineage entanglement (cf. Fox 1924: 299). A chief's death brought instability and uncertainty; the polity threatened to unravel. One of my consultants reported that, formerly, when a chief died, people in their sorrow lamented, "Now we are divided!" The appointment of a new chief would end this liminal return to dissolution.

Often, in Arosi, the forces of destruction and social fragmentation were not embodied in the person of a warrior. Instead, these forces took a variety of forms ranging from naturalized social processes of exogamy and patri-virilocality to the ad hoc actions of bellicose men. Normally these forces did not require a special human agent but were, and continue to be, regarded as operative in a continuous process of organic decay. Arosi view productive social relations as subject to an inherent law of cosmic entropy against which the *auhenua* must fight to retain both their own and other lineage members in their land. Accordingly, in addition to facilitating relations among convergent lineages, the chief would also strive to ensure the continued presence of the *auhenua* matrilineage in its land. In this respect, in order to be a successful architect of entanglement, a chief also had to be mindful of the autochthonous history of the *auhenua* and their precedence within the polity.

On behalf of the *auhenua*, the chief helped to counter the effects of low birthrate and the absence of lineage women that resulted from exogamy and patri-virilocal residence. Specifically, he sought to bring some of the lineage's children, and the lineage-owned personal names that they carried, back to their land. When facing a shortage of lineage women of childbearing age, the chief would purchase a young woman from elsewhere to be adopted into the lineage and to bear children who would reproduce the lineage. Without the organizational efforts of chiefs, lineages would have found it difficult to maintain a stable and significant presence on their lands. The Arosi verb *dauhenua*—"to hold the people and the land/village together"—succinctly expresses the function of a chief.

Sometimes, however, the natural course of social entropy was aided by a "bad chief" who, by definition, was one who failed to work against its dissipating force. A chief might, for example, have been ineffective at holding together the *auhenua*, their land, and the other people with whom they lived. Past chiefs who did not bring lineage children back to the land, who did not intervene in local disputes, or who permitted strangers to usurp the position of the rightful *auhenua*, are remembered as having been "bad chiefs." Ironically, in combating social entropy, a chief could become a center of excessive social gravity; if he did not hold the prerogatives of the non-*auhenua* to their proper limits, the necessary distinction between the *auhenua* and the non-*auhenua* on which his *auhenua*-based polity depended threatened to collapse.

It was precisely under such circumstances that the principle of dissolution might come to be embodied by an especially aggressive Arosi person. This occasional emergence of a warrior figure presents a contrast with depictions of Malaitan society as continually harassed by unpredictable opportunistic murderers engaged in internecine feuding, violent serial murders, and personal combats (de Coppet 1968: 54; Fox 1962: 33; Keesing and Corris 1980: 17–25). Arosi also had warriors, but these fighters killed traditional external enemies on set battlegrounds (cf. Bradford to BC, September 7, 1861, TBCP, Vol. 5: In-Letters, 1857–1866, set 24, item 8; Fox 1924: 305). A warrior was likely to have been a contentious and intimidating member of the *auhenua* lineage. Sometimes such an antagonistic and testy character was one of the chief's brothers who had established a reputation as a fierce killer of distant enemies. A "professional fighter" would provide the body of a victim, taken from a distant social group, as was required for consumption at certain feasts and initiations (Fox 1924: 306–307). Although, as a rule, he did not use violence against people within his own collective polity, a warrior might make threats, backed by his notorious reputation, in order forcefully to remind non-*auhenua* villagers that they lived on his lineage's land due to his lineage's generosity. As the defender of the identity and prerogatives of the *auhenua*, the warrior necessarily represented the narrow unilineal focus of their autochthonous history.[9]

Just as the centripetal pull exerted by the chief could become excessive, the centrifugal push exerted by the warrior could also exceed useful proportions. This possibility is imagined in a narrative I collected from several Arosi. The story describes the intolerable conditions created by the murderous behavior of Mwaeroobwani (Killer-of-olden-times). Mwaeroobwani was a monstrous giant whose forearm was the length of an ordinary man's entire arm. He killed indiscriminately and let no one come near the canyon where he lived in a cave surrounded by steep rocky cliffs. His violence was so terrible that even his wife could not bear him and orchestrated his demise. Mwaeroobwani is a hyperbolic figure of the anti-social isolation that can befall a person or social group that allows the forces of destruction and dissolution to override those of stability and cohesion (cf. Keesing 1985: 245). As in southern Malaita, "[t]hese two modes — murderous and peaceful — are inseparable at the level of the whole; that is to say, one is inconceivable without the other" (de Coppet and Zemp 1978: 116, author's translation).

Today, chiefs are no longer groomed from childhood and ritually installed; the men termed chiefs (Pijin: *sif*) in contemporary Arosi are elected officials with limited prestige and authority. The warrior, in his turn, has been curbed by law and reformed by the call to Christian brotherly love. Nevertheless, the memory of such figures remains alive. On many occasions George Huruani (b. 1911–), an elected chief for Tawatana, regaled me with accounts of the exploits of the most storied generation of Arosi leaders that included the chiefs Boʻorauaniara of Heuru (d. 1909) and Takihorotaʻimae of Wango (d. 1917), and the warrior Iʻahoroiasi of Tawatana (d. c. 1920). Takihorotaʻimae and Boʻorauaniara are famous because it was they who invited the Anglican Church to their villages during the last quarter of the nineteenth century, acted as middlemen between European traders and local villagers, and received the Union Jack when the British Solomon Islands Protectorate was declared on Makira in 1893. Owing to their mediating contacts with Westerners, these

---

9. An analogous pattern is documented in southern ʻAreʻare where the murderer is subordinated to the peace-chief and acts as executioner in the service of the latter. By contrast, in northern ʻAreʻare the murderer and peace-chief are independent figures, although the peace-chief may have been a murderer in his youth (de Coppet 1973: 16, 17; Barraud et al. 1994: 44–45). In Kwaraʻae, north central Malaita, "Warriors are remembered as dangerous and often impetuous men, but some of them were also regarded as guardians of morality who threatened and killed to uphold the 'law' and gain restitution for breaches of tabu. These warriors are now often compared to policemen" (Burt 1994a: 48; cf. Keesing 1985: 245–246, 250; 1992: 31–32).

Figure 2.1. Boʻorauaniara, Heuru, 1906 (Beattie Collection).
© The Trustees of The British Museum.

chiefs enjoyed an unusually far-reaching prestige that enabled them to establish larger and more stable regions of influence than previous generations of
chiefs. Iʻahoroiasi, for his part, is remembered as having been intimidatingly
tall and quick to anger, and people say that he was constantly policing the actions of others by threatening reprisals. People agree that he was an exacting,
dangerous, and even cruel person who killed a man who refused to pay compensation after having committed adultery with his wife, victimized relatives
of wrong-doers if they themselves could not be located, and abandoned his
own sister on Ulawa because he thought that she had become pregnant while
still unmarried. In contrast to Takihorotaʻimae and Boʻorauaniara who flour-
ished in the early colonial period, Iʻahoroiasi inevitably came into conflict with
British authority. George still remembers how the first British official appointed to Makira in 1918 had compelled Iʻahoroiasi to surrender a particularly fine Winchester rifle decorated with in-laid mother-of-pearl.

Ironically, the very influences and institutions for which they helped to provide a foothold served ultimately to erode the position of chiefs as well as warriors. Over the course of the past century, Christians—both missionary and
indigenous—have helped to eliminate the warrior and have dramatically

Figure 2.2. Takihorotaʻimae, Wango, 1906 (Beattie Collection).
© The Trustees of The British Museum.

transformed the chief with a new message of universal peace and unity. The call to Christian love and forgiveness, backed by British law, quickly forced the warrior into obsolescence. Not only did Christians seek to stop murder, theft, and violence; they also sought to dismantle many of the ritual contexts, such as canoe launchings and mortuary practices addressed to ancestral spirits, that had previously required a murder victim from a distant enemy. With their police function at home usurped by government agents, and their ritual function as killers abroad denounced by the Church, recognized warriors disappeared. Coincident with the demise of the warrior has come a redefinition of the role of the chief. Discerning the authority and mediating function of chiefs, early missionaries sought to work through these leaders to promote their own agenda. In doing so, however, they promulgated a new ideology of peace. In place of the Arosi ideal of stable social relations within a composite polity centered on strong representation of the *auhenua* in their land, the missionaries introduced a new ideal of fraternal love centered on parity and unity in Christ. Consequently, the structure of chieftaincy has been transformed, and many of the chiefs' pre-Christian practices have been curtailed. No longer anointed representatives of *auhenua* lineages in their land, village chiefs represent the constituencies that elect them to what has become a public office. No longer organizing feasts designed to map relationships among the separate groups within their polities (Fox 1924: 318–324), chiefs have ceded to the Church the role of presiding over eucharistic and festival meals that override social divisions and seek to equalize those who participate.

While Takihorota'imae and Bo'orauaniara are objects of great admiration to present-day Arosi, they have also become objects of dissension. Both are viewed as having been representatives and guarantors of stable *auhenua* line-ages in their territories. But the question, aptly formulated by one man, is: "Who anointed them chief?" That is to say, which lineages did they represent as the *auhenua* lineages at the centers of their polities? This is the point about which Arosi today disagree. These symbolic figures of a lost unambiguous order have become analogues to the coastal landscape itself onto which com-peting *auhenua* identities are projected. Remarkably, although these men died less than one hundred years ago, different Arosi matrilineages have grafted them into their genealogies or narrative histories in incompatible ways as they work to construct themselves as the lineages in whose service these men op-erated. Owing to the fact that a chief did not have to belong to the matrilin-eage that he represented, and that different lineages might contribute shell valuables for his anointing, these current conflicts furthermore raise the pos-sibility that such discordant constructions may have been contemporaneous with these men themselves. The possibility of supporting such divergent in-terpretations may even have constituted an important feature of precolonial Arosi chiefship as an institution.

Disease and Disorder: The Colonial Reorganization of Makira

Depopulation

The double refrain that the *auhenua* of the coast are all dead and that "we're all people who have come from elsewhere" correlates with a long and well doc-umented history of disease, depopulation, and spatial reorganization during the early colonial period.[10] After brief Spanish contacts with Makirans in the mid and late sixteenth century, it was nearly two hundred years before Euro-

---

10. Frazer (1973; 1981: Chapter 3) documents an analogous decline of landholding groups on the coast of northern Malaita in the context of depopulation and relocation.

Figure 2.3. Chiefship today: George Huruani, Tawatana, 1993.

peans chanced across the Solomon Islands again. It was not until the early nineteenth century, however, that whalers and traders incorporated Makira into their regular voyage itineraries. The first long-term European presence in Arosi was that of the French Marist missionaries who maintained a settlement at Makira Harbour for over a year spanning 1846–47. Representatives of the Anglican Melanesian Mission began to make yearly visits to Arosi from the 1850s, taking Islanders as pupils back to their school in New Zealand. As growing numbers of traders, labor recruiters, missionaries, and naval warships visited Makira during the last quarter of the nineteenth century, the island's inhabitants were increasingly exposed to exogenous illnesses and diseases, and Makira was soon identified as suffering from "very heavy mortality" (Hopkins 1922: 63). These diseases, often leaving Europeans unaffected, frequently took the form of devastating epidemics among Makirans who had little immunity against them.

References to these epidemics recur in a variety of sources, the earliest of which are the accounts given by Anglican missionaries. Returning to Arosi each year to bring "new life" to the Islanders, the missionaries found themselves documenting the inroads made by the diseases that they themselves were, in part, responsible for introducing (Durrad 1922: 5–7; Guppy 1887: 176; Hilliard 1978: 156, 268; Laracy 1976: 40, 67; MM SCL, April 2, 1923: 5).[11] Touring the Solomon Islands in 1882, the medical doctor Henry Brougham Guppy found cases of influenza and mumps, and in one instance linked the latter to a schooner that had called at Makira Harbour to return laborers from Queensland plantations (1887: 176). When the mission vessel Southern Cross returned to Ha'ani and Wango on Makira in 1884 the missionaries discovered that there had been "much sickness and several deaths" in these villages since the previous year (MM AR, 1884: 11). Visiting Arosi two years later, Richard Blundell Comins noted that never before had he "so many sick to see and minister to" (MM AR, 1886: 13). In 1896 the missionaries simply noted: "The people are not healthy" (MM SCL, August 1896: 4). The following year they recorded that at Wango village "nine persons have died

---

11. The irony of this situation was not lost on the Anglican missionary Fox who, in 1918, recorded that some Arosi were in the habit of invoking "a spirit called Sukarito" who was "not the spirit of a dead man, but a spirit who had never been a man, but once came down to the world from the sky, and who controls all sickness and diseases and is very much feared." Recognizing Sukarito as a local rendering of the name Jesus Christ, Fox insinuated that, owing to the diseases brought by the earlier Marist missionaries, the people of Makira had learned to associate the coming of Christ with the coming of disease (ABM R, June 1, 1918: 39).

since last year, and the people are very few" (MM *SCL*, December 1897: 4).
Heuru village was struck by dysentery in 1898, and in 1901 Robert Paley Wilson observed that, "[a]t Heuru there has been much sickness, and ten people have died" (MM *SCL*, July 15, 1901: 66).

When Charles M. Woodford was appointed first Resident Commissioner of the British Solomon Islands Protectorate in 1896 he was well aware of the disastrous effects introduced diseases were having in the islands (Bennett 1987: 131). In his first Annual Report, Woodford stressed the necessity of passing a regulation that would stop people from visiting the Solomons within three weeks after having left German New Guinea and the Bismark Archipelago, areas where smallpox and cholera were present (BSIP *AR*, 1897: 25–26). Soon after the establishment of the Protectorate, the Anglican mission ship *Southern Cross* was quarantined in order to prevent a measles epidemic (Woodford 1922: 71).

Woodford considered dysentery to be "the most fatal disease amongst the natives." He suggested that,

> The fact that natives are extremely careless about the quality of the water they use is probably the cause to which these deaths may be assigned; but the ignorance of remedial measures, and the almost hopeless disinclination of a native to submit to proper medical treatment and discipline, is a large contributing factor. (BSIP *AR*, 1898–99: 5; cf. Woodford 1922: 71)

But for many years afterwards, medical treatment was only available to a very small percentage of Islanders, such as those living close to the government station at Tulagi (Nggela) or near to a mission station. There was no government initiative involving trained medical personnel on Makira until the mid 1920s (MR, November 20, 1922, BSIP 9/III/4 B). In fact, the government had little presence in the Eastern District before 1918, and until then the only "discipline" known to Makirans was in the form of punitive expeditions and shellings of recalcitrant villages (Campbell to Barnett, November 11, 1916, enclosure in Barnett to Sweet-Escott, November 13, 1916, WPHC 1915–18: No. 3269/1916; cf. Corban 1972: 39; Sayes 1976: 194).

On Makira the epidemics continued intermittently. Fox noted that "[e]very few years dysentery passes through the bush villages, killing scores, or even hundreds ..." (1919a: 98). But Fox and his fellow missionaries, for the most part, could only continue to record the frightening extent of the epidemics and deaths: "Missionaries can only stand by and sigh" (MM *SCL*, June 1, 1921: 7). "In 1910 there were, near Pamua, 5 small bush villages, about 200 people, when the epidemic of that year was over no one was left alive in those villages" (Fox 1967: 47). Four years later Makira was "visited by a grievous epidemic of dysentery" that, according to one government official, killed at least one third of the population of the island (ADO to SG, September 18, 1928, BSIP 9/VII/3[a]; BSIP *AR*, 1914–15: 4; MM *AR*, 1914: 23–24; Sayes 1976: 201–202). It is probable that this epidemic began when a mission vessel landed a woman at Maro'u Bay who was suffering from dysentery (Kuper, n.d., BSIP 8/IX/6). The year 1916 was another "year of sickness" with Heuru, like other Arosi villages, suffering from "recurring attacks of dysentery" (MM *SCL*, March 1, 1916: 672, 673).

Fox recounts how, on one occasion, he was on a hilltop behind Heuru and was shown "the sites of forty-six once flourishing villages of which now only three remain, and most of these forty-six were inhabited fifty years ago before the great dysentery epidemic of that time" (1919a: 98). Heuru, a coastal village, was one of the most populous Arosi villages during Fox's time (1978: 212); ironically, *heuru* is the Arosi term for an abandoned village site. To Fox, the prospects for the survival of the inhabitants of Makira looked bleak. He thought it very likely that before too long there would "be no living people in the interior and only a few half-civilized, pidgin-English-speaking people on the coast" (1919a: 98; cf. O'Brien 1995: 199, quoting Rouillac, April 1900; MR, August 12, 1920, BSIP 9/III/4 A).

Although the British Solomon Islands Protectorate had been declared on Makira in 1893, it was not until early in 1918 that Frederick M. Campbell opened the Eastern Solomon's District Headquarters at Kirakira and began to bring the island's 8,000 people under government control (Bennett 1987: 112; K. Green 1976: 43; Sayes 1976: 194). While serving earlier on Malaita as the Officer in Command of the Constabulary, Campbell had been chiefly occupied with pursuing a project of pacification (Akin 1993: 137–138; Boutilier 1983: 59; Keesing and Corris 1980: 42, 66; Knibbs 1929: 187–192). On Makira, however, noting a lack of violence or "serious crime of any description," he focused on implementing paternalistic strategies designed to halt disease and depopulation (AR, January 4, 1919, BSIP 9/III/1 A). During four earlier visits to Makira Campbell had reported:

> The population is dying out fast, on my patrols inland I saw the remains of a good few villages and from enquiries amongst the natives, missionaries, and other white residents I gathered that fully one third of the population have died within the past 3 or 4 years, principally from dysentry [sic] and chest complaints due no doubt to their dirty state of living. (Campbell to Barnett, November 11, 1916, enclosure

in Barnett to Sweet-Escott, November 13, 1916, WPHC 1915–18: No. 3269/1916)[12]

Appalled by the "deplorable conditions of filth and insanitary [sic] surroundings" in which Makirans lived, Campbell sought to stem the spread of disease by dividing the island into administrative districts, appointing headmen for each district, mandating that domestic pigs be fenced, and charging people to clean their villages and clear small "roads" (i.e., broad footpaths) between villages. To counter what he believed to be the bush people's "nomadic" habits, Campbell collectivized Makirans into "substantial villages" that he thought would both improve the health of the inhabitants and increase the possibility of better government administration (AR, January 4, 1919, BSIP 9/III/1 A).

Campbell's specific actions must be contextualized with reference to the influential *Report of the Commission Appointed to Inquire into the Decrease of the Native Population* (Fiji 1896).[13] The Fiji report established the terms and parameters of the colonial discourse about depopulation well into the 1920s (Pitt-Rivers 1927: 50, 277; Rivers 1922: 88; Roberts 1927: 88; Thomas 1990: 154; Woodford 1922: 70). Enumerating a long list of causative factors and recommended remedies, the authors of the report suggested that the dispersal or "decentralisation" of the population was not simply caused by epidemics, as some people believed (MM *SCL*, March 1, 1916: 673), but was itself a significant cause of depopulation (Fiji 1896: 89–95). Ideally, "centralised" villages were to be located at elevated airy sites with good drainage (Fiji 1896: 84–89, 94, 157). The authors of the Fiji report also drew explicit connections between the spatiality of people's residence patterns and the development of each person's character and consciousness. They assumed that small scattered villages contributed to the psychological causes of depopulation: "mental apathy," "laziness," and "lack of ambition" (Fiji 1896: 72). In keeping with these assumptions, Campbell's measures were aimed at transforming the lives of "the most dirty and lazy lot of natives of any island in the [Solomon's] group" (Campbell to Barnett, November 11, 1916, enclosure in Barnett to Sweet-Es-

---

12. Skeptical of the accuracy of population estimates such as Campbell's, which were not based on census data, demographer Norma McArthur (1967: 345–354; cf. Groenewegen 1972: 1) proposes that population decline throughout the Pacific was not as high as has been believed. It should be noted, however, that official statistics for Makira show that the total population continued to decline from the first census in 1919 until the early 1930s (Bedford 1970).

13. Campbell, like a number of his fellow district officers in the Solomons, had served in the colonial government in Fiji prior to his arrival in the Solomons in 1913 (Boutilier 1983: 44; Golden 1993: 305).

cott, November 13, 1916, WPHC 1915–18: No. 3269/1916; cf. ADO to RC, September 18, 1928, BSIP 9/VII/3[a]). The new pattern of residence was designed to raise villagers from forms of organization based on indigenous "communism" to those based on Western "individualism" and "individual freedom" (Fiji 1896: 90, 91).

Colonial officials engaged in the discourse about depopulation were primarily concerned to promote living conditions among Pacific populations that they thought would lead to increased birth rates and to healthier adult populations. The discourse addressed what we might call the reproduction of healthy people. Underpinning this discourse was the assumption that the proper spatial ordering of daily practices and productive activities was a precondition for the reproduction of healthy people. Campbell's administrative strategies on Makira must be understood in terms of the assumption that depopulation was caused, in large part, by the Islanders' lack of spatial order. To Campbell, the observable forms of indigenous Makiran cultural order appeared as disorder, and his attempts to establish colonial order on the island were attempts to transform the spatial structuring of life on Makira.

Partition

In spite of the difficulties that he encountered in trying to travel around the Eastern Solomons District, Campbell was quickly able to institute an administrative hierarchy of district and village headmen that encompassed the district. He did so by mapping out bounded geographic sub-districts and by appointing a headman to be responsible for each of these. The activities of these headmen, in large part, gave tangible form to the sub-districts that had been diagrammed in the abstract on paper at district headquarters, and it was through these headmen that Campbell attempted to establish a spatial order for the reproduction of healthy people on the island.

Having opened the station at Kirakira, Campbell soon "divided the District into eight sub-districts." The sub-districts on Makira were called "Arosi," "Wainoni," "Ravo," "Funariti," "Haununu," and "Kirakira."[14] The neighboring islands of Ugi and Ulawa were also named as sub-districts (AR, January 4, 1919, BSIP 9/III/1 A; cf. K. Green 1976: 45). It is likely that Campbell, given his relatively limited experience on Makira, took advice from long-time missionary residents and plantation workers about how to split up the Eastern Solomons District into sub-districts (DO to ARC, May 4, 1918, BSIP

---

14. The "sub-districts" were generally referred to as "districts" in the colonial documents. Similarly, the headmen for these sub-districts were called "District Headmen."

9/VII/3[b]). The Arosi sub-district, for instance, is identical to Fox's (1924: 3–6) differentiation of this area from the rest of the island.

Fox asserts—and the villagers of Tawatana today concur—that Arosi was originally the name of only a small area of the raised beach to the west of Tawatana. But, he continues,

> in the neighbouring islands of Ulawa and Mala (at the Sa'a end) the name Arosi came to be used for all the western part of San Cristoval while Bauro was used by them for the coastal mass of the island, and Hanuato[']o for the whole island....
>
> In the *Threshold of the Pacific* I gave this name Arosi a rather wider sense than it has in native use so as to include the whole Western end of the island, where only one language is spoken, which I therefore call Arosi. It begins at Wango on the north coast and follows round the western end to Makira Harbour on the south coast. Near Makira Harbour rises the Wango River flowing out on the other coast at Wango and this river, running roughly south to north, forms the eastern boundary of Arosi, which thus includes the whole portion of the island, less than one third, to the west of Wango River. (Fox *BG*: A1; cf. 1924: 3–4)[15]

Fox's ethnographic description of the area that he named "Arosi" contains the proposition that this area and its inhabitants form a natural geographic, linguistic, and cultural unity vis-à-vis the rest of the island. But the fact that some groups of people within this area, in Fox's words (1924: 305), "lived always in a normal state of war," suggests that there were other ways in which the island might have been segmented. For example, sub-district boundaries could have been placed between "traditional" enemies. This possible alternative, together with Campbell's use of straight lines—as if drawn by a surveyor—to demarcate the boundaries of the other sub-districts, indicates that in creating these administrative sub-districts, Campbell was not simply describing pre-existing natural divisions on the island.

His mapping of the divisions on the island should be seen less as depicting divisions than as an attempt to create a number of similarly structured enclosed spatial fields for effective administrative regulation. Campbell was—to adapt Robert Sack's (1986: 19) definition of "territoriality"—"attempt[ing] ... to affect, influence, or control people, phenomena, and relationships, by de-

---

15. In tension with this account is the observation by the earlier Marist missionary, Father Léopold Verguet (1885: 193), that "[t]he name that the natives give to San Christoval is Arossi [*sic*]...."

limiting and asserting control over a [number of discrete but contiguous] geo-graphic area[s]." By such an act of geographic encompassment, Campbell sought to create order—at the level of the district as a whole—out of what he perceived to be the chaotic flux of Makiran existence.

This abstract delimitation of sub-district boundaries was given tangible form primarily by the activities of "District Chiefs" whom Campbell appointed to or-ganize life within their own sub-districts. At the beginning of 1919 he reported that during the course of the previous year he had "placed as reliable a native as it was possible to obtain with my short knowledge of them, temporarily in charge of each [sub-district] ... and call[ed] them District Chiefs."[16] In choos-ing district chiefs Campbell again relied on the Europeans who were already resident on Makira (e.g., Campbell to Babonneau, September 16 and 20, 1918, RCCNSI). All but one of the headmen he recruited had Christian names and several could "read and write in the native dialect," indicating that seven of the eight men whom he chose were mission converts. Campbell wrote that,

> These men are responsible to me for the general cleanliness and good order of their Districts, they have to visit all villages in their districts several times yearly and advise and instruct the inhabitants generally, report or bring before me all offenders, receive birth, death and mar-riage reports and forward [these reports] to me. (AR, January 4, 1919, BSIP 9/III/1 A)

Campbell and subsequent government officials frequently complained in their reports that their efforts to establish structures for indirect rule were handicapped by the lack of a hereditary indigenous elite upon which they could rely to fill positions of responsibility (AR, January 15, 1931, BSIP 9/III/1 B). Campbell recognized and accepted this situation and, as noted, relied in-stead on his own and other Europeans' judgment to identify responsible per-sons. But despite Campbell's example, later government administrators at-tempted to promote candidates for the position of district headman on the basis of their supposed noble pedigrees (AR, January 18, 1930, BSIP 9/III/1 B; QR, January 3, 1931, BSIP 9/III/4 C; ADO to SG, March 2, 1931, BSIP 9/VII/3[a]).[17] Similarly, as my older consultants recalled, colonial officials

16. The Arosi District Chief was Simon Suniabu of Bia village. See K. Green (1976: 42) for a list of all the District Headmen appointed in 1918.

17. Referring to Fox as the "local herald's office," these documents clearly show that such efforts were influenced and perhaps encouraged by Fox's (1924) ethnographic de-scription of the Araha lineage, the name of which happens to mean "chief" in Arosi, as an anomalous chiefly lineage that provided chiefs for all of the other Arosi lineages. In my

acted on a presupposition that village headmen ought to be recruited from the ranks of pre-existing village chiefs. "When [administrative officers] arrived [in our village] they asked us, 'Where is your chief?' And we said, 'It is [so-and-so], he is our chief.' And they would go and talk with him. But he wasn't our chief because we hadn't anointed him like anointing a person who is important in *kastom*." When it soon became apparent that these methods were misguided, district officers sought to avoid the appearance of "Government place men" and instituted the election of both district and village headmen; village headmen were popularly elected within their villages and, in turn, selected their immediate superior, the district headman (ADO to SG, March 2, 1931, BSIP 9/VII/3[a]). Commonly known as "bosses," village headmen "would serve until they were reluctant to carry on and then we'd vote for another. The important thing was that the district officer knew, even if the person worked for only one year." It is crucial to note, however, that these elected village headmen could not fulfill the role of the customary representative of the *auhenua*. Their authority was strictly a function of the government and could not serve to bind multiple lineages together under the ruling shadow of an *auhenua* lineage. "Don't call them *mwaeraha* [i.e., anointed chiefs]," Casper Kaukeni instructed me. "They were just a few [government] chiefs."

Concentration

It is no longer possible to give a full account of the pre-1918 spatial order on Makira. Nevertheless, some features of this order can be recovered by examining Campbell's reports and those of subsequent district officers while supplementing this documentary material with oral accounts collected in Arosi. In the early 1990s Arosi accounts of life in the bush prior to the opening of the government headquarters at Kirakira described people living in small widely dispersed settlements throughout the island's interior. These accounts indicate that people moved frequently—many moved to a new garden site every year—rather than living at one particular place for long periods of time. When asked where his ancestress, Rebianimae, was from, one man gave a typical answer: "She was a woman of the bush above Tawatana, but she didn't simply live at one place; they lived at many many different places." Campbell, observing such movements, described those who lived in the bush as "nomadic" because they changed "their place of abode yearly," and a successor, J.

---

own field research I found that Arosi of other matrilineages strongly deny that Araha ever held such an aristocratic position. Some Araha, however, seem to regard their lineage as endowed with special qualities for leadership. See chapter 9 and Scott 2005b.

C. Barley, similarly characterized Makirans as "an essentially restless and nomadic people" (AR, January 4, 1919, BSIP 9/III/1 A; MR, January 11, 1921, BSIP 9/III/4 A; cf. Fox 1924: 5). Other reports suggest that during this period Islanders "scattered" and changed their places of residence more frequently as a direct result of the epidemics (MM *SCL*, March 1, 1916: 673). In 1993, Johnson Bwaurari of east Arosi told me that, through his informal research into the origins of people now settled in Wainoni, he found that many people had moved from Star Harbour during a dysentery epidemic. Campbell's perspective on such settlement patterns accorded with that of the authors of the Fiji report (1896: 90), who saw in "[t]he tendency of the native race ... towards decentralisation" a form of spatial disorder that was detrimental to the reproduction of healthy people.

Campbell sought to bring Makirans together into "substantial villages" (AR, January 4, 1919, BSIP 9/III/1 A) that would be "easier to keep ... clean and healthy" ("Instructions to Native District Headmen," 1918, BSIP 9/VII/3[b]).[18] By the beginning of 1919 he could report that "already several fair sized communities are collecting" (AR, January 4, 1919, BSIP 9/III/1 A). Throughout the Arosi bush a number of "substantial villages" were formed. Tarorua of Tawaniaʻu village, whose family had lived in the bush prior to the establishment of colonial rule, recounted to me: "When the government came they called us together and we formed a large village at ʻAdoʻaiʻoʻo. We cut leaf from the abandoned villages to make that village." Later, following the instructions of the village headman, Heradodoi, they moved to Hunawarasi and then to Harahu-Taritari before finally moving down to the coast. At Dahui, approximately one and a half kilometers inland above Tawatana, another large village was formed by people from Mwanimaʻo and Taranaiauau. One consultant recalled that his mother, a resident at Dahui, had told him that the houses in this centralized village were all built in straight lines in conformity with Campbell's specifications.

Even though the government forced people to come together into larger villages, today the Islanders say that their forebears did not do so in a haphazard or passive fashion. Of the people who joined to make up the village at

---

18. The policy in question was also being implemented concurrently in other parts of the Protectorate. In fact, prior to his appointment to Makira, Campbell had visited the south coast of Guadalcanal where officials were engaged in a policy of encouraging hamlets to consolidate into larger villages and move coastward (Bennett 1974: 2.36–2.37). Although based on government directives, as Bennett (1974: 2.40) notes, these policies did not gain legal sanction until the King's Regulation of 1922.

'Ado'ai'o'o, Tarorua said, "Those who came together there were really only one group (*ruruha*)." That is to say, people brought their own sense of order to the new villages, coming together according to their matrilineal and other kinship relationships. This was true of those who settled in villages on the coast as well as those who gathered in new bush settlements like 'Ado'ai'o'o. The assertion that relocated bush people chose the villages where they settled, not by random chance, but in accordance with pre-existing connections to those villages or their inhabitants has, furthermore, played a central role in fostering the heterotopic construction of coastal land in Arosi today.

While bringing scattered groups into substantial villages, Campbell made Islanders build (or, in some instances, rebuild) their villages on what he considered to be "more healthy sites" (AR, January 4, 1919, BSIP 9/III/1 A). In the discourse about depopulation, sites with poor drainage were believed to compound the health problems caused by the damp tropical climate. Sites with good drainage and with elevated airy positions were preferred (Fiji 1896: 84–89, 94, 157). Accordingly, Dahui village was built on a hill. Wango village was moved to a more healthful location, as was the neighboring village of Ha'ani/Fagani in Bauro, and later, the residents of Etemwarore village moved to a new site called Tadahadi on higher ground. An elderly man, 'Ohairangi, explained to me what he understood to be the rationale for this last relocation. He recalled that many people died every year at Etemwarore because the village, he thought, was too close to the road.

Importantly, larger centralized villages—rather than spatially dispersed smaller settlements—facilitated the penetration of colonial regulation into many aspects of island life. The larger villages made work on government projects easier. Concentrated village populations served as small-scale labor corps that, under the direction of village headmen, were required to build clean orderly houses, enclose domestic pigs, make latrines, set aside Saturdays to tidy the village and build "roads" to connect neighboring villages. Such population clusters also offered greater "accessibility for inspection" by colonial officials, increased the possibility of better government administration, and facilitated constant "strict and searching supervision" (Fiji 1896: 89, 95, 114, 173). Tarorua remembered, for instance, how while his family lived in the bush at 'Ado'ai'o'o, government soldiers would often walk up to the village wearing cartridge belts and carrying rifles: "Those [villagers] who disobeyed [the government] had their houses burned; those who ran away had bullets whistling past them ... [But] we didn't fight the soldiers because we were scared of them." In corroboration of Tarorua's assertion I found no written or oral accounts of even small-scale attempts at violent resistance to these early government initiatives. That Makirans did find means of passive resistance is amply attested, however, in the constant complaints of district officers against the recalcitrance of Islanders to enclose their pigs or remain in their villages, and the apparent need to resort to coercion when orders to relocate were repeatedly ignored.

Supervision

The imposition of a further anti-nomadic regulation strengthened the centralization of villages on Makira:

> they are strictly forbidden under penalty of imprisonment to change their place of residence or to absent themselves for more than a month from their respective villages under which their names are registered without the express permission of the District Officer at Kirakira. (MR, January 11, 1921, BSIP 9/III/4 A)

This regulation was clearly difficult to enforce, however, for in 1921 Barley noted that people would often live in the bush and only return to their villages once a week when they were required to join in the communal village work (DO to RC, September 20, 1921, BSIP 9/VII/3[a]). This law was amended, and by the late 1920s people were not to be absent from their villages for more than seven days at a time (QR, October 4, 1930, BSIP 9/III/4 C).

People's movements from their villages of residence were increasingly circumscribed. They were discouraged from shifting their place of residence frequently, and extended visits to relatives presumably became more difficult. Each person was to reside in the village in which he or she was registered. But some, at least, sought to resist this form of coercion. In 1993 one man recalled, for instance, that his family had settled at the beach between Tawatana and 'Ubuna, but, "the government came and told us to move. When they came round again we were still there so they took [my father] Wakii'a to prison for four months."

Theoretically, the aim was to plot and map each Makiran as a permanently registered, almost immobile, resident of his or her village. By registering every Islander, Campbell sought to ensure that each person in the district would be located at a particular place and could be visited with relative ease during his district tours or during those of the police. Furthermore, by bringing people together and restricting their movements Campbell was able to collect a census in which he recorded the names of all the inhabitants of Makira.[19] Village

---

19. In the census completed in mid 1919 the San Cristoval District had a total population of 8,424. The population by sub-district was: Kirakira 1,040; Ravo 1,506; Arosi 1,365;

headmen were responsible for reporting the birth and death statistics to their district headman, who in turn reported them to the district officer (AR, January 4, 1919, BSIP 9/III/1 A; DO to RC, June 29, 1920, BSIP 9/VI/3[a]). These statistics were crucial for charting the rates of birth and death, the ratio of males to females, and, ultimately, the census material could be used to determine the success or failure of the measures taken to combat depopulation. With this data in hand Campbell quickly determined that "[i]nfant mortality is appaling [sic]" and that "something must be done to prevent this in the near future" (AR, January 4, 1919, BSIP 9/III/1 A).

Registering and fixing the location of individuals in conjunction with the census enabled District Officer Barley to collect the "Head Tax" in late 1921. On Makira the tax rate of five shillings was imposed "on all able-bodied native males between sixteen and sixty years of age" (Bennett 1987: 162; cf. MR, May 4, 1922, BSIP 9/III/4 B). Together with the concentration of villages and the registration of Islanders, the head tax was an attempt to foster the interrelated development of individualism and wage labor among Solomon Islanders who, in order to acquire the money needed to pay the tax, might have to make themselves available to European enterprises as wage-earning units (cf. Keesing and Corris 1980: 74–75). At the time, Fox observed that "[t]he people are and have always been communistic, and if the tax had been on villages (the same amount of tax) it would have been in accord with their own ways, but it is on individuals" (MM *SCL*, May 2, 1921: 9). To meet the demand for cash for taxes and trade goods, Arosi worked on trading and mission ships, taught in mission schools, or served the government. Some women entered domestic service on local plantations. Relative to other Islanders in central and southeast Solomons, however, Arosi preferred casual short-term employment on local plantations to indentured labor on other islands and many raised money sporadically by direct sale of small quantities of local produce such as copra, ivory nut, and trochus shell to traders (Bennett 1987: 168–187; cf. Philp 1978).

Missions

In a critical commentary on colonial reorganization projects, Fox noted that "bushmen ... were ordered by the Government to come down from their homes to the coast." "What," he inquired, "has the Government done for them? As far as they can see, nothing" (MM *SCL*, May 2, 1921: 8). Fox's critical

---

Haununu 460; Wainoni 1,673; Funarite 1,053; Ulawa 1,092; and Ugi 235 (MR, July 1, 1919, BSIP 9/III/4 A).

stance notwithstanding, Campbell's policies were working in tandem with already established Anglican and South Sea Evangelical Mission (SSEM) practice.[20] It appears, in fact, that a significant portion of the Arosi bush population had already descended to live on the coast by the time that Campbell tried to impose government on the island (MM *SCL*, October 2, 1916: 755; cf. AR, January 4, 1919, BSIP 9/III/1 A; Hilliard 1966: 218–219). The Melanesian Mission resolved "[t]hat small villages be, as far as possible, amalgamated into one or more central villages" (MM *SCL*, September 12, 1911: 220; cf. Bennett 1974: 2.31, quoting Wilson, August 1910; Ivens 1918: 191; White 1991: 114–115). Although both missions were based on the coast, in contrast to the Melanesian Mission's method of selecting one pre-existing village to form the core of a consolidated Christian community, the SSEM attempted to create altogether new villages. Invoking 2 Corinthians 6:17 to equate relocation with holiness, the SSEM called converts "to 'come out and be separate' " from their "heathen" neighbors "by making a separate settlement" around the new mission schoolhouse (Hilliard 1969: 51–52, quoting Deck, December 1912; cf. Bennett 1974: 2.32; SSEM *NIV*, 1911–13: 20). Consequently, by 1916 there were "not very many people in the [Arosi] bush" (MM *SCL*, October 2, 1916: 755), and in that part of Makira at least, coastal villages were "chiefly villages made by people who have came down to the coast to school [i.e., to the mission]" (Fox 1919a: 98; cf. Hilliard 1966: 158 n. 3; MM *SCL*, February 6, 1907: 103; November 10, 1909: 90; Sayes 1976: 117, 189–190, 229; SSEM *ND*, July 1914; SSEM *NIV*, 1916–17: 2–4). The old coastal communities of Wango, Heuru, Tawatana, and 'Ubuna, with their new Anglican churches, and villages such as Hada, Mwata, Rumahui, Manuasi, and Onehatare in which the SSEM established schools, already formed the nuclei of these collectivized villages.[21] Unlike the "very small" bush villages, the coastal settlements tended to be relatively large; Wango, for example, had a population of just under one hundred in 1919 (Fox 1919a: 98; cf. 1978: 469).

Several older people recounted to me a dramatic example of how the factors of disease, government policy, and missionary activities intersected to achieve the gradual and, at times, reluctant migration of Arosi from bush to coast. As already mentioned, during Campbell's tenure as district officer, the new amalgamated village of Dahui was built on a hill about one mile inland from Tawatana. As a prelude to his account of the unusual events said to have

---

20. Bennett (1974: 2.25–2.47; cf. Chapman 1987) and Bathgate (1975: 42–49, 60) document a similar conjunction of Protestant missionary and government practice on the south and west coasts of Guadalcanal during the same period.

21. The SSEM had first opened schools in Arosi in 1909 (SSEM *ND*, February 1912).

Figure 2.4. Mission school, Wango, 1906 (Beattie Collection).
© The Trustees of The British Museum.

transpired there, John Christian Tarorodo explained the origin of the village in this way: "Before, people didn't live together but lived all through different places. It was the government who told them to come together. That's why a large village was built at Dahui; people moved from places like Taranaiauau and settled at Dahui and cleared a road down to [Tawatana] which they called the 'government road.'"

When the village of Dahui was first formed the inhabitants still followed their ancestral religion. With multiple variants, Arosi tell the story of how an earlier generation abandoned this village for the coast and became baptized. All raconteurs agree that a representative of the Melanesian Mission, perhaps Fox himself, attempted to convert the residents of Dahui to Christianity, but his preaching went unheeded. The now Christian Arosi say that, as a result of the Dahui villagers' stubborn adherence to their own ways, Satan killed many of them. Casper Kaukeni relayed his mother's version of events in the following terms:

> Doctor Fox came to Dahui at a time when people didn't experience any problems. He tried to convert them, but while they accepted Fox

they didn't come down and get baptized and confirmed quickly. Fox tired of insisting that they should be Christian. Rarakemanu, a spirit of the ocean, killed many of the people there. The remaining people came to live in Tawatana and 'Ubuna and converted and were baptized. When people are baptized the priest makes the sign of the cross on their forehead with water. But the devil told a Malaitan woman called Dokus who lived in Tawatana that he was her friend. When the devil liked to kill one of the people of Dahui she'd dream about the incident the night before. In one dream he killed a pig in the morning and then its owner at midday. [The next day] everyone was frightened and hid inside their houses and peeped out of holes in the walls. There was a slight rainfall and when the sun appeared a rainbow formed. A white egret came from near the rainbow and walked through the station. People could hear the pig squealing when it was killed. The victim-to-be was very frightened. The egret came to his door and looked inside and the man died. The egret did follow the people who came down to Tawatana, but Dokus said that the egret would see the white mark [of the cross made when they were baptized] on their foreheads and would not be able to kill them. The egret disappeared when people converted.

According to another man, the frustrated missionary cursed the village saying,

"Well, you don't want to hear the word of God? You just go ahead and work then, and pray to Satan." He said this and came back down and everyone was killed by the spirit of the sea. They would see an egret and then a person would die. There was death every day. Bwaura'ini's children ran away and settled at Su'u [near 'Ubuna]. Ahota'i died there [at Dahui]. Tarani died when he came down. Tarokekerei came down [to Tawatana] and because of that the egret wanted to come into the house of Usumwara and Tahisau where she stayed. But during the morning the church bell was rung and the egret would fly away frightened. It tried to kill Tarokekerei but they hid her and she didn't see it. If she had seen it, she would have died. No one converted at Dahui. They didn't go back up to Dahui until they'd all converted. When they were Christian they went back up and the spirit fled. If a pagan had gone back up he'd have been killed. When they converted the thing was finished.

In these accounts Rarakemanu manifests himself in the form of a white egret; in other accounts he is said to be anthropomorphic. Tarorodo specified that

Figure 2.5. Rakerakemanu, *Ataro ni matawa*, Drawn by Oroanii'a, Wango (from, Fox, *Threshold of the Pacific*, 1924: 128). Used with permission of Kegan Paul.

Rarakemanu appeared to his victims in the form of a "white man" (*ai haka*, literally, ship person), whereas Paul Dururongo heard that the spirit entered the village as an egret but transformed into a man as soon as he arrived at the victim's house. Fox's ethnography and the speculations of several Arosi whom I interviewed suggest that this malevolent spirit may represent devastation by disease. Fox (1924: 249; 1978: 358) notes that consumption (*rakerake'a*) was thought to be caused when "the soul has been taken by Rakerakemanu, a sea spirit."[22] Indeed, it may be that this same spirit was always implicated in any appearance of a white egret in a village, an event which, according to Fox, was taken to presage illness (Fox to Rivers, May 24, 1918, Perry Papers, B2). In Father Abel Ta'aimaesiburu's version of events, when Dokus began to dream, "anyone who was slightly ill would die." Another man expressed his belief that illness had "changed into a spirit" at Dahui, and Casper Kaukeni considered that perhaps it was only malaria that had killed the people there. Comment-

---

22. Fox (1924: 247) also notes that dysentery was believed to be caused by another spirit called Wairabu. For comparative data on the relationship between spirits and epidemic disease on Malaita, see Akin 1993: 282 n. 57, 664, 694 n. 55; de Coppet 1981: 177–178.

ing that Rarakemanu could not enter the house of a baptized person, one man stated, "this proved to people that Christianity was something true; it was a demonstration of power." Seeking refuge from the ravages of disease in the protective fold of the coastal Christians, Dahui residents completed the second phase of a progressive descent from the bush that had originally been instigated by Campbell's directives.

In addition to anticipating and aiding the government's agenda of coastal collectivization, the missionaries divided Arosi into two parts. This was Fox's idea, designed to break the mission field into two spheres of influence to facilitate the separate and non-competitive work of the SSEM and his own Melanesian Mission. Seeking government sanction of a de facto regional split between the two denominations, Fox wrote to District Officer Barley in August 1920:

> I would respectfully suggest that from Pamua (or from Kirakira indeed) to Maro['] u should be held to be a sphere of the Melanesian Mission and from Maro['] u to Bia of Dr. Deck's Mission [i.e., the SSEM].... I think native opinion generally agrees with this too, they don't want the unnecessary sight of Christians fighting one another, I know I don't.... What I would like best is that the Government should recognize these two spheres, which are really spheres of actual occupation. (Takibaina [i.e., Fox] to Barley, August 23, 1920, enclosure in DO to RC, September 7, 1920, BSIP 9/VII/3[a]; cf. MM *SCL*, May 2, 1921: 7)

The boundary at Maro'u Bay suggested by Fox lies behind the current Area Council boundary between Arosi I and Arosi II.[23]

"Waste Land"

The current efflorescence of *auhenua* identities on the coast must also be linked to a colonially induced awareness among Arosi that land that appears to outsiders to be unoccupied and unworked is vulnerable to appropriation. If Campbell saw the lack of boundaries, roads, and fences and the fluidity of Makiran residence patterns as a species of spatial chaos, his colleagues in the Protectorate administration saw sparsely inhabited and undeveloped land throughout the Solomons in a similar light.

---

23. The original denominational division represented by this boundary remains largely intact as well. At the time of my stay in Tawatana village, for example, everyone was Anglican apart from two in-marrying women who were raised in the South Sea Evangelical Church in Arosi II and one elderly woman who was a Seventh-day Adventist.

As elsewhere in the British empire, colonial officials in the Solomons approached land and resource management informed by a long tradition of moral philosophy and law according to which unimproved land, even where inhabited, might justifiably be taken over and developed for the greater good (cf. Williams 1986: Chapters 7 and 8). Beginning with Woodford, colonial administrators sought, under shifting legal definitions and forms, to identify and purchase, or simply requisition, potentially productive land in the Solomons for purposes of commercial sale and lease or government protection. Pressed to generate revenue for the Protectorate and convinced that the indigenous population was doomed to near extinction, Woodford facilitated the alienation of over 400,000 acres between 1896 and 1912. Of these, approximately 240,000 acres were released to foreign holders of Certificates of Occupation under regulations that, at first, recognized the category of land "vacant by reason of the extinction of the original native owners and their descendants," and later defined "waste land" as "land which is not owned, cultivated or occupied by any native or non-native person" (Allan 1957: 37–38; BSIP *AR*, 1912–1913: 13; cf. Bennett 1987: Chapter 6; 2000: 41–42; Heath 1981: 62–66).

Objections by Solomon Islanders that much of this land had been incorrectly identified as ownerless compelled the Protectorate to repeal these regulations, and between 1919 and 1925 about half of this land was returned to indigenous claimants (Bennett 2000: 88). Nevertheless, although subsequent legislation in effect from 1914 to 1959 prohibited the sale of land to "non-natives," it permitted land "not in cultivation nor required for the future support of natives" to be purchased or "compulsorily acquired by the Protectorate Government for public purposes" (Heath 1981: 65). Still hoping in the early 1950s to circumvent the possibility of indigenous claims to land apparently unowned and unused, the government appointed Colin Allan Special Lands Commissioner "to recommend in what way the use and ownership of native land and land to which no validated claim is found to exist, can best be controlled" (Allan 1957: i). Following Allan's recommendations, a short-lived Solomon Islands Land Trust was established to manage "all lands which adjudication has shown to be vacant of interests amounting to full ownership" (Allan 1957: 288; cf. 1990: 171–172). Through all these legal transformations, as Bennett insightfully concludes, there ran a deep sub-text of "the Western settler view that idle land was anathema" (2000: 182).

By all accounts, the early land alienations of 1896 to 1912 inculcated a sustained wariness among Solomon Islanders that, despite the cessation of land sales to foreigners, the colonial government was looking for ways to dispossess Islanders of their land (Allan 1990: 172; Bennett 2000: 147, 151; Fox 1967: 67; Heath 1981: 68). As government administrators cynically recognized (e.g.,

Allan 1957: i), Islanders in many parts of the archipelago developed a strategy of defending their interests in land by denying the existence of waste land. In 1956, for example, the well-known Solomon Islands World War II hero, Jacob Vouza, advised the government that, on the island of Guadalcanal, "there is no waste land here. Every bit of land belongs to someone" (Allan 1957: 287; cf. Taro 1990: 54). And in 1974 Islanders from Malaita, Makira, Ugi, and the Eastern Outer Islands told the Select Committee on Lands and Mining that "there is no such thing as waste land" (Heath 1981: 71). This same committee reported that throughout the Solomons people condemned the old waste land policy as having been wrong "because every part of the Solomons was owned by some group, even if they did not use it at the time" (Heath 1981: 72). Separately but unequivocally, that is to say, people from diverse islands, including Makira, responded to the perceived threat of land loss with assertions that original customary landowners still held, or might at any time return to, all the lands that colonial agents were prone to misrecognize as empty or unused.

In fact, relatively little Makiran land—and none in Arosi—was recognized as waste land by the government during the Protectorate (Sayes 1976: 161, 164).[24] Notably, during the first two decades of the twentieth century several small tracts of coastal land in Arosi were sold by indigenous landholders, either directly to foreign companies or through government mediation, for the development of coconut plantations that are now defunct.[25] Although people I questioned about the status of these areas were unsure what parties may now have an interest in them, the legacy of these local transfers by purchase appears less disturbing to Arosi than the memory and concept of waste land appropriations elsewhere. Land sale invariably creates potential for disputes, but Arosi clearly find this prospect far less alarming than the idea that a land-grabbing agent may fail to recognize or choose to ignore their existence and claims to land.

Among Arosi, as elsewhere in the Solomons, fears of this type of predatory land seizure clearly antedated but were exacerbated by the Japanese invasion

---

24. In 1907 the government granted a Certificate of Occupation to Lever's Pacific Plantations, giving the company a 99-year hold on 2,000 acres of "what was supposed to be Waste Land" in Wainoni Bay, Makira. But when the Wainoni people claimed this land soon afterwards, Lever's allowed the Certificate to lapse (Woodford to im Thurn, July 4, 1910, WPHC 1875–1914: No. 61/1905, No. 1654/1911). The largest waste land concessions were in the western and central Solomons (Bennett 2000: 42).

25. These plantations are at Boro'oni (300 acres), Waimarae (500 acres), and Maru (200 acres) in Arosi I, and at Maro'u Bay (40 acres), Monaagai (450 acres, reduced to 77), and Hawa'a (32 acres) in Arosi II. For an account of the establishment and early history of these plantations, see Golden 1993: 271–272; K. Green 1976: 40–41; Sayes 1976: 160–178.

of the western and central Solomons in 1942. It is probable, as well, that through their own security measures during World War II and subsequent social services policy, British officials unwittingly contributed to an ongoing Makiran conviction that there were unspecified forces readying to take their island. As documented in the following chapter, these fears peaked during the post-war political movement known as Maasina Rule (c. 1946–c. 1952). Contrary to Bennett's assertion that Maasina Rule was "not focused on land matters" (2000: 141), in my research among Arosi I found that many people understood the movement and its practices as a campaign aimed to prevent a new influx of foreigners from usurping Solomon Islands land.

CHAPTER 3

"WHERE IS THE *KASTOM* LANDOWNER?": MAASINA RULE IN AROSI

Variously characterized as a politico-economic movement (Burt 1982, 1994a; Worsley 1968), a nationalist movement (Alasia 1989), a literary efflorescence (Laracy 1983), a quest for identity (Guidieri 1988), a reaction to status deprivation (Cochrane 1970), a counterhegemonic discourse of resistance (Keesing 1992), or a cargo cult (Allan 1950; Herlihy 2003), Maasina Rule as it developed on Makira has been one of the most important factors contributing to the reformation of *auhenua* identities and the production of heterotopia in the coastal villages of Arosi today. Maasina Rule precipitated the completion of population resettlement from bush to coast and sparked a drive to revive a selective repertoire of indigenous Arosi practices and values—two processes that advanced allied, but not always compatible, strategies for protecting Arosi land from appropriation by alien forces. In consequence, the movement left a legacy that continues to shape the Arosi landscape and the ways in which people understand their relationships to it. This legacy is evident in artifacts such as the previously mentioned handwritten *kastom buk* that "no one wants to hear about." The owners of this book say that its contents represent the genealogy of their matrilineage as collected in the context of Maasina Rule. Living analogues to this book, the knowledgeable people (*sae aidangi*) of today are people who gained their custom proficiency under the guidance of Maasina Rule leaders (cf. Allan 1957: 92). Ironically, however, this period of final relocation to the coast, although concurrent with a process of custom reification and a preoccupation with discerning and securing coastal *auhenua* identities, served countervalently to amplify the refrain: "we are all people who have come from elsewhere."

Bringing Maasina Rule to Arosi

The two decades following District Officer F. M. Campbell's departure from government service in mid 1919 were remarkable for their uneventfulness. District officers served on the island for only short periods of time; there were gaps in the administration; and for a number of years the district station at Kirakira was actually closed (K. Green 1974: 8–9). During several of these administrative gaps, Campbell was recalled from private life as a local planter to serve as Acting District Officer. His 1932 assessment of routine life in the Eastern District may be taken as typical for these decades: "The native population is most law abiding.... There were no outstanding events of any importance during the year, no boundary disputes and no causes of unrest or disturbance. There are no secret societies or similar organisations in this District" (AR, February 4, 1933, BSIP 9/III/1 C).[1]

Despite this atmosphere of tranquility, however, the government's regime of benign neglect had, from the beginning, fostered a variety of resentments. Even one of Campbell's early successors, J. C. Barley, sensible of the government's failure to deliver basic services and improvements, was reluctant to institute taxation in 1920 and acknowledged Makiran resentments as justified (MR, January 11, 1921, BSIP 9/III/4 A; cf. Bennett 1987: 269–270). The specific grievances catalogued by Barley included: taxation that, without visible benefit, compelled men to engage in low paying wage labor; harassment by past punitive expeditions as a means of government policing; demolition of houses deemed dilapidated and unsanitary; obligatory collective labor; restricted mobility; and the pitiless shooting of unlicensed or unhealthy dogs and unfenced pigs.

If, as noted by Campbell, Makira was free of "secret societies or similar organisations" in 1932, nevertheless, the conditions described by Barley in 1920 ultimately proved conducive to indigenous activism. There is significant documentary evidence that by 1939 some Arosi had embraced the agenda associated with the so-called "Fallowes Movement" (Barrow n.d.: Part III, 23). Originating on Santa Isabel and the central Solomons under the leadership of the former Melanesian Mission priest, Richard Fallowes, this movement advocated measures designed to grant Islanders representation through a "Native Parliament," redress economic inequities between Europeans and Melanesians, and develop educational opportunities for Islanders. Although Fallowes him-

---

1. For accounts of the markedly contrasting, and at times turbulent, history of Malaita during this same period, see Akin 1993, 1999; Bennett 1987; Burt 1994a; Keesing 1992; Keesing and Corris 1980.

self was deported back to Britain for fomenting discontent, a platform of demands survived in the Solomons and, in the minds of government officials,
became synonymous with his name. As articulated in a circular letter by an
Arosi advocate of the movement, Ham Monogari, these demands included:
higher prices for copra and shells, better wages for employees of the government, missions, and European company-owned plantations, and better teaching and education, especially the opening of a technical school (December 23,
1940[?], BSIP 1/III/F43/14 Sub File 1; cf. QR, July 1, 1939, BSIP 9/III/4 D).[2]
When Acting District Officer A. N. A. Waddell toured the island in 1940 he
found this social agenda sufficiently prevalent and disruptive to warrant sustained exhortation that Makirans should "forget the Utopian ideas that had
emanated from the fertile brain of Mr Fallowes" (QR, August 29, 1940, BSIP
9/III/4 E1). In July of that same year, Walter H. Baddeley (Bishop of Melanesia, 1932–47) received a letter from the office of the Secretariat of the Resident Commissioner in which an unnamed Acting District Officer for the Eastern District (probably Waddell) is quoted as having reported:

> The latest Fallowes rumour is that the King is to send Fallowes back
> to the Solomons by aeroplane with money to raise the price of copra
> etcetera. The King considered that it was too dangerous to send Fal-
> lowes by sea and has chartered a special air liner. This rumour em-
> anates from Reverend George Giladi of the Melanesian Mission who
> is said to have got the information from Dr. Fox. (Confidential letter
> to Baddeley, July 25, 1940, BSIP 1/III/F43/14 Sub File 1)[3]

By implicating George Giladi (also spelled Gilandi) in the spread of rumors
keeping expectations about Fallowes alive, this report, like Monogari's letter, locates ideas associated with the Fallowes Movement directly in Arosi. Giladi, himself a man of Santa Isabel where Fallowes had served as missionary, was resident
on Makira from 1921 until the late 1940s, first as a deacon and later as a priest

---

2. The extant copy of Monogari's letter, which is a typescript, has been annotated by
an unidentified hand: "Translation of letter circulating on Makira credited by some people
to John Pidoke (earlier involved with Fallowes)." This letter is very similar in form and initial content to another known to have been written by the government headman of Nggela,
John Pidoke (cf. Laracy, ed. 1983: 50–51), but Monogari appears to have adapted it and
addressed it specifically to the Arosi villages between Tawaiabu and Anuta in west and south
Arosi. I thank David Akin for supplying me with copies of both Monogari's letter and relevant pages from Lennox Barrow's (n.d.) "Outlying Interlude."
    3. Interestingly, Hilliard and Whiteman both cite personal communications from Fal-
lowes indicating that Fox was the only European missionary who "expressed any sympathy
with his aspirations" (Hilliard 1966: 224; cf. Whiteman 1983: 211).

in Arosi (MM *SCL*, May 2, 1921: 7; July 2, 1934: 15; March [read: April] 1, 1949: 37; cf. Fox 1958: 162). According to Hilliard (1978: 283), Giladi became actively involved in Fallowes's local "parliament" initiative after 1939.[4]

Although none of the Maasina Rule participants with whom I worked remembered the Fallowes Movement, this documentation indicates that there was probably some continuity between this earlier drive for social reform and Maasina Rule, and certainly the same long-standing neglect and inequities that had made Arosi receptive to the former made them likewise receptive to the agenda of constructive resistance offered by the latter. Furthermore, however, as well as reflecting Arosi interests in obtaining better wages, fair prices for their produce, and improving their prospects through education, the aims of the Fallowes Movement as represented in Monogari's letter foreshadowed yet another issue that would shape Arosi inflections of Maasina Rule: "Also take care of the little piece of ground that is left to you," he admonished.

The matrix of Maasina Rule seems to have been the military base on Guadalcanal where U.S. military personnel and Solomon Islanders interacted after American forces liberated Guadalcanal from Japanese occupation in 1942.[5] In response to the magnitude of the U.S. military machine and their perception that American servicemen treated them with openhandedness and egalitarian camaraderie, the early formulators of Maasina Rule conceived an agenda of indigenous autonomy and resistance to British rule backed by the hope of American intervention on behalf of Solomon Islanders. Bypassing the structures of British administration, Maasina Rule leaders on Malaita promulgated guidelines for an independent order with its own hierarchy of local and central chiefs. They called for Malaitans to construct and come together at new coastal villages, work and garden communally, withhold tax payments from the government, join in labor strikes and demands for higher wages, and codify custom laws for use in local indigenous courts. The stated aims of Maasina Rule founders were to achieve unity and an improved standard of living for all Solomon Islanders. Thus, at its inception, Maasina Rule exhibited characteristics of a civil rights as well as an incipient nationalist movement.[6]

---

4. For fuller treatments of the Fallowes Movement, also known as "Chair and Rule," see Herlihy 2003; Hilliard 1978: 281–285; Laracy 1983: 13–14; Laracy, ed. 1983: 49–52; White 1978: 119–245; 1991: 196–199; Whiteman 1983: 205–211.

5. For a fuller treatment of World War II in the context of Solomon Islands history, see Bennett 1987: Chapter 13. For a chronology of the war in Solomon Islands and Islander accounts of their wartime experiences, see White et al., eds. 1988.

6. For accounts and analyses of Maasina Rule on Malaita, see Akin 1993; Allan 1950; Burt 1994a; Keesing 1978; Laracy 1983; Naitoro 1993.

The proximity of the Pacific theater in World War II had only indirect effects on Makira; no combat took place on the island, and for the most part Arosi remained untouched by the battles on Guadalcanal. Relative to the number of Malaitans, only a small number of Makiran men enlisted to work with the Americans on Guadalcanal in the Solomon Islands Labour Corps (Laracy and White, eds. 1988: 124). It was not until the years following the war that its reverberations were felt in the form of ideas and practices that coalesced in the 'Are'are region of southern Malaita in 1944 and spread throughout the central and southeast Solomons. It is impossible to pinpoint the precise moment when Maasina Rule first gained adherents in Arosi. By 1946 sufficient inklings of and interest in the activities on Malaita prompted at least one delegation from Arosi to attend meetings on southern Malaita for information and instruction. In the early 1990s, when I asked him to tell me about the beginnings of Maasina Rule, Tomas Rehu'a recalled the launching and itinerary of one journey to Malaita in vivid detail.

> 'Arau[7] came and spoke to Takiwarita'iasi, the leader at Tawatana, and to the rest of the village. At that point we'd already stopped participating in the census and paying tax. 'Arau said don't write names [i.e., don't comply with the census] because we don't want our government. They had meetings in the "rings" [i.e., meeting houses built during the movement] in the villages and spoke about people from America being met in the night. News came from 'Arau, and Taki spoke to us.
>
> Then we left to go to Malaita in George Giladi's canoe *Goroha*. Giladi had blessed the canoe, and so even though there was a heavy rain and it was dark, the canoe was blessed and we could see Sa'a [bathed] in light. The following people went in the canoe: Ha'u from Hada [village]; John 'Arau, Tawari'i, Bebeni, and Rade from Tawaiabu; Habit Abeanimae, Maesipa'ewa and his wife Nunu, and Wakii'a from 'Ubuna; Rehu'a and Rex Taki from Tawatana; Apwahi from Heuru; Don and Rarekeni—a person from 'Are'are who had married here—from Tawaraha; Ha'aaru from Rumahui; and Beka Bo'ari from Heranigau.
>
> We left in the morning and we arrived at Sa'a [village] at about 3 P.M. We slept at Sa'a and there was a meeting there in the morning.

---

7. John 'Araubora (d. c. 1964) was the leader of Maasina Rule in Arosi. He had been educated at Onepusu (1931–35), the SSEM school on Malaita. He was recruited for training at the Keravat Demonstration Plantation near Rabaul, New Britain (1940–41) and then worked and as a Native Agricultural Instructor at Kirakira before returning to his village, 'Ahi'a, in Arosi II where he established the village school in 1945.

Then we went to Ro'one and we slept there before going to Maro'u. Aliki Nono'oohimae spoke to 'Arau who wrote what Aliki said.[8] We weren't with him; 'Arau did this on his own. When Aliki talked, he walked up and down, and a man called "Kastom" followed him up and down. The "Kastom" was a man with medicine to stop poisoning. This was Waiparo.[9] Timothy George was also there.[10]

We slept once at Maro'u then went back to Ro'one where we slept before returning to Sa'a and back to Makira.... When we came back they held a meeting in each village: at Tawatana, Heuru ... working in a new village every day up to Borodao.

Arosi was soon thereafter recognized as a center of Maasina Rule on Makira (DCCS to SG, November 26, 1946, BSIP 4/C91; DO to DCCS, May 16, 1947, BSIP 8/IX/6).[11]

---

8. Aliki Nono'oohimae (d. 1984), who was among those Malaitans who had served in the Solomon Islands Labour Corps on Guadalcanal, was one of the founders of Maasina Rule in 'Are'are (Akin 1993: 320–321; de Coppet 1985, 1998: 198 n. 32; de Coppet and Zemp 1978: 106–109; Fifi'i 1989: 52–55, 60–64; Keesing 1978: 49–50; Laracy 1983: 17–18).

9. Waiparo Haiware (d. 1962) of Takataka village was an important leader of Maasina Rule in southern Malaita (Akin 1993: 384; de Coppet and Zemp 1978; Fifi'i 1989: 104–105; Laracy 1983: 18; Naitoro 1993: 130–132).

10. Timothy George, an SSEM member who was born and educated in Queensland, was head chief on Small Malaita. He too became one of the main leaders of Maasina Rule on Malaita and co-authored the "first Order for the Island" in December 1945 (Corris 1973b; Fifi'i 1989: 62–63; Keesing 1978: 50–51; Laracy 1983: 20–21, 88–89; Scott 1990–91).

11. The word *maasina*, according to most authorities, means "brotherhood" (Akin 1993: 414 n. 32; Allan 1950: 27; Keesing 1978: 49; Laracy 1983: 19–20), or "relatives" (Naitoro 1993: 83 n. 23; cf. Fifi'i 1989: 60–61) in the language of 'Are'are. Naitoro (1993: 83 n. 23), noting that the 'Are'are term *ruru* refers to any type of cooperative activity, clarifies that there is no relationship between *ruru* and the English word "rule"; rather, "[t]he term 'Maasina Rule' came to be used as the movement grew and spread [from 'Are'are] to other districts, and began to assume an authority which was seen as equivalent to colonial authority." The British rendered Maasina Rule into English as Marching Rule (among other expressions) based on homophony, perhaps assuming that *maasina* was a Pijin form of "marching." Although one Arosi explained the meaning of the 'Are'are term to me, most Arosi were uncertain of the correct pronunciation of the term and of its meaning; they most frequently used *Maasinga Ruru, Maasing Ruru, Masingi Ruru, Masinga Ruru, Ismasinga Ruru*, Rule Revelation, and Marching Rule. There are no cognates for the 'Are'are word *maasina* in Arosi that would make its meaning in combination with the Arosi term *ruru* (meaning "group") transparent to Arosi.

It is beyond the scope of the present study to describe and analyze fully the rich and unique development of Maasina Rule once it took firm root in Arosi. What follows is not intended to account for all aspects of the movement or their possible interpretations; rather, it focuses narrowly on a small subset of those aspects that impinged directly on Arosi ideas of, and practices relating to, land and the organization of space. Adapting the imperatives of the movement as it prevailed throughout the central and southeast Solomons, the leaders of Maasina Rule in Arosi promoted the continued collectivization and regimentation of villages, a drive to divide and fill the coastal land, and the formalization of instruction in indigenous custom. The particular shape that Arosi thus gave to Maasina Rule is best understood, I propose, as a multiplex response to expectations of imminent foreign invasion fostered by government directives as well as by the framers of the movement itself.

It was this threat of invasion that appears to have motivated Arosi to concentrate population along the coast, not as a line of defense intended to repulse military force, but as a means of presenting their land as saturated and unavailable for alienation. The need to fill the land and hold it against possible usurpation furthermore raised issues of customary land tenure and corresponding *auhenua* identities. By its very nature the defensive strategy of filling the land forced the question, who is *auhenua* here? But decades of depopulation and colonial reorganization had combined to wipe out whole matrilineages and separate others from their ancestral lands, rendering ancestral entitlement to the coast ambiguous. In the context of this ambiguity, most Arosi appear to have been content to fill the coastline by placing people on areas of land, not according to their matrilineal attachments, but according to their broader relationship networks of inter-lineage entanglement. Some Arosi, however, fearing invasion and land loss, were galvanized to research the histories of their lineages and their connections to particular territories. These lineages began the work of collecting and recording lineage narratives and constructing themselves as the *auhenua* of the coastal land in preparation for the approach of strangers who would inquire: who owns this land? In so doing, these lineages helped to create the necessary preconditions for the present condition of heterotopia in Arosi.

Expectations of Invasion

The anticipated invasion took different forms in the minds of different people. This fact became evident to me as I sought out older people's recollections of Maasina Rule and its teachings. There was no discernible master version of the invasion. Some people had been taught that the invaders would be Americans; others had been warned that virtually anyone might come. Some people had believed that the newcomers would liberate them from British rule and assist them to "stand by ourselves, have our own government, tax ourselves for ourselves." Others had been alarmed by the repeated slogan: "If things turn bad then there'll be a war." But, as a number of men admitted, "We didn't know who was to fight whom." It had also been predicted that, following this war, the invaders, whoever they might be, might establish a state of commodification called *kolonia* in which everything would be bought and sold. Finally, some people's testimonies indicated that, at one time, they had looked for a combination of these, not incompatible, possibilities.

From the beginning, a component of Maasina Rule on Malaita had been the hope that American armed forces would come to the assistance of Solomon Islanders in their quest for self-improvement and prosperity, and this hope was also prevalent among Arosi. Although the British derided rumors of the imminent advent of Americans as fantastic mythology, it is likely that through their own safety instructions during the war and later public health directives they fed Arosi expectations of invasion and land usurpation. Sources indicate that, as the war drew closer to the Solomons archipelago in early 1942, the British government organized Islanders to maintain a continuous alert and state of preparedness for the possibility of a Japanese incursion. Security precautions included the construction of houses up in the bush as ready refuges in case hostilities reached their shores and the mounting of regular coast watching activities (AR for 1941, 1942, and 1943, BSIP 9/III/1 D and E; QR, June 30, 1942, BSIP 9/III/4 E1). Even after the war, these artifacts of wartime security remained prominent features of Maasina Rule in Arosi. Adherents of the movement maintained the bush refuges. "We made many houses in the bush. Each group (*ruruha*) had its own house. This was preparation in case another country came to fight us." Several of my consultants also described how they, or their relatives, had served as local "Harbour Masters" (*Haba Masta*) charged with the responsibility of monitoring all maritime activity near their villages and investigating the intentions of any people who might try to land.

The seemingly unlikely influence of government recommendations regarding public health may have inadvertently encouraged this post-war continuation of invasion alert. A document entitled "The Work of Native Councils" issued by Assistant District Commissioner (Kirakira) G. L. Barrow in mid 1946 exemplifies a didactic rhetoric used to impress upon Islanders the importance of basic nutrition and care for mothers and newborns (June 25, 1946, BSIP 8/I/F1/1). The tone and diction of this document indicate that it was addressed to the members of "native councils" to advise them of their duties and the rationales behind them. Under the heading "Children," Barrow addressed the problem of high infant mortality, underscoring the need for pregnant women to learn proper infant care by warning that underpopulation was rendering Makira vulnerable to outside land seekers.

> In these islands there are not enough people. There are 100,000 people in the Solomon Islands. There should be 10,000,000. Here there is plenty of ground and not many people. In some other countries there are too many people and not enough ground. People from those countries would like to come and live here and take the ground from the people who have it now. Just now the Government does not let them but it cannot stop them all the time. There is only one way to stop them and keep these islands for the people here—that is to have plenty more people here so that they will use all the ground. Then no one will want to take it from them.
>
> This is why it is very important that there should be plenty more children here and why the women must know how to look after themselves before the children are borne [*sic*] and how to look after the children properly when they are young.[12]

This warning, it should be noted, was not simply the disciplinary bogeyman of a paternalistic colonial administrator, but was rooted in already long-standing (and subsequently ongoing) debates as to whether the Protectorate should permit the importation of large numbers of Indian or Chinese laborers and, more generally, in social Darwinian discourses of resignation that the last remnants of Solomon Islands depopulation would be wiped away by an uncontrollable overflow from Asian overpopulation (Bennett 1987: 150–153; PIM December 1947: 64–65; April 1948: 5–6, 24; August 1953: 20, 89–94).

Many of my Arosi interlocutors stated that during Maasina Rule they had been instructed by movement leaders to fill up the coastal land in preparation

---

12. Scholars have previously pointed out that Aliki Nono'oohimae had been involved in government efforts to curb depopulation before the war, and that he himself acknowledged that fear of extinction had been a key motivating factor in his organization of the Maasina Rule movement in 'Are'are (Akin 1993: 321; Laracy 1983: 18). What this document by Barrow additionally suggests is that, on Makira at least, government measures to reverse the depopulation trend not only provided models for Maasina Rule activities, but also planted in the minds of Makirans the fear that, in their reduced numbers, they were easy marks for land-grabbers.

for the coming invasion. They frequently referred to this as blocking or protecting the land. Indeed, the description of these procedures given by Johnson Bwaurari, who had acted as "Harbour Master" for Tawatana village during the movement, suggests that to him the identity of the invaders was immaterial; what mattered was that Arosi should hold the land securely for themselves. In light of the Barrow document, it is perhaps significant that children were deployed to fulfill this function.

> All the land was split up. In *maasinga ruru* we thought any country could come—Africa or Malaysia, black people or white people too.... America too. Were they to come and do good or bad? I don't know. But if they wanted land we'd already taken up all the land, so many places were blocked. We were ready and children looked after places and women were prepared because we were to stand by ourselves and then, because of this, other countries would want to come.... At Tawatana the land was split up and I know in the area from Wai Boro'oni to Tadahadi it was too. But the arrangement of the land was done according to groups (*burunga*).
>
> I was the *Haba Masta* and when a ship arrived and its tender came ashore, I asked, "What do you want?" ... If a ship came, people would come to get me. I had a book, and if a ship or a yacht went past I'd make note of it.

Having listened with me to this account given by his father's brother, Casper Kaukeni, who had been eleven or twelve years old at the time of Maasina Rule, contributed his own personal memories of these measures:

> I remember Taenohu and Mauriasi telling Itamwaeraha and Tarosubani to make a garden in the land to the west of Mwanihau in case people came to take the land. Mauriasi wrote the young people's names against the pieces of land because they'd be alive for a long time to come. Tarokekerei was [placed with me] at Haurahu at that time because Nagi had planted coconuts there. If someone came and asked, "Does a person live here?" we were to say, "Yes." We thought: "Suppose they take the land from us."

Another man seemed to envision the possibility of two distinct invasions, one rapacious and one benevolent, the latter associated with Americans.

All the young women were married in case people from England or
Russia came.[13] Houses were built in empty spaces in case they came
and they took our lands. We did *maasinga ruru* so that we could live
well like you white people, but only America would do this [i.e., help
us]. They were to come and work for us but not take the island from
us. Our people watched over the village through the night in case
people would come in a ship while we were asleep.

American Makirans?

Some people's expectations regarding Americans included the notion that
the arriving Americans would, in fact, be the returning descendants of Makirans who had departed or been taken away from the island in the past. Repeat-
ing to me a story he had heard during Maasina Rule, a resident of 'Ubuna said
that originally there had been four lineages on Makira. In order to escape from
the depredations of four man-eating monsters, representatives of these lineages
had fled from the island to settle both in neighboring islands and further afield
"in America, Borneo, Russia, and England." Other people likewise knew narratives about the past that placed ancestors at far-flung locations from which
their descendants might return at any time. By his own account, the Spanish
explorer Mendaña took a family of Makirans to Peru in 1568 (Amherst and
Thomson 1901: 63, 92, 180, 207–208, 421, 424–426). When I interviewed Father John Espagne, a Roman Catholic missionary resident on Makira 1946–58,
he reiterated his earlier assertion to Hugh Laracy (1976: 123) that during
Maasina Rule many Makirans had theorized that black Americans were the descendants of the people Mendaña had taken away. One Arosi woman told me
that, when she had been a teenager, Maasina Rule leaders had taught her that
a second wave of unnamed explorers following Mendaña had arrived and abducted a woman of her lineage who had married in America and produced an
American branch of her lineage. More common, however, was a variant of this
story set in the context of the more recent history of the labor trade of the nineteenth century. According to this variant, Europeans had stolen people from
Arosi and taken them to America or other nations where they had established
Makiran lineages.

13. Cochrane (1970: 140; 1967: 210, 294) records that members of the San Cristobal
Local Government council told him that "Russians were expected to bring the 'cargo' in
1952," but "the Solomon Islanders expected to have to pay for it by giving the Russians land
for a base."

They told the story of how during the "blackbirding" days a steamer came and took a young girl and her mother.[14] They lived at Mwani-hau. It was during this period [i.e., the season when] people crack nuts. They were taking the shells off canarium nuts and saw the ship, so they ran down to the beach and were taken.... In *maasinga ruru* they said, "That woman and child were [our lineage] and they went to America and they married with people there and our lineage reproduced tremendously in America. They are just Arosi people; only their bodies are white." They came in World War II to Lunga [i.e., the American base on Guadalcanal] and they loved us. Because they loved us, they told us to do this custom (*ringeringe*) called *maasinga ruru* so that one day we'd live like white people, civilized.... Similar stories were told at different villages, at Tawaiboro, Heuru, and Haurango. We believed that they were the true lineage and that this was their land.

For many Arosi, the reputed generosity and kindness of American service-men toward Solomon Islanders on Guadalcanal took on great significance. This perceived benevolence performatively revealed the Makiran identity of the Americans by showing that they lived according to the precepts of the true *auhenua*. In search of additional signs that would prove the affinity between Makirans and Americans, Arosi also pointed to what they took to be elements of shared temperament and symbolism. In contrast to the British, who allowed three warnings before taking punitive action against a miscreant, both Makirans and Americans, observed Arosi, gave only one warning in their dealings with one another. When Arosi saw the eagle emblem on American military attire they identified this eagle with a well-known mythic eagle they regarded as an element of local custom and understood the Americans to be wearing a symbol of their ancestral island (cf. Meltzoff and LiPuma 1986: 58; Scott 1990–91: 60–61).[15]

Performing Population Plenitude

These diverse ideas regarding the nature of those who might come notwithstanding, the outward appearance of Maasina Rule in Arosi was not dissimi-

---

14. Although the term "blackbirding" has its origin in the African slave trade and strongly connotes the illegal kidnapping of Pacific Islanders prior to c. 1875, it came to be used by Europeans and Melanesians alike to refer to all forms of labor recruiting and transport of Pacific Islanders (Moore 1985: x–xi; cf. Corris 1973a).

15. Despite the partial homophony between America (Pijin: *Merika*) and Makira, to my knowledge, Arosi did not theorize a relationship between these names.

lar to that found elsewhere in the southeast Solomon Islands. As was typical wherever Maasina Rule was practiced, in Arosi, an intensive effort—described in one government report as a "frenzy"—was aimed at drawing the remaining bush residents down to the coast and consolidating pre-existing coastal villages and hamlets in accordance with newly prescribed designs (ATR, September 1948, BSIP 1/III/F14/35). Fred Ta'aru recounted to me that an order came from Malaita that the bush people were to come down to the coast and join in making large villages. 'Erihoro came down to Tawaiabu, Taritari to Heuru, and Wagau and Tara'oi came down to Asimaanioha (ATR, September 1947, BSIP 1/III/F14/35; [undated map of Arosi], BSIP 9/I 1; ATR, March 12, 1948, enclosure in DOSD to SG, March 12, 1948, BSIP 1/III/F14/35).[16] Don Ho'asi recalled how a Maasina Rule messenger, Nugata'i, came up from Heuru to Taritari and said, "We should come down and all live on the coast." Fifty years later, owing to this final descent, Arosi's bush interior is today almost entirely uninhabited, and nearly everyone lives in coastal villages.[17]

At the time of Maasina Rule, existing coastal villages were redesigned and enlarged to accommodate the influx of people from the bush. At Heuru, according to Ta'aru, "We only made houses on stilts and made kitchens at the back." The houses were built in two straight lines that met to give the village the shape of a "V." Ta'aru, who was one of the village architects, explained that the "V" stood for "village" (cf. ATR, September 1948, BSIP 1/III/F14/35). With 190 residents in November 1948 (Fox *D*: November 10, 1948), this refurbished village, like Asimaanioha, became one of several large villages that absorbed and replaced a scattering of smaller bush villages and dispersed coastal hamlets. Other magnet villages included Tawatana, which was rebuilt at Mwanihau on a bluff above the beach with houses aligned to form an "L," and 'Ubuna, where villagers rebuilt their houses to form two straight lines parallel to the shoreline. Although the resulting concentrations of population were fewer in number than the small villages they replaced, they were nevertheless

---

16. Ta'aru added that, after Maasina Rule, it was difficult for people to go back up to the bush, so new villages were subsequently formed along the coast. Villages, such as Waarau, Tawania'u, and Heraniauu, were slowly formed when groups of people who lived in the collectivized Maasina Rule villages relocated as a result of social tensions, conversion to Seventh-day Adventism, or, in one case, to establish a medical clinic.

17. Although the population of Arosi I lives along the coast, in Arosi II there are a few small hamlets in the bush behind Maro'u Bay. In contrast to the neighboring islands of Malaita and Guadalcanal, Makira as a whole has only a small inland population today. Most of the island's remaining bush settlements are in the East Bauro and Wainoni Bay areas (Herlihy 1981: 54; Ministry of Provincial Government and Rural Development 2001: 10; Provincial Planning Office 1988: Map 3).

understood as providing complete coverage of the land. By marking and maintaining boundaries between villages, residents ensured that there were no vacant interstices between them that escaped oversight (cf. Cochrane 1967: 17–20). In the words of Hoahoura'imae of 'Ubuna: "A boundary was placed at Ha'amami and one at Haurahu River forming the land that the 'Ubuna people looked after. Tawatana looked after the land from Haurahu River to Ruhuruhu, and Maranu'u village [looked after] the land from Ruhuruhu to Hau'ahe. The village would work and garden within its boundaries."[18]

Interpreters of Maasina Rule have frequently analyzed these activities either as imitative but autonomous continuations of precedents established by the British administration or as emulations of the order and regimentation seen at the American military base on Guadalcanal (Allan 1951: 80; but see Cochrane 1970: 92 n. 1). Without necessarily discounting the relevance of these influences, I would emphasize that most Arosi appear to have made sense of these mandated practices primarily as efforts designed to block the possibility of land seizure by a large influx of strangers (cf. Akin 1993: 343; Allan 1950: 46; Burt 1994a: 179–180). In addition to demonstrating to the British government that they had the capacity to plan and superintend their own social and physical order, Arosi were also, I suggest, engineering an appearance of population plenitude in the land (cf. Allan 1957: 250).[19] In many cases, by erecting houses in rows along the beaches, they were presenting a scene of total occupation to the eyes of anyone arriving by sea.[20] By labeling

---

18. Other people noted that "the boundaries placed during *maasinga ruru* were not customary boundaries [i.e., the boundaries of lineage territories]."

19. Several of my consultants glossed the place name Arosi as meaning "completed," or "full" and said that the area was given this name "because there are a lot of people here." Based on his research from the early 1920s, Fox (1978: 71) gives "continuous, unbroken, running the whole length" as his first definition of *arosi*. It strikes me as plausible that in the context of Maasina Rule, with its concern for peopling the coast, the people of Arosi may have been extending the semantic range of this term.

20. In the Annual Report for the District of Malaita, 1947, R. J. Davies indicates that there was a similar motive behind the construction of coastal villages on Malaita. He writes that the fear "that a 'colony' of foreigners was coming to invade Malaita and dispossess the people of their land, went a long way towards persuading the people of the necessity for building these villages. This would account for the haste with which they were constructed, their arrangement in long lines, and the fact that they are situated wherever these [*sic*] is a good landing place on the coast, in order to impress intending immigrants with the size of the population and persuade them to go away" (January 31, 1948, BSIP 1/III/14/36; cf. QR, July to September 1953, BSIP 9/III/4 F; Davies n.d., 88–89, 133). Malaitans directly expressed similar concerns in a document entitled "The Kwara'ae District Advising by D.R.D.V." Laracy, who reproduces the document, notes that this letter "was circulated about

and monitoring village boundaries, they were asserting proprietary precedence at all points. One man made this purpose especially explicit. "At the edges of the village," he explained, "there were boundary lines and these had signs marking the boundaries in case America came and tried to take the land. The notices informed us who looked after that piece of land and consequently who was going to talk to them about it when they came. We weren't going to let the land be taken."[21]

Raising *Kastom*

Another way in which Arosi sought to guard against the potentially inimical forces they believed might soon arrive was to "search through the *kastom* of the island" and raise "*kastom* to stand against *kolonia*." "We were to follow *kastom* again," recalled George Huruani. This recrudescence and objectification of custom was a general feature of Maasina Rule throughout the southeast Solomon Islands (cf. Akin 2005; Keesing 1992). In ways that extrapolated indigenous norms and practices from everyday life and subjected them to regimes of mission-style pedagogy, what Arosi cast as the revival of custom generally took the form of explicit schooling in social forms and values, treated as discrete types of transferable knowledge. Young people learned to sing songs, such as those that had once accompanied mortuary rituals, and to perform dances. Greater stress appears, however, to have been placed on the transmission of behavioral norms that emphasized cooperation and social cohesion. Salient themes included respect for elders, how chiefs ought to lead, how unmarried women should comport themselves, the rules of courtship and marriage, and, as one elder put it, all forms of "custom (*ringeringe*) by which villagers could live well together." Men and women who had been in early adolescence at this time recalled that, in addition to these basic precepts, their elders had stressed the importance of hospitality, gift giving, and reciprocity, instructing them in the proper ways of hosting guests, contributing to marriage exchanges, and participating in communal work.

---

the beginning of 1947" (Laracy, ed. 1983: 106–107). See also Burt's references to the fear of land alienation and the construction of coastal villages in Kwara'ae (1982: 386–387; 1994a: 179–181).

21. Without reference to Maasina Rule, Hviding (1996: 78) describes a remarkably similar response to the possibility of territorial incursion in present-day Marovo (Western Province).

Even before Maasina Rule some Makirans, stimulated in part by Protectorate initiatives to establish "Councils of Elders" and "Native Courts" that
could arbitrate disputes according to customary law, had recognized that even
practices unobjectionable to the Church were in decline. In 1941, the proposal
of Acting District Officer Martin Clemens that a Council of Elders might
gather in every sub-district to rule on matters of custom was met by Makirans
with "much doubt ... in some of the totally missionised sub-districts as to the
amount of work which the council would be able to do." To this indigenous
doubt, Clemens added his own observation: "It is true that in some parts of
the District, Christianity has made a clean sweep of native custom" (QR, July
3, 1941, BSIP 9/III/4 E1).[22] Later, by the time of the movement, general awareness of custom decline had become, among Arosi, an anxiety that people's
waning grasp on elements of their ancestral traditions, including even their
language, might threaten their ability to retain their land and way of life
against the encroachment of alien values. Unlike Clemens, however, Arosi did
not view Christianity as the source of such alien values or as the cause of the
demise of their custom. Rather, most Arosi viewed the Church as good because it had been mediated to them by their chiefs of old and was not at odds
with their *ringeringe*. "We thought that the *ringeringe* of the Church was almost the same as the *ringeringe* of the island. The chiefs were the ones who
brought the Church here—Bo'o[rauaniara] and Taki[horota'imae]. It was because of this that we accepted the Church. But we don't know where the government came from. It was the government that threw away our chiefs and
set up the headmen."

The true bearer of alien values was a supposedly Western-style government, along with the commercial interests it would support. An idea reiterated by many of my consultants was that *kastom* stood in direct opposition
to a condition they called *kolonia*. *Kolonia* was envisioned as an extreme form
of individualistic capitalism that the anticipated invaders might bring and

---

22. Although similar proposals had been forwarded for several years prior to the war,
documentary evidence suggests that a fully functioning "Native Council" was not established in Arosi until c. 1944–45 (ATR, December 1944, BSIP 9/I F1). This is to say that
the development of Native Councils charged with the adjudication of "land disputes and
other matters of native custom" was concurrent with Maasina Rule in Arosi (Barrow n.d.:
Part III, 22). Although government reports complain that Native Councils on Makira came
under the control of the movement, I have not been able to determine whether or to what
extent the Native Council of Arosi became an organ of the movement's agenda of custom
rehabilitation (AR, March 12, 1948, BSIP 9/III/1 E2). None of my consultants had served
on this council or mentioned its activities in connection with their reminiscences of
Maasina Rule.

impose on the island. Under the regime of *kolonia* everything would be bought and sold, and rightful landowners would be fraudulently dispossessed (cf. Allan 1957: v, 56).[23] Rosemary Magewa, expressing a view shared by many Arosi, represented this state of affairs as socially and morally antithetical to the *kastom*—or more frequently, *ringeringe*—enjoined by Maasina Rule.

> We call it *maasinga ruru*. It is simply a ruling *ringeringe*. We established a *ringeringe* to live by. It isn't like the *ringe* of the council, *kolonia* in which you have to buy everything: betel nut and tobacco. You just share. If you kill your pig, don't make [people] buy [the cuts of pork]. If someone is marrying, you give food, a pig, or a cow. And [the recipients] will do the same some day for your child. If you [came to visit], we'd make *susu'u*, *gori*, and *taumwa* [i.e., various types of pudding] and we'd climb up to get you coconuts [to drink]. You would eat without paying and we wouldn't leave you that day, we'd sit and talk with you. It shows respect. And when you went back to your house, my child would carry food after you.... *Maasinga ruru* was things people had forgotten: mutual respect, mutual love, generosity.

Arosi adherents of Maasina Rule turned to an idealized vision of their local *ringeringe* with its prescription for the sharing of produce and resources across a network of kinship and exchange relations as the requisite barrier against the alienating commodification of *kolonia*. Knowing *kastom* became an urgent necessity.[24]

> If we don't know *kastom* that will stand to block *kolonia*, then *kolonia* will come. In *kolonia* we will buy food and water, even from your cross-sex-sibling and your child. But before, and in *kastom*, you

---

23. Anxiety about the coming of such a regime was still evident in the Wainoni subdistrict of Makira in 1953: "The fear of becoming a Colony, although normally dormant, is, nevertheless, to these people a very real fear as it involves, in their minds, not only the theft of their lands but also their own virtual enslavement" (AR, January 15, 1954, BSIP 9/III/1 F).

24. Ironically, even as they were endorsing this emergency return to *kastom*, Arosi were also preparing for commodification by fixing and recording the price of everything in their possession so as to know what to charge if and when *kolonia* came. During a stay in the village of 'Ubuna I was shown a notebook from the Maasina Rule years containing an inventory of foods and their values in pounds sterling.

Figure 3.1. Rosemary Magewa: "If we don't know *kastom* that will stand to block *kolonia*, then *kolonia* will come."

would not do this. Under *kolonia* you buy a house and everything is sold between everyone.... So we thought we must be strong in *kastom* to stop this. Europeans would bring *kolonia* here, but America would not.

While it is clear that many Arosi understood return to *kastom* as a means of countering self-interested individualism with communitarian Maasina Rule values, there was another meaning implicit, though often uninvoked, in the notion that knowledge of *kastom* would have the power to block *kolonia*. Because a primary goal of the movement was to protect the land from theft or unfair alienation, the movement and its practices inevitably pointed to the issue of who should be recognized as the rightful landholders along the coast. Thus, raising *kastom* to block *kolonia* could mean identifying and putting forward the *auhenua* to welcome the Americans, stave off intruders, or, minimally, demand a just compensation in return for their land. One woman described how John 'Araubora had instructed her to this end. "It is a preparation for when they come and ask: 'Where is the landowner? Where is the *kastom* landowner, the *auhenua* person who has the land?' And ['Araubora] said if I didn't learn they will come and end up buying the gold of the island from a person of another island—a different person."

John 'Araubora, one of the principal Maasina Rule figures in Arosi, is still respected as having been a man of exceptional foresight and leadership. "He was our scientist," people said, meaning that he had superior knowledge and, especially, understanding of the ways of Europeans. Significantly, he was a SSEM mission-educated teacher at the village of 'Ahi'a on Maro'u Bay, an area that, since the 1880s, had been visited by several European gold prospecting expeditions. At least one of these expeditions, undertaken by two Germans in 1930, had explored up the 'Eteria river (Grover 1958: 83–84). Perhaps as an attempt to explain how these Europeans knew where to look for gold, 'Araubora appears to have theorized that Europeans must have been in possession of some memory or record of the Maro'u Bay region from an antecedent incursion. As several of my consultants recalled, he taught that the Arosi names for the cliffs at Rohu (on the northwest end of Makira) and the river 'Eteria are corrupted forms of the names Rome and Italy and constitute evidence that the ancient Romans had once visited and settled in Arosi for a short time.

'Araubora's concern that Arosi people might be cheated out of profits to be had from any gold yet to be discovered in their lands may have been sparked by more immediate events, however. After payable gold was indeed discovered on Guadalcanal in 1931 (Grover 1962: 172), former District Officer F. M. Campbell prospected there in the early 1940s, employing two dozen Makirans (IMA, July 28, 1941, BSIP 1/III/F48/9; cf. Clemens 1998: 291), including some Arosi. It is therefore likely that, not only 'Araubora, but other Arosi too were well informed about and interested in the possibilities for future mining developments on their own island. It is also likely that they were aware that one of the grievances expressed by supporters of the Fallowes Movement on Guadalcanal had been that they had seen no benefits in return for the gold extractions on their lands (Bennett 1987: 262). With visions of similar resources to be found on Makira and a desire to ready themselves to be recognized as the rightful beneficiaries, it is not surprising that, as they went about the task of positioning people throughout the coastal land, some Arosi interpreted this reorganization of space in ways that reflected their own self-understandings as the *auhenua* of the area.

It should be noted, however, that although this tendency was in evidence it was not universal. Some Arosi, for example, rather than attempting to sort the *auhenua* from the non-*auhenua*, chose to represent decisions regarding who was placed where as dictated by a variety of non-unilineal kinship relationships. As already quoted above, one man asserted that "the arrangement of the land was done according to groups (*burunga*)." Because the term *burunga* can mean both a matrilineage and any general group of related people, I asked him in which sense he was using the word in this instance, and he indicated the latter.[25] This is to say that he assumed that some kinship-based order or rationale lay behind the seating of people on the land, but did not inquire into the specific nature of people's links to the places they guarded.

In a statement seemingly indicative of a similar trust, another man, whom I will call Ruku, gave an account that suggests it was the ethic, or *ringeringe*, of the *auhenua* that discouraged close scrutiny of who was placed where.

> In *maasinga ruru* we knew who the *auhenua* lineages were, but we all must eat together [i.e., share things]. We knew the lineage that had things. But the [*maasinga ruru*] chiefs would not say who the *auhenua* were in case the people who had come would be ashamed. The chiefs just told us where to garden. We made these arrangements with the land in *maasinga ruru* because we knew that one day something would come here. That's also why we worked out the prices of things.

This statement should be taken with a degree of suspicion, however, because the man in question understands his own matrilineage to be *auhenua* in the land of his village. It may be that his assertion that there was no ambiguity during Maasina Rule concerning who was *auhenua* where represents only his interested point of view. Indeed, fifty years later when I recorded this statement, Ruku was engaged in a quiet tug-of-war with the representative of another lineage over the name and identity of the matrilineage thought by some to be *auhenua* in the area where both men live. These men are of different lineages, but each one claims that his lineage is this *auhenua* matrilineage. Today, the particularities of their dispute emerge in their readings of the events of the Maasina Rule period. Ruku, for his part, states that a member of his lineage, Haka, had been the Maasina Rule chief who, acting as a representative of the *auhenua*, had placed people on his lineage's land. Ruku's rival denies this, however, and states that it was really Haka's brother, 'Omesurimwara, who had been the Maasina Rule chief. Although the rival recognizes that 'Omesurimwara was a member of Ruku's lineage, he nevertheless asserts that the name 'Omesurimwara belongs to, and had been given to this chief by his lineage. Consequently, the rival constructs 'Omesurimwara's chiefship and activities during Maasina Rule as having been on behalf of his lineage as *auhenua*, rather than Ruku's.[26]

It is difficult to assess whether such competing readings of the Maasina Rule period represent attempted revisionist histories, or whether they reveal that

---

25. For a fuller discussion of this term, see chapter 4.
26. All of the personal names used in this account are pseudonyms.

conflicting constructions of placement in the land were contemporary with the movement itself. Another case about which I learned speaks more plainly in favor of the latter possibility. This case concerns the boundary marker erected between two villages during the movement. According to one consultant, this boundary marker became a source of contention when one man decided its placement infringed on what he considered to be his matrilineal land. In keeping with the Maasina Rule initiative to leave no unencumbered land between villages, the sign was originally staked at a place on the coast roughly midway between the two villages in question. Objecting to this placement, a man from one of the villages relocated it to a spot slightly nearer to the other. The next day, the man charged with oversight of this other village moved the marker back to its original site. On the following day, the first man again pushed the marker back toward the other village. The two men continued these maneuvers for several days. When I inquired what had motivated the man who kept pushing the sign back toward the other village, I was told that he thought his matrilineage was *auhenua* at his village and that his matrilineal territory extended beyond the midway point between the two villages. In other words, the land policies of Maasina Rule had impinged on and surfaced an *auhenua* identity.

In addition to these inklings of competing *auhenua* identities during the time of Maasina Rule, I also encountered evidence that members of at least one other Arosi lineage were intensively and secretly engaged in the work of recovering the genealogical narrative of their lineage so as to discover and preserve their own *auhenua* identity at their village and its environs. One woman of this lineage recalled that sorting out the matter of which lineages were truly of the island and which lineages had arrived from offshore had been a prominent feature of the village-wide Maasina Rule meetings she had attended. As she describes, one purpose of these meetings had been to commit such matters to writing.

> The [person who was called the] *claka* (clerk) wrote laws and where the lineages came from. That's where I learned the things I know. [They taught] the *kastom* generation of Makira—*kastom* so that they'd know the *auhenua* lineages [of the island], ... and they'd also know the coming here of the people on the island. That's what they taught most importantly, that's what they looked for. The first lineages were Atawa and Amaeo. That's the type of thing in which we were interested.

Alone among themselves, however, members of this woman's lineage took this interest one step further; they recorded for themselves a "*kastom* generation" specifically linking them to the area around their village.

This "*kastom* generation" is of particular interest, not only because it constructs this lineage as *auhenua* on the coast, but because it also constructs this lineage as the lineage of the Americans whose anticipated arrival it transforms into a welcome return. Recall that during Maasina Rule a number of Arosi, as well as other Makirans, theorized that America had become populated by the descendants of people who had been kidnapped or forced to leave the island long ago. Incorporating this idea into their lineage narrative, this particular lineage developed the view that they were of one lineage with the Americans. According to their "*kastom* generation," a female of their matrilineage, which was *auhenua* on the coast, had been taken to America where she had produced many children; when her children's children returned to their coastal land, the branch of the lineage that had remained in Arosi would be there to greet them, and they would all live together as one people. In view of this understanding of their shared *auhenua* identity with the Americans, this lineage's reclamation of an idealized *ringeringe* acquired the additional rationale of ensuring mutual recognition between themselves and their returning cousins (Scott 2007). One representative of this lineage articulated this rationale in the following terms:

> If people came and asked, "What's your *ringeringe*?" you could tell them and they could live like us. They said this in case some of our people that had been stolen came back and we'd recognize them. [The people who came] would ask whether you knew such-and-such a person and you'd be able to say you knew. That's why they had these meetings. They said sometime [those who are related] will come and they'll ask us about our lives here and we'd be able to tell them so they'd know too. Perhaps they'll ask about our *ringeringe* and you want to know.

As this concern for mutual recognition implies, however, the idea that the anticipated Americans would be the descendants of Makiran women could be a threat to Arosi who understood themselves either to have lost custom or to be non-*auhenua* where they were living on the coast. If the Americans could trace themselves to coastal women of old and were therefore legitimate landholders there in their own right, they might come and displace such interlopers. In fact, one of my consultants, who had been a young man during Maasina Rule, expressed his ongoing concern that the original inhabitants of the island might one day return but fail to recognize Arosi as authentic Makirans because they now speak only an unintelligibly corrupted form of the Arosi language. Reasoning along similar lines, another Maasina Rule veteran confided: "A little question we always asked, all the time, to this day, was, 'If the lineage of the woman of Tawatana who married at America returns, what will we people of Tawatana now say, we people who have all come [here]?' In our *kastom* there is nothing we could say."

The full extent of the impact of the Maasina Rule movement on how Arosi understand their relationship to the coastal land becomes apparent when it is taken into account that the man who posed this "little question" is a member of the very lineage that came to construct itself, not as *sae boboi*, but as the *auhenua* kinsmen of the Americans. In light of this fact, his voicing of the question appears disingenuous and signals the presence of two simultaneous levels of discourse about lineages and land already operative during Maasina Rule. On one level, the people who wondered openly what they as *sae boboi* would say to Americans returning to the coastal lands of their matrilineal ancestors were, in effect, articulating a consensus that none of them could claim to be the *auhenua* of the coast. On another level, however, the man who repeated this question to me is now, and was during Maasina Rule, adopting the language of the consensus while concurrently reserving to himself and his matrilineage an *auhenua* identity.

In 1973 the former leader of Maasina Rule in 'Are'are (southern Malaita), Aliki Nono'oohimae, explained in detail to de Coppet and Zemp the nature and aims of his program of custom revival during the movement: "The program that we undertook included the establishment of our genealogies, the maintenance of our laws in the land, and respect for our living as well as our dead. And for that purpose, we decided to survey the funeral sites that structure all our territory" (1978: 106–107, author's translation). More recently, de Coppet has stated unequivocally that these measures were undertaken "in response to the threat of confiscation of lands said to be 'vacant' (vacant land) by the British administration or later by the central government of the Solomon Islands anxious to launch large economic development projects" (1998: 190, author's translation).[27] Naitoro furthermore reports that the compilation of genealogies in 'Are'are during and after Maasina Rule was expressly aimed "to show the 'Are'are people as one community" (1993: 93) and as "all related genealogically" (1993: 131). Similarly, Burt (1982; 1994a: 215) de-

---

27. Jonathan Fifi'i (1989: 64; cf. Keesing 1992: 104), who had been appointed the Head Chief of Maasina Rule for Kwaio (to the north of 'Are'are), explained that during the movement: "We chiefs spoke about land. We talked about how, if we just stayed quiet, the Government would come in and take our land away. They'd lie to us, and they'd give the land to outsiders.... That's what we were worried about." Reflecting on both Fifi'i's explanation of Maasina Rule concerns and the recent history of Kwaio *kastom* politics, Keesing (1992: 124; cf. 1978: 54–55; 1982b: 361, 362) notes that "[f]or the Kwaio, writing down genealogies and histories of lands and shrines provides the foundation for their struggle to hold their homeland against invasion by plantation (and now logging) interests."

scribes how Kwara'ae (north central Malaita) efforts to record genealogies aim to unite all Kwara'ae by linking the genealogy of each landholding lineage to a single unifying origin narrative and tracing "their descent from the first ancestor" (1994a: 234).

The evidence of my consultants' testimonies suggests that the nature and aims of the movement in Arosi were essentially similar, but that in Arosi the activities of genealogy collection and territory delimitation were neither open nor aimed at unification. Below the outward appearance of cooperative coastal collectivization and placement of people in the land, Arosi began the work of assembling lineage narratives and correlating lineage identities with lands on a clandestine intra-lineage basis. Whether Arosi imagined that a new colonial regime would attempt to confiscate or commodify their land, or looked for signs of Americans arriving to liberate them and bring development, the situation urged that an *auhenua* lineage be present to receive the newcomers and to protect the interests of those living in the island. But already at that time, as in the present, assertions of *auhenua* identities, however necessary and desirable, could not be straightforward. They consisted instead in the inconspicuous but nonetheless socially disarticulating retreat of interested matrilineages to the solitary tasks of building up and protecting their own stores of legitimating genealogical and place-specific historical knowledge.

The contrast between Arosi and other regions of Solomon Islands regarding the means and form of customary land tenure revival and reification is significant at another level as well, however. It suggests that, while the fear of land loss that animated much of Maasina Rule clearly contributed to the objectification of customary land tenure in the central and eastern Solomons, this factor alone did not determine the shape that objectification took in any given context. The process of custom objectification, it appears, elicited preexisting differences among indigenous Solomon Islands land tenure practices. The will to hold onto land by appeal to *kastom* did not in and of itself promote either unifying or individuating descent-centered land tenure systems. Both are found. There appears to be little ground, in other words, on which to speculate that strategies to secure land via *kastom* politics created the Arosi system of landholding *auhenua* matrilineages and the poly-ontology it entails *de novo*. To the contrary, it might more reasonably be supposed that such a system would be less suited to the purpose of deterring outsiders from appropriating land than one that permits a community to present a vocal and united front as locally documented customary landholders. As an indigenous theory of being that inheres in Arosi understandings of relationship to place, Arosi poly-ontology appears, therefore, both to have informed and been reformed by the revivification of custom that accompanied Maasina Rule.

Maasina Rule activities on Makira had subsided by the early 1950s, and in the early 1990s many Arosi looked back on the movement with self-deprecating humor as a misguided endeavor. But the reality it highlighted for Arosi that land without an *auhenua* lineage anchored in it may be subject to random appropriation by outsiders remains in people's minds as an unresolved problem inculcating a sense of vulnerability to land loss (cf. Allan 1957: 56). Reflecting on the Protectorate government's settlement of Polynesian Tikopians on land west of Kirakira in the mid 1960s, one man gravely stated to me: "That's what happened at Wairaraha. The lineage was finished and the land was neglected, so the government took it and it became Tikopian land."[28] This could happen at Tawatana, he explained, because the people of Tawatana have all come from elsewhere on the strength of their relationships of "entanglement."

In view of the history of the last one hundred years, it is small wonder that Arosi today hesitate to construct their attachment to their homes and gardens on the basis of these relationships of "entanglement" alone, but seek instead to attach themselves inalienably to the land as the rightful *auhenua* there. The anticipated arrival of logging interests and even gold prospecting is, furthermore, contributing to this impetus. But if recent history and the possibility that land may be given new value help to account for why Arosi find it necessary to emplace themselves as the true *auhenua* in their land, it does not explain either the particularity of the practices they employ in so doing or by what Arosi criteria such practices are meaningful and appropriate. In order to · understand the nature and logic of these practices, it is necessary, I suggest, to attend not only to historical factors but also to their engagement with and transformation of the premises of Arosi cosmology and ontology. As a first step toward analysis of these premises, I begin in the following chapter with an examination of ideas and practices pertaining to human reproduction in Arosi and the tension between pure matrilineal consubstantiality and interlineage mixing they entail.

---

28. Lomas (1972: 10; cf. Sayes 1976: 168) describes the land used for this Tikopian resettlement as having been "taken from an abandoned [plantation] estate of some 2,000 acres of which only a very small area had ever been planted and which upon abandonment became Crown land."

CHAPTER 4

CUTTING THE CORD: REPRODUCTION AS COSMOGONY

Paradoxically, the unity and continuity of an Arosi matrilineage as a distinct entity depends on its intersection with other similarly distinct matrilineages. Casper Kaukeni expressed the problem in the following terms: "Even if the whole of Makira were full of people, no one could marry if everyone belonged to the same lineage. It would be," he stated laconically, "the end." This hypothetical situation, visualized in response to my questions about the tabu status of matrilineal endogamy, imagines a single lineage in a state of total isolation. Being entirely self-contained and unable to establish reproductive relations with other matrilineally defined human categories, the lineage would perish.

In this chapter I explore the ways in which Arosi poly-ontology entails an ongoing burden to construct unity—in the form of social polities—from diversity through the establishment and maintenance of productive and reproductive relations among matrilineages, understood to be the human transformations of multiple unique primordial categories of being. At the same time, I show how, as Casper's vision of lineage extinction suggests, these same relations are equally necessary for the continued viability of each matrilineage as a humanized category. The ever-present possibility of return to chaotic over-differentiation—the lack of relations among separate lineages— threatens to subvert, not only the cohesion of a synthetic sociality, but also the internal continuity of each constituent lineage within that sociality.[1] The persistent need to establish inter-lineage relations is, I suggest, most clearly represented in lineage origin stories that depict mythic groups of proto-peo-

---

1. Tony Swain (1993: 33, 50–53) also notes the potential dangers of what he dubs "monadology," a state of atomism that precolonial Australian Aborigines overcame through the construction of interdependent relations among autonomous places. Swain does not, however, identify these processes of coming into relationship as cosmogonic.

Figure 4.1. Casper Kaukeni: "Even if the whole of Makira were full of people, no one could marry if everyone belonged to the same lineage. It would be the end."

ple in atomistic asociality. These groups are what we might term potential or proto-lineages. It is only after representatives of these apparently autonomous proto-lineages come into relationship with one another that cosmogony, the formation of a comprehensive and internally ordered universe, occurs. Such an agglutinative cosmogony, or poly-genesis, is not a single foundational event, however, but a continuous process. Arosi poly-genesis requires constant renewal through practices that reinforce connections among the diverse categories.[2]

Furthermore, it is through the mediation of relationships between different categories of being that each category generates internal distinctions. Arosi express the consubstantiality and common descent of the members of an ontological category in terms of a lineage's shared umbilical cord or common blood. Differentiations and separations within a lineage—say, between a mother and child—that are critical for the reproduction of a category of being are established in cosmogonic moments, in the inception, fruition, or invocation of relations with other categories. In processes of mono-genesis, differentiation is often modeled as a spontaneous unfolding within a single primordial unity; in Arosi poly-genesis, however, separations within each independently arising ontological category are generated when one category impinges on another.

As previously noted, among Arosi there are no widely shared myths of cosmogony at a universal scale nor are there any all-encompassing cosmological narratives or rituals in which Arosi categories of being might find their "most abstract representation" (Sahlins 1985: xv). Nevertheless, Arosi models of cosmogony and ontology are accessible to analysis in quotidian forms of thought and practice that express Arosi assumptions about the poly-genetic nature of their sociality. Here I focus particularly on Arosi understandings and treatments of relatedness, conception, birth, exogamy, and other practices that, even when no longer regularly performed, can reveal the ontological presuppositions that continue to inform contemporary transformations of Arosi onto-praxis.[3]

Burunga and *Waipo*

Mika 'Aroha'i,[4] an eyewitness to the events he described, related to me that once, when there had been a land dispute in his village, a dried coconut frond

---

2. Here my discussion has been influenced by the distinction between "creation" and "true cosmos"—that is, between a primary generative act and a secondary structuring operation—that Brian K. Smith (1989: 50–69) develops in his analysis of Vedic ritual.

3. My analyses of practices that Arosi no longer perform—for example, killing a woman's first child or selling a person who marries within his or her lineage—are not offered as reconstructions of an idealized pre-contact system. Rather, I explicate past practices to which Arosi themselves refer and objectify when they conceptualize, discuss, and act in the current context.

4. This is a pseudonym.

was discovered thrust into the ground beside an important gravesite (*hera*) associated with one of the disputing parties. The leaves of the frond had been twisted and tied around the main stem in the manner of a coconut frond torch. This torch had been deliberately, but anonymously, fixed in the ground at a slant, pointing in a particular direction. Mika explained that the torch had been set up by one of the parties to the dispute so that it pointed toward the place where the other disputants' ancestors were thought previously to have lived. Angled as it was, the frond silently urged, "Go back to the place of your grandmother. Go back to the place of your lineage (*burunga*)."

While the actions of those who set up the torch reflect the often covert nature of Arosi land disputes, Mika's interpretation of the message of the torch indicates the matrilineal nature of Arosi lineages. Furthermore, his interpretation suggests that each lineage, *burunga*, is connected to a particular place to which its members may return; each lineage is made up of "the matrilineal descendants of the original people of a particular area" (*burunga i auhenua*).

In clearly denoting a matrilineage, Mika's use of the word *burunga* in the phrase quoted above accords with the principal sense of this word among Arosi. But Arosi also use this polysemous term in a variety of other ways (cf. Fox 1924: 10, 17; 1978: 110). Consequently, knowledge of how a particular person tends to use the term and of the speech context in which it is used are both vital to understanding the meaning of *burunga* in any given instance. Mika, like most Arosi, also employs *burunga* to reference collectively a number of different matrilineages that are known by the same name. Unlike the matrilineages they comprise, however, *burunga* in this sense are not unified and connected as such to particular places. I translate this use of *burunga* as "clan," but stress that, although such classifications of lineages are recognized phenomena among Arosi, I discovered no general Arosi theory as to why or how some lineages have come to share the same name. Arosi, in other words, do not account for the existence of shared clan names in terms of lineage schism; clans are not understood to be united by descent from an apical ancestress. While matrilineage and clan are the two most common referents of the term *burunga*, Arosi will also use this word to signify a situationally constituted group of people, such as the constellations of men surrounded by the families of their sons described in chapter 1.

During the course of more abstract discussions, several people offered explanations of *burunga* commensurate with the idea of a bilateral kindred in which each person is situated. They suggested that only a different and perhaps older term, *waipo* (or *waibo*, literally, umbilical cord, navel) should be used to refer to the matrilineage. Seeking to clarify this point, some even gestured toward their navels when they discussed matrilineages. Most Arosi use *waipo* in this way (cf. Fox 1924: 276, 352).

It should be noted, however, that Arosi tend to use the word *waipo* when describing the general nature of a matrilineage, but favor the term *burunga* when speaking about a particular matrilineage.[5] General discussions about the characteristics of matrilineages elicit phrases such as: "one umbilical cord" (*ta'i waipo*), "a cord" (*'e waipo*), "of a cord" (*ana waipo*), or "cords have …" (*waipo to'o …*). In these contexts, *waipo* tends to be used as a simple noun. Only occasionally does an Arosi person refer to his or her lineage as *waipogu* (literally, cord-my), whereas *burungagu* is commonly used. Nevertheless, a person who recounts his or her lineage's genealogical link to the land "narrates along the cord" (*mamaani suri waipo*). In fact, both the matrilineal nature of lineages and their connection to a particular place—indicated by Mika's comments about the torch—are conveyed powerfully by the concept *waipo*.

Another friend's explanation captured both of these aspects of the lineage:

> Each lineage is joined together with an umbilical cord: the children's umbilical cords are joined with those of their mothers and their mothers' umbilical cords join with those of their grandmothers and the grandmothers' umbilical cords join with those of their grandmothers too, and so it goes back. And the daughters are the young shoots of the runner; they are forever joined together like that too, and the runner or umbilical cord gets longer without end.

As indicated here, lineages are often conceptualized both as umbilical cords and as the "runners," "creepers," or "vines" of plants, and many Arosi use the expression *warowaro waipo* (literally, vine umbilical cord).[6]

Continuing his discussion, my friend explained that lineages are like the sweet potatoes runners we had recently planted or like the vines of yams. A few weeks before, having made mounds in a new garden, we went to a neighbor's garden to cut approximately six inches off the tips of runners growing from already mature sweet potato tubers. We planted these cuttings in the mounds throughout the new garden. Like a sweet potato runner that extends continually over the ground, the lineage, "planted" (*hasi*) or "anchored" (*huna*) in the land, keeps on growing without stopping. The leaves that develop at the sides of sweet potato runners and yam-vines but do not produce

---

5. When people refer to a specific matrilineage they frequently employ the term *burunga* with the first, second, or third person singular possessive pronoun suffixes—*gu*, -*mu*, -*na*, indicating "inalienable possession" or "direct possession." For a more detailed discussion of possession in Arosi grammar, see Capell 1971; Fox 1924: 22–23; BG.

6. Fox (1924: 72, 75) notes that the expression *waro ni noni*, "the string of people," is used in many other parts of Makira and on Santa Ana.

Figure 4.2. "Each lineage is joined together with an umbilical cord: the children's umbilical cords are joined with those of their mothers ... and so it goes back": Patsy Hatarageni and her baby.

Figure 4.3. "And the daughters are the young shoots of the runner; they are forever joined together like that too, and the runner or umbilical cord gets longer without end": Helen Kei.

further growth are likened to the lineage's sons; the growing tip is considered to be analogous to lineage women.[7]

---

7. Although Arosi do not use *waipo* to refer to the "sprouting tip" (*pwaopwaona*) of the sweet potato, they do use the term for the points at alternate sides of the bamboo culm—just above the sheath scar at successive nodes—from which roots, branches, and leaves spring. Bamboo plants, like lineages, "sprout to life through" a *waipo*. As noted in chapter 1, sweet potato is a recently introduced cultigen in Arosi, but the fact that my consultant

Each matrilineage is identified as belonging to a particular area—the place of its grandmother, in Mika's terms—where it is the "original lineage" (*auhenua*). Nevertheless, as noted above, matrilineages connected with different, non-contiguous, areas may have the same clan name. There is, for example, an Amaeo lineage said by its members to be connected to one area on the south coast of Arosi and another Amaeo lineage said to be connected to a completely different area on the north coast of the island. While some whom I questioned on this matter considered the possibility that the different lineages designated by the same clan name were "one some time in the past," they stated emphatically that if two lineages are connected to different places they are "one clan in name only." Thus, separate lineages that bear a common clan name, but that view themselves as *auhenua* in different places and cannot trace the ways in which they may have been related in the past, are considered today to be "mutually distinct" and unrelated people. Members of different lineages that share the same clan name can, as a result, intermarry.

At the same time, however, the concept *burunga*, in the sense of a clan, can be used to establish relationships between different lineages that understand themselves to be *auhenua* at different places. If two people meet and in talking find that their lineages share the same name, that discovery can form a basis for their relationship. This mode of relationship is characterized as sharing "a little love" due to the common name. On one occasion, this form of "love" was tangibly evident when members of a lineage contributed a shell valuable to the bride-price payment made by another lineage with the same clan name. But, in the current context of latent land disputes, acknowledgment of such a connection can be considered perilous. The man whose lineage had received the shell valuable contribution was anxious that I should not divulge the details of the event to a wider audience and stressed that his and the other lineage were "completely different." On another occasion I recorded a lineage narrative that told how the ancestors of one lineage asked a person of another lineage with the same clan name to come and reside with them. Such invitations are, however, quite rare today. Some Arosi express fear that their actions will be seen by other people in their villages as evidence that they are not *auhenua* in the land where they reside if they cultivate close relations with a lineage from elsewhere that shares their clan name. They are afraid, in other words, that their distinct lineage identity will be compromised and that

---

here consistently referenced both sweet potato and yam together suggests that there is continuity between this discourse and indigenous yam cultivation. For discussion of analogous botanic metaphors in other Austronesian-speaking contexts, see J. Fox 1988, 1995, 1996.

they will become assimilated in the minds of their neighbors with another lineage from another locale.

The term *burunga*, then, in addition to signifying "matrilineage," can be used to invoke an array of possible forms of relationship: a clan, an extended bilateral kindred, or a contextual social group. In contrast, the term *waipo* references only the unilineally defined continuity of a matrilineage's connection to a specific area of land. This linguistic distinction between two aspects of a matrilineage is, I suggest, one of several symbolic registers indicative of a tension between an Arosi insistence that a matrilineage as *waipo* is singular and whole and a simultaneous Arosi recognition that a matrilineage as *burunga* is constituted by a plurality of lineage intersections (cf. Macintyre 1989: 134; Thune 1989: 153–157, 172). That Arosi have in the past and continue in the present to perceive and seek to mediate this tension is evident, I suggest, in a variety of Arosi ideas and practices surrounding ultimate origins, conception, gestation, parturition, and childhood, and furthermore in nightmarish representations of the anti-cosmogonic consequences of endogamous marriage.

Anthropogony: From Chaos to Kindred

Chaos: Proto-lineages

Members of one Amaeo lineage tell a particularly instructive lineage origin myth that crystallizes the Arosi understanding of human reproduction as a paradoxical cosmogonic process in which matrilineages, as the loci of unique and enduring ontological categories, come into being through their relationships with one another. Variants of this myth tell how the Amaeo matrilineage came into being through the union of two mythic quasi-human beings, a *pwapwaronga* and a *masi*. In popular tales and alleged eyewitness accounts, Arosi describe *pwapwaronga* as a wild autochthonous people who are less than one meter high.[8] They are said to live in caves and speak their own language. Stories tell how *pwapwaronga* do not have fire and must therefore eat their food uncooked. According to those who say they have seen them, *pwapwaronga* have long fingernails and long uncut hair that can hang over their faces and make them look like tree stumps. They are also thought to have a keen sense of smell, eyes that shine like flashlights, and to be physically very

---

8. See also, Fox 1924: 138–147; 1962: 22–23; 1978: 348; 1985: 75–76; Bernatzik 1936: 247.

strong. I was told that, owing to the noise of guns and dogs in recent years, *pwapwaronga*, who are shy and retiring by nature, no longer live close to Arosi villages but have retreated into the bush. In their original condition, these small people were subject to a self-destructive form of generation. Surprisingly, in spite of their reputation for exceptional intelligence and all-knowing wisdom, *pwapwaronga* did not know how to give birth properly. When a female was parturient they simply cut the child out of its mother's womb. The mother had to be killed so that the child could be delivered. This obstetrical dysfunction is, I suggest, an embodiment of their primordial ontological isolation and lack of connection with other categories of being. It was not until a female *pwapwaronga* married exogamously with a male *masi*, the representative of another category of being, that the *pwapwaronga* could reproduce without the mother having to be killed. Together the *pwapwaronga* and the *masi* are said to have produced a truly human baby girl (*inoni mora*, literally, true human).

Unlike *pwapwaronga*, who are believed still to inhabit Makira and are occasionally reported to have been glimpsed by villagers, *masi* are said to have become extinct.[9] Storytellers depict *masi* as living in houses and cultivating gardens as humans do today. The small *masi* were remarkably stupid, however. Many of the stories I recorded describe how the stupidity of the *masi* leads to their deaths. For example, in one tale they launch a canoe over a cliff, and all on board are killed. In another story, often told as a source of amusement, a company of *masi* cut down the branch of a type of sago palm. Fearing the branch would be damaged when it hit the ground, they try to catch it but are crushed to death when it falls on top of them. Typically these stories do not describe *masi* as interacting with other human-like beings; rather, engaged in their various absurd and suicidal activities, *masi* form "a tribe by themselves" (Fox 1924: 148). Moreover, particular *masi* in these narratives are distinguished neither by name nor in terms of their kinship relations with one another. The stories simply present "the *masi*" as a homogeneous group of comically foolish people (cf. Ivens 1927: 409–410).

The Amaeo origin myth pictures a primordial condition of over-differentiation among original categories of being. With the exception of the *pwapwaronga* who married the *masi*, *pwapwaronga* can be characterized as a potential lineage, a group in sterile isolation. They are, as Fox (1924: 139) aptly

---

9. See also, Fox 1924: 148–154, 345–346, 369–370; 1962: 21–22; 1978: 292; 1985: 74–75; Ivens 1927: 409–414; and Ouou 1980: 14–15. Ugi island, called Uki ni Masi, off the north coast of Makira is reputed to have been populated by a particularly large number of *masi*.

notes, not "quite human." In this isolated state, the *pwapwaronga* are unable to negotiate the termination of unity between mother and child in order to reproduce without absolute and fatal self-replacement. It is only when a *pwapwaronga* comes into reproductive relations with the representative of another analogous proto-lineage that true cosmogony and anthropogony occur. No longer limited by a closed monadic body, the *pwapwaronga* acquires an open body through which she becomes both a link to other categories and the source of a particular matrilineal continuity. The exogamous marriage achieves both inter-category connection and proper intra-category differentiation. Cosmogony and anthropogony occur simultaneously.

Blood and Waipo

The Amaeo origin myth presents exogamy as the solution to the tension between unity and diversity expressed in the self-destructive reproduction of the *pwapwaronga*. More generally, Arosi birthing practices reiterate the resolution of this tension in everyday life. A human birth forces Arosi to address the competing values of unity and distinction in the mother-child relationship. The unity of mother and child made tangible in the umbilical cord provides the basis of Arosi statements that a lineage is "simply one" and that people are "one because of the lineage." At the same time, however, a separation must be introduced if the lineage is to reproduce successfully. The umbilical cord joining the mother and child must be cut if both are to live.

Arosi say that a foetus develops when the father's blood "forms up together" with that of the mother. The joining or mixing of the father's and the mother's blood is believed to be necessary for conception, and more specifically, the flow of this mixture of blood through the umbilical cord itself is deemed necessary for the reproduction of the matrilineage/*waipo*. Because a child is the site of this confluence of bloods, he or she is said to be "one blood," not only with his or her matrilineage, but also with the matrilineage of the father, and to be furthermore "entangled" by blood with an extensive bilateral kindred. Arosi think and speak of blood, in other words, as a medium of combination of different matrilineal categories; blood is thus primarily an idiom of interrelatedness centered on the person. At the same time, however, there is blood and there is blood. If every person is the site of the blending of many bloods, it is also the case that every person is the site of the washing out and replacement of some bloods by others, and in all of this, as Martin Toku observed to me: "It is important that the blood of the woman keeps going." That is, when passed on through the umbilical cords of women, the special "power" (*mena*) that inheres in matrilineal blood alone remains constant. Generally assimilated in discourse to the idiom of the *waipo* itself, the power within matrilineal blood is granted an overriding integrity even as it undergoes constant combination with other bloods.[10] For Arosi, therefore, there is a fundamental difference between their connection to members of their own matrilineage and their connection to other kin. The former is regarded as an inherent, permanent unity of being; the latter a socially achieved temporary intermingling of bloods. Whereas the members of a *waipo* are "simply one," relatedness to a matrilineage and its ancestral spirits through a male diminishes generationally, as does relatedness between the descendants of two opposite sex siblings. After a debated number of generations, the descendants have become "different people." One man pointed this contrast precisely: "A *waipo* is long; the father's blood is just short."

After noting the initial input of paternal procreative substance, Arosi tend to de-emphasize the contribution of the father and his connection to the development of the foetus. One man characterized the father as "placing" (*nuga*) his seminal fluid and then simply carrying on living as he normally would. Others, uncomfortable with this depiction of complete aloofness on the part of the father, pointed out that the father does work together with the mother to make gardens and grow food that both the mother and the foetus will eat.[11] Nevertheless, Arosi accounts of pregnancy, although recognizing the crucial role of the father, focus on the mother, especially the illness and pain that she experiences as the foetus develops and at the time of birth. In fact, several friends enacted graphic accounts of the mother's experience of gestation, parturition, and childcare after birth to provide rationalizations for the matrilineal nature of Arosi lineages.

---

10. Two of my consultants used the Pijin phrase *blad laen* (blood line) to refer to the unique continuity of a matrilineage. Such a metaphor is consistent with the Arosi assumption that mother's blood, although itself a mixture of bloods, nevertheless carries a unique power that is passed on through a continuous line of umbilical cords. It is at odds, however, with the way Arosi also speak of blood as the substance a person shares with members of his or her bilateral kindred. Perhaps because the opposition between *waipo* and *'abu* (blood) permits a clearer distinction between given matrilineal consubstantiality and achieved temporary sharing of substance, this Pijin term for a lineage, which was probably promoted by colonial discourses (cf. Hviding 1996: 136; Tiffany 1983), has not gained wide usage.

11. If the father were completely aloof, the child would be termed a "fatherless child" or "a child of an unmarried woman" (*gare a'osi* or *gare pwai'o'ora*). It should be noted that, in Arosi, the simple act of feeding a child can neither establish nor alter that child's matrilineal identity. For contrastive data from elsewhere in Melanesia, see Lederman 1986: 34; A. Strathern 1973.

While the combination of the father's and mother's blood at conception is thought to be essential, the foetus is considered to be part of the mother's body. Growing in the mother's womb, the foetus is nourished by her blood. When the mother eats, the "goodness" of the food is thought to travel in the mother's blood through the umbilical cord to feed the foetus and cause it to increase in size. Together, a mother and her child are said to form a unity: they are "simply one" (ta'i moi). Because mother and child are understood to be consubstantial, things that the mother eats can have an effect on the child's health, not only in the womb, but even after the child has been delivered. For the first five or six years of her child's life, the mother (and her child, but not the father) must abstain from eating certain types of fish, as these would cause her child to become ill with shaking fits. Arosi express this unity between mother and child through the concept of *waipo*.

Arosi attend especially to the fact that, even after the baby has been delivered, "the umbilical cord still stays in the mother's womb," joining mother and child until it is cut by the midwife. A sliver of bamboo is used to cut the *waipo* near to the child's navel.[12] When the placenta (*ngasi*; sometimes called, metaphorically, the "child's bed" *be'a ni gare*) has been expelled, the long part of the *waipo* that is attached to the placenta is buried expressly so that it will "rot" (*ngabo*) like a corpse.[13] The four- or six-centimeter end of the *waipo* still attached to the child is knotted and dabbed with lime and the liquid from the inside of a young betel nut, or it is smeared with a piece of vine. These treatments are said to help the sore to heal. This short part of the *waipo* falls off after about a week. According to some of my consultants, in the past, this part of the cord was often dried by a fire with the idea that this process would also promote the healing of the child's navel. In explicit contrast to the placenta, this portion of the *waipo* is often "planted" (*hasi*) so that it will live and grow. When a cord is to be planted, a cut is made in the husk of a sprouting coconut

---

12. The *waipo* is no longer cut in this manner if the pregnant woman is able to travel to a rural health clinic. While women previously gave birth in dwelling houses in which coconut mats had been placed around the walls, today most births occur in the clinics.

13. On neighboring southern Malaita, 'Are'are also leave the placenta to "rot" like a corpse (de Coppet 1985: 85–87). Fox (1924: 178) notes that in Arosi "[t]he 'ahui (afterbirth) is buried in the bush, and I never could hear of any more notice being taken of it." Arosi do not regard the placenta as potentially dangerous, nor are they concerned that a placenta might be used in magic. For contrastive ethnographic reports from Santa Ana, see Bernatzik 1936: 116–117; and from Ulawa and Malaita, see Akin 1993: 34–35, 472, 884–885, 904; Burt 1994a: 57–58; Hogbin 1939: 30–31, 114; Ivens 1927: 77, 277, 282, 289, 324; 1930: 105, 117, 220; Keesing 1982a: 64; 1983: 19; Köngäs Maranda 1974: 183; Maranda and Köngäs Maranda 1970.

near the new shoots, and the cord is placed in this hole. The nut is planted, and both the child and coconut palm will grow up together. Later, as the child matures, its parents will point to the coconut palm and teach their child, "Here's your umbilical cord," and will tell their relatives, "There's my child's umbilical cord."[14]

Stating that they plant a child's umbilical cord as a "memory only" so as to gauge the age of the child by the growth of the coconut palm, Arosi are not overly anxious if a cord is not actually planted. Neither are they distressed if, once the umbilical cord is planted, the resulting tree blows down in a cyclone or is cut down when the village expands. In short, Arosi have a relaxed attitude with respect to the planting of the umbilical cord; many cords are never planted and the precise location of others is often forgotten.[15] Parents can plant their child's umbilical cord anywhere they choose, but often do so on a piece of land close to where they reside at the time of the birth. They do not make a point of returning to the mother's land to plant the child's umbilical cord.

Because the planting of the physical *waipo* need not connect the child to the land of his or her matrilineage, we might interpret the practice of planting a *waipo* as iconically representing the general rootedness of Arosi lineages in the island as a whole. One woman suggested, however, that an umbilical cord/coconut palm could be used as evidence presented in a land claim, and that a person might refer to his or her *waipo*/palm in order to support a claim,

---

14. When referring to a child's umbilical cord or to his or her navel, a person will use the possessive pronouns -*na* and -*gu* to indicate "inalienable" or "direct possession" (for example, *waipona*, literally, cord-his/her). This is the construction used for all parts of the body. In contrast, the statements quoted here concerning the coconut palm as *waipo* indicate "alienable" or "indirect possession" by the addition of the morpheme *a*- to the possessive suffixes (for example, *waipo ana*). This is what Lynch (1973: 76) termed "overlap": the same noun can be possessed in more than one type of possessive construction. Given the long and ongoing debate over the nature of possessive constructions in Austronesian languages—are they noun class or relational systems, or both? (e.g., Lichtenberk 1985; Lynch 1973, 1982; Pawley 1973; Pawley and Sayaba 1990)—it would seem injudicious to offer an interpretation of the different possessive constructions documented for the noun *waipo*. If the current case does involve noun classes, however, the use of the possessive marker of one class with a noun of another class could function as a "grammatical metaphor" to intensify the connection between the possessor and the object possessed (David Dinwoodie, personal communication, March 12, 1998).

15. For a contrasting example from elsewhere in the Pacific, see Williksen-Bakker's (1990: 235–236) discussion of the Fijians' anxious concern that a child's umbilical cord be planted in the land—ideally but not necessarily "one's own"—and their belief that misfortune will befall the child whose umbilical cord does not take root successfully.

saying "Here is my true place, the place I have." Therefore, despite the apparently indifferent attitude Arosi have toward planting an umbilical cord, a *waipo*/palm has at least the potential to be used to index a lineage's connection to a specific place. But, the realization of such a potential depends on the right conjunction of socio-cultural circumstances and semiotic conventions. The capacity of the *waipo*/palm to index an *auhenua* connection to a specific place "remains *indeterminate* until one places it in the framework of a context, where 'context' entails intersubjective contracts, ongoing discourse, and a horizon of background experience" (Hanks 1996: 86, italics in original).[16]

Practices involving the planting of the umbilical cord and/or placenta in land where the newborn has a privileged connection are well documented for many Pacific contexts (e.g., Merrett-Balkos 1998; Saura 2002; Stewart and A. Strathern 2001: 90–96; Williksen-Bakker 1990). On the strength of this documentation, one might suppose that there was once a stronger imperative for Arosi, not only to plant umbilical cords, but to do so in the children's matrilineal territories, and that the present relaxed attitude is only the necessary consequence of the current ambiguity about who, if anyone, is *auhenua* on the coast. While such a reconstruction cannot be falsified, neither is there evidence to support it. Fox (1924: 178) devotes an entire chapter to "Birth and Childhood" but says only of the placenta that it was buried in the bush without subsequent notice. Among the customary practices Arosi lament as lost, the ability to plant the umbilical cord in matrilineal land is not one of them. Furthermore, although I was made privy to considerable secret information relative to people's narrative constructions of their *auhenua* connections to coastal land, no one ever confided that he or she had discreetly planted a child's cord at a particular place precisely in order to create the circumstances necessary for the resulting palm to become an index of the child's *auhenua* identity there. Nor did anyone complain that the planting of a cord by someone else had infringed on his or her *auhenua* territory. Accordingly, as further developed in chapter 6, I suggest that, for Arosi, the planting of an umbilical cord/coconut palm simply objectifies an *auhenua* person's given connection to Makira. It is as an icon of this given connection to the island that the *waipo*/palm entails a capacity to become an index and a means of a matrilineage's ongoing emplacement in a particular area.

---

16. I do not mean to imply that only the indexical relation between a *waipo*/palm and a lineage's connection to a specific place is based on conventionality. Although an icon— like all relations based on similarity—may appear natural, it is "to a degree conventional" (Hanks 1996: 45).

This double aspect of the *waipo*/palm as both icon and potential index may also be represented in the analogy between a matrilineage and a sweet potato runner that I cited previously. Recall how my friend used the sweet potato runner imagery to convey the "anchored" nature of a lineage in its land, and to compare the runner's growing tip to the ongoing continuity of matrilineal reproduction through women. One month earlier he had, in a seemingly inconsistent manner, employed the same analogy to liken the cutting of the umbilical cord at birth to our cutting of the tips of the sweet potato runners growing from mature tubers in an established garden. As described, we planted these cuttings in the newly hoed mounds in our freshly cleared garden and waited for the cuttings to form tubers. Without cutting and transplanting, the runners would not be productive and yield healthy tubers. While sweet potato runners quickly spreading across a garden evoke the continuous nature of a matrilineage, Arosi horticultural practice demonstrates the necessity of introducing discontinuity—literally a "cut"—before the sweet potato runners, and by analogy the lineage, will reproduce successfully. Similarly, if the sweet potato runners metaphorically express the anchored nature of lineages, the transplanting of cuttings to form new gardens points to the possibility that members of a lineage could move into or lay claim to new areas of land on the basis of newly planted umbilical cords. But, as my discussion of Arosi attitudes toward planting umbilical cords suggests—and as my analysis of the formation of ancestral shrines in the following chapter shows—a matrilineage's anchoring in the land is not primarily constituted by planted umbilical cords.

The Midwife As Sacrificer

In contrast to the cutting of sweet potato runners, which is effected without ceremony, the midwife's activities are more elaborated. Fox, for example, writing around 1920, gave the following account of a midwife's interventions:

> As soon as a baby is born the mother is given cold and hot charmed water to drink, and the baby is washed in cold charmed water.... The umbilical cord ... is cut by one of the attendant women (*ha'ahasusu*), who says to the mother "I cut this for you" (*au tapurua tana'o*). If some other woman wishes to adopt the baby it is she who cuts the cord, and to do so, and also to shave the baby's head, is formally to adopt the child; women will rush off as soon as they hear that birth is near, so as to be ready to do this, for adoption is common. (Fox 1924: 178)

Like Fox, I was unable to identify particular women who regularly acted as midwives. Nevertheless, my own inquiries corroborated what Fox's account implies: it was common practice for a woman in labor to be attended by an assistant who cut the umbilical cord and washed the child. Esther Bwairageni explained to me, however, that because large numbers of births are now occurring in clinics, women have little experience at performing this role and "very few" are willing to help if a birth happens to take place in the village. Many middle-aged and older Arosi identify the midwife who was involved in their own birth as the person who "bathed me" (*mwa'anuhi 'au*). While the midwife generally did not take a child away from its biological mother, she assumed the position of an adoptive classificatory "mother vis-à-vis the child" (*ha'iinada*). Thus, many older Arosi count themselves among the children of the woman who bathed them at birth; they reminisce that as youths they were welcomed at the midwife's home and would, on occasion, go to her house to be fed. Later in life they reciprocated with small gifts such as tobacco or a small shell valuable. The relationship (*haito'oranga'i*) is, in sum, characterized by "love" (*haita'ahi*) in its substantial and tangible Arosi forms: shared sustenance and gifts.

The nature and strength of the relationship between a child and the midwife who assisted in his or her birth can vary and can be subject to different interpretations. In some cases the relationship is quite strong: the child has been named and adopted by the midwife, and the child believes that the midwife is his or her biological mother. In other cases, by contrast, no relationship is recognized, and the child does not know who attended his or her birth. Between these two extremes it may happen that the midwife will name but not adopt the newborn, establishing a relatively strong relationship with the child. Consequently, a child named after a midwife's deceased relative may also receive access to the nut trees of his or her dead namesake. Just as the strength of the relationship between the child and the midwife can differ, the nature of the relationship between the child and the midwife's living relatives is also open to interpretation. For example, one man recalled that he became suicidal when told that he could not marry a woman at whose birth his maternal grandmother had assisted. Other villagers thought that he was too closely related to the woman in question, in part, because of his grandmother's involvement in her birth.

Whether acted on or not, the para-parental nature of the relationship of a midwife to the child she delivers is assumed. The strength of this assumption is evident when verbal expression of the full potential of the relationship is found even in the absence of a sustained or practicable relationship between midwife and child. In an interesting, though admittedly exceptional, case that occurred around 1950, a man, Charlie Kuper of Santa Ana, acted as "midwife." Kuper was ferrying Harry Taʿai's pregnant wife, Ariringa, to the mission clinic at Kerepei (Ugi) in his boat when she went into labor and gave birth to a girl. Kuper reputedly held the baby up, exclaiming in Pijin, "*Bebi blong mi nao!*" and gave the child his mother's name, Kanana.[17] Even in this unusual circumstance, Kuper expresses the acknowledged claim of the midwife to parental relationship to the child. Today, the analogously anomalous situation of rural health clinic births is a source of humor that indexes the nature of the midwife as a maternal double. Arosi occasionally find it amusing to speculate that the nurses in the clinics who act as midwives could potentially be considered the mothers of many children. The nurses, however, have not sought to assume, nor have they been given the position of adoptive mothers toward all the children who are born in the clinics.

While Arosi do not consider their birthing practices to be a type of *hoʿasi*— the Arosi term that Fox (1978: 217–218; cf. 1924: 112–123) translates as "sacrifice"—recent theories concerning the structure of sacrifice provide a productive model for analysis of the midwife's role and the differential treatment allotted to placenta and cord. Informed by the work of authors who have elucidated the cosmogonic or anthropogenic nature of some forms of sacrifice (e.g., Lincoln 1986, 1991; B. Smith 1989; Taylor 1999), I suggest that Arosi birthing practices reprise the crucial transition in Arosi cosmogony from presocial monadic isolation among pure categories of being to a socio-cosmic order of interrelated categories.[18] Specifically, I interpret the activities of the now largely obsolete Arosi midwife as concretizing an Arosi conceptual principle according to which the transition from unity to plurality within a matrilineal category requires the mediation of an external agent.[19] Refiguring and

---

17. Charlie Kuper was the second son of the German-born trader Henry (Heinrich) Kuper, who settled on Santa Ana in the early twentieth century and married Kafagamurirongo of Santa Ana (Bennett 1987: 180; Bernatzik 1935: 8–14; Byer 1996; Golden 1993: 299–300; Mead 1973a: 52). Charlie Kuper married Sibasau of Tawatana, Arosi.

18. From this perspective, as Lincoln asserts, "the (purported) presence of divine recipients [is] an accidental rather than an essential feature of sacrifice, i.e. one variable among many, but hardly *sine qua non*" (1991: 204; cf. Valeri 2001: 260, 263–264).

19. In Lau (Malaita), by contrast, the differentiation between mother and child appears to occur autogenetically, without the intervention of a midwife. During the month of seclusion observed by mother and newborn after childbirth, the baby is thought to separate spontaneously from the mother. This separation, Köngäs Maranda notes, is expressed by Lau through the idiom of the child's blood. At birth a newborn's blood is said to be simply the blood of his or her mother. Then, during the course of the first month of life, a baby's blood regenerates and "changes gradually, until it is all new at the end of the month" (Köngäs Maranda 1974: 187; cf. 1970: 159).

reiterating the categorical rupture of exogamy, the midwife intervenes to sever the link between mother and child, manipulating the umbilical cord in ways that precipitate her own nature as a sacrificer and the nature of the cord as a sacrificial victim.

The period immediately after a baby has been delivered entails the temporary realization of a form of Arosi socio-cosmic disorder (cf. Merrett-Balkos 1998). Lacking differentiation, mother and child exist in a state of complete identity.[20] As we have seen, while the placenta remains in the womb and the umbilical cord continues to join mother and newborn, the baby is regarded as consubstantial with its mother. In this condition, mother and child precariously approximate the condition of the *pwapwaronga* among whom mother and child are fatally over-identified. They have regressed away from true humanity toward proto-human categorical solidarity and isolation. The actions of the midwife signal, however, the obviation of this *pwapwaronga*-like predicament with the successful negotiation of a passage from oneness to multiplicity. This passage, I suggest, marks an important moment in Arosi anthropogony and cosmogony that is formally comparable to the sacrificial division, discernible in many myths of mono-genetic cosmogony, of a primordial unity as the foundation for a phenomenologically multiform universe. In the act of cutting, the midwife effectively sacrifices the umbilical cord, the icon of undifferentiated matrilineal essence, in order to produce human persons who are both inter-lineally constituted and matrilineally identifiable.[21]

Once separated from one another by the act of cutting, cord and placenta come to index two crucial but contradictory processes of sacrificial "transformative negation" (Lincoln 1991: 204; cf. Valeri 2001: 254).[22] First, the burial of the placenta to rot like a corpse underscores the negation of complete iden-

---

20. On neighboring Ugi and Small Malaita, "[t]here are many stories of infant prodigies who did wondrously or ever [*sic*] their umbilical cord was cut. Winding it round their middle they started off on the quest of adventure" (Ivens 1927: 78, 433–440; cf. 1911–12: 138–143; Fox 1924: 156–160). Such tales suggest that a certain power resides in this condition of non-differentiation between mother and child.

21. The idea that the umbilical cord in a routine Arosi birth is comparable to the victim of a cosmogonic sacrifice of original unity gains credibility when juxtaposed with myths from other Austronesian-speaking contexts that figure a cosmogonic separation of sky and earth in terms of the cutting of an umbilical cord that binds them together (e.g., Lewis 1988: Chapter 3). Among the Laboya (Sumba, Indonesia) this macrocosmic umbilical cord is understood to be simultaneously a great python (Geirnaert-Martin 1992: 39–41; for non-Austronesian parallels in Melanesia, see A. Strathern and Stewart 2000: Chapter 5).

22. Contrary to Babadzan (1983), who analyzes birthing practices throughout Polynesia, I do not take the placenta and the umbilical cord to be inherently distinct. Rather, like

tity between mother and child already expressed in the cutting process. Second, the planting of the umbilical cord to become one with a growing coconut palm simultaneously negates that negation by affirming the continuity of matrilineal essence in the newborn child. The treatment of the placenta as though it were a corpse again recalls, but more fully parallels, the plight of the *pwapwaronga*.[23] Like the *pwapwaronga* mother who must be killed in order for her child to be removed from her womb, the placenta marks the death and passing away of an earlier phase of absolute oneness.[24] Although involving a death in exchange for a life, the death of the *pwapwaronga* mother is not properly a sacrifice, however, in that it effects no transition from one ontological state to another. The physical removal of the *pwapwaronga* child from the body of its mother cannot be said to negate their identity, as there is no progression from a state of unity to one of duality and relationship. No series of connected beings emerges; there is only static displacement. This defective mode of reproduction amounts to what may be called a defective mode of sacrifice. Among fully human beings, by contrast, the disposal of the placenta serves as a symbolic substitute for the killing of the mother and communicates the first half of the paradoxical message that matrilineal integrity has died but lives. The second half of this message is located, not only in the survival of the mother, but also in the new coconut palm tree growing up with the planted umbilical cord. Whereas the death of the *pwapwaronga* mother replaced one monad with another, the sacrificial cutting of a human umbilical cord at once achieves the death of total unity between mother and child and the reproduction of a matrilineage whose internally diverse representatives embody an array of interlineal relations. It is not a case of either/or but of both/and; the continuity of the *waipo* depends on the cutting of the *waipo*.[25]

Saura (2002), whose observations also pertain to Polynesia, I suggest that in Arosi, they must undergo a ritual separation, which I furthermore identify as a form of sacrifice.

23. Ivens's (1927: 415; cf. Ouou 1980: 13–14) comment that the *muumuu* of the adjacent island of Small Malaita—who appear to be very similar to the Arosi *pwapwaronga* (Codrington 1891: 354–355; Fox 1924: 139)—are called the "broken afterbirth" may point to an implicit recognition in a related context of the type of analogy I am drawing between the doomed *pwapwaronga* mother and a human placenta.

24. De Coppet (1985: 85–87) observes that, on Malaita, 'Are'are treat the afterbirth like the corpse of a "murder victim."

25. Stewart and A. Strathern (2001) have discerned similar transformative processes with systematically different meanings in the treatment of the umbilical cord in Hagen and other contexts in the Highlands of Papua New Guinea. In these contexts, characterized by agnatic clans associated with territories, the planting of the umbilical cord in the "ground of the father" effects a transformative autochthonization of the child in paternal clan land

The both/and message legible in the differential treatment accorded to placenta and umbilical cord is additionally conveyed in the emphasis Arosi place on another of the midwife's tasks—that of washing the mother's blood from the newborn. Like the cutting of the cord itself, this action accomplishes the separation of mother and child by demonstrably removing from the child the physical substance of its mother. At this stage in the birthing process, both of the midwife's chief actions—cutting and washing—perform and represent differentiation. Significantly, however, Arosi subsequently refer to the midwife who helped in their birth, not as the person who "cut my cord," but as the one who "bathed me." This mode of expression is not accidental, but indicates, I propose, a shift in consciousness required for the completion of the process of anthropogony.[26] At this stage, Arosi clearly mark the transformative separation of the child from its mother by foregrounding the past act of bathing.[27] As a result, the concept *waipo*, although also implicated in the actualization of separation, is left in the background to continue to point to its primary referents: the unalterable connection between mother and child and the enduring encompassing oneness of a lineage.

Apparently referring to areas of Makira east of Arosi, Fox reported to Rivers: "Property in gardens, nuts, coconuts and pigs goes always to the sister's children. The father's sister also has a special place (e.g. cuts the umbilical cord) ..." (Fox to Rivers, December 4, 1915, Perry Papers, B2). As noted already, neither Fox nor I found any prescriptive norm as to who should cut the umbilical cord in Arosi. Yet the analysis I have developed here for Arosi makes sense of what Fox found to be true elsewhere on Makira and suggests

---

that overrides but nevertheless continues to figure, as a natural symbol of maternity, the child's permanent "tie to the mother and her group" (2001: 94; cf. A. Strathern and Stewart 2000: 73).

26. My analysis of Arosi shifts in focus between the signifiers employed during birth is informed by Valeri's approach to Hawaiian "sacrifice as an objectified process of consciousness" (1985: 73).

27. Fox (1924: 178, 253) briefly draws attention to an analogous transformative practice that was performed at death: in the pre-Christian past a person was paid to wash the flesh from certain types of human corpses before the bones of the deceased were placed in a shrine or in a relative's house. The presence of such structural analogies between birth and death are, however, difficult to trace and analyze in Arosi today. For documentation of intriguing transformations of these analogies, see Guidieri's (1980: 121–122) analysis of the relations among childbirth, death, and different types of decay in Fataleka, north Malaita. Bernatzik (1936: 116) also draws attention to the importance of washing the newborn on Santa Ana.

that the two situations may represent neighboring developments of related practices on an island noted throughout for its matrilineal descent categories. If, as I have argued, the one who cuts the cord reprises the cut in absolute matrilineal integrity that exogamy introduces in order to make matrilineal continuity possible, then the one who cuts the cord is a stand-in for the father, the true sacrificer. The significance of the act would thus seem to urge that the ideal midwife would be a woman of the father's matrilineage. This would bring the adoptive prerogative of the midwife into focus as a function of her status as a kind of mother from the father's matrilineage (cf. Fox 1924: 21, 61). But as well as seeming to prescribe that a woman of the father's matrilineage should perform it, the significance of the act endows it with a performative quality such that whoever cuts the cord thereby becomes a virtual exemplar of the matrilineal category of the father as the category that severs in order to sustain the matrilineal category of the child. Thus the situation in Arosi, where the role of midwife is not prescriptive but replete with performative implications, may be a complementary transformation of the prescriptive situation Fox found in other parts of Makira.

Cosmos: From "Stupidity" to "Knowledge"

I have argued that the establishment of relationship between two categories of being through exogamous conception and the differentiating activities of the midwife at birth are crucial moments of Arosi anthropogony. But for Arosi, the reproduction of true humans, like the production of a socio-cosmic whole, is a continuous process, irreducible to one or even two foundational moments. In fact, a child is not considered a complete embodiment of humanness until it has been fully socialized. Arosi conceptualize this process of socialization or stage of anthropogony as a transition from a state of ignorant foolishness to one of knowledge and responsibility.

Arosi say that a child is born *bweubweu'a*, stupid, lacking in sense or practical understanding. When autobiographically narrating their earliest memories in everyday parlance, Arosi regularly refer to the time of childhood as "when I was still stupid." Only as a child grows and is taught by his or her mother and father does he or she come to have *aidangi*, the knowledge, intelligence, and understanding of a fully mature person. Arosi stress that children, being *bweubweu'a*, lack knowledge of the tabus associated with sacred sites in the land and are thus unable to exercise the requisite self-discipline to refrain from acting inappropriately at localities where such restraint is said to be necessary. For this reason children are thought to be particularly susceptible to illnesses caused by spirits who are offended by the tabu violations that

Figure 4.4. The young son of Barnabas Boʻosae and Eunice Huna. Today, parents continually express concern that children are not learning custom.

result from childish ignorance. Furthermore, young children must be taught to whom they are related so that they will know whose houses they can and should frequent. As children grow into young men and women they must be instructed that if they "eat in a house" they should not "think to have sexual relations with a person of that house." In other words, they should not attempt to marry a relative. To contract a marriage of this type is, to paraphrase one Arosi, to act as if one has no mother or father, like a *gare pwaiʻoʻora*, a "fatherless child."

Today parents often bemoan that other parents do not teach young children the nature and extent of their kindred networks. The problem is then compounded when children are separated from their families for long periods to attend secondary boarding schools where they can receive no parental instruction of this kind. One man who lived beside the Mauriasi Memorial Primary School at Tawatana explained the problem to me in terms of his own experiences.

> The fathers of children who come here to school [i.e., men to whom he is related] will often come to visit me later and ask: "Did my children come to visit you when they were at school?" Nowadays I often have to answer, "No!" If a child doesn't come and visit me or even just say something, I'll wonder, "Does that child still understand me to be his relative?" If he does visit with me, I'll know he's still related to me; he loves me. But these days, when people don't visit

one another, young boys get someone pregnant whom they should visit [i.e., someone to whom they are related] and later they'll get married.

Arosi fear that this scenario is occurring with increasing frequency.

The "stupidity" or "ignorance" of young people who attempt to marry a relative appears to parallel the predicament of the child whose father is not known. In the past, if a father doubted whether it was his procreative substance that had led to the conception of a child, he might kill the newborn baby. Doubt concerning the paternity of the child frequently attended the first-born in particular, and some first-born children are said to have been killed by their mothers' husbands.[28] Documenting a term no longer in use today, Fox (1924: 30, 177; 1978: 50) records that Arosi designated the first-born by the compound noun *ahubweu*, "thickhead" or "stupid one." He reports: "The first-born baby they say will never be strong or clever, and is probably not the son of this man [i.e., the mother's husband], but of someone else; it is best to kill it at once" (Fox 1924: 177; cf. Espagne 1953: 27). While all children are born "stupid" and "ignorant," unlike other children who are regarded as capable of becoming knowledgeable and intelligent, the first-born child was thought to be irremediably stupid. Other children have the potential gradually to acquire knowledge of their ancestral spirits, their kindred, and whom they can and cannot marry, but the first-born whose paternity is suspect cannot be situated in such a network of relationships. Rejected in former times by his or her mother's husband, such a child was unable to acquire the knowledge needed to establish relationships with paternal relatives; he or she was doomed to perpetual stupidity. When exposed at birth rather than killed outright, the first-born was sometimes saved by a person who adopted the baby by "buying the mother's breast [milk]" with shell valuables. When the child was weaned the adopting parent would take and raise the child as his or her own.[29]

Like the first-born of earlier times, the increasing number of "fatherless children" among Arosi today do not have access to adequate knowledge of whom they may or may not marry and, consequently, regard a wide range

---

28. Citing Fox (1924: 177), Bernatzik (1936: 117 n. 128) explicitly states that, in contrast to Arosi, inhabitants of the Star Harbour area did not regularly kill the first-born. He reports, nevertheless, that a new husband was disinclined to raise children from a woman's previous unions and moreover reserved the right to judge whether a subsequent child was his (Bernatzik 1936: 189).

29. Arosi no longer talk about or treat their first-born children in this manner. Significantly, however, older consultants observed that, when such children had formerly been killed, their umbilical cords were left uncut (cf. Saura 2002: 136–137).

of people as eligible partners and spouses. This is likely, Arosi fear, to lead unwittingly to tabued marriages that will be replicated and compounded by the offspring of such unions, establishing a pattern undermining to the premises of Arosi social order. In this process of social breakdown, the most dangerous form of union is one in which two members of the same matri-lineage—in disregard of their common substantial natures—attempt to marry endogamously. Somewhat counterintuitively, to attempt such a union internal to a single matrilineage is referred to as "cutting the *waipo*" (cf. Thune 1983: 349). Despite this locution, however, the cutting of the *waipo* figuratively enacted in endogamy is the precise functional inverse of the cutting of the *waipo* literally performed by the midwife. Whereas the latter ensures matrilineal succession, the former precludes it. Rather than a cut that signifies life-giving convergence among lineages, endogamy is an anti-social, anti-anthropogonic, and ultimately anti-cosmogonic cut that signifies a dead ending.

Anti-cosmogony, or Dangerous Liaisons

Although a marriage that Arosi consider proper is one that joins members of two different matrilineages, an Arosi marriage involves more than the matrilineages of the bride and groom. An Arosi marriage normally brings together two distinct, though frequently overlapping, person-centered bilateral kindreds. There is no exclusive Arosi term for these kindreds; the members of these groups are said to be "related to" (*haito'oranga'i*) either the boy or the girl.[30] These relationships are formed through blood, the exchange of shell valuables, the sharing of food, the giving of a name, or by acts such as serving as midwife or wet-nurse. Increasingly, couples will simply elope; ideally, however, when a couple wish to marry, the people most closely related to the boy will go and ask the girl's closest relatives if she can and would like to marry the boy. If the answer is yes, a wider circle of the boy's kindred will contribute strung shell valuables and Solomon Islands dollars to make up the bride-price and they will go to "buy the woman" (*hori urao*) from her kindred. When they present the bride-price, the boy's kindred are feasted by the girl's kindred. More extensive groups, usually whole villages in addition to relatives from elsewhere, will participate in the subsequent marriage feast that is held on the same day as the wedding service in the church.

---

30. As noted above, some Arosi use the term *burunga* for these kindreds and make an explicit contrast with the lineage (*warowaro waipo*).

Figure 4.5. Alan Tarosubani organizes the distribution of food at a bride-price payment.

Arosi say that one should marry a person to whom one is "not related"; a marriage between people who are considered to be related in any way is characterized as "wrong" or "disobedient." Nevertheless, as noted above, older Arosi worry that an increasing number of youths want to marry people within their own kindreds. Today, these marriages are frequently permitted because relatives fear that young people might commit suicide if they are forbidden to marry. Everyone remembers a number of Arosi who committed suicide in recent years when they were told that they could not marry.

While two particular people might be forbidden to marry because they are relatives "entangled in blood," Arosi stress that the descendants of these people will be able to marry "some day." Because every child is formed from the mixing of the mother's and the father's blood, the "mix" (*dorari*) of different generations of descendants' blood keeps changing. As a result, the shared blood that constituted a particular relationship is thought to become increasingly diluted in the children of each successive generation. During a village meeting convened to discuss *kastom*, one elderly man explained that the process is similar to pouring sea water slowly into a bowl of fresh water: soon the fresh water becomes salt water. The rate at which this process of dilution occurs varies depending on local histories and the geographical proximity of the parties concerned. If a couple have a common ancestor within five ascending generations, however, their proposed marriage is likely to be challenged as inappropriate on the grounds that the boy and the girl are still relatives "after the one blood." Relevant to the previous discussion of childbirth, it here becomes explicit to what degree a mother's blood and a father's blood are both composed of many bloods mixed together. The bloods that mix when a child is conceived embody or "join together" two networks of relationships formed by the "entangling" of many people in previous generations. A person is the site of a rich plurality of relationships.

In contrast to the descendants of these person-centered kindreds who eventually become "different people" and can intermarry, it is "absolutely tabu" for members of the same lineage to marry. Up until the early years of the twentieth century, a person who attempted to marry within his or her lineage was either killed or sold to another lineage elsewhere. Some of my consultants, unable to recall a term for such marriages, suggested that no one had ever married endogamously. If older Arosi are concerned that people today are attempting to marry within their kindreds, they are quick to point out that people simply cannot marry a member of their own lineage.

The penalties formerly prescribed for someone who attempted to marry within his or her own matrilineage suggest that such a person was seen to be acting as if he or she belonged to another lineage. No one would kill a member of his or her own lineage, but people who tried to marry endogamously denied the substance of their own being (cf. Thune 1989: 176 n. 13). As a result, their nature and identity became ambiguous and perhaps even danger-ous. No longer recognizable as belonging to a particular category of being, such people were subject to remedial killing. Alternatively, the lineage could objectify what the person's acts already manifested and sell the offender to an-other lineage elsewhere on Makira or to the people of a neighboring island. The act of selling saved the person from death by ontologically transforming his or her nature and substance; the person who was sold became "one" with the lineage that purchased him or her.[31]

Referring to a particular past case, Peter Itamwaeraha explained the trans-formation that occurred if someone were sold in this manner:

> They bought the blood in her body with shell valuables, the hair on her head with shell valuables, they bought her whole body, and they did not call her [name] Mwara lineage. No! They released her from the Mwara lineage and she went into the Amaeo lineage. It was the shell valuables that made her go into the Amaeo lineage with the two of them [those who bought her]; it was as though she was their sis-ter [and] they had come out of the one hole, it was as though they were brother and sister.

Itamwaeraha's graphic account indicates that once a person had been pur-chased he or she was regarded as one who had originated from the womb of a woman of the lineage that made the purchase. In fact, this practice was termed "buying to lengthen the lineage" (*hori urui burunga*). The members of a lineage would often seek to buy a woman if there were few children who could continue the lineage and the lineage's future existence was threatened. Purchasing someone, whether male or female, was an act of transubstantia-tion through which the person bought became attached to a new umbilical cord. In the case of the endogamist, the umbilical cord denied by this form of "cutting the *waipo*" was replaced by another life-giving umbilical connection. This transformative act was effected by many lengths of shell valuables metaphorically termed "bags of valuables." Accounts indicate that ten or twenty strung shell valuables were paid to those who sold an offender. Al-

---

31. People were also sold if they were guilty of other "serious offences" (Fox 1924: 36). Nevertheless, as if in testimony to the serious nature of endogamy, I found it difficult to document the other offenses that prompted lineages to sell their members. The only other case I recorded involved a young woman who had previously been purchased from Bauro but was sold again when she was accused of having urinated in a container used for carry-ing drinking water. For an earlier description of what may have been a regular institution of selling children, see Verguet 1885: 205–206.

though people from several different lineages might have contributed shell valuables to purchase the person, he or she could only be bought for one lineage, otherwise his or her dangerously ambiguous ontological state would remain unresolved. The purchasing lineage might seek to return resources contributed by other lineages, but even if it did not, the person thus bought—whether young or old—became a child of the purchasing lineage alone.[32]

In the words of one man, "a *waipo* is set apart and is one." Overemphasizing and retreating to this separateness and unity, endogamous marriage secludes a lineage and is seen to short-circuit viable human reproduction. Thus, despite their apparent preference for lineage integrity, endogamous couples are appropriately said to "cut the umbilical cord." That is to say, they terminate the growth potential of their lineage by removing it from relationships of inter-lineage exchange; they "cut the peaceful productivity" or "goodness" of their lineage. In contrast, exogamous couples cause a changing mixture of blood to flow through the mother's *waipo*. Carrying multiple entangled relationships, this blood reproduces the lineage as the vehicle of a vital and distinct ontological category in relationship with other homologous matrilineally sustained categories. In short, endogamous marriage is tantamount to another type of reversion to the primordial condition represented by the *pwapwaronga*: a chaotic state of categories in sterile isolation. Admitting that secret endogamous marriages had occurred within her lineage, one Amaeo woman even averred that, as a consequence, members of her lineage were becoming progressively smaller with each generation and had "nearly gone back to [being] *pwapwaronga* again" (Scott 2007).[33]

This anti-cosmogonic vision is also realized in the fates of the victims of a dangerous type of phantom pregnancy believed to be caused by spirit possession (*bwauni adaro*). If possessed by a malevolent non-ancestral spirit—*adaro wawauru*, *adaro ni hasimou*, or *adaro ni mou*—a person may begin to exper-

---

32. During the course of the twentieth century a few Malaitan descendants of Malaitans sold to Arosi in the previous century occasionally visited the Arosi descendants of these same purchased Malaitans. These visiting activities do not imply, however, that the Arosi descendants of the person sold are also members of the lineage that sold their ancestor. For contrastive material on the transformations of headhunting captives in what is now Western Province, see Hviding 1996: 91; McDougall 2000; Thomas 1991: 48.

33. Describing three such marriages as "wrong," she explained in general terms that a large number of shell valuables had been exchanged so as to keep these forbidden unions secret. She suggested to me that these valuables were the reason that I was unable to find independent verification of the endogamous nature of these marriages. Other members of her lineage (and other lineages) denied these accounts and argued that these marriages were demonstrably exogamous.

ience erotic dreams that, for a man, may be accompanied by nocturnal emissions. In their first few dreams, the victims of this condition will have sexual relations with strangers, but after an increasing number of dreams, they will begin to have relations with distant relatives. If the condition is not treated, the possessed person progressively dreams of erotic encounters with people to whom he or she is more and more closely related. People who find that they are beginning to have such dreams may cure themselves by confessing the nature of their dreams to the person with whom they dreamed they had sexual relations (this is said to make the spirit "ashamed"); by confessing the dream to an Anglican priest; or by chewing a betel nut with leaves picked from a place where people or dogs have urinated. Finally, if no action is taken, the afflicted will begin to couple with their "opposite sex siblings" (*asida*), "mother" (*inada*), or other people within their own household. At this advanced stage no cure appears to be possible.

The spirit possessing the person is believed to change its form, assuming the likenesses of the dream sex partners, and ultimately causing a female victim to become pregnant. If a male is possessed his penis swells, he begins to urinate puss, his stomach becomes hard, and eventually when his penis bursts his genitals are the site of a large open sore; death follows. A possessed female's stomach becomes swollen; she is "pregnant with a spirit child." Attempts to cure this condition are thought to be hopeless. In a recent case, for example, medical interventions at Kirakira provincial hospital proved ineffectual. Soon the unfortunate woman will give birth to an unformed shapeless progeny whose characteristics people likened to that of a pig's liver. "No woman," Harry Ramo commented to me, "can survive this."

These malefic spirits cause possessed Arosi to be lured in their dreams into a form of reproductive activity that is fatal: coupling with their closest relatives. The lack of ontological differentiation between a spirit-possessed woman and her simulacra sexual partners—members of her own *burunga*—is concretely modeled, I suggest, in the undifferentiated and shapeless form of the resultant "child." Furthermore, the still-born "child" does not have a father whose procreative substance has mixed with that of its mother at conception; rather, the "child's" father is a spirit in the form of a male relative of the mother. Intriguingly, although I did not find a stated connection between the killing of the first-born child and such spirit pregnancies, there is another infrequently used Arosi word for the first-born that may indicate such a connection: *gareurutaora*. The term *urutaora* refers to the meteorological phenomenon of precipitation and sunshine occurring at the same time (Fox 1924: 177; 1978: 460). Accordingly, *gareurutaora* might be translated "sun-shower child." Arosi stories associate these weather conditions with the appearance of dangerous spirits and represent the rainbows caused by such conditions as spirit pathways. These ideas suggest that cases of doubtful paternity or "fatherless children"—whether first-born or otherwise—may sometimes have been understood to involve a pregnancy caused by spirits.[34] In any case, the danger posed by the sexual content of spirit-induced dreams appears to derive from their suggestion of endogamy. Relative to the proper mode of reproduction through exogamous relations between lineages, this form of deadly and abortive intercourse is contrastively anti-anthropogonic. Inverting the production of an ordered universe, anti-anthropogony and anti-cosmogony coexist simultaneously wherever there is a chaotic over-differentiation among diverse categories of being and a concomitant lack of differentiation within such categories. For Arosi, such a condition would be—to echo the words of Casper Kaukeni quoted at the opening of this chapter—"the end."

---

34. Spirit pregnancy is also documented for Santa Ana and Santa Catalina by Bernatzik (1936: 117), who records that if a mother became sick during delivery, the newborn was left to die because it was thought to be, not a real child, but an evil spirit seeking to torment the mother to death. Bernatzik also reports that multiple-birth children were assumed to be evil spirits and were therefore put to death.

CHAPTER 5

RE-PRESENTING
AUTOCHTHONOUS HISTORIES

Like the discourses and practices associated with routine human reproduction, people's everyday activities in the land offer insight into Arosi assumptions about cosmogony and ontology. Simple acts and events—such as
going to or avoiding a place, monitoring a child's activities in a place, varying
one's language or experiencing different emotional states depending on whom
one is with at a place—all reveal that land and the powers thought to inhabit
it remain ontological and social categories despite a recent history of dislocation and the acceptance of Christianity.

This chapter provides historical and ethnographic accounts of the types of
ancestral places, powers, and practices in relation to which many contemporary Arosi are quietly constructing their matrilineages as the *auhenua* of their
coastal villages. Arosi who understand their matrilineages to be *auhenua* on
the coast inhabit a landscape full of the vestiges of past acts and agencies that
orient their daily conduct and define their existential natures in the present.
These vestiges—ancestral ossuaries, shrines, abandoned villages, or old nut
trees tended by deceased forebears—are valued as relics of ancestral precedence. Emplotted and memorialized in lineage narratives, they are also available as live points of reference for the continued emplacement and subjective
experience of matrilineal identities. Although seemingly inert objects, often
derelict, overgrown, or imperceptible to those to whom they are not significant, these elements of the Arosi landscape represent the dynamic processes
through which Arosi matrilineages once became—and, moreover, may go on
becoming—the *auhenua* in a particular area of land. Like the cosmogonic
processes that establish and support social relations between matrilineages,
these processes of emplacement are not confined to a distant primordial
epoch. Lineage narratives not only describe how ancestral figures formed matrilineal territories through their multilocal cosmographic activities; additionally, even the spontaneous partial allusion to such a narrative, in conjunction with evaluative commentary on recent incidents in the land,

performatively reproduces a lineage as inseparably wedded to a particular territory. An illness, an accident, the alleged appearance of a spirit, or a presumed sign of ancestral support can provoke local interpretations that, drawing on lineage narratives, serve to form and reform a lineage's relationship to its land. Asserted by lineage members to be unquestionable in their social and historical detail, these situationally invoked narratives repeatedly and creatively call into existence lineage ontologies anchored in the landscape.[1] As elsewhere in island Melanesia, a lineage and the land it takes to be its territory are partners in a mutually constituting and sustaining relationship mediated by the recollection and recognition of ancestral places, powers, and practices (e.g., Guidieri 1980: 62–63; Hviding 1996: 132–133).

The dynamic quality of matrilineal emplacement notwithstanding, no Arosi person would allow that a matrilineage that was not native to Makira could ever become *auhenua* simply by arriving on the island and leaving physical testimony to its impinging presence on the land. Only lineages thought to have originated on Makira are characterized as being truly *auhenua* in their intrinsic natures and thus able legitimately to engage in acts of progressive emplacement as the *auhenua* of a specific part of the island. A number of Arosi highlight what they take to be the autochthonous nature of genuine *auhenua* lineages by depicting them as arising from the interior of the island and descending to the coastal land: "Some lineages came down here. Those are the true lineages, the true lineages of the island, those people who came down here ... they sit on top of the island ... the Adaro, Amaeo, Araha lineages simply came down." Such an emphasis on spatial interiority allows members of these and other lineages to distinguish themselves from people they believe have come from other islands. Some Arosi suggested to me that the Aoba lineage, for example, had come from the island of Aoba (Ambae) in what is now the neighboring nation of Vanuatu. Quick to contradict this idea, however, representatives of the Aoba lineage say that their lineage originated at Hoto, a mountain in the Makiran bush.

Similar to these delegitimating claims about the Aoba lineage, there are additional discourses that cast some of the other lineages now prevalent in the

---

1. To borrow the terminology developed by Michael Silverstein (1998), local interpretations of events in the land both "presuppose" understandings based on the "intersubjective reality" formed among lineage members who share the same lineage narrative and "entail" (i.e., create or call into being) an intersubjective reality among lineage members that forms the basis of further discursive and non-discursive social action. Here, my argument has also been influenced by Nancy Munn's proposal that "sociocultural action systems (or activities through which they become operative) do not simply go on *in* or *through* time and space, but that they form (structure) and constitute (create) the spacetime manifold in which they 'go on'" (1983: 280, italics in original; cf. 1986).

coastal villages as allochthonous. Much muted controversy, for example, surrounds lineages that share the principal name Mwara, which means Malaita. Some Arosi call one Mwara lineage Mwara Rihurihu, signaling their view that this lineage's founders arrived from Malaita in a canoe and "coasted" (*rihurihu*) around Makira before landing and establishing themselves on the island. With the same implication, others call another Mwara lineage Mwara Harutariu. They say that the founders of this lineage were Malaitans who, when blown off course in their canoes while returning to Malaita from a visit to Ulawa, "paddled on" (*haruta riu*) until they reached Makira.[2] Another tradition identifies a *burunga i Henuaasi* (lineage of The-sunken-island) as the descendants of refugees from Te'o, a small island submerged by a tidal wave but said to have formed a "fourth sister" to the existing Three Sisters group north of Makira.

But none of the members of the matrilineages so described accept these names and their connotations. People who know that others say they are *burunga i Henuaasi* eschew this lineage name and maintain that they are members of one of the recognized autochthonous matrilineages. One woman of a Mwara lineage that some call Harutariu rejects this epithet and explains that the name Mwara itself does not refer to Malaita but is a variant of the Arosi word '*amara* meaning "barren." She and other members of her lineage say that they bear this name because, in the past, women of this lineage tended to have only one child. A man of another Mwara lineage that is also sometimes called Harutariu agrees that his matrilineal ancestors arrived from Malaita but insists that they were only returning to Makira after several generations of residence away from their matrilineal land. Calling his matrilineage Mwara Auhenua, he was at pains to stress to me that his lineage, "didn't come down here [from the east] and it didn't come up here [from the west]. It is *auhenua* because it didn't come from any place. It didn't come here from Mwara out there, it didn't come up here.... This is the place where it was created."[3]

---

2. Although most Arosi differentiate between Mwara Rihurihu and Mwara Harutariu, some clearly regard these names as two different ways of referring to the same Mwara lineage. Moreover, some people also use the names Mwara Tatare (Mwara-drifting-on-the-sea) and Mwara Urawa (Mwara Ulawa) to refer to these lineages.

3. Similarly, O'Connor (1973: 47–48, 79–80) notes that the coastal people of southeast Guadalcanal were unwilling to have their lineages characterized as having come from another island (cf. Meigs 1984: 7–8). An assumption that these biases in favor of autochthony are cultural processes rather than natural reflexes or inevitable strategies for claiming land gains support from the contrasting situation on the island of Ranongga (Western Province). According to McDougall (2000; 2004: Chapter 4), although Ranonggans engage in land disputes, they also emphasize their allochthonous origins.

Auhenua is frequently defined as meaning simply that "it [i.e., a lineage, a custom, a bird, etc.] hasn't come from another island." One man described a member of an *auhenua* lineage as "like a boulder that was created with the island. It didn't come from another place, it can't be carried off, and it will not be moved. If the island burns the stone will burn too. That's *auhenua*: there isn't a place where it has come from." To indicate that no one can truthfully tell a story of a genuine *auhenua* matrilineage that depicts it as having migrated to Makira from an offshore point of ultimate origin, this man said: "Nobody has their history."

Anticipating the themes of the next chapter, it may be inferred from these discourses that the possibility of becoming *auhenua* through dynamic processes of transformative emplacement presupposes a prior static condition of being *auhenua* as a given primordial connection to Makira. By reason of such a presupposition, another Arosi man could state with equal and unqualified conviction: "An *auhenua* lineage has history." That is, as opposed to a history linking it to alien origins, an *auhenua* lineage has an autochthonous history of coming into being as coming into place. In a spatial register, the relationship between the static and dynamic dimensions of the Arosi understanding of autochthony is analogous to the relationship between *waipo* and *burunga*. The static dimension of *auhenua* prioritizes a given unalterable Makiran essence as the basis for Makiran identity and synthetic sociality; the dynamic dimension situates this essential basis in a wider spatial field of perpetually renewable interconnections.

Sites of Narrative and Negotiation

The ongoing production of the relationship between a lineage and its land is evident in the way Arosi who view themselves as *auhenua* seek to illustrate what makes their lineage autochthonous in a particular territory. In such a context people do not simply resort to an assertion of ultimate origin in the island; they describe the graveyards, shrines, and tabu places that their ancestors established in the land over the course of several generations. To reiterate what the consultant quoted above said: "An *auhenua* lineage has history ... [theirs is] a history of movements, of placing stones, and of consecrating their places." Although such narrative descriptions are often simply called *histori* (in Pijin) or *mamaani* (in Arosi), Rosemary Magewa used the particularly apt expression *mamaani auhenua*—"an autochthonous history"—to characterize processual accounts of how a lineage becomes *auhenua* in a particular area of land.

At one level this process is expressed in the formal titles given to lineage narratives if they are written down. It is now relatively common for lineages to have a school notebook or "exercise book" containing a genealogical list or "generation," notes on shrines, burial sites, and the names of once-worshipped sharks and the people who propitiated them. The covers of these books bear titles, often printed in English, that stress the dynamic character of a lineage's connection to an area of land. Representative titles include: "THE HISTORY BOOK FROM [the lineage's name] ABOUT [a named area]," and "HISTORY BOOK OF TRIBE FOR THE [lineage name] AT [a particular locality] GEN-ERATION."[4] These lineage history books, like similar documents on the island of Santa Isabel (White 1991: 35), have been written to be at the ready in the event of land disputes. Although the contents of these books usually cannot be recited in full from memory, in the Arosi context, they are comprehensive and tangible objectifications of the mutually constitutive processes of lineage and land formation. In contrast to Santa Isabel, where the information contained in such books appears to be of little relevance to social life outside the context of disputes over land (White 1991: 35; cf. Burt 1998), such books in Arosi codify knowledge that otherwise informs lineage members' understandings of their daily activities in the land in ad hoc and piecemeal ways. Even if particular lineage members know relatively little of their lineage narrative, their interpretations of their relationships to objects and events in the land presuppose the existence of a more encompassing written or oral account. In consequence, Arosi lineage narratives are incompletely analyzed if understood only as tokens to be deployed instrumentally in land disputes.

The production of the relationship between a lineage and its land is expressed in these lineage histories whether they have been transcribed or are "storied" among members of a lineage. In addition to describing the burial sites, shrines, and tabu areas throughout lineage land, these narratives sometimes trace the actions of the ancestors who established or formed these places. Each site is known variously as a *dora maea* or a *dora ta'a*. In these locutions *dora* means a place or locale. Since the mid nineteenth century, the word *maea*

---

4. Although the titles are often written in English, the contents of the books are invariably in Arosi. All of these books are dated, indicating either when the book was written or when the author of the book first heard the narrative. I saw seven books containing lineage histories; the oldest was apparently written in 1965, and the latest was written in 1993 in response to my research. Another lineage narrative to which I listened had been recorded on an audiocassette by lineage members. These objectifications clearly impinge on the nature of memory and the relative authority of different narratives, but because they are subject to tropical heat and moisture, loss in cyclones, and destruction by vermin, they tend to perish quickly and thus do not eliminate the dynamics of variation over time.

has been used in translations of Christian prayers and catechisms to gloss "holy" (Patteson, in Gabelentz 1861: 235–242), and currently many Arosi give this as its primary meaning. *Maea* can also be defined as "respected," "set apart," "dedicated" (to the ancestors or to the Christian God), or "invested with powers" (derived from the ancestors or the Christian God). *Dora maea* are thus respected places that have been shaped by the powers said to have been placed in them. Anglican churches are considered to be *dora maea* and, as such, entail tabus—do not spit, do not talk, do not shout, do not urinate, do not eat, etc.—that if broken, Arosi say, will cause the offender to have a feeling of having done something wrong or to become ill. Many Arosi draw comparisons between churches and ancestral *dora maea*.

Villagers also occasionally refer to ancestral *dora maea* as *dora ta'a*. In using this expression, the speaker incorporates into his or her discourse a phrase introduced with Christianity and intended to express a judgment that the powers associated with *dora maea* are Satan's work; such powers are, some European and Melanesian missionaries taught, *ta'a*, "bad." Nevertheless, Arosi use of the phrase *dora ta'a* does not necessarily represent simple concurrence with this position; rather, the speaker often appears to be using Church discourse for his or her own purposes. As one man explained: "When people say that a place [formed by the ancestors] is *ta'a* they mean that it is still powerful. But it is only *ta'a* from the point of view of the Church."

As the expression *dora ta'a* suggests, the different types of ancestral sites that I treat below are not only constituent elements of matrilineal narratives; some have also been important loci of missionary intervention in Arosi life. Accordingly, as well as providing descriptions of their physical characteristics and Arosi accounts of their initial formation, this discussion of ancestral sites also treats the colonial practices that impinged on these sites and explores the resultant variety of Arosi interpretations of their present status and nature. By introducing the ancestral burial grounds and places for sacrifice in the context of Arosi colonial history and its legacies, I begin to explore the issues addressed in chapter 7, namely, the conditions that facilitate the cosmographic processes through which lineages relocated from the bush during the first part of the twentieth century are now becoming *auhenua* on the coast.

Burial Grounds (Hera)

> In the centre of the village is a mound, surrounded by a wall of stones, reserved to all appearance for the reception of the shell of the

[canarium almond] nuts before mentioned; but, I afterwards ascertained that it was a place of interment for the dead. Growing close to this mound were several sombre-looking trees, whose leaves were almost black. On my plucking one of the branches, the natives showed signs of uneasiness, and motioned to me to throw it on the grave, which I accordingly did. There must be some mystery attached to these trees. (Webster 1863?: 87–88; cf. Verguet 1885: 207, 208, fig. 91)

The Arosi burial sites called *hera* are physically quite different from today's Christian graveyards (also known as *hera*) in which people are buried in their own plots in a designated area at the margins of the village. Pre-Christian burial sites contained the bones of many people and—as John Webster's account from his visit to Makira Harbour in 1851 indicates—were often placed in the middle of a village. Many such structures remain visible today at abandoned village sites along the coast and in the Arosi interior. One can count, for example, at least five stone burial places in different parts of the contemporary village of 'Ubuna (cf. R. Green 1970: 91–93). *Hera* are similarly found scattered in and among the small hamlets, coconut plantations, and wooded areas that form Tawatana village today.[5]

One particularly well-documented burial ground is in 'Omaaraha, a hamlet of Tawatana. Located at the shore, this hamlet is close to the break or passage in the reef at the mouth of Tawatana's stream. The site of the *hera* lies just behind the main path that runs west following the beach down to 'Ubuna. Unkempt and overgrown, to me this site was barely distinguishable from the surrounding area without the aid of friends familiar with its position. Contrasting with this condition of relative obscurity, Fox's detailed account describes what once must have been a substantial structure. He called the burial mound a *heo*, acknowledging that this was a "seldom used" term (1924: 218):

> It is a solid stone structure with a rubble interior rather lower now than the outer walls, which were 5 feet or 6 feet high. It is about 55 feet by 33 feet, and runs north to south. It has no cave, but a *giru bwara* or oblong grave was made in different parts and in this was a wooden bed, while a thatch roof covered the whole and a bamboo

---

5. Daniel Miller's (1979: 88–107; 1977) archaeological site survey conducted in 1977, although limited to a coastal strip 200 meters wide, documents the frequent occurrence of *hera* in current villages and coconut plantations along the north coast of Arosi. These sites are plotted on the map drawn by Miller (1979: 88). Archaeologist Roger Green (1970, 1974) also surveyed this coastal area in 1970.

fence surrounded it. By the *giru bwara* were placed two small stone pillars, one for men, one for women..., also another curious stone whose use is not known. The dolmen [under which skulls were placed] is a fine one, the covering slab of stone being 4 feet by 2 feet. The *hera* was to the east, the *oha* to the north, and a house for the keeper of the dead to the south of the *heo*. (1924: 221)

Although Fox (1919b: 39) notes elsewhere that the word *hera* is "usually the name for the village burial place," in this and other descriptions of 'Omaaraha he indicates that the term applies equally to the *heo* itself and to the "large oblong cleared space" (1919c: 104) or "courtyard" east of the mound used for dance performances (1924: 218, 219; 1978: 209). His use of the past tense to describe the adjacent structures made of wood and thatch—the *oha* (canoe house) in which offerings to the dead were placed and the "keeper of the dead's house"—suggests that they, like other such houses, had "long since decayed" (Fox 1924: 220). In fact, by the late 1910s when Fox was writing, the mound itself had already "been partly demolished by the Government," an act Fox judged to be "a piece of vandalism without excuse" (1924: 221; cf. Fox to Rivers, May 28, 1919, Perry Papers, B2).

In 1977 when Daniel Miller (1979: 97, site SB-2–35) visited Arosi, he recorded that the 'Omaaraha "site is still further disturbed from the state that Fox described and half of it is now covered by a [normal residential] house." By 1993, Michael Ngaraediri's house—the one to which Miller refers—was gone; his family now lives in a new house about thirty meters from the *hera*. I was informed that the cyclones of the 1970s and 1980s had not only destroyed a dyke that had run between the village and the beach, but that the waves crashing up to the village had also damaged the 'Omaaraha *hera*. As a consequence, the large stone that Fox characterized as a "dolmen" was no longer apparent and had perhaps been covered by rubble. At least part of one of the stone pillars that Fox (1924: 288) described was visible, and during my stay in Tawatana a villager propped the pillar up in a vertical position. But finding the *hera* little more than a jumble of many stones, I had difficulty discerning the once distinctive shape of the mound Fox had described. Some bones were visible among the assortment of stones, dead vegetation, and encroaching creepers. As people independently volunteered information about the *hera* or answered my questions, everyone agreed that it had once belonged to one particular lineage. Whether or not this lineage is extinct or represented by people now living in the village is a tacitly debated question.

Figure 5.1. Examining the *hera* at Mwageresi.

Lineage burial *hera* can take various forms.[6] For example, the *hera* at the former village of Mwageresi, just to the west of Tawatana, lies approximately twenty meters from the beach in what is a coconut plantation today. Here two large slabs of rock lie across a circle of stones to form a small hollow mound on the floor of the plantation. The sides of this chamber are about one and a half meters by one and a half meters, and it is approximately half a meter high. This form of construction, I was told, is called a *hausuru*. The ossuary at Mwageresi contains two human skulls, a couple of broken jawbones, and a small number of other human bones. Other coastal *hera* are situated on top of the distinctive limestone crags that dot the north coast of Arosi. A typical exemplar is Hausi'esi'e, the *hera* involved in my unwitting arousal of a dormant land dispute (see Prologue). As at Mwageresi, at Hausi'esi'e the ossuary site consists of a stone circle. At the time of our visit, one of my guides, Andru Ba'ewa, called this circle formation an *ariari*. Later, an older man, Basil Bunaone, suggested to me that, here too, large stones had once lain across this circle to form a *hausuru*, but that these top slabs had been destroyed in the past.

6. Fox (1919a: 176; 1919b; 1919c; 1924: 218–228; cf. Riesenfeld 1950: 130–139), R. Green (1970), Miller (1979: 90, 97–107), and Verguet (1854: 153, 155; 1885: 207–210) describe and provide sketches of various types of Arosi *hera*. Philp (1978: 131–132) also gives brief descriptions of some Arosi burial sites.

Hera are also located throughout the island's interior. I visited one such burial site called Hera ai Mari'o at Mwanima'o, an abandoned bush village above Tawatana. This *hera*, sited on a level elevation, consisted of a mound that was about one and a half meters higher than the surrounding ground. The flat face of the *hera* mound was circular with a diameter of approximately four and a half meters. Some small trees were growing on the mound, but once Mark Tahini'o'o had cleared them away with his bush knife we could see an oval depression in the center of the mound. Harry Ramo noted that a shaft had once descended from the surface to the center of the mound. As this was no longer visible, it had either subsided or been filled in, causing the depression on the mound's surface. Ramo also suggested that a small stone enclosure had formerly sheltered skulls at one end of the flat mound face.

The burial *hera* scattered throughout the Arosi landscape index pre-Christian mortuary practices that most Arosi can describe only in general terms based on recollections they have heard from members of a previous generation. Their accounts make clear that corpses were treated in a variety of ways. Sometimes corpses were placed in large food bowls that had holes through which the rotting flesh and fluids could drain; alternatively, they might be encased in long strips of wood from the betel nut palm, placed in caves, or exposed on rocks or in a tree. All of these mortuary practices enabled the relatives of the deceased to collect his or her bones and set them in their *hera*. Others, however, did not. Some bodies, for example, were tied to a stone and buried at sea.[7] People also informed me that bones were often reserved and kept in houses. Once people had joined the Anglican Church, however, church leaders exhorted them to gather these bones and place them together with those already in their ancestral *hera*.

Ancestors As Powerful Presences in the Land

Arosi assume that the dead whose bones are deposited in *hera* remain powerful presences in the vicinity of these sites. In a variety of manifestations, these dead ancestors continue to interact with the living. Often, as at Hausi'esi'e, when my guides approached a *hera* that they wished to show me, they asked permission for our visit from the ancestors they assumed were aware of our arrival. But in spite of such precautions, Andru Ba'ewa, one of my escorts to Hausi'esi'e, dreamed afterwards of being pursued by a person

---

7. Fox (1919a: 176; 1919b; 1919c; 1924: 210–217; cf. 1962: 63–65; *AMM*: 21, 83–84) and Verguet (1854: 152–156; 1885: 207–210) give detailed accounts of mourning practices and modes of treatment of a corpse in pre-Christian Arosi. See also Codrington's (1880/81: 300–303) and Webster's (1863?: 93) brief descriptions.

with a bright light. On another occasion, after taking me to a different *hera*, this same man told me he had dreamed that someone was coming to kill him with a spear. The threatening people in his dreams, Andru explained, were the spirits of the dead, called *adaro*, who inhabit the *hera*. In the world of everyday experience, *marewana* (from the root *marewa*, light), Arosi can glimpse *adaro* or find evidence of these spirits who dwell in another corresponding realm of reality. In their dreams, however, Arosi may enter and act in this usually unseen realm of the spirits, *rodomana* (from the root *rodo*, dark, black, night). Accessing this spirit realm in his dreams, Andru was re-experiencing our visits to the *hera* and seeing the *adaro* who, unknown to us at the time, had been unsettled by our actions. Additionally, when Arosi fall ill they sometimes explain their illness in terms of the existence of spirits. If a person's symptoms—often fevers, weight loss, diarrhea, or general disorientation—fail to respond to the treatment dispensed by the local health clinics, people may begin to suspect that the illness is caused by the intervention of spirits. Perhaps the afflicted has unwittingly stumbled across a *hera* in the bush, and the spirits of the dead have obstructed or removed the "shade" (*nunu*) from his or her body. Such a diagnosis is confirmed when a dream-curer sends his own shade to rescue that of the sick person. During his dream, the curer may find the patient's shade being held at a *hera* by the ancestral spirits who reside there.[8]

It was to these ancestral spirits—now most frequently called *adaro* but said formerly to have been known as *hi'ona*—that the pre-Christian Arosi offered sacrifice (*ho'asi*).[9] As Fox records, sacrificial offerings of yam, taro, banana,

---

8. Arosi consider every living human body (*abe*) to have two spirit entities; each has an *adaro* and an *aunga* (also called *nunu* in the context of illness). The attributes and functions of the two spirits are sometimes not clearly differentiated, but both are thought to be essential to the life of the body. Generally, Arosi speak of a body's *adaro* only in the context of discussing a person's death or when discerning signs of a dead person's presence. At death, a body's *adaro* is thought to remain as a social actor on Makira, but it is also thought to travel simultaneously to Marapa, the island of the dead in Marau Sound (eastern Guadalcanal). Apropos to the theme of matrilineal unity on both sides of the grave discussed below, Mr. Ben Mononga'i told me of a *kastom* story he knows according to which *adaro* encounter two people on Marapa who direct them to the place of their matrilineage. The body's other spirit, the *aunga*, is today thought to be the entity resurrected by the Christian God and taken to "paradise" after the body's death.

9. Today the term *hi'ona* is sometimes used in conversation to refer to the Christian God. The Holy Spirit is called the *hi'ona maea* both in conversation and in the Arosi Anglican prayer book. Some Arosi today theorize that the prevailing use of the term *adaro* to refer to ancestral spirits is a product of Christian theological efforts to distinguish between a spirit (*hi'ona*) considered worthy of worship and other spirits (*adaro*; Pijin: *devol*, devils) deemed to be associated with Satan. But as Father Augustine Taukerei, an Arosi-born

pig, dog, fish, and pudding were "made in many places, in the shrine of the village, in the sacred grove, in the canoe-house, in the guest-house, at rocks in the sea or on the land, by pools, under trees, and in the peoples' own houses" (1924: 114; cf. Codrington 1891: 129–130; Verguet 1854: 159; 1885: 212). At the 'Omaaraha burial site, for example, "[t]he first-fruits of the gardens were hung up in this *oha* [canoe house] as offerings to the snake spirit (*hi'ona*) and sacrifices were offered on the *hau suru* ['dolmen'] to the *hi'ona*" (Fox 1919c: 104, spelling of Arosi terms amended). Today, *adaro* are also thought to continue to reside at some of these sites throughout the island. These ancestral shrines are variously called *dora anai suho'asi, hera,* and *birubiru.* The phrase *dora anai suho'asi* (or *suuho'asi*) literally means "a place for burned sacrifice." Although the word *hera* often refers to burial sites such as those already described, it is also, and just as frequently, used to denote places that were not necessarily burial sites but that were set apart as places where sacrifice was offered. This type of *hera* constitutes one form of *dora anai suho'asi. Birubiru* is the word used to designate coastal shrines. In conversation, however, these terms are sometimes used interchangeably. For example, although some people specify that *birubiru* can only be found on the coast, a number of people described certain bush *hera* as *birubiru.* Also, while most people specified that food offerings given at *birubiru* were uncooked, a few nevertheless occasionally called these shrines "places for burned sacrifice."

One *dora anai suho'asi* is located in the bush near the confluence of two streams. As is true of all such sites, there is only one proper path into the shrine. I was told that this shrine is a raised mound on which two species of nut tree sprout from a single tree trunk. On the mound, as at many "places for burned sacrifice," there is a stone. The name of this stone is also the name of a black snake with a shortened tail reputed to live at the shrine. It is said that when sacrifice was offered, the snake emerged from the stone. On my inquiring why a snake would appear, a man whom I will call Warimakira explained that his lineage's ancestors had taken the bones of a number of their relatives and placed them on the stone. Then, in an act that Warimakira com-

---

Anglican priest, explained to me, although he believes *adaro* and the *hi'ona maea* to be opposites, strictly speaking, both are *hi'ona.* In light of this present semantic debate, the earliest published description of Arosi religious practice should be taken into account. Verguet appears to use the terms *adaro* and *hi'ona* interchangeably (e.g., 1854: 158). In his word lists, however, Verguet (1885: 230) glosses *hi'ona*—which he transcribed *Jona* (1848: 446) and *Iona*—as an "idol" (1885: 230), "god" (1854: 184–185), or "type of divinity" (1854: 187) and *adaro*—which he transcribed *Ataro* and *Attaro*—as "spirit" (1854: 184–185).

pared to the laying on of hands by an Anglican priest when blessing or confirming someone, his ancestors had prayed to their relatives and, in so doing, established the shrine, believing (*suri ha'ahirihiri*) or trusting (*'u'uri*) that a snake would henceforth live there.[10] Having completed their formative act (*ha'amaeaa*, literally, to make *maea*), they removed the bones, leaving only the distinctive tree, the stone, and the snake at the shrine. Such snakes, many people agreed, were—and are—the spirits (*hi'ona*) of the particular lineages that established and made offerings at the shrines.

Warimakira's lineage also claims another shrine in the bush where, unlike the one just described, certain words are tabu. Warimakira instructed me that if a person requested, "hand me a rope [to climb a coconut or betel palm]" in the locality of this shrine, when his companion handed him a rope it would become a snake. "Some of the ropes at that place are snakes" that frighten ignorant interlopers away. Similarly, it is said that at other *hera* snakes will appear if a person utters the ordinary words for frogs, eels, or prawns; at these places one should use alternative words for these animals. Elsewhere, the terms regularly employed to refer to a digging stick or stake for husking coconuts, and the verb meaning to make a rope from a creeper, should not be used, lest snakes become visible.[11]

When I questioned Arosi about why a lineage's different *hera* might have distinct tabus, I was told that the ancestors established each site after their own wishes or according to their trust. In one woman's understanding, an ancestor shaped each place with tabus that then became the "original custom of the land" (*ringeringe auhenua*). Embedded thereafter in the land, custom was passed down from one generation to the next in the form of knowledge about tabus and places in the lineage's land. Although Arosi regard the tabus associated with each *dora maea* as part of the intentional, premeditated plan of the person who initially formed the site, it is possible that many tabus objectify the accumulation of actual experiences in the area. By analogy with word tabuing on Malaita (cf. Keesing and Fifi'i 1969), the institution of some place-specific tabus in Arosi may have been the result of decisions made by people

---

10. Although Arosi frequently employ the term "belief" (*hinihini*), many stated that this concept had been introduced by the Christian missionaries. Rather than having been concerned with defining or achieving different states of belief, pre-Christian Arosi are said to have conceptualized their relationships with their ancestral spirits as based on "trust" (*'u'uri*).

11. Throughout Arosi—as in other parts of the Solomons (e.g., White 1991: 38)—the sudden appearance of a large number of snakes is thought to be an indication that the tabus of a locality have been broken.

after some local precipitating incident. As such, the tabus may index a history of what are now forgotten events at particular places.[12]

Owing to the presumed power of spirits who dwell at the different types of *dora maea*, people who are not descended from the ancestors thought to be resident at a particular location are usually reluctant to go there. As John Christian Tarorodo admitted when asked whether he would visit the shrine at the old bush village of Mahumahu, "I would be extremely afraid." As previously mentioned, a number of Arosi compare the *adaro* in a *hera* to a radar system: the power (*mena*) of the spirits emanates from that site into the surrounding area; the spirits observe everyone in the vicinity and can protect or punish people as they deem appropriate.[13] Arosi who venture onto unfamiliar land frequently carry items they call *buru adaro* that are thought to provide protection against these spirits. *Buru* include small objects such as a Christian cross that has been blessed by a priest, an ancestor's tooth, or a piece of wood—often from a species of tree known as *buru*—that has been endowed with prophylactic power through a set of magical procedures. One consultant, elaborating the metaphor, likened these *buru* to radar blocking or jamming devices installed on American bomber planes during the Gulf War of 1991.

Another man proposed that the *adaro* who reside at burial sites are like immigration officials who inspect closely anybody who enters their land. *Adaro* literally "oversee their places." He made this observation when, as we walked through the bush, we heard the repetitive song of a medium-sized red parrot. The parrot was challenging us in the Arosi language from somewhere up in the forest canopy: "Who are you?" My companion shouted an answer: "It's just us, and here's our young friend, Michael Scott, who has come to write our *kastom*." Hearing his reply, the bird stopped calling and we went on our way. What we had heard, I was later told, was either the sound of an *adaro* ventriloquizing through the bill of the bird or an *adaro*

---

12. Although I was unable to pursue a systematic study of tabued words throughout Arosi, the apparent physical homology among the objects and some of the animals whose names are commonly tabued may suggest a further homology among these objects and animals, the ancestral snakes, and the lineage/umbilical cord.

13. *Mena* is the Arosi variant of the Oceanic term *mana*. Scholars (Keesing 1984; Burt 1994a: 54–55) who have sought to uncover pre-Christian (and pre-anthropological) Melanesian understandings of this concept would suggest that my Arosi consultants' uses of the term *mena* to describe a power radiating from a place incorporate a Western tendency to "metaphorically substantivize power." Although this may indeed be the case, in the present analysis I am primarily concerned to document how Arosi currently use the term *mena* to describe their ancestral sites.

Figure 5.2. The *hera* at Haunaraha.

that had taken the form of the bird. The *adaro* was looking after its area of land, and if we had not identified ourselves we would have become confused, angry, unable to find our way, and would have fallen ill. Members of another lineage explained that in a few places *adaro* may assume the form of a dangerous pig.

Because of the potential dangers posed by the presence of *adaro*, when parents take their children up to the bush they teach them where they should avoid going to the toilet—an action that if done on a *hera* would undoubtedly cause an *adaro* to make them unwell. More generally, they point out areas where youngsters and strangers should not wander and localities in which they should not use certain tabued words or even speak loudly. "Don't shout," Tarorodo warns his grandchildren. "Do what I do or else you'll see something." Children who do not listen and adults who make mistakes or do something wrong are thought likely to become sick. In one case that occurred soon after my arrival in Arosi, a man felling trees in an area that was generally said to belong to another lineage suddenly dropped dead. In the discussions that followed his death, many people judged that the spirits at the nearby *hera* had killed the man because he should not have been working on that land.

Although the spirits associated with a graveyard or a shrine would frighten and perhaps even kill strangers whom they do not recognize and who violate the tabus and prohibitions of the place, they protect and guard their own descendants. Even though no one openly claims to make sacrifices at their ancestral *hera* today, ancestral spirits are still revered and are thought to continue to look after their descendants. It may seem that ancestors' relatively quiet acts of protection and love would be more difficult for Arosi to demonstrate than the spirits' clearly punitive actions against strangers. But if spirits' actions are judged from one perspective to be disciplining punishments that cause some people to leave a place, the same actions, when viewed from another perspective, can be portrayed as protective measures ensuring the spirits' descendants continued access to their land. Analogously, if one person's shade is said to be abducted from his or her body and held by *adaro* at a *hera* because the person broke a tabu, another person's shade is said to be held because an *adaro* loves the person so much that it wants him or her to live with the *adaro* in the *hera*. To take a common example, if parents do not lovingly provide for their child, the spirit of the child's dead grandmother or grandfather may take the child's shade in an effort to care properly for him or her. If a dream-curer does not reunite the child with his or her shade, the spirit's love will kill the child.

Some people state that they are reassured of the continued presence of ancestral guardians by identifiable snakes that are normally resident in particular *hera*. These same snakes will occasionally appear in their houses or accompany them when they travel. Other people are said to be able to call a bird or a snake out of a *hera*. More often, however, Arosi illustrate their ancestors' love for them by pointing out that they do not have an uncomfortable feeling when they visit a *dora maea*, and that the *adaro* there do not act punitively toward them. One woman described how such a "sign" (*ha'ara*), or argument from silence, transpires: "I can go and shout from the top of the *hera* and the things that you're afraid of will not be seen. To show I have the *hera*, I'm not afraid of it, I can climb up there today.... So I went up there but nothing happened to me.... No one saw a snake. But when others go there they see snakes and run away. They feel bad and they can't see straight." Although she is a Christian, this woman's relationship with her *hera* recontextualizes a pre-Christian Arosi assumption that an uneventful period of time was a sign of ongoing ancestral support and protection; illness and trouble, conversely, necessitated sacrificial offerings to the ancestors in order to reestablish such a state.

Ancestors and Anglicans: Uncertain Powers on the Coast

Like the Anglicans on Santa Isabel about whom White (1991: 38) writes, Arosi are sometimes uncertain whether ancestral powers and tabus continue to be efficacious at particular sites throughout the landscape. Although virtually everyone assumes that the old shrines and burial sites in the bush interior are still powerful, many wonder if this remains true of those sites located along the coast at which Christians have performed rites of exorcism or which are seen as subject to the authority of Christians living in their vicinity. Because most of the *dora maea* in the bush were simply abandoned when people moved down to the coastal villages, these sites are thought to persist as loci of unquelled ancestral power. Coastal *dora maea*, by contrast, were often sites at which the ship-borne missionaries directly challenged and sought to supplant the power of the local spirits when establishing their own spiritual beach-heads on Makira.

As part of a diffuse mission strategy designed to force Arosi to break ancestral tabus, put the power of ancestral spirits to the test, and replace ancestral shrines with Christian altars, many churches—such as the ones at Tawatana and 'Ubuna—were built near to ancestral shrines. As the district priest explained to me in 1993, the siting of the first church at 'Ubuna early in the twentieth century had caused the power of the adjacent shrine "to go down a little," or had even caused the spirit at the shrine to disappear completely. Similarly, missionaries often sought to have their houses built on or near places of sacrifice in order to shake "the faith of the heathen party in the power of their ghosts" (MM *IV*, 1886: 31) and compel villagers to commit single-mindedly to the Christian God. But despite forcing people to dismantle thatched structures in which ancestral relics had been housed and encouraging them to remove the bones to burial *hera*, the Anglican missionaries do not seem to have undertaken systematic campaigns aimed at the deliberate desecration of more permanent shrines in Arosi.[14] Rather, their treatment of pre-Christian ancestral sites was inconsistent, varying according to the nature of the locale and even the individual missionary involved. While some sites were intentionally desecrated, others were left undisturbed, and elements of others were visibly incorporated into church structures, leaving room for diverse interpretations of their present power and nature.

One example of such an artifact of the intersection between the concrete markers of ancestral presence and missionary practice is a large red stone, "about 2 feet square" (Fox 1924: 282), that Robert Paley Wilson (missionary to San Cristoval, 1896–1906) removed from an ancestral shrine and embedded in the chancel steps of the Heuru village church in 1903. The stone, called Hauwaibina, or simply Waibina,

> had magic powers, the chief being that it could give power to people to eat to repletion without any unpleasant consequences. People going to a feast used to come and touch it with their spears or with a pearl shell knife for slicing yams, and then, according to tradition, they went and ate fabulous amounts of food at the feasts. (Fox 1924: 283)

They also performed rites at Hauwaibina to ensure success in raiding and warfare (Fox 1924: 283–284). The stone, Wilson wrote at the time, "is now to be dedicated as part of this chancel to the honour and glory of God, and is a symbol of those formerly offering sacrifices on it, who, having been brought out of heathendom, are now stones in Christ's Living Church" (MM *SCL*, March/April 1904: 42; cf. Coombe 1911: 230).

Missionaries' intentions notwithstanding, villagers' attitudes toward the old shrine and repositioned stone reflect a broad pattern of ongoing respect for ancestral powers. Fox (1924: 283) reports that even after "people became Christian" and the "*hera* [from which the stone had been removed] was dismantled," the area of the shrine was still regarded by villagers as powerful, and

---

14. In contrast, on Santa Isabel the Anglican missionary Henry Welchman clearly envisioned a campaign of shrine and burial site defilement (White 1991: 103).

Figure 5.3. Interior of St. Paul's Church with Hauwaibina visible as dark block in chancel steps, Heuru, 1906 (Beattie Collection). © The Trustees of The British Museum.

the fruit of the "sacred coco-nut" associated with the shrine was "never eaten." Furthermore, the red stone is still said to be powerful. If Bishop Cecil Wilson (MM *SXL*, September 1905: 103), who dedicated the Heuru church, viewed the "old ghost stone ... [as] a trophy taken in the battle with heathenism," Arosi interpret the stone's placement in the church quite differently. An elderly man effectively characterized local ideas about the stone and, by extension, offered one possible interpretation of other ancestral sites in the context of Christianity. He attributed the following words of explanation to an unidentified missionary: "The sacred powers of your grandfathers remain [with the stone], I will place it also with the sacred powers of God." In this formulation, both ancestral and Christian powers are thought to coexist even though the physical positioning of the stone in the church suggests that the ancestral powers have been subsumed under those of Christianity.

As the history of the site indicates, however, the nature of this encompassment remains uncertain or, to borrow White's (1991: 108) phrase for analogous situations on Santa Isabel, it is "not fully guaranteed." Currently, one face of the partially buried stone Hauwaibina remains visible in the steps at the site where the old church stood; no trace of the building is left except these steps and some blocks of coral. The church has been moved, and the site of the former church is no longer specially dedicated to the Christian God. Nevertheless, people continue to perform rites at Hauwaibina if they want to gorge themselves on their hosts' food without feeling full when they go on a visiting party to another island (as was done in the first part of the twentieth century), or when they are the recipients of a feast in a distant village where they have gone to pay for a bride. Like warriors of previous generations who sought ancestral support before a raid, young men who play football will sometimes go to the stone before an important inter-village game to ensure a victory. Although many Arosi state that "power resides in this stone," one Heuru resident expressed his doubts to me that Hauwaibina could still be really powerful when people no longer follow the "customary ways" (*kastom ringeringe*).

The current practices of Arosi-born Anglican priests also contribute to people's uncertainties about whether the coastal shrines and burial places remain sites of ancestral power, creating contexts in which Arosi can formulate diverse and potentially competing interpretations regarding the existence, extent, and source of power at any given coastal place. Two Arosi priests independently told me that Anglican missionaries and priests have not in the past,

Figure 5.4. Altar steps encompassing the stone of Hauwaibina, former site of St. Paul's Church, Heuru, 1992: "Power resides in this stone."

Figure 5.5. Altar at the new St. Paul's Church, Heuru, 1992.

and do not now, simply set out at their own initiative to "spoil" ancestral places with holy water— an important element in an exorcism. Rather, they "leave aside things that are *auhenua*, and don't disturb them" unless they have expressly been asked by a descendant of those who established the place to "chase away the spirits" (*tari'i adaro*), "take the power out" (*ha'amoria*), and "bless" (*ha'agorohia*) an ancestral site. When the priest performs these rites, the Christian God is thought to "lift the power" (*rehia mena*) of the spirits.

Nevertheless, it is possible for some Arosi to maintain that ancestral power still resides at a site even after the priest has performed an exorcism. People may argue, for example, that the priest was asked to perform the rite by strangers (*sae boboi*), and that he was not invited to conduct the exorcism by the true descendants of the *auhenua* ancestors who made and worked the shrine. In such circumstances, those who quietly regard themselves as the true *auhenua* can judge the priest's actions to be ineffective and maintain that the Christian God did not make the area safe for interlopers. One friend, who had not been consulted before Casper Uka (Assistant Bishop of the Diocese of Central Melanesia, 1975–?) performed an exorcism at a shrine he regards as belonging to his lineage, secretly stated to me: "God does not help them if they invade." "God follows the person whose words are about true things," a younger woman explained. "God doesn't help the liar, doesn't help the corrupter, doesn't help the thief, doesn't help the arrogant person who says, 'But I have this place ...'" On another occasion she elaborated: "If you come [i.e., if you are not *auhenua*] it is difficult for you to try to make the power [at a shrine] disappear, even if you pray, because God follows the straight, the proper way, the true; so you won't be able to come and spoil the *auhenua* of the people here." Thus the Church and God are not always united in action. If the representatives of the Church act mistakenly as the agents of an interloper, the Christian God will nevertheless protect the interests and follow the wishes of the true *auhenua*. Whether the priest was acting on behalf of the *auhenua*, and whether his actions were actually efficacious in any particular exorcism are questions subject to interpretations that reference the assumed contexts of different lineage narratives.

Even if the ritual actions of a priest and others who perform exorcisms — including catechists and healers[15] — are considered successful, this does not necessarily mean that the site in question is no longer regarded as the locus of a potentially dangerous or protective power. Occasionally, Arosi use the term *ha'amaeaa* to describe the Christian rite performed by a priest at a burial site or shrine. In this context *ha'amaeaa* — which I have previously translated as "to invest with powers" — can be glossed as "to bless" or "to sanctify." As in White's analysis of a semantic equivalent in the Cheke Holo language of Santa Isabel, one possible construal of this term implies that the priest literally eliminates the ancestral presence from the site. White records that

The act of "blessing" is termed, literally, "making sacred or tabu." ... Note the inversion of meaning expressed in the act of blessing: a Christian "making tabu" is used to negate an ancestral one. The indigenous concept of ..."tabu" implies a prohibition backed up by threat of ancestral retribution. In this sense, the shrine was already a sacred or tabu place regarded as powerful, dangerous and restricted. The Christian "blessing" does not so much remake the area as sacred or tabu (as the term "making sacred" would imply) as it neutralizes

---

15. Strictly speaking, catechists are licensed Church officials who conduct daily church services and provide Christian teaching when an ordained priest is not present. In many Arosi villages, however, locally appointed unlicensed "readers," who are frequently called catechists by villagers, conduct daily services in lieu of trained catechists. Here healers include people who use customary healing practices (such as the dream-curing mentioned above), most of whom have sought a priest's blessing for their activities, and also groups of villagers engaged in the lay "Healing Ministries" that work in conjunction with the Church.

Figure 5.6. Martin Toku, veteran of the Healing Ministry, Tawatana.

the harmful ancestral powers, thus ending the restrictions associated
with the threat of spirit attack against trespassers. (1991: 108)

White goes on to acknowledge that the ultimate efficacy of a priest's actions remains questionable. Like the Arosi, the people of Santa Isabel may still consider a shrine to be dangerous after an exorcism.

In Arosi, interrogation of these Christian practices may go beyond the question of their efficacy to ask what it means for such rituals to be successful. Even when there is a general consensus that a particular blessing has achieved a result, there is considerable latitude in the determination of what that result has been. As noted, the power of the ancestors may be thought of as having been completely neutralized. But some Arosi appear to view the blessing of a shrine as an act that actually replaces the ancestral spirits with the Christian God. Thus, for example, if someone becomes ill after visiting a site that has been blessed by a priest, people may interpret the illness as having been caused by the Christian God, who is now thought to act alone to protect the land of the *auhenua* from interlopers. One consultant explained: "At first [i.e., in pre-Christian Arosi] they said that their *kastom* spirits [chastened strangers who acted inappropriately], but we today don't; it is the spirit that we call God." Another interpretation suggests that the priest's blessing of a shrine makes the ancestral spirits subservient to the Christian God. From this point of view, the spirits continue to act as they have always acted, but they have now become God's agents in protecting the land for the *auhenua*. Some Arosi go further and—implicitly suggesting that the blessing of a shrine changes nothing—argue that unbeknownst to the pre-Christian Arosi, the spirits have always acted on behalf of the Christian God: "Before, the pre-Christian Arosi called it a spirit (*adaro*); then they didn't know the true thing that we call God because the god (*hi'ona*) they called a spirit (*adaro*) isn't a spirit (*adaro*) but is [the Christian] God (*hi'ona*)." As I explore more fully in the concluding chapter, these last two interpretive options, which together represent the point of view of many Arosi today, effectively equate the will of the *auhenua* with the will of God.

More generally, Arosi sometimes suggest that shrines and burial sites located on the coast are no longer powerful simply because a large number of church-going Christians live nearby, making the Church quite "strong" in the vicinity of these sites. But subjective judgments as to what constitutes regular church attendance or the critical number of Christians needed to outnumber and overwhelm spirits can also contribute to people's ongoing uncertainties about the possible dangers of ancestral sites. Thus, while a lone Christian who breaks tabus and acts improperly in the bush will undoubtedly "encounter a problem," Arosi suppose that if many—although it is unclear how many—Christians went into the bush, the spirits would "clear away." Conversely, people often assume that the coastal spirits have already cleared away or are "hidden" until someone falls ill or encounters signs that they understand to be evidence of the continued presence of spirits. Such occurrences may lead people to question whether they attend church regularly enough, whether they have fallen into sin, or whether their village as a whole is as strongly united in its commitment to the Christian God as it should be.

Shark Shrines (Birubiru)

Other ancestral sites that occasion such equivocation are the coastal shrines called *birubiru* at which sacrificial offerings were formerly given to ancestral sharks (*ba'ewa*). One such *birubiru* is at Tawatana in a sandy area between the *hera* at 'Omaaraha and the village stream. Located a short distance from the church, this shrine is in the center of the seaside plaza now used for village meetings. Today, a large tree at this *birubiru* provides shade for villagers attending meetings, participating in communal work, or relaxing in the late afternoon. With these activities in mind, people have leveled the site, forming a small platform by filling the area behind a short retaining wall with pieces of dead coral and sand. Although villagers—both male and female—do not observe any form of prescribed or tabued action at this site, one elderly man told me that on occasion a spirit that sounded like a fire burning could be heard at this *birubiru*. Another man informed me that he had been told that a "shark stone" (*hau ba'ewa*) had previously been located at this site. A shark stone was located in most *birubiru*. In the past, these stones were usually referred to simply as sharks, *ba'ewa*.

Many of these shark stones were worked into cylindrical form. Those that I saw varied from about twenty-five centimeters to about seventy-five centimeters in length, and from about ten centimeters to about thirty-five centimeters in circumference. Although one partially buried stone, identified to me as a shark stone, did not appear to have such a tubular shape, most of the stones had been smoothed and rounded. The length of one stone had even been worked into a flowing S-curve. The stones used in these carvings are said to be "stones of this island [of Makira]," meaning that they—and by implication the lineages that offered sacrifices at them—were "formed on this island" and did not come from elsewhere. Arosi testimony indicates that such stones are "representations/images of the sharks" to which sacrifice was offered at these shrines. Some people said they knew of a local *birubiru* composed of a dyke surrounding a rectangular mound of earth on which a number of shark stones had once been placed. I was unable to visit this shrine, however, because these people told me it had become overgrown and they had not been able to locate it recently. In view of this situation, others noted archly that ancestral *adaro* can conceal a *birubiru* or *hera* from the people of another lineage. Another *birubiru*, called Birubiruuha, stands near Raoa village; it has a very distinctive mushroom-shaped rock that protrudes about forty-five centimeters up from the otherwise flat platform of the fringing reef. In the pre-Christian past, offerings would have been placed in the shallow bowl-like depression still visible on the top of this rock.

Like the stones found in bush shrines, the shark stones associated with *birubiru* are thought to be invested with ancestral power so that, if one of these stones were manipulated, the spirit-shark associated with the shrine would act in a particular way. If, for example, the husk of an enemy's betel nut or a piece of his food were placed in front of the shark stone the enemy would soon fall victim to the spirit-shark. Similarly, Fox (1924: 286) tells how these stones were sometimes pointed at an enemy's village in order to cause an enemy to die. At the same time, the spirit-shark may be thought to protect members of the lineage that established the coastal shrine. Such guardianship is dramatically illustrated by stories told by members of some lineages that describe how young children were formerly left under the sea with the spirit-sharks for safekeeping when their parents went to work in the gardens.

In pre-Christian Arosi, interactions with spirit-sharks were conducted by "shark-men" (*sae baba'ewa'a*) who were invested with the power to sacrifice to sharks. Shark-men were often named after particular spirit-sharks and experienced a special affinity with those sharks. A shark-man's life would be inextricably linked to that of his shark: if the shark were speared its namesake would also feel pain, or if the shark were hungry the shark-man would feel hungry too. Today, people like Gordon Hidawawa, who have been given the names of the shark-men of the past, are still thought to be under the protective watch of the spirit-sharks. Even apart from the influence of such names, Arosi suggest that anyone in a lineage that previously sacrificed to spirit-sharks could potentially reestablish a sacrificial relationship with his or her lineage sharks.

Although some *birubiru*—such as the one at Tawatana—are no longer thought to be dangerous, those who claim to be members of the lineage who founded a shrine can continue to interpret their own good fortune—at fishing, for example—in the vicinity of the shrine, or conversely others' lack of success there, as the result of the shrine's continued power. Thus, in spite of what Miller (1979: 105) judged to be the "spoilt" or "ill-defined" condition of many *birubiru*, Arosi still view many of these sites with caution, believing them to be potentially powerful. As a friend commented to me when we were strolling along the beach past a rock said to be a point at which victims were formerly pushed to spirit-sharks: "I don't play around [by pretending to make an offering] at a *birubiru* in case somebody gets eaten by a shark." In fact, one man who was recently attacked by sharks was reputed to have crossed over an underwater *birubiru* while carrying a magic leaf to which the sharks objected. Clearly, *birubiru*, like *hera*, are subject to diverse interpretations. As traced out in chapter 7, the uncertain status of these sites enhances their susceptibility to conflicting incorporation within interdependently evolving lineage narratives.

Trees (Ruruunga)

Similar in some respects to *hera* and *birubiru* are certain examples of the trees known as *ruruunga*. Broadly speaking, *ruruunga* are those trees (excluding coconut palms) from which people regularly collect nuts or fruit during the appropriate season and to which they understand themselves to enjoy access by one recognized criterion or another. Some *ruruunga*—usually very mature trees—can stand as signs of matrilineal rootedness in the land and serve as bearings around which Arosi who see themselves as *auhenua* can affirm and experience their matrilineal relationships to land.[16] Some knowledgeable people will point to specific nut-producing trees when recounting the actions of their lineage predecessors in the land and can occasionally name the ancestors who planted them. In particular, they mention canarium almond trees that are known by distinguishing names. These names, although they often describe the physical characteristics of each tree and its nuts, do not merely designate a species of tree but serve to individuate each tree, much like a personal name. "Tree-with-the-forked-trunk," "Tree-with-the-bent-trunk," and "Tree-with-the-hard-nuts" are representative names. The nut of the canarium almond has always been highly valued as an ingredient in many Arosi puddings that are still made and that were formerly used in competitive feasting exchanges. In places where the trees have not been tended by lineage members for a number of generations, the fallen nuts of an old tree will take root around its base and ensure a form of arboreal continuity. Today, however, few of these uniquely named trees remain along the coast where they are said to have been uprooted by recent cyclones or to have been cleared to make way for coconut plantations. Nevertheless, these trees—named or unnamed,

---

16. Nevertheless, those who understand themselves to be the *auhenua* of an area will also recognize that some of the fruit and nut trees in the land they regard as theirs were planted and/or tended by members of other lineages and will not attempt to collect the yield from those trees.

present or absent—form part of the lineages' narratives that tell of ancestral activities in their land.

"Just One Snake": Matrilineages As Multilocal Systems

"I don't want to story properly because [if] I story properly … you just know [what will happen]." Fearing that other villagers would overhear and dispute the land claims implicit in the story of his lineage, this is how one elderly man interrupted himself after beginning to recount for me his genealogical lineage narrative. Similarly, most people with whom I spoke declined to tell me their lineage narratives at locations where non-lineage persons might hear. Such self-censorship also means that when variant interpretations concerning the powers of any given shrine are sometimes aired in the village, people generally do not articulate fully the lineage narratives on which such interpretations are based. I found that those who were willing at all preferred to narrate their lineage's genealogy and history in the relative seclusion of their gardening areas above the village. More frequently, I learned particular narratives in a disjointed fashion as I walked through land with a friend or from responses to seemingly unrelated questions that I asked while alone with someone or sitting apart with a group of closely related people.

In contrast to most Arosi, who can only trace the descendants of an apical ancestress three or four generations back, the particularly knowledgeable people described in chapter 2 can name the matrilineal descendants of an ancestress who is six to twelve generations removed from themselves. One friend—somewhat guiltily confessing to me that he did not know the whole story of his lineage—characterized his lineage's narrative as a "guideline" to who is who in his lineage. Acknowledging that he could not explain how four different segments of his matrilineage were related, this man directed me to a younger relative whose account began with a more remote ancestress. Although a progenitor in some cases may be a primordial being such as an animate rock, a snake, or a spirit woman, a genealogical account is usually not explicitly linked to a primordial proto-person or place of ultimate origin, but simply begins with an ancestress who is fully human. Taking for granted—if unaccounted for—the existence of other marriageable people (cf. Fortune 1932: 31), a knowledgeable person will start with an apical ancestress and "only narrates along the *waipo*," that is, through women. As one woman explained after sharing her lineage history with me: "The story I have told you is that of my matrilineage (*waipo*). I was just taught about my lineage (*bu-*

runga). I haven't narrated the children of the males of the lineage." Although the names of male lineage members are given and husbands are sometimes mentioned, such accounts focus primarily on the matrilineal descendants of apical women, "because history only follows [the *waipo*]." If at any point there is a set of female siblings, the narrator tends to trace the descendants of the eldest sibling before returning sequentially to trace the descendants of her sisters. Because the same names reappear in successive generations, for the sake of clarity, narrators specify that a particular person is the first, second, or third person to have held the name.

Fuller lineage accounts describe ancestral movements over geographic space. The narrators, having specified the village on the island at which the apical ancestress resided, trace the movements of her descendants around the land.[17] For example, one lineage narrative tells how one generation of lineage members moved down from a village in the interior to establish a village on an empty stretch of coast. The next generation moved back up to the bush village again and then, after six generations, lineage members returned to the still vacant coast. The lineage's members moved up and down from the bush to the coast along a path. This oscillation between bush and coast is a common pattern of lineage movement, and, as a result, a multiplicity of lineage paths striates the island. Each of these lineage paths today is known by the name given to the lower end of the path. Another lineage narrative, analyzed in greater detail in the following chapter, begins with the account of a mythical animate rock and traces her descendants. But in this example, all the members of the second generation leave the island with the exception of one daughter who is instructed to return to her land: "You go back to our land and you reproduce for the land, you who are a girl." The narrative then traces this girl's descendants and names the places where each of them lived. In some generations, daughters are described as having been told to settle in different sites throughout the lineage's land: "The mother of these four sisters placed them throughout their [lineage's] land." Other generations of descendants are said to have founded new villages or to have returned to the village of their grandmother.

A third lineage narrative demonstrates the lasting link between a lineage and its land. The narrator began by stating that two female siblings lived in a

---

17. Arosi appeals to autochthonous histories exemplify what James Fox (1997: 9) terms topogeny, defined as "the recitation of an ordered sequence of place names." In Arosi today, however, such appeals often make only oblique reference to implied accounts of topogeny and lack the types of ritual recitation contexts described by Fox for other Austronesian-speaking societies.

coastal Arosi village. One of the siblings gave birth to only one daughter, and when this child grew up she did not have any children of her own. Although the other sibling gave birth to two boys and two girls, only one of her daughters went on to have children. This daughter married and moved along the coast away from the lineage's land. She, in turn, gave birth to only one daughter who went even further afield; she moved to Malaita to reside with her husband. The narrative recounts that, over the course of the next few generations, all the lineage women resided away from the lineage's land with their husbands on the islands of Ulawa or Ugi. Finally, a direct matrilineal descendant of the first woman to move away from the lineage's land returned to her ancestral land on Makira after her lineage had been absent from their land for five generations. The narrator explained to me: "She came back when she was already a young girl and ready to marry. When she came back the people at [the named village] knew she was the lineage of the land."

During the course of these genealogical narrations, people well-versed in lineage knowledge may mention a *hera* or *birubiru* when they give the name of a particular male lineage member; males typically "work" (*tau'aro*) these *dora maea*. In my experience, however, the narrators catalogue and describe *dora maea* after they have completed the genealogy. In fact, it is the description of shrines and burial grounds that constitutes most of the lineage knowledge that is passed between lineage members. As a result, many lineage members will know whether certain words are tabu in the vicinity of a *dora maea*, and what form the spirits might take at that place; they may even know who worked a particular *dora maea* and who was the last person to offer sacrifice at the site. For them, however, this knowledge tends to be disarticulated from an encompassing account of the lineage's genealogical history.[18] Consequently, even if a person knows that a shrine was founded by someone called Saewari, or has heard that Saewari's bones were placed in a burial ground, he or she is likely to be uncertain whether the Saewari in question is the first, second, or third.

Although most conversations concerning *dora maea* tend to focus on the characteristics of a particular site, some people can narrate the sequence in which their lineage shrines were formed. For example, on one occasion while I was in the gardening area above the village with Bwaa, an older friend, he began to describe how Tara, one of his lineage ancestors, formed a number

---

18. Non-lineage persons who live in close proximity to a *dora maea* and who know little of the genealogical history of the site, may also know the tabus associated with the site so that they can conduct their daily activities without encountering problems.

of different shrines.[19] Bwaa explained how Tara had taken small red stones from the lineage's first shrine near the coast at Wanga and moved them about the land to establish additional shrines at which his lineage could make offerings to their ancestral spirits. First, Tara carried the stone called Haurumu from Wanga down to the beach at Toga and, from there, carried it along the beach to Marawa. Returning again to the central shrine at Wanga, Tara then took other stones and carried them further up into the bush, placing the stones at Do'o, Wara, Meramera, To'ohi, Wawara, and finally at Raaraamaa where he died. At each of these sites Tara formed a shrine where lineage members who were already living in adjacent villages could make their offerings of pork and food. Prior to the establishment of these shrines, lineage members had to go to Wanga to offer sacrifice. The new shrines were either made on top of naturally raised areas or they were built up with mud. Tara placed one of the stones that he had carried on top of each mound. These stones were said to be the images of the lineage's ancestors in the form of a shark named Ba'ewamamahui.[20]

The radial pattern of dispersal from a central shrine that Bwaa described is not as clearly marked in the other lineage narratives that I recorded. Often a narrator would describe one *birubiru*, name the sharks and tabus associated with that site, and then simply mention that sacrifice was also offered to the same sharks at one or two other *birubiru* that his or her lineage had established. In general, therefore, Arosi lineages—unlike many Malaitan descent groups—are not concerned to distinguish between "a traditional founding shrine and a series of branch shrines at subsequent settlement sites" (Keesing 1982a: 86; cf. Burt 1994b: 320–322; Maenu'u 1981: 13–15), even though such a distinction is implicit in a lineage's genealogy (cf. Guidieri 1980: 63–65). Although each of a lineage's *dora maea* is formed differently and may require that a person observe different tabus than at the lineage's other *dora maea*, each *dora maea* is part of a larger system of lineage shrines. In fact, as Bwaa's narrative indicates, the formation of one shrine is only intelligible in terms of this multilocal system. It is by virtue of an episodic series of ancestral actions, as briefly described in this lineage narrative, that these sites are threaded together along an umbilical cord as the network of focal points that constitutes a lineage territory.

The fact that a lineage's *dora maea* constitute a multilocal semiotic system finds expression in a number of different ways, however. In some lineage nar-

---

19. I have changed both personal and places names throughout this account.

20. Fox (1924: 116–117, 263) gives similar accounts of the multiplication of *birubiru* along the coast. He also notes that—presumably as a result of such processes—"[t]he bushmen ... worshipped the spirits of the sea as well as of the land" (1924: 115).

ratives, for example, a shark or a snake that is said to reside at one shrine is characterized as traveling to a different shrine. Spirit-sharks are often said to change into snakes to travel on land. Thus, as many people explained, the snakes at some shrines in the bush are actually the same as the sharks to which people once offered sacrifice at the coastal *birubiru*.[21]

Making the relationship between the lineage spirits at different shrines more explicit, some Arosi state that each lineage has its own particular spirit entity: "It goes with the lineage, a lineage and its spirit (*hi'ona*), a lineage and its spirit" (cf. Hogbin 1964: 94). When I inquired of one man about the seemingly different snakes that he said appeared at his lineage's different *dora maea*, he told me that they were "just one snake." The formative action of making a *dora maea*, as described above, is said to have involved placing the bones of a number of ancestors on a stone and investing the locality with their power. It is not the case, however, that through this process the place came to be associated with the spirit of only one particular ancestor; rather, the snake that appeared at the site represented the spirit of the lineage as a whole. From the perspective of the lineage, the ancestors whose bones were used to form a plurality of *dora maea* are "just one" because they are "one *waipo*, a *waipo* is one." Although lineage members used to sacrifice to certain named ancestors conceptualized as distinct spirits—their grandmothers and grandfathers—these ancestors also represent a condition of ontological unity within the matrilineage.[22]

---

21. Apropos the question of hierarchy among a lineage's shrines: one man pointed out to me that for some lineages the distinction between an original and subsequent shrines is implicit in the fact that lineage members may say of a snake at a bush shrine that it is the shark from a coastal shrine in alternative form, but would not acknowledge the inverse possibility. The apparent ontological priority of the shark in this non-reciprocal transformation confers an apparent chronological priority on the coastal shrine. Compare Fox on the name of a house for making sacrifices (*ruma ni asi*): " ... the expression *ni asi*, belonging to the sea, is a strange one, for the same name is given to it in the bush" (1924: 114–115).

22. Fox (1924: 93 n. 1, 235, 236) also recognized the tension between Arosi conceptions of ancestors as distinct spirits—each with a "personality" (1924: 236)—and as forming, what he termed, a unitary "immortal essence" (1924: 235). Concerning this latter state, Fox (1924: 235) writes, "[the dead] may return to the world of the living, [where] they will have a serpent incarnation...." But for reasons that will become apparent in chapter 8, Fox (1924: 235) identified this "immortal essence" with an all-encompassing "supreme being" or "supreme God" rather than with each distinct category of being. Keesing (1982a: 82; Keesing and Fifi'i 1969: 158) describes an analogous tension in Kwaio between the recognition of distinct ancestors and the practice of clustering ancestors together as collective sources of power. For other Solomon Islands contexts, de Coppet (Barraud et al. 1994: 61–65), Guidieri (1980: 142–147), and Monnerie (1998: 103–106) also analyze the simi-

As in several of the Melanesian contexts discussed in the Introduction (e.g., Fortune 1932; Macintyre 1987, 1989; Thune 1989; A. Weiner 1978, 1980, 1988), this unity of the matrilineal category prevails on both sides of the grave. Just as living lineage members regard their ancestors as aspects of one spirit entity, the ancestors are thought to recognize their living lineal descendants as bearers of this same essential oneness. It is also supposed that this condition of oneness is evident to the ancestors in the children of lineage males as a product of their father's matrilineal blood. Recall, however, that this blood—the medium of oneness in such non-unilineal cases—becomes increasingly diluted in subsequent generations. After a small but negotiable number of generations, the ancestors, like the living, will view these descendants of lineage males as having become unrelated "different people." Owing to trust in the ontological affinity between ancestors and descendants, members of a lineage and the children of lineage males can go freely and without danger to any of a lineage's *dora maea* where it is assumed that the ancestral spirits will know them and will neither frighten them nor cause them to become ill or die.

The character of a matrilineage as an ontological type comprising a multitude of tokens of its type is reflected in the character of the snakes to which many lineages—including the Adaro, Amaeo, Mwaa, and Mwara—formerly made offerings at their *dora maea*. These snakes, I suggest, iconically signify the power that resides in the undifferentiated oneness of the lineage. Several consultants made the point that if a stranger were to chop such a lineage snake in two and "throw the two pieces away, the snake would just form together again and go back to its place." Like the physical umbilical cord, which remains intact as a symbol of matrilineal continuity even after it is cut in the process of human reproduction, these ancestral snakes likewise figure, by their elongated form and their gift of self-regeneration, a single and unbreakable line of descent through women. It is this oneness of being—shared among the spirits of the lineage dead, the builders of their burial sites and shrines, and their living descendants—that confers coherence on a lineage's multiple *dora maea*.

Arosi naming practices likewise reference narrative repositories of ancestrally established patterns in ways that both transformatively reproduce matrilineal emplacement and index the Arosi model of a matrilineage and its spirits as a microcosmic mono-ontology. Today, most Arosi children are given two names: an English language-based Christian name and a local language-based

---

larly dichotomous nature of an ancestor as both an identifiable personality and an amorphous state of being.

name.[23] Fox (1924: 54, 62) records that in the early twentieth century Makirans' baptismal names were not subject to the same practices as their local
names. Since this remains true today, the following discussion refers to the
latter type of name, sometimes called the "island name." A lineage recycles its
own exclusive set of island names. Knowledge of this set of names is an important part of a knowledgeable person's repertoire, and he or she is able to
list the names from memory. I was told that a lineage-specific name should,
ideally, be reassigned to a newborn child only after its previous bearer has died
(cf. Fox 1924: 179) and, aside from the few exceptions I analyze in chapter 7,
this was the practice. Appropriately, the same Arosi term, *adaro*, means both
an island name belonging to a deceased person and an ancestral spirit. If an
ancestor with a particular name formerly lived in a certain locale, his or her
name is regarded as connected to that area of the lineage's land. In some cases,
this connection is elaborated by traditions that the ancestor in question was
the one who established a shrine or placed tabus at the site that consequently
bears his or her name. Thus, by virtue of their spatialized genealogical form,
lineage histories often narrativize the correspondences between lineage personal names and certain locations.

The affinity between a name and a place is linked to the affinity thought
to inhere between a name and a field of relations that encompasses both living relatives and ancestral spirits. Because they embody a given essential oneness, all members of a lineage, along with the recent descendants of lineage
males with whom they share "one blood," can use the full extent of the area
they regard as theirs in confidence of ancestral recognition and protection.
Yet, within this state of ontological unity, personal names differentiate people by calling forth the specific constellations of social relations formerly realized by past bearers of the names. It is precisely in this context of a unified field of being within which persons become individuated through the
elicitation of certain sets of possible relationships that Marilyn Strathern's
(1988, 1992) model of Melanesian sociality best fits the Arosi situation. Re-
cycling a personal name—an *adaro*—revivifies a distinct ancestral spirit—
an *adaro*—both of which presuppose a set of social relationships convergent
in a particular area of the lineage's land. The name and the ancestor simultaneously link the child to that land and the field of relationships it entails.

When an *adaro* (name of a deceased) that could potentially be given to any
one of a number of same-sex children is actually given to a particular child,

---

23. Some Arosi names are built on or incorporate semantic elements drawn from other
languages in the Solomons (cf. Fox 1924: 179). A few people have English language-based
middle names. Many people also receive nicknames during the course of their lives.

relatives will address this child using the same kin terms that they had once used to address his or her ancestral namesake. Although Harry Ramo, for example, addresses most of his brothers' daughters as *mau*, he addresses one of these children as *ina* (mother) because this girl was given his mother's name, Maesiʻino. By the same principle, Esther Bwairageni calls one young girl *wawae* (grandmother) because this girl was named after Esther's grandmother. These children embody not merely one isolated dyadic relationship, but a whole system of relationships activated by the names that they have been given. As they grow up they will literally "eat food on account of the name." They will be empowered to make decisions about the same area of land and nut trees that their deceased namesakes oversaw. Other people will therefore come to ask them where they may build their houses, make their gardens, or which trees they may cut down. In other places, they—and even their own children—will be invited to gather nuts or make copra where their ancestral namesakes are still remembered as important relatives.

The way in which personal names mobilize systems of relationships that extend into the spirit realm is also exemplified in the references my consultants often made to men who had been named after ancestral shark-men. As noted previously, Arosi suggest that any member of a lineage that formerly sacrificed to spirit-sharks can potentially reestablish a sacrificial relationship with these lineage sharks. But a man like Hidawawa, who has been given the name of a shark-man, inherently has influence over his namesake's shrine and spirit-sharks. The spirit-sharks, according to Arosi, protect him simply "because he has the name of a person like that."

Because giving a lineage's personal name to a child bestows special authority over a portion of the lineage's land and access to certain nut trees, these names should, ideally, only be given after all the members of the lineage have consented to the naming. This consent has to be given by both the living and the dead. Fox (1924: 178) records that Arosi formerly selected a child's name by a type of divination through which they sought to discover which "ghost ... wishes the child to be called after him." Although Arosi no longer seek consent by divination, people say that if the ancestor whose name is being given does not approve of a naming, he or she will cause the newly named child to fall ill. Sickly children are, consequently, often renamed.[24]

---

24. As discussed in the following chapter, ancestral names are often given to the children or grandchildren of lineage males; that is to say, the names are bestowed on children who are not part of the lineage. It would appear that childhood illness is more likely to be interpreted as ancestrally wrought if the child is not a member of the lineage from which the name originated.

At the same time, names are continually being added to a lineage's list of *adaro*. It has always been true that some children are not given a name associated with a lineage ancestor but are named after an event, a perceived characteristic, a relative's nickname, or something their parents have done. Occasionally, the name of an admired or well-known ancestor will provide the root from which new descriptive names are derived. For example, the name and deeds of one renowned warrior, Iʻahoroiasi, has given rise to the names Iʻatarogari (The-news-of-Iʻahoroiasi-goes-around) and Iʻahaingahu (Iʻahoroiasi-knows-how-to-kill). I was told that, due to the high birth rate in the last three decades, an increasing number of children are being given such newly coined names. Once a person with an innovated name has died, however, his or her name may become one of the names belonging to his or her lineage. Owing to a variety of factors, including fluctuations in lineage birth rates and lineage members' discretion, it is often the case that only some of a lineage's personal names will be assigned to living people at any given period; any remaining names are held ready to be given to newborns. Most lineages' personal names are thought to have been reused only a total of two or three times. It appears, therefore, that as new personal names are incorporated into the lineage repertoire while others fall into abeyance, and as certain areas of land are worked while others are neglected, the reproduction of a lineage and its land is subject to continual transformation.

By endeavoring to give their names to children, the members of a lineage seek to ensure that living people will continue to look after all of the different areas and local powers they regard as constituting their territory. Frequently, a personal name will be given to a newborn child with a view to eventually bringing the child to live at a particular village associated with his or her namesake. Through the practice of naming, a lineage intentionally activates sets of relationships that place living representatives of the lineage in diverse locales throughout its territory. At the same time, keeping the names of ancestors alive memorializes and perpetuates the distinct identities of dead ancestral spirits locatable at specific sites vis-à-vis the amorphous and territory-wide collective lineage spirit. The lineage's set of personal names serves, in short, as an important vehicle through which the lineage's spirit entity is manifested as named ancestral spirits and the lineage's territory is parceled into smaller spheres of control.

The lineage narratives that Arosi shared with me articulate how their matrilineages actively appropriated territories and produced lineage members—both new offspring for the future and dead ancestors of the past—who became emplaced in a changing landscape. Like the generation of children through exogamous unions among the living, the generation of ancestral *adaro* through disposition of remains and commemoration in the land was vital to the formation of matrilineages that were thereby constituted, not only in relationship to one another, but also in relationship to their own defining places. The burial and enshrinement of ancestors in the past made the Arosi landscape a spatiotemporal medium through which combinations of matrilineages, territories, and spirits came into being as discrete but interconnected unities. These activities anchored a lineage in its land and gave it a history. Today, Arosi no longer place the bones of the dead in lineage *hera* or make offerings to spirit-sharks at *birubiru*. Yet, with daily reference to these types of *dora maea*, they continue to reproduce their lineages' relationships to land as they rehearse parts of their lineage narratives, teach children about the acts of their ancestors, observe the tabus associated with particular places, interact with animals they spontaneously encounter, interpret illness and death, or give ancestors' names to their children. The past is everywhere and always integral to their lived environment and their imaginative world, providing the concrete and conceptual points of reference through which Arosi are maintaining by reconfiguring their lineage identities in the present.

CHAPTER 6

BEING AND BECOMING *AUHENUA*

Having described in the previous chapter how Arosi are reproducing themselves as the *auhenua* of the coast in ways that reference often imperfectly known but nonetheless presupposed lineage narratives, I suggest in this chapter that these processes of emplacement furthermore imply two distinct Arosi visions of primordial coming into being. Arosi themselves do not reflexively isolate or name these visions of primordiality as units of *kastom*. Rather, what I term here utopic and topogonic primordiality are analytical constructs based on a variety of Arosi representations of the static and dynamic dimensions of the concept of *auhenua*.

The Arosi vision or mode of primordiality I call utopic refers to the ways in which Arosi express the general quality of being *auhenua* to Makira as a given and unalterable matrilineally reproduced condition. These forms of expression are not only assertions of absolute autochthony, they are also the clearest indices of Arosi descent-based poly-ontology. Arosi accounts and figures of autochthonous Makiran lineage origins, such as the Amaeo origin story discussed in chapter 4, ascribe ontological autonomy to a plurality of *auhenua* proto-lineages depicted as coming into being independently at separate but generic points or bounded domains on the island. Although emphatically Makiran, each such generic point or domain may be analytically defined as utopic in the strict sense of the term: it is, as yet, not-place. Spatial analogues of the proto-lineages they mark as ontologically individual, these primordial not-places—serial types still unformed by human agency—are proto-places. They are indeterminate potentialities, open to receive their "first lineage." As the adamant unwillingness of Arosi to be cast as members of matrilineages without such credentials indicates, strict Makiran origin of this kind and the unique ontological identity it confers are taken to be the necessary preconditions for subsequent and ongoing matrilineal emplacement in a specific area of Makiran land. A variety of Arosi representations assert both the enduring precedence of primordial not-places and their displacement by lineage-specific territories created when lineage ancestors shaped the land through actions that were literally and conceptually place-generative.

Building on James Fox's (1997) concept of topogeny—a narrative of ancestral movement and place making—I call the second Arosi vision of primordiality the topogonic mode of primordiality. This mode of primordiality, which is legible to analysis primarily through the types of autochthonous histories discussed in chapter 5, refers to a dynamic epoch in which ancestors achieved poly-genetic humanity and sociality by establishing relationships among matrilineages and between matrilineages and their unique areas of land. Although equally a vision of origins, in contrast with utopic primordiality, topogonic primordiality represents a vision of relative rather than absolute origins. It blurs, therefore, into ethnohistory and the ongoing present itself. The topogonic activities in which the ancestors are said to have engaged to establish proper sociality are models, not only for replication, but also for the innovation of analogous topogonic activities through which Arosi endeavor to continue to maintain proper sociality. At the same time, what amount to topogonic activities original to the present may be endorsed as consonant with, even prescribed by, the activities through which the ancestors made an implied initial transition from utopic to topogonic primordiality.

What begins to transpire more fully from this analytical breakdown of Arosi ideas about primordiality is the likelihood that heterotopia is not just a function of Arosi postcoloniality. The potential for mutually disqualifying constructions of geographic space, it seems, may be inherent in this distinctive Arosi conceptualization of cosmogony as a transition from one mode of primordiality to another, understood as necessarily repeatable, open-ended, and generative of new means for the maintenance of proper socio-spatial order. Whereas the cosmogonic events envisioned in utopic primordiality allow multiple matrilineages to claim to be *auhenua* without necessarily coming into conflict, the cosmogonic events envisioned in topogonic primordiality allow for the possibility—even the probability—that more than one Arosi matrilineage will, over time, represent themselves as having become *auhenua* in relation to the same terrain. It will be the task of chapter 7, therefore, to show how the current state of Arosi heterotopia represents a magnification of this indigenous cosmogonic tendency under postcolonial conditions that are intensifying Arosi efforts at socio-cultural reproduction through semantically revalued transformations of ancestral topogonic activity.

Utopic Primordiality: Proto-lineages in Proto-places

Arosi occasionally use the words *pwaranga* (empty) and *dadara'aa* (free, unclaimed) to describe areas of land abandoned by an *auhenua* lineage or cleared of its ancestral powers. But they do not directly identify—in myth or otherwise—the original utopic state of their island as a whole.[1] As in 'Are'are (Malaita), in Arosi, "locality cannot even be conceived of without the apical ancestors and their subsequent deeds" (de Coppet 1985: 80; cf. Guidieri 1980: 57–64). Nevertheless, Arosi assumptions about the initially utopic nature of their island become apparent situationally through a number of discursive and non-discursive forms of social action. Such assumptions surface, for example, when a person recounts how his or her lineage was the first to inhabit a particular area; when someone conceptually conflates lineage territories with pre-existing bounded domains; when parents justify their selection of a site at which to plant their newborn's umbilical cord; and in stories that describe a disjuncture between the site of lineage inception and the formation of lineage territory. Discernible in these moments and forms, the models of utopic primordiality here identified are congruent but unintegrated in Arosi thought or practice and are nowhere reconciled within a single narrative or other framework.

The most detailed representations of the imagined condition I call utopic primordiality are lineage-specific accounts of autochthonous ultimate origins on Makira. Although some of these accounts contain similar narrative material, Arosi regard them as unique narratives of unique origins. Several lineages say that they are the progeny of human daughters born to snake-grandmother figures; others depict their ancestors as having been rock-people who were materially one with the island; one lineage claims that it was sung forth on the island by a bird; and, like the Amaeo lineage whose myth is described in chapter 4, a second lineage also traces itself to a union between a *pwapwaronga* and a *masi*.[2]

---

1. In contrast, the Fataleka of Malaita have a concept, *boro*, which can refer either to an original chaotic negativity or to a particular unmarked and uninhabited space. Guidieri (1980: 43, 62) glosses this concept as an "abyss," or a "black hole."

2. O'Connor (1973: 42–49) reports that the matrilineages of the Bota Moli and Veeru Moli Districts of neighboring Guadalcanal have similarly diverse origin stories. Strikingly, the word she glosses as "lineage" means "one beginning" (1973: 45–46). Likewise, Fox notes (1924: 75) that in Star Harbour (east Makira) the locution used to refer to what he terms a clan "was explained to mean 'a string stretching out from one beginning.'" See also Allan 1957: 85, 91.

To elaborate a particular case, members of one lineage tell the story of a female spirit, an *adaro*, who lived in a well. One day a man climbed the canarium almond tree (*ngari*) near to the well in order to collect nuts. His mother and father had died and left him alone with no one to pound the soft covers from the shells of his nuts. When he had climbed the tree, the female spirit called: "Let your *ngari* nuts down [in baskets] and I will remove their skins." Looking around, the man was confused because he could not see anyone. Then he noticed what looked like a young woman with fair hair and a light complexion, "a beautiful spirit woman." "Where do you live?" he asked. "Just here in the well," she replied. She brought water for him to drink. Soon they thought that they would like to get married. The man suggested that they go to his village, but the woman refused, fearing the villagers might kill her. So the man went to the village and told everyone what had happened. The spirit woman then came to feast and be married. This is the beginning of one of the lineages called Adaro. Hezron Sinaha'a, who first told me the myth, indicated that the spirit woman was her great-grandmother.

Taken together, the diverse types of autochthonous progenitors in such myths constitute what I have termed proto-lineages, living in sterile isolation, overly differentiated, and not yet engaged in productive social relations with one another. In this mode of primordiality, a proto-lineage is likewise not yet connected to the particular domain that will become its lineage territory. Just as it is not a lineage of true human beings, its site of ultimate origin is not a true lineage territory. Although a point of lineage origin must be imagined as having been somewhere on the island—such as a well in the bush, a village inhabited by animate rocks, or the site where a snake gave birth to an ancestress—it is nevertheless a proto-place, a place without a peopled past endowing its features with names and creating landmarks that are the vestiges of ancestral words and deeds. One proto-place of lineage origin is functionally indistinguishable from the multiplicity of other proto-places that give rise to the multiplicity of other proto-lineages.

Although distinct in style and content from tales of ultimate origins, genealogically ordered autochthonous histories also present images of utopic primordiality in accounts of first advent in a particular area of land. Such accounts emphasize that, prior to the time of initial incursion, the land in question was empty and had no identity as a place. A commonly held principle of first occupancy, according to which "the land is the land of the lineage that arrived first," presupposes an empty or pre-social physical geography that has not been transformed by the activities of another lineage. The island's rivers, ridges, cliffs, soil, and trees are understood to have existed prior to the settling, cultivating, and multifocal territory-producing human activities examined in the previous chapter. When Arosi speak of this pre-social state, they specify that some part, rather than the island as a whole, was the unsettled and unused "virgin forest" (*wabu*) that lineage ancestors were the first to clear (cf. Fox 1924: 301). The original vacuity of the land is given exemplary expression in one man's statement concerning his lineage's descent from the island's interior to the coast many generations ago: "When we [i.e., his lineage ancestors] first came down, no other lineage was at the coast here." It was only after recounting the formative actions of his ancestors in this vacant land that he could explain to me: "So, this is our land here along the coast; we have shrines and burial grounds, and no other lineage has such things here."[3]

The Arosi model of static origins I term utopic primordiality may also be inferred from Arosi descriptions of the relationship between a lineage and its land that seem to conflate the dynamically achieved ancestral territories mapped in lineage narratives with pre-existing bounded domains in which the lineages originated. In such descriptions, Arosi highlight rivers, the watercourses of streams, ridges, and rocks as evidence of a given and stable partitioning of the island.[4] These fixed units are not to be confused, I was cautioned, with newer and relatively transitory attempts to divide the land. Such innovations include the boundaries between present-day villages established by colonial officials in order to apportion responsibility for clearing coastal footpaths; the recently demarcated borders between small plots of land on which coconuts have been planted; and unmarked—some would say, notional—boundaries between the coast and the bush. In contrast, when Arosi treat lineage territories as defined by geophysical features, they speak of relatively large territories that are permanent and antecedent to any human activity in the land. One older man, who is known locally for his interest in Arosi custom, listed the rivers on the north coast of Arosi that he believes serve as lineage territory boundaries. He explained that one lineage's land lies from Maro'u Bay in the west to the Waiaroaha river in the east (about eleven kilometers along the coast); another lineage's land is between the Waiaroaha and

---

3. The original emptiness of land and its settlement by mythic pioneers is well documented for Malaita (e.g., Burt 1994a: 24–25; 1994b: 318–319; Burt and Kwa'ioloa 1992: 6–9; Burt and Kwa'ioloa, eds. 2001: 15; Codrington 1891: 61; de Coppet 1981: 176; 1985: 80; Frazer 1973: 19; Guidieri 1980: 41, 62–63; Ivens 1930: 291–292; Keesing 1992: 23–25; Maenu'u 1981: 131; Naitoro 1993: 30; Ross 1973: 115, 160). Citing examples from other Austronesian-speaking populations, Peter Bellwood (1996) has theorized a mutually informing relationship between such "founder-focused" representations of polity formation and experiences of initial expansion into new territories.

4. For brief discussions of topographic features said to antedate humans on Malaita, see Burt 1994a: 26; de Coppet 1985: 80.

Waimarae rivers (about five and a half kilometers); and a third lineage's territory is bounded by the Waimarae and the Wainaraha (about twelve and a half kilometers). Although this man did not specify the inland extent of these territories, some people suggested that they reached well into the bush, even to the highest central ridge that runs northwest to southeast through the length of Arosi. Interpreting other topographic landmarks as parsing the land differently, however, many Arosi would dispute both whether these rivers are actually lineage boundaries and whether the territories he describes correspond with the particular lineages he named. Having described an alternative set of boundaries, Peter Itamwaeraha summed up the import of such divisions as evidence of how each lineage originated in its own already bounded domain on the island: "The spirit of God placed the lineages on the land, it split the land for us; these divisions in the land already existed."

This image of different proto-lineal categories of being arising from their own discrete areas on the island is analogous to the way in which some Arosi describe the production of fish, shrimp, and crabs. These sea creatures are said to be released from an organism called I'abwari that lives under the sea north of the small island of Bio about sixteen kilometers from the north Arosi coast. I'abwari, I was told, looks like an underwater reef. Occasionally, it floats up near the surface, and at such times people can fish near its edge. During different seasons, I'abwari is thought to bear various species of fish, prawns, and young crabs. Each species of marine animal is, in the words of one friend, released from its own "room" (*banihoro*) in I'abwari. The immature fish are said to leave I'abwari in bag-like membranes or wombs (*'ahu'ahu*) containing many little fish of the same species. The bags, if they do not open prematurely and are not attacked by hungry fish, wash onto the Makiran coast where they split open and release their loads. The origin of sea creatures in I'abwari and the origin of matrilineages on Makira are, I suggest, semantically parallel. Although I'abwari and the island seem to constitute natural unities, neither entity is thought to engender an ontological relationship among the various categories of being that it fosters. Rather, both cases depict a state of original speciation. Just as each type of sea organism arises in its own room during its particular season, each lineage originates in its own bounded territory as distinct and unrelated to any other on the island. In short, the one: Makira, gives rise to the many: the disparate unrelated Arosi proto-lineages.[5]

---

5. The analogy, of course, breaks down at the point of reproduction. Arosi do not think that different species of marine life inter-breed with one another in the way that Arosi matrilineages reproduce exogamously. Nevertheless, as I explore in chapter 8, some Arosi make a more or less explicit analogy between I'abwari and Makira itself when they speak of the

The fact that Arosi representations of lineage territories as preconstituted segments of land refer to specific named geophysical features may seem to belie analysis of them as evidence of an Arosi vision of a condition accurately construed as utopic primordiality. Some of my consultants pointed especially to named rivers as though they defined the particular territories of several local matrilineages. Yet these representations of static pre-constituted, even God-given, lineage territories do not align, either conceptually or spatially, with the dynamically innovated ancestral territories represented in lineage narratives and referenced in daily life through the vestiges of ancestral activity. They are utopic to the extent that they employ real geophysical features to inscribe idealized lineage territories on the land, much as Itamwaeraha did when he took a stick and drew a line of contiguous rectangles in the sand to illustrate customary land tenure as a system of matrilineages identified with areas of land. Despite their association with known local features, such idealized lineage territories are generic spatial blocks. Arosi insistence on the cosmogonic priority of these blocks is, I suggest, ideationally similar to the act of planting an umbilical cord and points to another medium through which Arosi imagine a condition of given ontological diversity. In this geophysical medium, pre-socially bounded spaces mark the a priori ontological diversity of the lineages they contain. Like a planted umbilical cord, such a sealed off site of autochthonous manifestation can be anywhere at all on the island. But in this medium of expression, original plurality is reinforced by the idea that each lineage was seated in its own discrete cell-like zone on the island. No two lineages are siblings born from the same compartment on the island.

The seemingly unrelated practice of planting a newborn's umbilical cord with a sprouting coconut may also be interpreted as momentarily bringing to the surface the foundational but now overlaid emptiness and utopic quality of the island as an underlying field of reference for generalized autochthonous Makiran identity. As discussed in chapter 4, Arosi often plant a child's umbilical cord on a piece of land close to where they reside at the time of the birth. Despite the fact that an umbilical cord is a strong and unambiguous fig-

island as having the form of a snake called Hatoibwari. Prompted by a consideration of the word *bwari* in both names, Casper Kaukeni offered the following etymology of I'abwari. The name I'abwari is composed of two elements: the word *i'a* refers to fish, whales, and porpoises, and the word *bwari* means spider. Casper observed that when he had previously caught spiders and cut open their white stomachs he had found large numbers of little spiders to which they would have given birth. He suggested that the word *bwari* in these names stressed the productivity of the organism. When I shared his suggestion with other Arosi they found this to be a felicitous explanation.

ure of a matrilineage, parents do not insist on indexing matrilineal connection to a specific place by attempting to plant the baby's umbilical cord in what the mother regards as her matrilineage's land. The parents' latitude to plant a cord anywhere they choose can be seen as an occasional symbolic return to a context of pre-social vacuity in which their action is not in conflict with the history of any specific lineage in any identifiable area. In this symbolic suspension of all relativity, the sprouting umbilical cord/coconut palm becomes an icon of the general rootedness of an autochthonous matrilineage in the island; it is a figure of the simple fact of original germination somewhere in the island, understood as the criterion for being *auhenua*.

As previously noted, however, if a person were to refer to his or her umbilical cord/coconut palm as evidence of ancestral connection to a particular place, this icon of primordial emptiness could be transformed into an index of alleged sustained habitation in a given area. Potentially available as support for a lineage's claim to be rooted in a specific place, an umbilical cord/coconut palm can become a recent addendum to a long history of ancestral movement and activity, and thus an index of the process of becoming *auhenua* at that site. Such a semantic shift from iconically standing for a former state of utopic asociality to indexing a history of topogonic socialization of land parallels an ideal transition from one mode of primordiality to another. The potential for a similar transition inheres in the incommensurability between Arosi representations of lineage territories as pre-existing, ontologically differentiating bounded units and representations of lineage territories as the products of human activities shaping the islandscape into socialized areas peopled by the living and the dead. A lineage narrative traces a trajectory of movement through space that establishes a lineage on a homeland not identifiable or coterminous with its ground of origin. Yet, despite this disjuncture between a pre-existing area of initial containment and an achieved lineage territory, the image of a naturally bounded context of origin persists as an icon of an antecedent utopic condition. Like the randomly planted umbilical cord, this icon has the potential to become an index of a particular lineage's ancestral territory.

The incommensurability between ideal bounded contexts of origin and lived lineage territories is only one of several indicators that Arosi imagine a necessary and even painful disjuncture between a lineage's place of absolute beginning and its ancestral territory. This disjuncture is most commonly expressed by the unmarked quality of a lineage's place of origin. Thus, although some lineages can point to a specific place of origin—perhaps by naming the well from which an ancestress emerged, or by identifying the village formerly inhabited by living ancestral rocks—most narratives leave the locale of ultimate beginnings in obscurity (cf. Hviding 1996: 132). Members of the Amaeo

lineage, for example, simply state that the two mythological proto-human beings, the *pwapwaronga* and the *masi*, reproduced together on the island, but
lineage members do not trace themselves to a known place of origin. Some
lineages appear to lack accounts of their ultimate origins altogether (or they
chose not to disclose them to me).[6] Yet even those lineages that link themselves
to a definite place of origin tell stories about a rupture from that place that accounts for the dispersal of lineage members away from their point of first appearance and out over land that their ancestors altered and appropriated.

Recall that the self-contained Arosi proto-lineages must establish productive
and reproductive relations with one another if they are to generate truly human
children. The production of truly human offspring requires the successful mediation of a tension between the oneness of mother and child and their necessary separation at parturition. To greater or lesser degree, all of the lineage narratives I learned that locate a lineage's origin at a still recognized site reflect an
analogous tension between a lineage's connection to its site or source of origin
and its dislocation, even expulsion, from that site or source. Thus the processes
of social cosmogenesis are mirrored in those of spatial cosmogenesis. I have argued that the myth of the birth of the first fully human ancestress of the Amaeo
matrilineage may be analyzed as the outcome of exogamous intersection between representatives of two proto-lineages. This intersection introduces a
break, figured by the cutting of the umbilical cord, in the absolute integrity of
the two proto-lineages that allows for the paradox of matrilineal continuity
through mixing. Similarly, the formation of a fully human matrilineage also requires what I would characterize as a kind of figurative intermarriage between
a proto-lineage and the land that will become its territory. This union between
an emergent social group and its land likewise seems to entail a severing of the
natal tie between a proto-lineage and its proto-place of issue. This theme of geographic parturition, along with the importance of the chain of events through
which a proto-lineage comes into relationship with new spaces as well as other
social beings, is especially evident in the following lineage origin narrative.

The text given below is translated from the "Custom book"—as it is described in English on the cover—belonging to one Arosi lineage. Variants of
this myth, sometimes introduced in recitation by the title "The Journey of
Hauhuari'i," are widely known throughout Makira and south Malaita (cf. Fox
1924: 289; Keevil 1972: 1–3; Mead 1973b: 221). Of the six versions of this

---

6. It should be noted that many people were quick to provide origin stories for lineages
other than their own; they simply stated that the lineage in question was from another island. All of my consultants agreed, however, that Amaeo and Atawa had originated on
Makira.

story that I collected, only this one incorporates the myth into an account of a lineage's ultimate origin. In all variants, the word *hau*, meaning a rock or a stone, is prefixed to the names of the characters and indicates that the protagonists are lithomorphic.

Hauwewe was the mother of Haurae and Hauhuari'i. Hauhuari'i was a boy and Haurae was a girl.

Haurae and Hauhuari'i both left their mother at their village at Rorohu [in the center of the Arosi bush]. They did so because their mother told all the people to clear her garden. When they had finished their mother only boiled [leafy greens called] *wewe* for them. That is the thing [for which] the brother and sister were angry with their mother. They argued among themselves. And their mother told her two children: "You two get your own food and you two kill your own pigs. The thing that I eat I make for the people here." And she drove away her two children: "You two go away from me."

"Yes, we'll go, but your place will be there, where you stay," [Haurae and Hauhuari'i replied.] And the two went out following [a large river called] Waimarae.

When they came out they met a rock. Who? Hauwa'asiha. They said to the rock: "You clear away from our path." And Hauwa'asiha said, "You can still pass and go out; are you carrying a *haa* [i.e., a large bed on which a pig is placed for use as a battering ram]?" Haurae and Hauhuari'i then came out, but [the rock] still draws in its waist so that the two of them could pass.

The two continued to travel out and they met Hauniboo. And they said to Hauniboo: "You clear away from our path; we are going out." And Hauniboo said: "You two just go out." And Hauniboo moved out of the path of the two of them, and they came out.

They continued to come out following the river and they also met Haunihioro, and they said to Haunihioro: "Clear out of our path." And Haunihioro also cleared their way.

And they still came out following the river. They met Haunitaraidoru and they said to Haunitaraidoru: "You clear away from our path." And [the rock] said: "You two just come out past [me]." They came out and they flattened Haunitaraidoru.

Then the two of them came out to the mouth of Waimarae and they came down to [a named point of land projecting out into the sea] and first they rested with Hauwewe's sister [I have withheld her name]. Her village was at [I have withheld the name of this village].

All right, Haurae and Hauhuariʻi left for Malaita from [the named point of land]. They went out and reached Malaita, and Hauhuariʻi said to his sister: "You go back in to our land [on Makira] and you reproduce people for the land, you who are a girl."

Haurae went back and arrived at the [point from which they departed] and went inland following Waimarae as far in as [a named place]. And entered a ... fork of the river and came out following the river to the mouth of [another river] and lived there.

And she married [a man whose name I have withheld]. They only had one girl..., and Haurae said to her child there: "You go back and you reproduce at our land [at Hauwewe's sister's village]."

All right, his sister had gone back, and Hauhuariʻi looked back here [to Makira] and still saw Rorohu village [where they had left their mother] and [he] traveled [on] cutting Malaita and [he] looked back and did not see Rorohu and stayed there [on the eastern side of Malaita] until now.

This story describes a family argument that precipitates an initial schism between two rock children and their mother. The two children become angry when, in return for assistance in clearing a garden area, their mother offers her neighbors the meager fare of her habitual diet, the wild plant whose name she shares: *wewe*. The children's anger may be understood, I suggest, as a response to what they view as their mother's anti-social, and hence static and sterile, behavior. In ways that mark her as existentially similar to the primordial people discussed in chapter 4, the mother is unable to establish proper relations with the undefined social group that also lives at Rorohu. In fact, her name, Hauwewe (literally, Rock-greens), combined with her limited culinary practice, is indicative of a self-contained pre-cultural state of endo-cannibalistic isolation: she eats the uncultivated leafy greens whose name she bears, and it is this vegetable that she offers to the people who have helped clear her garden. When Haurae and Hauhuariʻi become angry with their mother, she drives them from their place of origin. At the same time, however, by making their mother stay and mark the place from which they are departing, the two children contrast their own mobility with the primordial immobility of Hauwewe.[7]

The two siblings' movement out and away from their mother at Rorohu maps the necessary separation between a proto-lineage and its proto-place. In

7. De Coppet's discussion of the emergence of ʻAreʻare apical ancestors and of the killer's actions indicates that a similar conceptualization of "the oneness and immobility of origins" exists in south Malaita (Barraud et al. 1994: 64; de Coppet 1985: 80–83).

a manner parallel to the successful production of people, with its concomitant element of separation, this lineage origin narrative concerns the successful production of a territorially situated lineage and suggests that this process involves a departure from the site of absolute origin. Hauhuari'i and Haurae's egress along the course of the river is a spatial analogue to the birth and parturition of a true human being. The problem of reproduction among primordial people—demonstrated in other narratives by the apparent lack of a birth canal among *pwapwaronga*—appears to be revisited in this lineage account in the theme of the obstacles to the rocks' movement. Nevertheless, the siblings are able to overcome these obstacles and emerge successfully to settle in new places.

The two rocks' subsequent trajectories seem to match the normal fate of the descendants of lineage males and those of lineage females with respect to their relationship to their lineage's land. A male, like Hauhuari'i, ensures that his lineage's land remains peopled by sending (or bringing back) lineage women to the land of his lineage, but he marries a woman from another lineage and must produce children whose land is elsewhere. I interpret two related elements in this story—Hauhuari'i's application of a vision test to measure the sufficiency of his movement away, and the radical geological break in the island of Malaita that his travels create—as symbolic of his inability to reproduce children who will appropriate land for his own lineage. The image of Hauhuari'i looking back from Malaita and still seeing his mother's village figures the possibility that recent descendants of lineage males can return to live with the lineage of their male ancestors. Such recent male descendants still see their paternal kin as relatives and are seen by them to be part of their bilateral kindred. When, however, Hauhuari'i splits Malaita in half and loses sight of his ancestral village, he comes to represent future, more distant, descendants of lineage males who are no longer thought to be related to the lineage—they have become "different people"—and cannot return to the land of their forefather. The territories formed and occupied by the descendants of Hauhuari'i will be as separate from those formed and occupied by his maternal kin as Small Malaita (Mwara Kekerei) is from Big Malaita (Mwara Raha). In contrast, the descendants of lineage females, such as those of Haurae, will form a lineage territory that represents balance between continuity with their lineage's site of ultimate origin and a new beginning in a new location. It is this balance, I suggest, that is represented by the otherwise enigmatic figure of the maternal aunt to whose village Haurae sends her own daughter. Being a maternal kinswoman, this aunt, along with the coastal land on which she resides, symbolically reconciles the simultaneous unity and separation between Haurae and her mother by marking out a new spatial starting point for the matrilineage that both links and distances Haurae from her mother.

Topogonic Primordiality: Matrilineages on the Move

In the second mode of primordiality, lineages come into relationship with the expanses of land that become their proper lineage territories. Haurae, echoing what her brother had told her, directs her sole daughter to go and reproduce at a particular place in their land. This daughter, in turn, marries and gives birth to a number of daughters who subsequently have children of their own. The exercise book in which this story is written continues by presenting the ensuing generations of this lineage in the following format:[8]

I____, child of Haurae, also married and had the children: S_1____[Da], S_2____[Da] and H____[Da].

H____'s children were—   1. T_1____[Da]

   2. T_2____[Da]

   3. T_3____[Da]

   4. T_4____[Da].

S_2____'s children were—G____[So] whose father was A____. M____[So] was a brother of G____; but M____ just went out from [a place called] A____, he was [a type of animal].

S_1____

Her children were—   1. I_1____[Da]

   2. I_2____[Da]

   3. I_3____[Da]

   4. M_1____[So] was a boy.

---

8. In order to respect my consultants' wishes I have coded the personal and place names in this translation. I give the initial letter of each personal and place name and use subscripts—numbers for personal names and letters for place names—after the initial letter, to differentiate those beginning with the same letter and semantic element. This style seeks to represent the fact that sets of sibling names often share initial semantic elements. I have also added the notation [Da] to denote a daughter and [So] a son.

H_____ lived at T$_a$_____.

S$_2$_____ lived at H$_a$_____.

S$_1$_____ lived at E_____.

H_____'s children —

T$_1$_____ lived at T$_a$_____.

T$_2$_____ lived at H$_b$_____.

T$_3$_____ lived at T$_b$_____.

T$_4$_____ lived at B_____.

T$_2$_____ (No - 1) lived at H$_b$_____ and her children's names were —

        1. 'U_____[Da]

        2. R$_1$_____[Da]

        3. A_____[So], a boy

        4. R$_2$_____[Da]

        5. M_____[So] another boy

'U_____ married and only had one child, T$_5$_____. T$_5$_____ lived at I_____.

R$_1$_____ walked up to settle a new village and lived at T$_c$_____.

[Etc.]

The children of each successive generation move out and live at different places that have not previously been mentioned in the lineage narrative; or, alternatively, a person is said explicitly "to settle a new village." Later in the narrative, a set of siblings is said to have "come down again [i.e., from the bush]" to live at a place inhabited by members of a previous generation.[9] Having recounted the places where people in the first six generations of the line-

---

9. The explicitly stated concern not merely to reproduce (*ha'atabara*) children, but to reproduce them for particular places, is a theme common to all lineage narratives. For ex-

age lived, the narrative does not explicitly state where the subsequent generations lived. Of the twelve generations recounted, it appears that these earliest generations spread out and inhabited what became the full extent of the
lineage's territory. As is characteristic of this type of narrative, the pre-existence of marriageable people residing in or near this land is assumed but left
unexplored. The land is functionally empty, pre-social, and utopic, ready to
be shaped by the lineage. Although this narrative does not include such details, Arosi listeners (or, in this case, readers) understand that, as their matrilineal ancestors moved out into the land, they were also engaged in making
burial sites and placing the remains of their dead throughout the landscape.
Rather than providing stories about such deeds, the last two pages of the "Custom book" contain a list of the shark shrines and "places for burned sacrifice"
that the ancestors of this lineage established and record the names of those
who offered sacrifice at each site.

This narrative, unlike many lineage narratives, conjoins utopic and topogonic primordiality within a single continuous account. Ironically, however, this
juxtaposition highlights the apparent irreconcilability of these two different
visions of the island. The account is able to place these visions side-by-side by
framing them in two distinct genres. The first part of the narrative gives a detailed and vivid description of the rock people's subjective attitudes, dialogue,
and actions. This form of narrative elaboration is common to all accounts of
ultimate lineage origins. The second part, in contrast, simply provides a
sparse, schematic catalogue of human marriages, the names of children, places
where they lived, and the shrines that they formed. There are no embellish-
ing descriptions, no dialogues, and no episodes of interpersonal conflict.
These two narrative structures provide two different "eyes"—to borrow
Medvedev's metaphor for genre—through which to see different aspects of
"reality" (Bakhtin/Medvedev 1985: 134).

The two genres visualize contrastive modes of action that are located in different spatiotemporal contexts.[10] In the first genre, the movements of
Hauhuariʻi and Haurae leave imprints of separation behind them, but the two
rocks do not stop to construct ancestral shrines. The dramatic impact they
have on the landscape is cosmographic at a regional scale, not topogonic at a
lineage-specific scale. This vision of utopic primordiality is temporally as well
as spatially indeterminate; neither space nor time is punctuated or measured

---

ample, another written lineage narrative notes: "All right, [our lineage] with different lineages reproduced people for the area of land that starts at [place name] to [place name]."

10. Arosi do not use separate terms to distinguish between these genres. Both types of
narrative genre are termed *mamaani* (a story, a narrative, or a history).

by the establishment of fixed lineage landmarks or the succession of generations. In the second genre, Haurae's descendants occupy the land and settle
new villages. They transform the land by building ancestral shrines and forming tabu places. Time is cumulative. Unlike the names Haurae and Hauhuari'i,
which are never reassigned, names from the second part of the narrative are
recycled, and the name of a lineage ancestor is often given to a descendant. If
the same personal name is used more than once during the course of the narrative, each instance of use is numbered sequentially (No - 1, No - 2, etc.). In
short, the two genres in this lineage narrative conceptualize utopic and
topogonic primordiality as two distinct modalities of space, time, and agency.

This disjuncture between accounts of ultimate origins and accounts of a
lineage's transformative engagement with place was further highlighted for me
when my own investigations appeared to induce an anomalous synthesis between the two in one consultant's narrative. When I first interviewed a man
whom I will call Asimaho, he could only recount the topogonic movements
of his recent ancestors, but was unable to link his description of their activities to an account of his lineage's emergence on the island. In a subsequent interview, however, he spliced his discussion of the formation of shrines and
burial sites together with a story depicting the very beginning of his lineage.
Afterwards, Asimaho explained to me that, during the months between the
two interviews, his lineage ancestors had appeared in a dream to another
member of his lineage. In the dream the ancestors had taught his relative the
story about the absolute origin of their lineage and how it was tied to their recent history. Mediation between the two modes of primordiality required the
intervention of ancestral spirits, moved, in this case, by the promptings of the
ethnographer's line of questioning.

As already intimated, the two modes of primordiality are further legible in
two contrasting Arosi images of spatiality: one that maps space as a series of
static enclosed domains and one that constructs space as a system of localities
inter-linked by human mobility and ongoing action. Not unique to Arosi,
these two images of spatiality commonly coexist in societies throughout the
southeast Solomon Islands. On Malaita, Ross contrasts the ways in which
Baegu orient their daily activities around "landmarks and the known or recognized areas immediately surrounding them" (1973: 118) with their "general
tendency to think of space as broken into units enclosed by rectangular borders" (1973: 111). Guidieri (1972: 324; 1980: 64–67) similarly distinguishes
a tension between the plurality of Fataleka funerary sites and pathways, and
the ideally unchanging clan territories in which they are enclosed. In a more
general survey of "land models" on Malaita, Ulawa, and Makira, Cochrane
(1969: 340) notes that "usufructuary privileges were defined in terms of ...

centers or focal points—especially ancestral shrines to which individuals were ritually related or trees to which they were economically related." But these "focal definitions," Cochrane (1969: 340) continues, are also "combined with boundary definitions, such as streams and other unmistakable landmarks." While Arosi likewise conceptualize a lineage's land both as a set of connected focal points and as an enclosed area, it also appears to be the case that these two models correspond with the alternative descriptions of primordiality. On the one hand, it is when Arosi need to recount the topogonic actions of their ancestors that they tend to describe a multilocal network or string of focal points—shrines, burial grounds, village sites, specific trees, and their connecting paths—that collectively constitute the lineage's land. In these, often pragmatic, contexts of narration, natural boundaries recede in importance and ancestral focal points come to the fore. On the other hand, it is generally in abstract formulations or stylizations that Arosi depict the pre-existing, permanent boundaries that confer distinct ontological identities on proto-lineages in the utopic mode of primordiality. The former of these two perspectives is most salient. Many of the people I interviewed were well able to document the location and nature of their lineage's shrines, but were unable to trace the boundaries of their lineage's land.

It is significant moreover that, whereas some Solomon Islands societies appear to conflate these two models of spatiality, Arosi do not. Hviding has noted the practice of placing ancestral shrines to delineate or powerfully reinforce marine boundaries in Marovo Lagoon (Western Province). He reports that in Marovo "skulls were not placed on any given [coral islet], but usually on special islets in or near passages that constitute a group's traditional boundary" (1996: 252). In Arosi, however, I found no instance in which a shrine or ossuary was employed to index a boundary. The fact that Arosi can point to the island's pre-social physical geography to refer to the boundaries of a particular lineage's land, but do not use shrines and burial grounds to mark these boundaries, emphasizes the conceptual and practical disengagement of the two models of spatiality and their correlation with two distinct modes of primordiality among Arosi.[11]

---

11. The analytical constructs of utopic and topogonic primordiality are comparable in some respects to Eric Hirsch's (1995) constructs of "background potentiality" and "foreground actuality" in his theorization of landscape as process. For example, what I describe as situational shifts in consciousness from multifocal networks to boundaries in Arosi references to matrilineal territories could be analyzed as Arosi attempts "to deny process" by realizing "in the foreground what can only be a potentiality and for the most part in the background" (Hirsch 1995: 22–23). The parallelism between the two sets of constructs

Trunk and Branches

Represented in lineage narratives such as the one analyzed above, the second mode of primordiality comprises several simultaneous cosmogonic processes. Drawing on Arosi arboreal metaphors of trunk and branch, I suggest that these processes graph perpendicular axes of generative relationships that intersect at, bring into being, and come to depend on, lineage territories. The processes that anchor particular matrilineages in particular places through the transformation of utopic land into socialized lineage territories constitute a vertical axis fusing lineages with land. Concurrently, processes that forge productive and reproductive relations among diverse matrilineages in the land of one encompassing *auhenua* lineage constitute a horizontal axis entangling multiple humanized categories of being.[12] In this context, it is significant that Arosi distinguish between two ways of moving across the land. People who are not part of the *auhenua* lineage of a place (i.e., *sae boboi*) are said to drift or float (*sahe*) over the surface of the land and seem barely to make contact with the earth. A few consultants suggested that people who have come to a lineage's land from elsewhere merely "sit" on the land. By contrast, lineage forebears are said to have moved into new places and to have rooted the lineage firmly in the ground by establishing shrines, burial sites, and tabu places. Using what he identified as the Arosi "picture word" for this contrast, one man explained: "They become the *ahui*, the base or bottom of the tree. They are the most important part, where life comes from, the original part, the center part. This is the part that must touch the ground; all the others are the branches (*raaraa*)" (cf. J. Fox 1994, 1995, 1996).

In this section I explore the production of emplaced matrilineages—the vertical axis—and the production of social polities—the horizontal axis—with reference to three important nexuses between the two: funerary sites and their related practices, access to and control over nut-bearing trees, and nam-

---

breaks down, however, to the extent that Hirsch (1995: 22) identifies foreground with "everyday social life ('us the way we are')," i.e., history, and background with "potential social existence ('us the way we might be')," i.e., myth. As a model of an Arosi vision of mythic but dynamic processes of coming into being that blurs into ethnohistory and "everyday social life," topogonic primordiality collapses these criteria of distinction. Furthermore, I do not offer utopic and topogonic primordiality as universally generalizable elements of a framework for the cross-cultural study of landscape.

12. Although analyzing somewhat different aspects of 'Are'are land tenure, de Coppet (1985; cf. 1976; 1981: 177) similarly employs the image of vertical intersection with a surface plane.

ing patterns. This examination of the dual-axis Arosi cosmogony reveals that, for Arosi, the solid grounding of lineages in the land is indispensable to the formation of *auhenua* lineage identities, and that the existence of *auhenua* lineage identities is, in turn, regarded as the *sine qua non* for viable relations among lineages who must inevitably live together in land where only one among them can be *auhenua*. Once discerned, this dual-axis system of relationships begins to render the current situation of heterotopia in Arosi intelligible. Without the *auhenua* at the nexus of their polities, Arosi begin to experience their sociality as disordered and fear that land will fall vulnerable to usurpation by newcomers. As the consultant who explained the "picture word" *ahui* to describe the centrality of an *auhenua* matrilineage in its land put it: "Our land must have an *ahui* so that it will not be lost." It is precisely the absence of recognized connections between lineages and areas of coastal land that has returned the contemporary Arosi landscape to the practical equivalent of a utopic condition, a primordial state of chaotic vacuity. Struggling to achieve, or as they see it, to reinstate proper social order and the security of land, Arosi lineages compete to construct themselves as the true *auhenua* in order to provide a central point of reference and foundation for community with their neighbors in the land.

Informed by their autochthonous histories, Arosi understand the various formative interventions of their ancestors in the landscape as the means by which they rooted themselves as the *ahui* in their lands. The ancestors came into being as they came into the land, shaping it and being shaped in return into representatives of true matrilineages, each with an exclusively emplaced past. Because of the mutually constitutive relationship among a lineage, its dead, and its land, land that is as yet unmodified and has received no dead functions as a void or black hole that threatens to consume a lineage's identity (cf. Guidieri 1980: 62). Cochrane (1969: 340) also seems to have discerned that incursions into empty "virgin land" could not have been based on "the kinship system" because this land was, as yet, "not thought to be owned by anyone."[13] Utopic land must be claimed from this pre-social condition and made into humanized places. To humanize a space in this way is to become *auhenua* there.

According to lineage narratives, Arosi matrilineages took possession of vacuous and unmarked land primarily through the enshrinement of their de-

---

13. Cochrane's (1969: 340 n. 30) observations are based primarily on data that he collected in the Bauro bush (Makira) and in Fataleka (Malaita). See also Bathgate's (1985: 84) brief description of the way in which the Ndi-Nggai came to inhabit "unclaimed land" in West Guadalcanal.

ceased. Although Arosi do not describe the phenomenon in this way, it may be said that pre-Christian funerary practices gave birth to ancestors. These past acts created an ongoing legacy that unites ancestral and current practices as analogously topogonic. Thus, whether performing mortuary ceremonies, carefully placing the relics of the dead in the land, remembering and offering sacrifices to the spirits of the dead, observing tabus, respecting and referencing ancestral sites in daily life, or reusing ancestral names, generations of lineage members actively produce and reproduce relations with ancestral spirits in their land. At the same time that the original deposition of ancestral relics in the land molded and determined the character of the topography, the land in turn became the medium through which ancestral spirits came into being to interact with the living. The process of becoming solidly and permanently rooted in the land is inseparable from, and dependent on, this process of deploying the dead throughout the land. Land that is not inhabited by the spirits of the dead remains utopic, amorphous, and incapable of supporting an *auhenua* lineage identity.

Just as lineage forebears are imagined as the sources of *adaro* in the sense of ancestral spirits who inhabit the land, they are also imagined as the sources of *adaro* in the sense of personal names that initially and repeatedly serve to personalize areas of land as intimate to a lineage. Names and naming both originate in and perpetuate topogonic processes relative to the vertical axis of Arosi cosmology. Recall that new personal names are continually being innovated, and each name has the potential to be added to a lineage's list of names. This can occur, however, only when the first person known by the innovated name has died. Passing the name of the deceased on to another person differentiates this second person from other members of the lineage by mobilizing within him or her the specific constellation of relations formerly realized by the deceased. Furthermore, the name of the deceased associates the living person with the locale previously inhabited by his or her namesake. The reuse of the name, at the same time, contributes to the perpetuation of the deceased's distinct identity as an ancestral spirit who inhabits a particular area.

Similarly, by establishing villages, clearing gardening land, and planting or tending nut trees, lineage ancestors embedded themselves in and reconfigured previously utopic land. As they settled in new places, old villages were left to decay. As they cleared and planted new gardens, old gardens became covered by secondary growth. But despite these vicissitudes, like the lineage's shrines, these places are amenable to reference as vestiges of past emplacement with lasting consequences. They form part of the ongoing topogonic process that fuses a lineage with its land. Thus, a lineage's knowledgeable people can catalogue the villages in which their ancestors lived, remember the names of the nut trees they harvested, and occasionally mention the areas in which they made their gardens.

The process of establishing this essential and abiding vertical connection between a lineage and its land may be compared to lineage exogamy. Both are necessary for the production of true human beings. As the lineage multiplies and occupies the land, it objectifies itself in the lineage territory that it creates. If marriage with other categories of being produces an internally differentiated primordial essence embedded in a fully human matrilineage, the wedding of a lineage to its land produces a tandem extension of that essence embedded in the land as differentiated ancestral powers.[14] The vertical axis of Arosi cosmology is the locus of a multifaceted process of coming into being. Along this axis, the making and re-making of matrilineal people, places, and powers cooperate to embed *auhenua* lineages in their land.

At the same time, a variety of physical and social phenomena represent the nexus between these vertical processes of cosmogony and concomitant horizontal processes of cosmogony. Beyond exogamy itself, among the many objects and practices that may be understood as points of intersection between these axes, the most salient are the burial sites established by the lineage pioneers, the old nut trees carefully tended on lineage land, and the distribution of lineage-controlled personal names. An *auhenua* lineage's relationships of cooperation with members of other lineages finds clear expression in the latter's access to, and in some cases, control over the *hera*, nut trees, and names that anchor the *auhenua* in their land. Yet even as these three phenomena represent the binding together of different lineages in an aggregate social cosmos, they also map a relationship of hierarchical encompassment founded on the theoretical precedence of the *auhenua* in their lands.

The central foci of the vertical connection between a lineage and its land—the burial sites established by lineage pioneers—can also serve as the central nodes of horizontal connections between an *auhenua* lineage and members of other lineages who live on their land. In ways that probably idealize the extent

---

14. With respect to 'Are'are, de Coppet (1995: 248–256; cf. Breton 1999: 573–574; Naitoro 1993: 43) observes the symmetry between marriage and reproduction, on the one hand, and funerary practices and the production of ancestors, on the other. In Arosi, however, this symmetry is formal and does not entail the various transformations of "sociocosmic relations" that de Coppet discovers in 'Are'are cosmos and society. For structural parallels between the generation of living descendants and the production of new ancestors in other Solomon Islands contexts, see also Keesing 1982a: 63, 68–74; Köngäs Maranda 1974; Maranda 2001; Monnerie 1996: 91–174; 1998: 99–101. A few brief comments that Fox (1924: 30, 178, 235) made might be read to suggest that he also observed this parallel on Makira.

to which relations between *auhenua* and *sae boboi* were formerly transparent and uncontested, my consultants explained that, in the pre-Christian past, the bones of deceased people who were not members of the lineage of the land—including in-marrying women, the children of lineage men, and people whom the lineage had settled in the land—could be placed in the lineage's burial sites. Those wishing to place the bones of such people in the lineage's burial grounds were supposed first to ask permission from the *auhenua* and give them strung shell valuables in return.

Similarly, according to my consultants, the social hierarchy between *auhenua* and non-*auhenua* in a given territory was mapped by the spatial arrangement of round or oblong stones placed in the burial sites of the *auhenua*. Each lineage was associated with a particular type of stone. A stone of the type identified with the lineage of the land was placed at the center of the *hera*. This central stone indicated to which lineage the *hera* and the surrounding land belonged. When the bones of members of other lineages were placed in the *hera*, the stone types identified with each of their lineages were also placed in the *hera*, but these stones were set around the periphery of the site. The *hera* remained identified with the lineage whose stone was at its center, because "one *hera* cannot be divided [among different lineages]." Through their concentric design, burial grounds tangibly represented the various social groups that the *auhenua* lineage succeeded in drawing into and encompassing within its orbit.

In some lineage territories, burial sites and shrines established separately by the non-*auhenua* further marked the horizontal axis of cosmogonic relations among lineages. Some people, referring to what they regard as their own lineage's land, stated that members of no other lineage had made separate *hera* on their land; the bones of the non-*auhenua* were simply placed in the burial sites of the *auhenua* lineage. A few people even suggested to me that the non-*auhenua* could not give offerings to their own lineage's spirit because they were living on another lineage's land. But, an equal number of consultants reported that their lineage had allowed non-lineage residents on their land to establish their own *hera* and shrines. For example, one elderly man explained: "People who are not part of the lineage of the land can pray and make burned offerings [to their ancestral spirits] in the area in which they live even though they are not *auhenua* there. They show respect to their own ancestors' bones; they also have shrines and spirit-sharks." Another man clarified that, "other lineages come and live here, so they also have shrines and burial grounds here. Yet, they have burial grounds where they came from too; that is their land."

Although the non-*auhenua* in these cases may have been permitted to build their own shrines and make their own burial sites on another lineage's land, the *auhenua* lineage of that land encompassed them. "The newcomers stay there on account of the people who are *auhenua*." The *auhenua* lineage welcomed and settled the newcomers on their land, and the latter would "seek the protection of the *auhenua*" against murderers and local spirits that might injure them. The encompassment of outsiders by the *auhenua* is said to be based on the principle of spatial and temporal precedence (cf. Burt 1994b; J. Fox 1994, 1995). This principle was first drawn to my attention by a friend who, during our earliest conversations, frequently referred to the *auhenua* in English as the "number ones" and the putatively later arriving *sae boboi* as the "number twos."

The Arosi principle of *auhenua* precedence elides the fact that, from an analytical perspective, a lineage that claims to be the "first" to have inhabited an expanse of land must have brought representatives of other lineages with them; they must also have encountered other marriageable people in the land. If the lineage had neither brought marriageable people to the utopic land nor found them there in the first place, it would have been in danger of reverting to the self-contained isolation of a proto-lineage. It is not only the characterless nature of utopic land that threatens to consume a lineage's identity; the lack of marriageable people also poses a threat to lineage viability. Implicit acknowledgment of this conundrum is found in lineage narratives that describe a lineage's apical ancestress marrying a representative of an unidentified category of people who already inhabit the land. In other words, inherent in the very narratives that Arosi use to establish one lineage's precedence in the land is a representation—necessarily unexamined by lineage members—of the premise that no lineage could, on its own, be first.

Nevertheless, in accordance with the prerogatives said by Arosi to be conferred by precedence, the *auhenua* reputedly treated the non-*auhenua* as though they were their own children and designated land that could be used by the newcomers to build houses and make gardens. The non-*auhenua* lived under the "ruling shadow" of the *auhenua* and under the discipline of the ancestral *auhenua* spirits in the land. As Hauni of 'Ubuna village explained to me: "They all intermarry, but in the teaching they know that this place is that of the *auhenua* lineage." Therefore, even if there were representatives of a number of different lineages living in a territory, each with different burial sites and shrines, the *auhenua* lineage "held them together" in their land.

In addition to burial and enshrinement in the land, the newcomers might also be given access to some of the established nut trees that members of the *auhenua* lineage tended. Over time, however, the newcomers and their descendants would plant new nut trees and take care of trees that took root naturally in their garden areas. If certain non-*auhenua* especially helped the *auhenua* to prepare for feasts or assisted them in warfare, the *auhenua* might give sole access to a grove of nut trees to these people. Other nut trees might be given in exchange for strung shell valuables. A lineage's land would accordingly contain trees belonging to outsiders as well as to the *auhenua*. Because children gain access to nut trees through both their mothers and their fathers, the children of any union between the *auhenua* and those resident among them would have access to the trees at which their parents and grandparents gathered nuts. Whether or not such children were members of the *auhenua* lineage, in tracing out their access to various nut trees, they mapped out the extent of their bilateral kindreds. Many people recounted to me that when they were young their parents took them to gather nuts at seven or eight different groves of trees. At each site they encountered a different constellation of their relatives. From the perspective of each of my consultants, the people he or she met at a grove of nut trees constituted a subset of all the people with whom he or she was "entangled" in blood. Consequently, the *auhenua* lineage's nut trees, like its burial grounds, were loci of its relationships with people of other lineages. But like the burial grounds, only certain people— usually members of the *auhenua* lineage—would have the power to regulate access to these trees.

More than simply giving people who are not *auhenua* access to burial sites and to nut trees, Arosi naming practices ensure that the children of lineage males will even control some of these nexuses of relationship. As we have seen, a lineage has an exclusive set of personal names, and each of these names bestows on its bearer special authority over a portion of the lineage's land and access to certain nut trees. These names are not only given to members of the lineage, they are also given to people who are related to lineage members through blood. Sometimes a lineage male, acting in accord with other members of his lineage, will give one of his lineage's personal names to one of his children. When a married woman has children, the right to name them alternates between people in her own bilateral kindred and people in her husband's kindred. People of the father's kindred usually name the first-born child in return for having paid the woman's bride-price.[15] This child is known as the "child who kills the valuables" (*gare mae ni ha'a*).[16] After the father's side

---

15. In the few cases in which no bride-price is paid, the woman's "side" can name all of her children. The payment of bride-price entitles the man to take his bride to his place of residence. Thus, if a man does not pay bride-price, the couple will usually remain at the woman's place of residence.

16. The first-born will be the head of the sibling set that forms "one group." As the eldest sibling matures, he or she will start to keep track of the long-standing exchange rela-

has named the first-born, the second-born will generally be named by the mother's side, the third-born by the father's, and so on. Any of the names that are given to the children from either the mother's or the father's side can be lineage personal names. For example, members of the father's lineage who contributed a large part of his bride-price payment may choose to give one of their lineage's personal names to one of his children.

The act of naming an infant for a lineage ancestor enables those who gave the name to take the child to live with them in the area where the child's namesake formerly lived. But even if the child does not reside permanently at this place, he or she will frequently visit his or her namesake's place. When grown, the child will oversee the area formerly looked after by his or her namesake. If, through such naming processes, a lineage name is given out to a non-lineage child, it may be retrieved by bestowing it on a lineage child in a subsequent generation. When this occurs the name is said to have been "brought back" (*waa aho'i*) to the lineage with which it originated. Thus, through the distribution of lineage personal names among blood relations, people who are not members of the lineage on whose land they live can nevertheless be empowered to make decisions about access to particular trees and residence sites in the land of their host lineage.

Heterotopia Past and Present

Some of my Arosi consultants seemed to acknowledge that the forms of social entanglement (*haikawikawi* or *haia'ia'i*) between an *auhenua* host lineage as the "trunk" and its guests from other lineages as the "branches" of a social polity may have, in some instances, enabled the lineage of a guest to take over as the new *auhenua* if a host lineage became extinct or appeared to have abandoned its land. Although the details of such past successions are difficult to recover, they are not unheard of. In one case, the last woman of an *auhenua* lineage was "purchased to lengthen" another co-resident lineage that subsequently succeeded her birth-lineage as the *auhenua*. A person regarded within his lineage as knowledgeable about custom described a second case to me. He simply stated that two other lineages, each in its own turn, had previously been *auhenua* in the land, but because the women of these lineages were unable to produce children for the land, his own lineage, which was also living

---

tions in which the sibling set is collectively enmeshed, organize the bride-price payments for younger brothers, speak and act on behalf of the sibling set, mediate their access to their relatives' nut trees, look after the group as a whole, and make sure their affairs are straightened out.

in this area had—apparently by default—become the *auhenua* lineage. In a third case, an elderly couple, who represented the remnant of an *auhenua* lineage, invited a man of another lineage to live with them. When the man and another member of his lineage gave the couple two strung shell valuables, his lineage became the *auhenua* of the land.

Such accounts of land transfers from one lineage to another exist in tension with the simultaneously held conviction that, once a matrilineage has become anchored in its land, this relationship is fundamentally unalterable. Despite the clearly dynamic nature of lineage-land formation as represented in lineage narratives, when Arosi speak in general terms about the nature of any lineage's relationship to its land, they assert that this connection is an unchanging state of being. I was told, for example, that "the name of a lineage cannot be lost from its land" even if lineage members have not inhabited the territory for two hundred years or more. If a territory has been unoccupied for many generations, the matrilineal descendants of those who once inhabited the land may still return and tell how the area was—and continues to be—their lineage's land. One woman who had made herself a specialist in the history of her lineage recounted to me that, after an absence of four generations, her lineage was welcomed back and acknowledged to be the lineage of the land by the other people who were living there. "Suppose we do not accept them back [as the *auhenua* lineage of the land]," one man explained to me, "then we would not be following our *kastom*." In any case, he continued, the ancestral spirits of the lineage, who still inhabit the land, would recognize the returning people as part of their lineage. Such formulations indicate that Arosi see the essential identity of a territorial landscape as immutable once it has been set by a lineage, regardless of whether or not living representatives of that lineage reside on the land. Some Arosi even proposed that if a lineage becomes extinct, or if its members lose the narrative of their connection to their territory (*mosu*, literally, to break, as of a string or rope), no other lineage would be able to form itself over that land. People who are not members of the lineage of the land could only look after the land of an absent or defunct lineage. Or, to paraphrase another man, if a lineage loses its connection to the land, then that land is lost; the land falls into desuetude as a living lineage territory. The connection achieved between a lineage and its land in the topogonic mode of primordiality is regarded as so firm and so vital that the demise of the lineage suspends its land in a spatiotemporal limbo.[17]

---

17. Apparently analogous images of territorial limbo have been documented elsewhere in Oceania. For example, Ravuvu (1983: 76; cf. Bonnemaison 1994: 166, 334 n. 18) records that in Fiji, "[a] land without people is likened to a person without soul." Without the peo-

Yet wherever land is seen to be empty of an *auhenua* matrilineage, Arosi cosmic and social order abhors such a vacuum and seeks to fill it (cf. Guidieri 1980: 57–58). Proper inter-lineage sociality, from an Arosi point of view, cannot form up and be managed without the orienting center of gravity that an *auhenua* lineage provides, and land without an *auhenua* lineage lies subject to takeover and dispute. Thus, at any given place, someone has to be *auhenua* in order for Arosi to achieve satisfactory cosmos and society there. There is consequently an ongoing "struggle against indeterminacy" (Guidieri 1980: 57). To reiterate how one consultant captured the twin imperatives to ground matrilineal identities in territory and to hold onto territories by means of matrilineal identities: "Our land must have an *ahui* (trunk) so that it will not be lost." Similarly, one woman confided to me that she would be afraid to leave her land empty (*pwaranga*), lest strangers attempt to colonize it for a new polity based around their lineage instead of hers. Land of ambiguous matrilineal tenancy is unstable and conducive to social chaos; it necessarily becomes a stimulus to projects of topogonic self-emplacement that are, ironically, as potentially threatening as they are remedial to social order.

It stands to reason therefore, although no data exist to prove such a hypothesis, that in the precolonial past as well as in the present, events such as lineage decline, extinction, and absence due to mobility—or even the appearance of these situations—gave rise to heterotopic constructions of bush as well as coast wherever land could be construed as free of legitimate *auhenua* occupants. Despite Arosi claims that the ancestral spirits of a lineage can never be eradicated from its land and that another lineage will never be able to reform this land, it appears likely that those who had once been *sae boboi* could subtly appropriate the land and ancestral sites of their former *auhenua* hosts. Arosi descriptions of such past transitions negotiate the issue of residual ancestral powers in the land differently. Some people seem to suggest that one lineage could simply inherit from another in its own right without problems. Others suggest that transformative continuity between the two lineages was achieved and recognized by the ancestral powers through processes of adoption or the payment of shell valuables. But there was probably always room for controversy. Those who disputed the *auhenua* status of any lineage or wanted to claim such status for themselves could argue that such successor lineages were only guarding the land in lieu of the true *auhenua* who might yet return.

---

ple, he continues, "[l]and becomes lifeless and useless." To form a contrasting pair with the concept of "topogenesis" implicit in James Fox's (1997) coinage of "topogeny" to describe narratives of place generation, James Weiner (2001: 234) has coined the term "topothanatia" to describe "the death, withdrawal, effacement, or covering over of places."

The current situation of universal heterotopia on Arosi coastal land is thus, I suggest, the result of indigenous Arosi socio-spatial dynamics intensified and proliferated by the relatively sudden and large-scale production of socially ambiguous land in the recent colonial past. Rather than placing coastal land in an indefinite and intolerable limbo, however, the alleged demise of the true coastal *auhenua* has, in fact, functioned to reinstate a virtual utopic primordiality of virgin land ready to be shaped and socialized by virtual proto-lineages. Reclaiming and reprising the deeds of their ancestors, a multiplicity of Arosi lineages are strategically—though without apparent cynicism—innovating neo-cosmogonic activities along the vertical axis in sincere efforts to re-order and stabilize the ongoing cosmogonic activities along the horizontal axis that continue to form the everyday pursuits of contemporary Arosi people. But as the following chapter explores, these efforts at socio-spatial renovation are leading unintentionally to a socially divisive retreat from the latter in favor of the former.

CHAPTER 7

PRESENT PRIMORDIALITIES

Ethnographers and theorists of colonial contexts have observed that, for colonizers and colonized alike, the colonial encounter and its aftermath can precipitate a perceived return to an imagined primordial condition. Thus, with reference to colonial projects comparable to District Officer F. M. Campbell's reorganization of Makira in the early twentieth century, John Noyes observes that European colonists mythologized colonial spaces as empty, unbroken expanses of chaotic wasteland into which they brought rationalizing order (1992: 6, 136; cf. Sack 1980, 1986; Williams 1986: especially Chapters 7–9). But if the indigenous spatial order of the colonized appeared to the colonizer as a chaotic wilderness to be tamed, Rhys Jones's (1985: 207) representation of the reaction of an Australian Aborigine from Arnhem Land to the city of Canberra illustrates how the spatial order constructed by the colonizer can appear to the colonized as a destructive regression to chaotic vacuity. To the eyes of Frank Gurrmanamana,

> Here was a land empty of religious affiliation; there were no wells, no names of the totemic ancestors, no immutable links between land, people and the rest of the natural and supernatural worlds. Here was just a vast *tabula rasa*, cauterised of meaning ... in his own words "this country bin lose 'im Dreaming." ... This land and its people therefore were analogous to the state of all the world once in some time before the Dreaming, before the great totemic Ancestral Beings strode across it, naming the places and giving it meaning. Viewed from this perspective, the Canberra of the geometric streets, and the paddocks of the six-wire fences were places not of domesticated order, but rather a wilderness of primordial chaos.

Also interpreting the point of view of the colonized, Geoffrey White suggests that the inhabitants of Santa Isabel (Solomon Islands) remember early Christian missionaries and their first converts as analogous to legendary ancestral figures and experience the colonial transformation of their moral and social order as comparable to "the primordial events commonly depicted in creation mythology" (1991: 136; cf. Errington and Gewertz 1994; Turner 1988; Young 1997). Capturing a different aspect of the recreative potential of return to primordiality, Joël Bonnemaison characterizes "pagan resistance" to colonialism and the John Frum movement on Tanna (Vanuatu) as sharing nostalgia for a mythic egalitarian "paradise lost" (1994; cf. Clark 1997: 79; Lattas 1998). Building on this evidence for an imaginative link between the experience of colonialism and conceptualizations of primordiality, I provide in this chapter detailed case studies of how the colonial convergence between British and Arosi spatializations of primordial chaos has created a postcolonial condition in which Arosi are elaborating and significantly revaluing received models of socio-cosmic order production in response to a virtual resurgence of utopic indeterminacy (cf. Scott 2005a).

Mindful of the recent colonial search for "waste land" on which to impose European schemes of order, Arosi continue to see in formerly depopulated, socially reorganized, and spiritually destabilized coastal land an approximate return to the original condition I have analyzed as utopic primordiality—a situation that is eliciting a variety of neo-topogonic responses with hetero-topic outcomes. The normal processes of Arosi poly-genesis are inherently on-going and impossible to achieve definitively. The logic of these continuous processes has emerged with particular clarity, however, as colonial interventions have produced a socially and morally depleted landscape in which the potential for lineages to become *auhenua* in supposedly empty places has received added stimulus and opportunity. During the past century and a half, land in Arosi has fallen into social limbo at a rate and on a physical scale that is likely to be unprecedented. Even as the coastal *auhenua* were decimated by diseases and replaced with dislocated bush lineages, missionaries and their converts were beginning to counterbalance, nullify, or simply neglect the ancestral powers said to inhabit the coastal land. Consequently, although only a few Arosi would concur with Pierre Maranda's (2001: 114) Lau Lagoon consultants in northeast Malaita that the demise of pre-Christian religious practices has left coastal places "empty" of ancestral powers, many are now prone to question whether such spirits—if they still exist—continue to have power over the living. Such uncertainty is, for all social intents and purposes, tantamount to indeterminacy. Along with these historical changes, moreover, the ethic of the *auhenua*, which discourages overt claims to *auhenua* status, is contributing to the construction of the coast as effectively utopic by compelling villagers to give outward consent to the proposition that coastal land is unencumbered by customary landholders. At the same time, however, Arosi anxiety that their current disposition in a functionally, if not literally, empty landscape is superficial and incoherent is augmented by fears that such open, imperfectly socialized land may be taken by outsiders. Experiencing this chaos of vacuity as both an obstacle and an increased incentive to the reproduction of their emplaced identities, representatives of the diverse Arosi matrilineages are developing novel variations on the topogonic activities of ancestral pioneers and putting them into practice as the means to anchor their lineages in otherwise lifeless, meaningless, and potentially alienable land.

Arosi responses to the utopic present may be divided into two broad categories. First, while openly assenting to the general opinion that the coastal *auhenua* are extinct, Arosi lineages may secretly construct themselves as the true and only *auhenua*. A very few people have gone so far as to build new "ancestral" shrines in the coastal land in accordance with pre-Christian topogonic practice. For the majority of Arosi, however, the process of becoming *auhenua* on the coast consists in the narrative appropriation of existing burial sites and shrines into their autochthonous histories and the withdrawal of their lineage personal names from circulation outside their lineages. Second, some people's responses to the postcolonial revivification of utopic primordiality explicitly express their dissatisfaction with this first set of options, which they view as contributing to an unstable, uncertain, and conflict-ridden situation. As an alternative to hidden strategies of self-construction as *auhenua*, several relatively wealthy Arosi have purchased land in sparsely populated areas elsewhere on the island. In so doing, these people have sought expressly to liberate areas of land from all vestiges of previous occupants—both living and dead—thereby eliminating the possibility of future claims on the part of any returning *auhenua*. By using cash to make land clearly and absolutely utopic, these innovators are effectively founding new lineages whose identities will come to be formed in that land. At the same time, others propose what they hope will provide a more general solution to the current situation. Starting from the consensus that there are no coastal *auhenua*, the proponents of this solution advocate a systematic shift to a father to son mode of land inheritance that would, they argue, reflect and codify the de facto residence and landholding patterns already in practice. Responding to a distinctively Arosi vision of chaos, all of these people are, in their diverse ways, striving to establish the necessary conditions for a new and viable socio-spatial order.

Producing a Heterotopic Landscape

For the most part, the process of becoming *auhenua* along the coast today is an invisible one, impinging only on each matrilineage's unique narrative construction of the landscape without altering the configuration of the land or the disposition of objects within it. I learned, nevertheless, of a few reports of open conflict involving the construction of new "ancestral" sites and the physical manipulation of existing shrines. Performed covertly in anticipation of possible court hearings, this type of topogonic activity is particularly difficult to document. The new structures need to be built in secret so that other people will be convinced that the sites are evidence of a long-term ancestral presence in the land.[1] In recent decades, the relatively portable shark stones associated with *birubiru* appear to have been especially susceptible to relocation, as all the incidents about which I learned involved these small carved rock forms. In fact, without ever pursuing the matter in court, people occasionally complained to me that they could have pointed to ample evidence of their lineage's ancient presence in a particular area if interloping pretenders had not absconded with these elements of their ancestral shrines.

The most notorious case of shrine creation occurred approximately thirty years ago. I first learned about this case while a friend and I were walking from Tawatana to a neighboring village to visit Bwaaniwai, an elderly party to the incident.[2] My traveling companion told me that the supposed shrine builder, whom I will call Mae, stole a shark stone from an old shrine near the village that was our destination. Allegedly, Mae took the stone to use as the centerpiece of a *birubiru* he was secretly constructing about nine kilometers away from Bwaaniwai's village. When he had completed his *birubiru*, Mae argued in local court that it was an old shrine that proved his ancestors had formerly lived in the land he was claiming. My friend expressed the generally held opinion that Mae had won the dispute thanks to the counterfeit *birubiru* he had made. Later, after Mae had died, another person who claimed to know where Mae had acquired the shark stone told Bwaaniwai to take the stone back to where it originally belonged. When I interviewed Bwaaniwai, he confirmed the details of my friend's account of Mae's theft and described how he himself had retrieved the shark stone. He allowed me to photograph the stone and told me some of the traditions associated with it. He explained that when the last person who had worked the shrine had died, the spirit-shark had gone wild and had "just swum away." Some months following my conversation with Bwaaniwai, yet a third person, who lived near to Bwaaniwai's village, gave me the same basic account of the theft of the shark stone. But this man asserted that, although Bwaaniwai currently had the stone in his custody, it did not belong to Bwaaniwai's lineage. He went on to give me a detailed narrative account of his own lineage, the shark stone, and the spirit-shark. Advising me

---

1. See Guidieri (1980: 63–64) for a brief discussion of the interrelationship among relic theft or "foundational appropriation," secrecy, and silence in Fataleka (Malaita).

2. I have changed all Arosi personal names in this account.

that several of the people who had recently manipulated or kept custody of the stone had dreamed that they were the victims of shark attacks, this man wryly noted: "If I worked this *birubiru*, all these people would truly have been eaten by the shark."

Other examples, although sparse in detail, run along similar lines. One young man stated his belief that, like Mae, one of his fellow villagers had moved a long white shark stone from a neighboring village and surreptitiously relocated it to a disputed area of land. My consultant in this case, who was himself a party to the dispute, suggested that the man had sought to fabricate a false shrine. At the time of our conversation, this old dispute had not been settled, leaving the alleged stone-tampering as a continued annoyance on this man's mind. This lack of resolution is typical of such accusations, which tend to remain at the level of grumbled grievances in the absence of incontrovertible proof. A middle-aged woman (whom I will call Wari), who claimed to have been the victim of shrine theft, went so far as to characterize the present state of tensions surrounding land claims to a perpetual, if undeclared, state of war. On hearing her assert that unknown pillagers had carried off her lineage's shark stones, I asked: "Can people just steal these shark stones and not suffer bad consequences?" Wari answered: "They don't live well or long because of it. But you know war; they want to win."

All of these cases illustrate the ambiguity surrounding local interpretations of pre-Christian shrines. Early in my research, Casper Kaukeni offered the opinion that, in pre-Christian times, people did not lay claim to shrines belonging to other lineages because they feared that such an action might provoke a spirit-shark attack. But now, he said, because Christians have chased the spirits away, people are no longer afraid to claim other lineages' shrines. But when Peter Itamwaeraha, who was listening to these observations, suggested that the situation was really much more complex than Casper's characterization had allowed, Casper was quick to agree that people remain nervous about going near to another lineage's shrines. Accordingly, when the subject of Mae's alleged shrine pilfering came up in another conversation among a group of men not directly involved in that conflict, Harry 'Abu wondered aloud why Mae had not instantly been attacked by the spirits when he stole the shark stone. John Selwyn Toraai responded by pointing out: "He *is* dead. The shark stone killed him." Episodes of shark stone theft and the debates they trigger indicate that, while some people may have become emboldened to interfere with other lineages' shrines—perhaps owing to faith in the power of the Christian God to displace or protect against the power of spirits—still others insist that such trespassers against the relics of the ancestors eventually suffer the consequences of their temerity.

Although many Arosi, like Casper, state that acts of tampering with other people's shrines are purely a product of the Christian period, Wari's equation of these activities with warfare signals that they may represent a measure of continuity with past Arosi martial tactics. Fox (1924: 286) provides evidence that the seizure of shark stones was, in fact, an element of pre-Christian Arosi warfare: "In the bush near 'Ado'ai'o'o I saw a *hau ni ba'ewa* [shark stone], which had been captured in a fighting expedition from a village near Waimarai [*sic*, read Waimarae]. It was a long white stone about 2 feet 6 inches in length and closely resembling a shark in shape. It could still be used to work magic by pointing it towards an enemy's village, which would cause him to fall when [climbing a tree for] nutting." Like the misappropriation of shark stones today, the practice of shark stone capture in the past appears to have been an attempt to undermine an enemy lineage's connection to its land while, at the same time, enabling the perpetrator lineage to dominate and employ foreign spirit powers to its own advantage in its own land. If being Christian has made it easier for Arosi to alter ancestral sites or to explain why such violations are not immediately punished, Christian faith alone cannot account for the possibility of shark stone theft in contemporary Arosi. Rather, a diversity of Christian outlooks has produced a climate of skepticism mixed with wary deference toward the ancestors that serves to invigorate the neo-topogonic possibilities inherent in the dynamic nature of Arosi poly-genetic cosmogony.

More typical than the physical manipulation and creation of new shrines is the intangible process of incorporating pre-existing shrines into lineage narratives. This subtle narrative reformation of ancestral sites was most evident to me when representatives of two or even three lineages would tell me their genealogical histories, each describing what, for me, were the same shark stones, shrines, and ossuaries. Lineage representatives recounted how these sites were made by their own ancestors whose spirits continue to reside in their vicinity. These different narratives, moreover, placed the contested sites within different multilocal systems that gave each site a distinct identity. Sometimes, based on partial knowledge of the narrative of a lineage they regard as inter-lopers, consultants would make a special point of alerting me that the other lineage in question was "telling lies" about particular ancestral sites. Although such allegations were common, no one with whom I worked acknowledged that his or her lineage might likewise be engaged in the discursive co-opting of another lineage's ancestral sites. Instead, all voiced a common concern not to broadcast their lineage narratives for fear that elements of their accounts might be used against them in this way. "We don't write the history of our lineage because of a little habit of the people who have come here (*sae boboi*)," one woman informed me. "In our *kastom* it is all right for anyone to come into your house and rest there. But if they saw our written *kastom* they'd take it away and teach themselves [about our lineage and incorporate elements of our history into their account]. This is theft, theft of the history of another lineage. So if you are true, you don't write your history." Despite the palpable air of intrigue and conspiracy surrounding these discursive strategies, those who pursue them appear to do so with a sincere conviction that they are the true *auhenua* and that general acceptance of this fact would, if other lineages only recognized it, be socially, materially, and even spiritually beneficial to all (cf. Scott 2005b).

One of the clearest examples of the subtle narrative reformation of ancestral sites and the concomitant production of a heterotopic landscape occurs in an area of land that stretches along the Arosi coast for about seven kilometers and extends up into the bush for about eight kilometers. Three lineages are independently and inconspicuously constructing themselves in this land in irreconcilable ways. Their three accounts all overlap on the ground. Each narrative describes certain specific shrines that are also featured in the other two narratives, but contextualizes these contested shrines within different larger networks of shrines. At the same time, each narrative populates the contested shrines with different spirit-sharks and associates them with the deeds of different ancestral figures (see Figure 7.1).

Lineage A has a primary *birubiru*, Eta, which is located on the slopes above the site of an old littoral village.[3] Although not in the physical center of the lineage's territory, Eta is a symbolic center for Lineage A because it marks the birthplace of the lineage's mythical apical ancestress. "Our lineage came from Eta," a member of Lineage A instructed me. In addition to this central shrine, Lineage A also lays claim to a small constellation of shrines connected to one another through the cult of a particular spirit-shark named Misu. According to traditions maintained by Lineage A, an ancestor named Ramo used to offer sacrifice to Misu and another spirit-shark called Uhi at a coastal *birubiru* called Rua. Rua is located near a small promontory in the eastern part of the lineage's land. Representatives of Lineage A told me that the lineage had other *birubiru* strung along the coast to the west of Rua, but they did not give me any details about these shrines. They did, however, identify two bush shrines as falling within their orbit. Ascending into the bush above Eta, one first en-

---

3. In the paragraphs that follow I have withheld the names of the lineages, used Arosi numbers to refer to the various shrines, and changed the personal names of the people and spirit-sharks in the three accounts. At points, my description is necessarily imprecise so as to render these three lineage narratives less recognizable to Arosi readers. I do not claim to have complete knowledge of each lineage's network of ancestral sites; consequently, there may be additional points of intersection not represented here.

counters the shrine called Oru where a shark stone and a resident snake are both said to be images of the same spirit-shark, Misu, to whom Ramo sacrificed on the coast. Still further up in the interior of the island beyond Oru lies the shrine known as Hai.

An elderly man knowledgeable about Lineage B's narrative told me that the symbolic center of his lineage's territory was Rua, the shrine located near the small finger of land jutting into the sea at the eastern end of Lineage A's supposed territory. "Rua," he explained to me, "is the central *birubiru* and [our other shrines were] spread out from there." Adjacent to Rua *birubiru* there is a place where two women "fed" the spirit-sharks in the pre-Christian period. This consultant told me that at Rua shrine the "leading" spirit-shark is called Bareʻo. He only mentioned Misu—Lineage A's leading spirit-shark—when I pushed him for more details. Misu was, he said, just one of several lesser

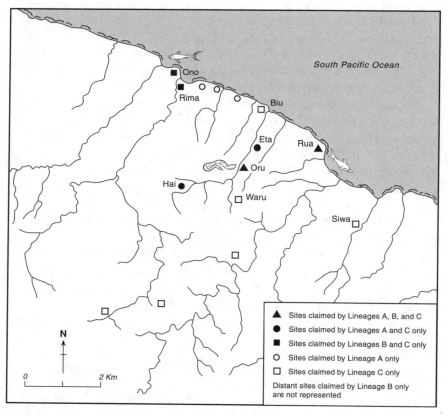

Figure 7.1. Schematic representation of overlapping matrilineal perspectives on an area of land.

sharks at Rua. For Lineage B, Bareʻo is also the head spirit-shark at Oru *biru-biru* in the bush. This man also named three *birubiru* that out-marrying members of Lineage B had been permitted to establish on the land of other lineages in east Arosi, Bauro, and Ugi. Each of these shrines had a different head spirit-shark, and taken together with Oru, formed a network of satellite shrines around Rua. Tied in to this constellation is another *birubiru* to the west situated on a similar coastal outcropping of land. I learned about the western part of Lineage B's territory from a younger female member of the lineage who told me that two different spirit-sharks dwell there at the shrine called Ono. One of the spirit-sharks is distinct in that it has a hybrid animal form. Additionally, at a village very near to Ono, there is a *hera* called Rima that Lineage B regards as one of its ancestral burial grounds.

Lineage C, like Lineage A, began in the area of the Eta shrine. For Lineage C, this area is associated with a man called Saemwane. This lineage ancestor transported shark stones out from this nucleus to establish other shrines down the coast to the west and then up into the bush. The lineage offered sacrifice to one spirit-shark—Misu—at each of these sites. Saemwane first went along the coast placing stones at Biu where Uraowari lived and at Rima where a brother and sister lived together. Saemwane also carried shark stones up into the bush starting from Eta and moving progressively up into the bush to establish shrines at Oru, Waru, Hai, and three additional sites. At all of these shrines, members of Lineage C offered uncooked pig and food to Misu. The lineage gave burned sacrificial offerings to Misu at the Ono shrine in the west of the territory and at the Siwa shrine near the eastern extent of the land. Like Lineages A and B, Lineage C claims the Rua *birubiru*. A recognized Lineage C authority told me that two male ancestors, Memeapu and Ria, looked after the offerings to Misu at that site.

Because each lineage uses different rivers to demarcate the eastern and western boundaries of its land, the three lineage territories are not absolutely congruent. Nevertheless, the three lineages independently construct their overlapping identities over the same core terrain. The main nodes of intersection among the three accounts are Rua *birubiru* on the coast and the Oru shrine in the bush. Each of the lineages claims the spirit-shark Misu as a power uniquely associated with its lineage either as its only spirit-shark (Lineage C), or as one among a distinctive group of related sharks (Lineages A and B). Four additional sites are contested by two out of the three lineages. Lineages A and C both refer to the Eta shrine as the starting point for the dispersal of their lineages, and also claim Hai shrine. Equally invested in these two focal points, Lineages A and C nevertheless situate them in very different multilocal networks. In contrast to Lineage A, which has no shrines further away from the coast than Hai shrine, Lineage C extends its territory to three more shrines higher in the bush beyond Hai. Situating Ono shrine within their different lineage narratives, and stating that different spirit-sharks dwell at the site, Lineages B and C both consider the shrine to be a place where their lineage ancestors offered burned sacrifices to their sharks. Representatives of Lineages B and C also told me that Rima was an important ancestral site.

In this particular case, all of the lineages concerned additionally assume the same lineage name and identity, and each regards the other two lineages as mere upstart impostors. When I interviewed them, representatives of each lineage would, to a greater or lesser extent, seek to undermine the other lineages' accounts. Typically they would state that the other lineages had really come from elsewhere and ought to be known by lineage names other than the one they were claiming; that the interlopers had stolen elements of their shrines; or that "they were just telling stories" that were patently untrue.

In other similar cases that I recorded, lineages interpreted the narratives of potential rival lineages in ways that suggested that these narratives, instead of demonstrating the rivals' autochthony, showed that the lineages were strangers transplanted to the island. For example, recall the lineage narrative that began with a family squabble between two rock children—Haurae and Hauhuari'i— and their rock mother—Hauwewe. Hauwewe sparked the argument when she offered nothing but wild cabbage to feed those who had helped her to clear an area for gardening. In the version of this lineage origin story analyzed in the previous chapter, the two children told their mother to remain at Rorohu village while they traveled down to the coast past four other rocks that obstructed their passage. In a rival lineage's version of this myth, however, the following words are attributed to Hauwewe when her children reproach her: "If you were a stranger like me, could you feed people properly?" Having thus identified Hauwewe as a foreigner, the man who gave this version of the story then pointed out that, even according to the other lineage's version, their apical ancestress "is at Rorohu till today." In his estimation, however, "No one thinks highly of Hauwewe; they step on her and press her into the ground." In this way, competing lineages attempt to invalidate each other's narrative constructions of the land, not only at the level of specific ancestral sites, but also at the level of the framing of whole lineage narratives.

In addition to shrine and narrative elements, lineage personal names are particularly susceptible to surreptitious assimilation by rival lineages striving to become *auhenua* on the coastal land. Representatives of different lineages informed me that certain personal names associated with the coastal land belonged solely to their lineages and not to the other lineages they suspected of having designs on them. I sometimes heard people bemoan that their lineage had lost control of land due to naming: "Our old people named different [non-lineage] people with our lineage's personal names, and [now these people] have taken our land." But a situation that members of one lineage characterize as name "theft," another lineage portrays as the return to their land of a personal name that had been given out to a non-lineage relative in a previous generation.

These conflicting perspectives are well illustrated by Lineages D and E with respect to a personal name that both lineages consider to be connected to a particular part of the Arosi coast. The disagreement centers on whether the name—which I will refer to as Atana—belongs to Lineage D or E (see Figures 7.2–7.3). Representatives of both lineages state that the first person to bear this name, Atana 1, lived at a place called X where his matrilineage was *auhenua* and that, following the Arosi custom of lineage exogamy, he married a woman of a different matrilineage that was *auhenua* elsewhere. Furthermore, both lineages agree that Atana 1's son, Bwaru, having no children of his own, bestowed his father's name on the firstborn of a woman, Urao, who lived at a place called Y. As a result of this naming, Urao's son, Atana 2, currently controls the land at X. Lineage D maintains that the woman, Urao, and Atana 1 were both mem-

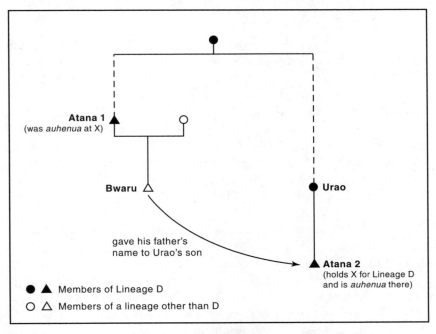

Figure 7.2. Lineage D claims that the name Atana and the territory it controls are rightfully held by one of its own members.

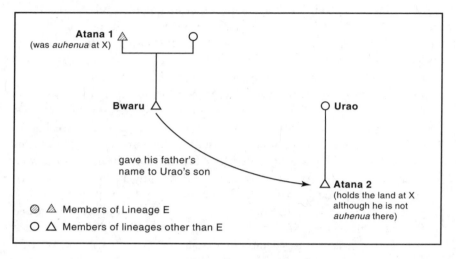

Figure 7.3. Lineage E claims that the name Atana and the territory it controls have been wrongfully "sent away" to a member of a different lineage.

bers of their lineage and that the places X and Y both fall within their larger ancestral territory. Therefore, from their point of view, when Bwaru named Urao's son Atana 2, Bwaru was simply keeping the name, along with oversight of the place X, within the lineage to which they belong. In contrast, Lineage E maintains that Atana 1 was a member of their lineage, but that Urao was not, and that her son Atana 2 now looks after part of their territory although he is not of their lineage. They argue that, although Bwaru, as the son of Atana 1, was welcome to live at X, he was not *auhenua* there and had no authority to give his father's name to Urao's son. Therefore, from Lineage E's point of view, Bwaru "sent part of their land away" by improperly bestowing one of their lineage's personal names.

Present-day Arosi naming practices both respond to and compound this type of dissension. Seeking to secure their ties to coastal land through naming, Arosi matrilineages are working aggressively to regain control over the personal names they understand to be as much a part of their unique ancestral inheritances as their sacred sites. Fearful that other people will appropriate their lineage's personal names and, with them, portions of their territories, knowledgeable people "hold firmly" onto names that are not currently in circulation and warned me against disclosing them to others. For the members of some matrilineages this means building up their *auhenua* self-under-

standings in the form of esoteric caches of personal names withheld from distribution even within their own lineages. Those who advocate this strategy
seem to think that, beyond protecting their names from theft, it also recoups
the essential power of the names for the lineage even when the names are not
put to use to place lineage members securely on lineage land.[4] At the same
time, some lineages are attempting to "hold firmly" onto names by bestowing
them on lineage children even when non-lineage relatives bearing those names
are still alive. This appears to be a method of counteracting the power that
non-lineage persons currently known by the lineage's names may try to exercise over the lineage's land. Although Arosi acknowledge that this practice is
contrary to custom, those who engage in it justify it as a necessary effort "to
bring back" the names and areas of land rightfully belonging to their lineages.

The heterotopia-producing activities documented in these case studies represent, I suggest, new variations and actualizations of the ancestral place and polity-
making processes envisioned as proper to the topogonic mode of primordiality.
By constructing new sacred sites, incorporating existing ones into autochthonous histories, and reclaiming lineage-specific personal names, representatives
of Arosi matrilineages are revivifying the power of topogonic action in competing efforts to come into being as emplaced centers for new social polities on the
coast. But this is not to say that Arosi are merely reenacting routinized mythic
paradigms or that Arosi socio-cultural order is essentially unchanging. When
Arosi engage in these practices they are drawing on received forms that they understand to be repositories of ancestral power, but they are not taking these forms
as scripts for the repetition of ancestral acts. Rather, in their postcolonial setting
of semantically evacuated coastal land, they are finding new potential meanings
inherent in these received forms and recapturing them for the present in ways
that alter and even invert their apparent previous social and moral messages (cf.
Kapferer 2003).

---

4. Annette Weiner (1992) identifies names as among the "inalienable possessions" that
Trobriand Islands matrilineages temporarily loan out to one another in ways that risk permanent loss. I would describe Arosi names as mobile extensions of matrilineal essences
rather than "possessions," and would argue that Arosi attempts to reclaim names represent
efforts to defend matrilineal power and integrity from a culturally particular—rather than
a general universal—form of "loss and decay" (A. Weiner 1992: 7). Nevertheless, I take the
processes of alternating distribution and retraction that Weiner describes in relation to such
elements of value as comparable to those in which Arosi engage in naming (cf. A. Weiner
1976: 126–127). This comparative data suggests, furthermore, that the current Arosi re-
tention of names, although apparently novel in its extreme form, captures and privileges
anti-social meanings already inherent in such forms of engagement in and withdrawal from
inter-lineage exchange.

Although informed by ancestral models in their struggles to achieve new transitions from utopic to topogonic primordiality, Arosi are unintentionally eliciting the socially fragmenting potential intrinsic to those models in ways that may be original to the present. Whereas autochthonous histories describe how the foundation of socio-cosmic order depended on processes that established horizontal relations among matrilineal categories as well as vertical relations between those categories and areas of land, the current drive to store up knowledge of such histories creates only lineage-cum-land identities as integral to themselves and as prerequisite to, rather than the outcome of, proper social relations. Similarly, whereas, lineage personal names might formerly have been used to specify ties with non-lineage kin, moves today to retrieve names from circulation outside the matrilineages represent, not only changes in practice, but also a devaluation of non-lineal relatedness that again seeks to reaffirm lineage-cum-land identities by extricating them from the very entanglements through which, according to narratives of ancestral activity, they were formed in the first instance. Instead of promoting fully neo-cosmogonic dual-axis processes of coming into being, these reframings of ancestral practices tend to conflate the mythic vision of a proto-human category of being arising in a discrete but utopic space with the reified image of a matrilineage seated in its territory as a preconstituted entity. Although variations on topogonic activities, these practices may be viewed as, in fact, promoting processes of anti-cosmogony that complete rather than remedy the postcolonial return to utopic primordiality.

The Arosi reification of the relationship between a matrilineage and its territory as a static isomorphism is similar in some respects to what Thomas Ernst (1999) describes as "entification" among the Onabasulu (Papua New Guinea). Ernst shows that, when Onabasulu represent themselves as clearly and permanently defined socially and territorially bounded "clans," they are drawing on a cosmogonic myth according to which the dismemberment of a primordial being created the culturally significant number of seventeen social and spatial units. Acknowledging that this tradition was not invented *de novo* in the contemporary context of fossil fuel extraction, Ernst (1999: 88) argues that, as part of "an emerging politics of difference" through which they are positioning themselves to benefit from gas and oil revenues, Onabasulu are reinterpreting this myth in ways that strategically redraw and fix social and spatial distinctions among themselves and between themselves and their neighbors. Although Onabasulu say that their social and spatial divisions are "authentic" and unchanging, these divisions are, according to Ernst's analysis, only a present contingent configuration and subject, therefore, to remixing and repartitioning with the changing circumstances of the future.

There is a critical difference between the Onabasulu and Arosi cases, how-ever. The Onabasulu cosmogonic myth that Ernst (1999: 92–93, 96 n. 3) pres-ents appears to describe how an original unity came to be internally differen-tiated to produce distinct clan groups to whom distinct territories were allotted. Thus, although Ernst does not appeal to the Melanesian model of so-ciality to account for the process of entification, as it occurs among the On-abasulu at least, entification may be amenable to analysis as an example of what those employing various versions of the model term de-pluralization or de-composition. Onabasulu engagement with agents of the Papua New Guinea government and Chevron Oil have elicited particular subsets of pos-sible relations from within a socio-spatial field that Onabasulu myth repre-sents as originally unbroken. In contrast, Arosi ontology posits an original plurality of categories in need of external relations. The reification of lineage-cum-land identities among Arosi involves, therefore, not an ideology accord-ing to which a single category of being was partitioned and its segments em-placed once and for all, but an ideology according to which multiple categories of being appeared in and have always been identified with pre-segmented areas of land. In both contexts there is equally a denial of change, but in Arosi the process of reification draws on visions of primordiality and ontological as-sumptions that make it the disarticulation of a sum back to its pre-existent parts, not the redrawing of boundaries within a fluid whole.

Like Arosi heterotopia itself, the fragmenting effect of neo-topogonic prac-tices is inadvertent and brought about in the course of what Arosi represent to themselves and others as efforts to follow *kastom* in order to restore the condi-tions necessary for *auhenua*-centered and harmonious multi-lineage polities able to protect land from alien encroachments. It is this reordering project itself that ironically demands an initial retraction of social ties, a pealing back of socio-spa-tial order to its elementary principles. The colonial processes that have rendered coastal land utopic have severed matrilineages from their lands but not from one another. Deracinated matrilineages, in effect, only partially instantiate the orig-inal plurality of isolated ontological categories proper to utopic primordiality. The anti-social dimensions of Arosi revaluations of ancestral precedents thus serve as the implicit preliminary means to the greater social end explicit in their neo-topogonic dimensions. The former work to fulfill, as far as is humanly pos-sible, the approximate return of matrilineal essences to pre-human asociality. So recovered, they have the potential to become the multiple starting points for fresh processes of emplacement and entanglement that should, at least in Arosi the-ory, yield cogently and transparently *auhenua*-centered polities.

But Arosi social reality is failing, so far, to follow Arosi social theory in the present, if it ever did in the past. Indeed, the bivalent nature of Arosi neo-topogonic projects highlights a conundrum: any attempt to reconstitute the poly-genetic order of an Arosi polity by identifying the emplaced *auhenua* matrilineage on which it is said to depend is likely to backfire by throwing that polity into disintegrative chaos. However much Arosi may declare that an *auhenua* lineage in its land is indispensable to proper social order, no one wants to permit a matrilineage other than his or her own to gain acknowledged ascendancy. There are consequently two countervailing and mutually intensifying incentives always at work, both aimed ostensibly at allowing the representatives of multiple matrilineages to live peacefully and productively together on the coast. On the one hand, there is an incentive to stifle any claim to be *auhenua* by pointing to the sources of ambiguity that support the no-*auhenua* consensus; on the other, there is an incentive to establish clear and confident *auhenua* centers of authority as the hidden but true and stabilizing underpinnings of Arosi society.

The way in which these two incentives reinforce one another is well illustrated by a recent incident in Arosi politics. Several Arosi recounted to me that, not long before my arrival, an elderly man whom I will call Timothy Karu had called together the inhabitants of his village. He initiated this meeting in order to refute statements made by one villager that permission to plant gardens on a certain area of local land needed to be secured from a man in a neighboring village who represented a particular matrilineage. Karu wanted to set the record straight, at least as he saw it, regarding who was who in the village. When the villagers had assembled he began to tell them where their grandmothers had come from. In presuming to inform them of their matrilineal histories he was implicitly stating that the people of his matrilineage were the original people of the land, and that everyone else lived in the village through the goodness and hospitality of his lineage. Immediately, the villagers who had gathered to listen to him became indignant. "All right!" they exclaimed, "We'll leave here and go back to the bush!" Talking among themselves, the villagers noted that no one who was truly *auhenua* would behave so arrogantly. They believed that Karu was telling them they had no right to live in the village.

At that point Karu's elder brother, Barnabas Abenga'i, who is an elected village chief, stood up and, contradicting his brother's implicit claims, said: "We are all people who have come, so we're all equal here. The *auhenua* are long dead and now no one here is *auhenua*. We are just off-shoots from them." He went on to negate Karu's claim that their lineage was antecedent to everyone else's by pointing out that his own name, Abenga'i, belonged to a now defunct lineage that had preceded theirs in the area. He exhorted everyone to live together peacefully as they had done for many generations. The villagers were mollified by what he said because, as they said: "He made everyone feel good; that's the work of a chief, to bring everyone together."

Although his actions at the meeting proved highly divisive, Karu was, in fact, attempting to overcome what he regards as the confused state of inter-lineage relations in the land by inserting his own lineage as an ordering center. His motives were both self-serving and, ostensibly, for the good of the village as a whole. Concerned that his lineage's land is being overrun by others, and eager to demonstrate that his lineage is *auhenua*, Karu used his professed knowledge of variant accounts of his neighbors' autochthonous histories to differentiate clearly between the *auhenua* and the non-*auhenua* in the village. He was willing to risk giving the appearance of arrogant self-promotion because a composite village polity, as he himself later stated to me, can survive and thrive only when an acknowledged *auhenua* lineage serves to collect and shelter other lineages under its benevolent auspices. Ironically, however, his emphasis on autochthonous histories, and thus on the separate Arosi categories of being that they delineate, had the inevitable, if unintended, socially fragmenting effect of under-valuing and weakening the ties of inter-lineage entanglement among the residents of his village.

Effectively severing these ties of entanglement, Karu's attempt to correct other lineage narratives exposed the heterotopic construction of the shared village land and threatened to dissolve the tenuous no-*auhenua* consensus-based village polity that masks that construction. By insinuating his claim to be *auhenua*, Karu denied the validity of other unspoken claims and laid bare the coexistence of diverse irreconcilable *auhenua* identities in the village. When the villagers responded that they would return to the matrilineal territories to which he had assigned them in the bush, their intended dispersal surfaced the deep poly-ontology of Arosi cosmology. Had they carried out their threat to go their separate ways, their departures would have signaled an anti-cosmogonic retreat to the primordial chaos of isolated, unrelated matrilineal categories seated on self-contained sites of autochthonous origins.[5]

But Barnabas's conciliatory stance averted this anti-cosmogonic dispersal. Rather than invoking autochthonous histories that distinguish among lineages, Barnabas gave precedence to the history of lineage entanglements in the present residence pattern. Furthermore, by suggesting that all of the villagers are equally newcomers to the coast, he attempted to reinstate the consensus

---

5. Of course, most villagers did not accept Karu's accounts of where their lineages had originated. Their exclamations that they would retreat to the bush expressed, therefore, their indignation at Karu's speech rather than their assent to its contents.

that no authentic descendants of the coastal *auhenua* can be identified with certainty. Like the historical factors to which Arosi point to justify it, the no-*auhenua* consensus serves to return coastal land to a functional condition of indeterminacy, amorphousness, and vacuity in which multiple lineages can engage in the kinds of neo-topogonic projects described above that over-value vertical connections between lineages and land as though they were autonomous from and prior to horizontal inter-lineage relations. The consensus both requires and permits all would-be *auhenua* to engage in these processes surreptitiously. For such would-be *auhenua*, it produces a safe and uninterrogated condition in which they can quietly construct and conceal their identities as the true coastal *auhenua*. Thus, Barnabas's reaffirmation of this consensus not only enabled the members of different lineages to return to peaceful and productive coexistence as horizontally enmeshed peers; it also enabled each lineage silently to retain its claim to a unique vertical connection to place undisclosed.

Notice, however, how the villagers' reaction to Barnabas's intervention suggests that over-valuation of entanglement to the neglect of individual lineage identities can also undermine the cohesion of Arosi polities. Arosi poly-ontology implies that unifying relations are predicated on distinct prevenient categories of being. Thus, when Barnabas attempted to re-unify the villagers by eliminating the necessary distinction between *auhenua* and non-*auhenua*, the villagers re-introduced this dichotomy by stating that Barnabas was acting in a manner befitting the true *auhenua*. Barnabas performatively embodied the social values that have come to be associated with the *auhenua*: namely, bringing people of disparate origins together to live peacefully on their land. By exhibiting these qualities, Barnabas counteracted the chaotic effects of his brother's divisive claim and restored the possibility of ordered relations among the lineages. At the same time, he served as a suitable substitute for a representative of an actual *auhenua* lineage. The villagers did not proclaim Barnabas to be a literal *auhenua* representative; that would have been to accept the claims of his brother, Karu. Rather, they appropriated Barnabas as a useful virtual *auhenua* who provides an acknowledged central base of authority to which a multiplicity of lineages can attach themselves and construct a network of inter-relationships.

Once Barnabas was firmly instated as the virtual *auhenua*, his appeal to the no-*auhenua* consensus and the ties of recent entanglement no longer constituted a decentering denial of distinctions, but a cosmogonic stance that permitted the villagers to reconstruct a landscape simultaneously empty and full of *auhenua*—a landscape that Barnabas himself has come to mirror. Although Barnabas disavows any claim to be *auhenua*, the reasons that some lineages offer for why they elected him chief express a variety of ways in which they either assimilate him into their lineages or view him as a legitimate token of their claims to be *auhenua*. The lineage that understands Barnabas's Arosi name it be one of its unique lineage names views his chieftaincy as an emblem of its identity as *auhenua*. At the same time, the lineage to which Barnabas's mother belongs is satisfied that he represents its status as *auhenua*. Like the heterotopic Arosi landscape today, Barnabas's chieftaincy is a composite of multiple latent and overlapping lineage identities.[6]

The mutually conditioned character of the usefulness of ambiguity and the desire for transparency again raises interesting, though ultimately unanswerable, questions about the nature of Arosi leadership and land tenure in the precolonial past. If, as speculated in the previous chapter, indigenous processes of lineage extinction and mobility probably gave rise to situations of heterotopia in the past, it follows that the goal of achieving clear *auhenua*-centered polities—especially in such situations—has often been aspirational and difficult, if not impossible, to realize. Accordingly, it may be that the polity-building work of precolonial Arosi chiefs included allowing for a certain degree of ambiguity regarding which lineages they represented as the *auhenua* of the land, leaving scope for representatives of different lineages to content themselves with different understandings of the structure of their polities.

Alternatives to Heterotopia

Because Barnabas himself has been made a replica of the heterotopia fostered by the no-*auhenua* consensus, the net outcome of Karu's momentary rupture of consensus has been the maintenance of the status quo. Appeal to the ethic of the *auhenua* as the pretext for promoting Barnabas as a stand-in for the lost *auhenua* failed ultimately to eliminate competing covert claims and unite disparate lineages in a stable village polity. There is still no legitimized *auhenua* lineage vertically anchored in the village land, hence there is still no possibility for clearly centered horizontal relations among the lineages. But from the point of view of most Arosi, this status quo is ultimately unsatisfactory because it leaves coastal Arosi communities subject to a basic and worrying fragility. The overlapping but isolated universes generated by neo-

---

6. Barnabas and John Taro (also a pseudonym) were elected "first" and "second chief" some time in the mid 1970s. Taro, the village's second chief, appears in similar ways to be a token representative of a subset of competing identities.

topogonic activities are prohibited from coming into proper relations with one another by the no-*auhenua* consensus that facilitates them. And this consensus alone cannot solidly ground an extended polity composed of representatives of different lineages or enable it to withstand the disintegrating effects of competing *auhenua* identities if circumstances bring them to the fore. This situation is untenable not only because of anticipated outside pressures on the land that threaten to elicit openly conflicting claims, but also because of the atmosphere of local friction that people experience as intimidating, frustrating to hoped-for development initiatives, hurtful, and contrary to the moral values of custom and Christianity. In a bid to escape from the burdens of secrecy, uncertainty, and mutual suspicion associated with the heterotopic condition, therefore, a minority of Arosi have begun turning to alternative neo-topogonic strategies that have in common an impetus to carve out unambiguous and indisputable allocations of land.

One such strategy—the contracted purchase of land—is open only to the very few Arosi who are able to acquire the necessary resources. Take the example of a man whom I will call George Saeniha'a. After a career as an educated professional that provided him with a cash income far greater than that attainable by most Arɔsi, Saeniha'a recently purchased land in Haununu, a sparsely populated area on the south coast of Makira. He explained to me that he hoped this land would be an incontestable bequest for all his children. "My children have this land; it is their land," he stated emphatically. In setting this land apart through purchase he intended, not only that no previous land-holder would be able to contest his children's control of the land, but also that even members of his and his wife's own lineages and their bilateral kindreds would have no stake in the land. "It is not [my brother's and sister's] children's land," he made sure to clarify. The placement of his children alone on this land will mark a severance from past ties to other lands and lineages and the beginning of a new matrilineage.

Saeniha'a has a blueprint in mind for the structure and organization of this new matrilineage that, according to him, follows customary Arosi practice.

> My two sons will oversee the land for the women, but I will make a woman the leader/head. My sons will protect the land, but my first-born daughter, I will make her the leader. It is she who will step in to correct things if something goes wrong. Because my sons will give bride-price for women of other lineages to come and live here, their children will not have the land and will not be boss, though they can live there. It's my eldest daughter's children who will be boss. When one of my sons protects the land he will not be doing so for his chil-

dren but for his lineage. As a man, he will act to protect the land while the women will be quiet. They will say: "Our grandfather and grandmother gave money for this place, that is why we have the land here." So we will follow women, since if we follow the men the land will leave. But if my eldest daughter doesn't have a girl, we'll name a boy and he'll look to bring a child of one of my other daughters back to the land through naming. Even if they have gone far away they can still come back; even if they've been away one thousand years they can still return to the land as long as they can still trace the story of their connection to the land.

Independently of both his lineage and that of his wife, Saeniha'a is, in effect, establishing on this land a new matrilineage that begins with his daughters. The small group of siblings that he plans to settle on the purchased land is, I suggest, in a similar position to that of the primordial proto-lineages situated in proto-places. Starting from scratch, they will have to enter into cosmogonic relationships with other lineages and transform the purchased land into a lineage territory from which they receive their identity and to which they give their imprint. As in mythic accounts of ultimate lineage origins, this new lineage has been designed to begin with an apical ancestress, his eldest daughter who, he hopes, will continue to reside on this land even after marriage. For the purpose of founding this new lineage, Saeniha'a wants to reinvent his daughter as though she had no previous existence outside the purchased land; it is as though she had emerged from this land with no antecedent identity.

In order to circumvent the uncertainties and disputes endemic to the Arosi coast, Saeniha'a was compelled to look beyond Arosi to find land where an apparently undisputed *auhenua* lineage existed with the power to sell part of its territory. In such a context, return to utopic primordiality is not the result of a consensus that the land is empty of *auhenua*, nor is it solely attributable to belief that Christian faith may have neutralized the power of ancestral spirits. Rather, return to utopic primordiality is intentionally induced by representatives of the *auhenua* lineage who actively open the land to the newcomers in exchange for cash or shell valuables. I was not present when Saeniha'a bought his land, but another woman described to me how a member of an *auhenua* lineage might free purchased land from the power of the lineage's ancestors.

If non-*auhenua* decide to buy the land, then when the person who has the land receives the money he'll go and open (*tahangia*) that land. The spirits there know him because he is *auhenua* of that place. [He will address his ancestral spirits saying:] "I place these people here because they gave me money to settle here, they bought me with the money; my power (*mena*) is with them and when they live here they'll live freely. If someone wants to take them to court or spoil them, I'll help them. You spirits, don't disturb them, because I placed them here. They bought my power and so they stay here. Look after them well." These people will stay there unhindered; they can walk over a shrine and nothing will happen to them. The Holy Spirit makes it a good place to live.... It is the *auhenua* lineage that can do this; a person from another lineage cannot. It is the lineage that worked in this power that can take the power away. But it will not be finished simply following this person's plan. No, he'll say a prayer to ask God to lift back the power from that place. But if another lineage comes and asks for the power to be lifted back it wouldn't happen.

The process this woman described may have antecedents in situations, such as those considered in the preceding chapter, in which a lineage on the brink of extinction bequeathed its land to another lineage through the mediation of shell valuables.

It remains to be seen, however, whether Saeniha'a's experiment in new lineage formation will prove to be a successful topogonic alternative to heterotopia. Any number of possible scenarios could threaten the establishment and continuity of the new lineage in its land. It may happen that the lineages of Saeniha'a and his wife may refuse to accept the anti-cosmogonic schisms necessary for the neo-cosmogonic founding of the new lineage and will insist on regarding the new lineage as part of a larger kindred with binding obligations. It is not inconceivable that members of the birth lineage of Saeniha'a's children will seek to claim the new land as their own, or that members of Saeniha'a's lineage will try to live on the land on account of their familial connections. At the same time, the new lineage may have to stave off encroachment by relatives of the *auhenua* lineage from which the land was purchased. Still another lineage could claim that it—and not the lineage that sold the land—was, in fact, the true *auhenua*, calling the legitimacy of the sale into question. In short, it is possible that within a few generations other people will begin to construct themselves as *auhenua* on this land, and Saeniha'a's descendants will find themselves in the same position as the coastal Arosi today.

A second alternative to the confusion and latent conflict of heterotopia is an increasing tendency among Arosi to appeal solely to paternal filiation as the basis for one's access to and use of land and its resources. This tendency is jointly promoted by the supposed demise of the coastal *auhenua* and by the fact that recourse to paternal connections provides a safe and legitimate means of asserting one's right to live and garden at a particular place. Owing to the practice of patri-virilocal residence, the choice of grown children to continue to reside with and enjoy the support of their patrikin rather than settle where their matrilineage is *auhenua* has always been an option. Today, however, in the absence of agreed on *auhenua* matrilineages along the coast, the practice of sons staying to work coastal land previously worked by their fathers or paternal grandfathers has become the dominant and least controversial residence pattern. Pointing to this pattern, a small but vocal minority of Arosi has begun to advocate an official acceptance of a father to son mode of land inheritance as a permanent solution to the apparent breakdown of matrilineal land tenure with a view to eliminating the potential for conflict inherent in the current heterotopia.

As already described, Arosi trace their present distribution along the coast to a socio-spatial reorganization during the mid to late nineteenth century under the auspices of "senior men" or "the people of old." Owing to this neo-topogonic event of an earlier era, the Arosi coast now comprises a set of contiguous land parcels called *odo* that encompass the coastal hamlets and extend in parallel strips up into the gardening land above them. "The people of old," it is said, gave jurisdiction over each *odo* to a particular man and placed him at the corresponding hamlet. The long-term effect of patri-virilocal residence over several ensuing generations is the present demographic pattern of older men in village hamlets surrounded by their sons and their sons' families.[7]

Arosi usually describe their connections to the land and to things in and on the land in terms of the metaphor of eating. People who eat (*ngau*) in a particular place use the nut and fruit trees there. They make gardens, build houses, and even establish plantations there. Arosi justify their eating at a particular place by tracing their kinship relations with those who have previously lived on or used the land there. If they establish their connection to a place by telling the narrative of their matrilineage, they say that they "eat through the mother" or "eat through the lineage." Eating through the mother denotes a permanent and inexhaustible connection to a place or thing by virtue of the unity of being within a matrilineage. If, in contrast, they establish their connection to a place by calling attention to where their fathers or other patrikin have lived and worked the land in recent memory, they say that they "eat through the father." But eating through the father denotes only a transient connection to a place or thing that is said to become exhausted within three to five generations. In describing the basis of their connections to the present-

---

7. These hamlet-based groups exhibit characteristics of what Barnes (1962: 6) termed "cumulative patrifiliation." Because these groups do not understand themselves to be of one substance within themselves, it is perhaps best to avoid labeling them "incipient patrilineages" (Oliver 1989: 1040).

day *odo*, many Arosi assert that they eat through the father. In fact, the expression "we all just eat through the father" is a common way of saying "we are all strangers here."[8]

The necessity of eating through the father in default of recognized matrilineal connections to the land emerged early on in my field research in what was to be the first of many conversations on this topic to which I was a party. Selwyn and I were relaxing together with Jems on Jems's verandah.[9] As I had recently arrived in the village, the two of them were eager to make sure that I received from them what they considered to be orthodox instruction regarding Arosi custom. Jems explained that, according to custom, "a person can eat through the father or mother; it's up to the person. In olden times when a woman married away [from her lineage's territory] her children would come back [to her land] so that her lineage would continue at that land. Today, the children do not return." Selwyn then interjected: "We only eat through the father today." On hearing this, Jems was quick to clarify: "This is only because we don't have the lineage whose land [our village] is on. I think that at some places the lineage is still there and has not disappeared, and at these places people eat through both mother and father."

In light of the ongoing production of heterotopia in present-day Arosi, it is not surprising that, having made this pronouncement on one day, Jems revealed to me on a later occasion when the two of us were alone that he, in fact, continues to eat through both his mother and his father in the village hamlet where he resides. In other words, although he can construe his occupation of land in his hamlet in terms of his father's residence there, he ultimately rests his claim on his understanding that his mother's lineage is the true *auhenua* where the hamlet is located. Jems is not alone in appearing to accept the idea that everyone now eats through the father while secretly subordinating his own paternal connections to land to an encompassing covert *auhenua* identity. In this way, some Arosi have enlisted the phenomenon of eating through the father as an aid to constructing and concealing their identities as *auhenua* on the coast. Like the no-*auhenua* consensus itself, the opinion that everyone must now eat through the father can be used to cloak one's hidden assumption that, at the same time and at a more fundamental level, one also eats through the mother.

---

8. Some Arosi say that the expressions "eat through the mother" and "eat through the father" misrepresent actual practices by oversimplifying the connections through which people gain access to gardening land, residential sites, and nut trees. As described in chapter 1, people gain access to land and its resources through a wide range of social entanglements that are not comprehended by this dichotomy.

9. Selywn and Jems are pseudonyms.

This situation in which open declarations of eating through the father co-exist with covert constructions of eating through the mother has prompted a small contingent of well organized men in east Arosi to spearhead an initiative to codify father to son land inheritance as normative Arosi custom. Pronouncing all pretensions to eating through the mother insupportable on the grounds that the *auhenua* are dead, this contingent asserts that eating through the father is the only valid criterion currently operative in determining who controls land. Arguing that de facto Arosi practice ought universally to replace the now impracticable system of matrilineal land tenure, they offer this plan as a remedy to the social tensions and muted hostilities among Arosi today. In effect, like Saeniha'a, they seek to liberate themselves from the heterotopic configuration of land tenure and to establish a new order unburdened by incompatible matrilineage-based views of reality along the coast. Rather than taking refuge in land made utopic elsewhere, however, these neo-topogonic innovators represent their project as a fait accompli.

This initiative is both similar to and different from other documented cases of proposed change or gradual drift from matrilineal to patrilineal land tenure in other parts of Melanesia (e.g., T. S. Epstein 1968; Foster 1995: 91, 256 n. 28; but see Nash 1974). Some of my Arosi consultants expressed their own formulations of what anthropologists have termed the matrilineal puzzle, complaining that it is difficult for people to maintain their connections to their supposed matrilineal territories when they are usually born and frequently live with their fathers and their fathers' relatives. One man went so far as to say that: "Whoever invented our *kastom* must have been crazy!" (cf. McDougall 2004: 179–180). Furthermore, as will become evident in the discussion that follows, what the east Arosi contingent is proposing entails a split between father to son land inheritance and matrilineal identity that is analogous to what Foster (1995: 91) analyzes as an opposition between patrilineality as the social logic governing *bisnis* (commercial enterprise) and matrilineality as the social logic governing *kastam* in the Tanga Islands (Papua New Guinea). In east Arosi, the opposition is cast in terms of land as the concern of men and their sons and "love" as the essence of a matrilineage. That said, however, the authors of this plan to formalize father to son inheritance promoted it, not as a remedy to problems inherent in matrilineal land tenure *per se* or as a means of facilitating commercial enterprise, but as a remedy to divisions, disputes, and jealousies caused by the demise of matrilineal land tenure, with the added bonus of facilitating success in court actions over land.

My knowledge of this plan derives from a short stay in the east Arosi village of Tadahadi in June 1993. I stayed in the village only three days to visit the relatives of a friend from Tawatana who accompanied me. Unexpectedly, at the conclusion of an otherwise uneventful morning at church, my Tawatana friend and I found ourselves caught up in an unusual event. In the midst of the closing announcements, a middle-aged man of the village, Ishmael Taroiara, asked everyone to gather after the service for a meeting to talk about *kastom*. He justified the convening of this meeting by saying: "We need a *kastom* of love and not division. *Kastom* and the Church work together and aren't at odds, and together they will bring renewal."

As people filed out of the church and began chewing betel nut under the shady trees nearby, Taroiara set up a diagram drawn on a large piece of white poster card showing his visual representation of Arosi practice today. As a preamble to his commentary on the diagram he said: "This is a talk that I have constructed after research with our old people, and I want all of us to listen, even the young people, so that we can all teach our children our *kastom*. I will talk, but the old people will answer any questions." He had invited a number of senior men—'Ohairangi and Siro of Tadahadi, and Wakiri and Martin Ringehuniramo of Wango—to support his position. Turning to his diagram, Taroiara began to develop the thesis that among Arosi today a matrilineage is "love" (*haita'ahi*) based on oneness of substance, but that "property," which he equated with land, is held and transmitted only through men.[10]

On the left-hand side of his diagram, under the rubric "love," Taroiara had drawn three rectangles in a vertical column representing three generations of a matrilineage. He explained that, although these generations are united by love, they do not constitute a landowning entity.

> What is the idea of a lineage? It is a group of people who have love. And so from them come out respect and honor. The mother teaches love so that the children will have respect and honor. This is the character or the life of a lineage. One umbilical cord is a group that comes from one mother, and they are one lineage, and each successive generation connected through women is a lineage. The lineage is love because it is a oneness. A lineage is one person (*ta'i inoni*); they aren't related.[11] They eat together because they are one, but if you want to eat from the nut trees through the lineage you should ask first. The people of a lineage visit among themselves. They eat with each other.

---

10. Arosi gloss the word *toto'ora* in English as "property" (cf. Fox 1978: 449). On his diagram and throughout his talk, Taroiara equated *toto'ora* with "land" (*ano*).

11. Taroiara is suggesting that because a lineage is ontologically one its members are not related to one another in the same way that non-matrilineal kin are related to them (i.e., through blood).

They have each other and live with each other because they are one umbilical cord. But the lineage does not have land and it doesn't have a narrative about land. A lineage and a continuous umbilical cord are one thing.... Before, they didn't know God and they sacrificed to ancestral spirits, but God had given them love since he is love. He gave them love within one lineage. A lineage is power (*mena*) and sacred (*maea*); it teaches the right way to live and get along as the living of one person. There is a lot of honor and respect in the lineage. They will not fight among themselves within a lineage, unless you break the custom (*ringeringe*). The lineage eats through people not through land. [Members of a] lineage live with one another because they are one people and not because of land. A lineage is a sacred thing. The lineage must eat with each other since they make themselves sacred to themselves. But they don't visit among themselves because of land but because of people.

At this juncture 'Ohairangi underscored the point at stake: "Land and lineage—they're different!" This thesis that land and lineage are separate and unrelated elements had emerged in an interview I had conducted four days earlier while at another village in east Arosi. The man whom I had interviewed had expressed the following conceptualization of a matrilineage:

A lineage travels. Remember, eating and lineage are different because a woman moves away at marriage and the children eat property through their father. In contrast, eating through the mother isn't forever, it's only certain things. But the lineage does not break. Eating is on the side of the father and lineage is on the side of the mother.

Only in the aftermath of Taroiara's meeting did it register to me as significant that this man credited 'Ohairangi as the source of his *kastom* knowledge. Several months later, another young man who was visiting Tawatana from east Arosi articulated a similar view of a matrilineage as a free-floating entity without permanent ties to land. Explaining that the word *huu* refers to a large box-shaped nut that drifts through the sea and can wash ashore anywhere, he described a matrilineage as a *burunga huu*. Using this poetic image, he compared women, who marry away from their natal places and can therefore end up anywhere, to these drifting nuts. They float from place to place and consequently have no place that is theirs.[12] Taken together, the testimonies of these

---

12. Interestingly, Fox (1978: 230) provides a number of different definitions of *huu*. In addition to identifying *huu* as the *Barringtonia speciosa*, he glosses *huu* as solid, rock, last-

representatives of the "eat through the father" party make clear their position that matrilineages are incapable of topogonic activity.

On the right-hand side of his diagram, under the rubric "property = land" (*toto'ora* = *ano*) Taroiara had drawn a parallel column of three rectangles representing three generations descending from fathers to sons. Moving on to this column, he explained how a father passes his land to his sons, not through his lineage, but by virtue of the bride-price he pays for his wife.

> A father buys children with strung shell valuables. Why does a man buy children? Because the male is a dry tree; he can't make his group longer. So he buys a woman and buys children [with the bride-price]. He buys a woman because he wants children and he must marry a [woman of a] different lineage. The father has land but the woman doesn't have land. Children don't have land through their mother, [because] a lineage doesn't have land. It isn't the land of the lineage; people have land through their father. People in [the third generation] often say that the land they live in [i.e., the first generation's land] is that of the lineage, but in fact it is not, since they [i.e., the first generation] also lived through shell valuables.

Again 'Ohairangi spoke up: "They [i.e., a man's children] have power to live on his land through the shell valuables [given as bride-price for their mother]." Together, Taroiara and 'Ohairangi were forwarding the idea that the payment of bride-price severs a child's connection to its matrilineage, wherever it happens to reside, and secures the child for the father's land. Although they were ready to accept the existence of certain exceptions to this general rule, they averred that the bride-price blocked the ability of children to return to and reside at the place from which their mother had come. According to this interpretation, paying a bride-price literally breaks the connection with maternal land. In the aftermath of the meeting this was a suggestion to which some people voiced strong objections.

Agitated by his characterization of this diagrammatic scheme as *kastom*, villagers at the meeting seemed not to hear Taroiara's concession that the coastal land had once been held by an *auhenua* matrilineage.

---

ing, inexhaustible, the beginning, origin. Under this last gloss he gives the example *huu i burunga*, "origin of clan." Although I never heard anyone else use the phrase *burunga huu* to refer to a matrilineage, Fox's definitions raise the possibility that this man was reinterpreting a locution that could also be understood in ways precisely opposite to his intentions.

> The lineage's land has existed from olden times. People change but
> the lineage's land doesn't change. Today, however, we can't trace back
> to the original lineage and we are not the original lineage. Here we
> are talking about what we do today.... From the beginning, the land
> was that of the lineage. The lineage's burial sites and shrines do not
> change, they have been there from the start. It is the people who
> change through marriage. As a result, they always sacrifice through
> their grandfather and their father.

Rather than denying that in former times matrilineages had held the land,
Taroiara saw himself as simply pointing to the fact that the extinction of the
auhenua has resulted in a separation between matrilineages and land tenure.[13]
He has, furthermore, taken it as his mission to evangelize on behalf of this
separation. Preaching the reframing of matrilineages as based purely on common ontology, along with the acceptance of father to son land inheritance as
normative practice, he offers the separation between "love" and "land" as tantamount to a gospel message in keeping with the will of God and guaranteed
to bring peace to Arosi.

> [In pre-Christian times] lineages already grasped the light from God,
> but they didn't know it. So we live not with love but with dispute
> today. Follow this plan that I'm talking about and we'll eat together
> and work together in the likeness of God. The *kastom* that has divided
> us has made us kill, for as the Bible says, if you are angry you have
> already killed.

He concluded his presentation with an itinerant agenda for the future. He had
already given this talk at Wango, he said, and he intended to continue northwest along the coast with stops at each village until he reached Asimaanioha,
or even 'Ubuna. "I want us all to have the same account of the true way of living, from Borodao [the village at Wango] to Asimaanioha, so that we won't
have divisions."

As the meeting began to break up, Martin Ringehuniramo gave a parting endorsement to Taroiara's recommendations, saying: "I am on the local court, and
it follows this *kastom*. If you follow the *kastom* that Taroiara is describing you'll
win!" These words of advice point to the importance of the legacy of British
colonial law in the current Arosi debate surrounding eating through the mother

---

13. In contrast, some people who espouse the "eat through the father" position maintain that Arosi matrilineages were never rooted in the land.

versus eating through the father. Modeled after British colonial law, Solomon Islands law favors the rights of persons and groups with a recent and demonstrable history of occupation in the land (Tiffany 1983: 284–285). Yet this clear incentive to conform one's practice to the system favored by the courts does not appear to override other concerns. Owing to a variety of objections and forms of resistance to this plan, it seems unlikely that Arosi as a whole will convert to Taroiara's revised version of *kastom* in the near future. In conversations pursuant to this meeting, I heard repeated rejections of Taroiara's interpretation of the meaning and function of bride-price. Contradicting Taroiara, people denied that bride-price can truly break the connection between a person and his or her matrilineal place. They pointed to a number of practices that, according to their understandings of Arosi *kastom*, permit children to return to the land of their matrilineage: naming, prestations given by the bride's kindred after receiving the bride-price, and even the birth of the first-born child itself. In light of these practices, they simply were not convinced by Taroiara's efforts to cast bride-price as a mechanism through which men could reproduce children for their land. One man emphatically drew my attention to what he considered to be a grave omission. Taroiara and his supporters had failed to mention that, at least in the past, *auhenua* matrilineages regularly and purposefully endeavored to recruit the children of their lineage women back to their land.

Following a different line of thought, another man was concerned that this plan would make it impossible for the people now living on the coast to claim the bush territories they had left behind at the time of colonial reorganization. Because he understands eating through the father to provide only a shallow and short-lived connection to place, and no one has lived in the bush for several generations, he is of the opinion that no one can claim to eat through the father there. People can only return to the bush on the grounds of perpetual connections through their mothers. Thus, if Arosi do away with the principle of eating through the mother, the bush land is lost. Aware that people had already begun to talk about reappropriating the bush, either in the context of recurrent rumors that gold might be discovered there or simply because of recent population growth, this man was anticipating a serious challenge to Taroiara's recommendations.[14]

---

14. Now, as pressure on the available coastal gardening land grows, Arosi increasingly talk about returning to live in the interior of the island. But, citing a variety of reasons—from the lack of primary schools and medical clinics in the interior, to the logistical difficulties of transporting produce and goods to and from ships—people have, as yet, been unwilling to reestablish villages in the bush. Given that Arosi have not lived in the bush for several generations, people have limited familiarity with bush locales, abandoned villages,

The ultimate obstacle to these recommendations, however, remains the unwillingness of the would-be *auhenua* to relinquish their covertly constructed identities as the true *auhenua* of the coast. Whenever confronted by the assertion that all Arosi "only eat through the father," these would-be *auhenua* complacently conclude that people who say this must be in-marrying strangers where they live. But the would-be *auhenua* remain confident in their identities. As one Tadahadi villager who had attended the meeting in silence insisted to me the very next day: "I live here through my matrilineage."[15]

Like the heterotopia-producing reframings of ancestral topogonic activities, the alternatives to heterotopia outlined above, simultaneously reproduce and transform customary Arosi land tenure. One might suspect that Saeniha'a, in his rejection of the conflicts and instabilities of heterotopia, has exchanged customary Arosi lineage interdependence and collective lineage land tenure for Western modes of individualism and private property acquisition that deny the inalienable connection between a matrilineage and its place. Yet, the use of Solomon Islands dollars to purchase the land has clear antecedents in the transformative use of shell valuables and, furthermore, does not alter the bivalent meaning of *auhenua*. Saeniha'a is able to install his children in a new place with the hope that they will become *auhenua* there, not only because he has money, but because he is recognized as an autochthonous person of the island and, for now, the people of Haununu agree that the purchased land is empty of *auhenua*. Using cash to eke out a space ostensibly stripped of its preceding significations, Saeniha'a optimistically anticipates a time when his children will move to this new land and topogonically form themselves as a new

---

or former sacred sites there and only occasionally reference them in their daily experiences in the land. As a consequence, the bush itself is now becoming utopic (cf. Merlan 1998: 111–113), and any future attempts to settle or develop land there are likely to generate the same types of neo-topogonic heterotopia-producing practices now prevalent on the coast. Bathgate (1985: 101) describes an apparently analogous historical context and the matrilineal practices implicated in the strategies of the Ndi-Nggai for reclaiming bush land in west Guadalcanal, but gives no indication that these strategies involve or produce conflicting claims.

15. On account of the brevity of my visit at Tadahadi, I had little opportunity to discover extensive background information about Taroiara or to situate him in the context of local parties and conflicts in the village. Moreover, being an unknown quantity in the village, it was difficult for me to conduct systematic follow-up interviews with the villagers who attended the meeting. On the following Tuesday, I sat with Taroiara for about two hours, at which time he told me that his mother was a local woman but that his father was from Santa Isabel. He said that he could continue to live in Tadahadi but could not claim land on Santa Isabel because his father had not paid bride-price when he married his mother.

auhenua matrilineage on the south coast of Makira. His aim is not to set them up as an autonomous nuclear family, but to plant them as a new trunk that will acquire branches—new inter-lineage entanglements.

Taroiara's plan to institute father to son land inheritance is a response both to the utopic condition created by the demise of the *auhenua* and to the heterotopic condition created by what he takes to be the recent formation of pseudo-*auhenua* identities. But unlike the inadvertent architects of heterotopia and Saeniha'a, Taroiara seeks fundamentally to alter the premises and processes of Arosi topogony; or, more accurately, he argues that they have already been altered. His topogonic project is retroactive. Divorcing matrilineages from land, he effectively argues that they have no topogonic function. Still, like all Arosi, he continues to maintain that matrilineages are the bearers of unique ontological substance and that, unlike the matrilineal bond, connection through males is of limited generational duration. He suggests that the reason men must pay bride-price is to overcome this lack of continuity through males and enable them to reproduce for the land in which they are living. Over time, the practice of paying bride-price constructs landholding social units based on father to son inheritance. But these landholding units are explicitly not categories of being modeled after and replacing the lost *auhenua* matrilineages in their territories as the fundamental building blocks of Arosi poly-ontology. Rather, diachronically speaking, they are purely territorial placeholders made up of a succession of representatives of multiple matrilineages joined together through men and their bride-price payments. This system of land tenure shifts topogonic activity away from matrilineages engaged in processes of becoming *auhenua* through the construction or co-opting of shrines and burial sites and locates it in the payment of bride-price from one generation to the next. Through the payment of bride-price, landholding units that lack ontological continuity achieve an anchored presence that, although stable, requires perpetual reconstitution.

But once divorced from land, what becomes of matrilineal essence in Taroiara's system? Conceptually deracinated from their territories, matrilineal ontological categories remain suspended in a state of merely being *auhenua* on Makira but never able to become *auhenua* in any particular territory. In the remaining two chapters I explore how the idea of a landless matrilineage, as a model of abstract ontological oneness, is implicated in the ongoing tension and negotiation between Arosi poly-ontology and the Christian myth of human mono-genesis.

CHAPTER 8

THE SEVERED SNAKE:
SCALES OF ORIGIN

I have so far identified at least two trends with the potential to promote a shift toward the conception of Arosi people and social order as constituting one all-inclusive lineage. Although operative in different practices, ideas, and modes of expression, these trends have both emerged in the context of Arosi dialogue with and appropriation of Christian teaching and the institution of the Church.

First, as described in chapter 1, communal work projects organized under the auspices of village churches are fostering village-wide and trans-village community identities that, in many contexts, transcend matrilineage and kin-based identities. By invoking ideals of Christian fraternity and unity as the rationale for cooperation, the leaders of such communal work projects are extending the ethic of cooperation said to be characteristic of a single matrilineage or kin network to encompass whole and sometimes several proximate villages. In many respects, this trend produces a social configuration that resembles the ideal structure of a multi-lineal polity centered on an *auhenua* lineage in its land, but consists instead in the coastal norm of a village comprising multiple kin-based hamlets clustered loosely around a focal church. Yet, with the churches at their centers, the many Arosi villages are further united at the level of the Church understood as one ecumenical family in Christ.

Second, as described in the previous chapter, Ishmael Taroiara is enlisting the idea of Christian love to redefine the nature of an Arosi matrilineage. No longer understood as a lineage anchored in an ancestral territory, a matrilineage, according to Taroiara, is simply a geographically dispersed group of people who share love because they are one. For Taroiara, a matrilineage, construed as oneness and love, becomes a model for the way in which the Arosi people as a whole ought to understand themselves and live together. Matrilineal oneness and love, he suggests, are in accordance both with God's plan and with Arosi custom, but in the past, Arosi have only partially comprehended the harmony between God's will and custom. Here Taroiara's theory of a matrilineage as love amounts to a theological ethno-history according to which, even before the arrival of missionaries, God had already imparted some knowledge of himself to the Arosi: "Before, they didn't know God, and they sacrificed to ancestral spirits, but God had given them love since he is love. He gave them love within one lineage." Thus, the matrilineage has been the locus of a revelation, but the content of that revelation—oneness and love—has been held exclusively within lineages. Now, Taroiara promises, his plan to institute father to son inheritance will break down the barriers among lineages, allowing them to experience together the oneness and love they had previously held to themselves; now they can all "eat together and work together in the likeness of God."

In addition to these trends, however, I also encountered a striking and singular mythic representation of all Makirans as members of one great endogamous lineage—an image that complexifies the issue of whether and how Arosi understandings of Christian themes of unity may be impinging on Arosi poly-ontology. When I interviewed Wilsman Warioha of Asimaanioha village in east Arosi, he expounded to me a complex theology of the island entailing a mono-ontological view of humanity. He explained to me that, before the missionaries came, Arosi had put their trust in a spirit-snake called Ha'atoibwari who was "the spirit of Makira." Warioha expressed his understanding of the complete identity between Ha'atoibwari and the island through a variety of statements, each conveying a slightly different aspect of the relationship between the two. "Ha'atoibwari is a snake," he said, "the spirit of Makira." "Ha'atoibwari is the image (*nununa*) of the island; ... Rohu [in the northwest] is the tail and Star Harbour [in the southeast] is the head." "In the beginning, the island was placed as a snake." "[Ha'atoibwari] forms up even now as the island ... the snake's image." "Ha'atoibwari isn't of Mwara or Ugi, alright, [Ha'atoibwari] is of Makira, this island." "Ha'atoibwari holds the *kastom* of us people on Makira." As well as being the island, Ha'atoibwari was the source of everything in the island: "Its radiant power (*rarahana*) placed stones, placed fish, placed trees." In response to human trust and petitions, Ha'atoibwari provided fish, game, good harvests, healing for the sick, and protection in war. Rather than directly addressing Ha'atoibwari in prayer, however, pre-Christian Makirans sought aid through birds, stones, trees, sharks, and snakes, which they regarded as small extensions or projections (*papasu*) of Ha'atoibwari. These creatures and objects were messengers (*ha'ataari*) of Ha'atoibwari. Similarly, in Warioha's system of spiritual beings, ancestral spirits were equally projections of the snake and its power. Warioha's explication of the unity among the island, Ha'atoibwari, ancestors, and other spirits culminated in a narrative according to which a primordial male and female were the progenitors of all people on Makira.[1]

When the island was placed it looked like a snake and it was called Ha'atoibwari. And the two people there that originated from (*hasubu mai*) ... No! didn't originate (*ai'a hasubu*), that dwelled (*awa*) on the island were Hauhunaari'i and Hauhunaaraha. They lived up to the east. That is the image of Ha'atoibwari. Alright, the two stones rose up (*suruta'e*), Hauhunaari'i a woman and Hauhunaaraha a man. They rose up in the east at Hautawaraha—you know, east at Gheta. They followed the hills in the bush [as they moved down the island]; they didn't travel along the coast. They stayed at a hill and they had two children: one girl, one boy. And they arose again and they came down to the second hill and they had two more children: one girl, one boy. Coming down again to the third hill and they also had one girl and one boy. The two of them [i.e., Hauhunaari'i and Hauhunaaraha] lived through the places there and they shouted saying: "You all, [when] marrying you go beyond two villages, [then at] the third village you can marry among yourselves." After speaking, they both went on again. They both came down again arriving at the hill coming down toward us and again they had a girl and boy, coming down until opposite Wango in the bush. That was the last of their children; they didn't have any more children.

And they placed shell valuables at that place. Alright, it is the shell valuables the two of them placed up there in the bush that [people] use to make valuables at Waiwora [near Makira Harbour]; but, if they hadn't carried [the valuables] here, [people] would make valuables at Su'u Namuga [i.e., at the eastern end of the island]. And they left it and they came down to Rohu and they stayed at that place there [at the cliffs at the western end of the island]. They didn't have a child there. They were already old and they didn't have any children and then they both died. Alright, and then their many children married. They went down the other side [of the island] and they came down

---

1. Warioha characterized his narrative as a *mamaani usuri*. In contrast to *mamaani 'oni'oni*—stories that are said to have been made up and often concern animals—*mamaani usuri* are said to have been passed down from "olden times" and to describe events that have actually taken place.

this side [of the island], and they lived in the villages at the lower ends of their paths [down which they'd descended from the bush to the coast]. Starting at Bauro coming down, coming down, coming down reaching Rohu they live at the lower ends of their paths. They have the coast and they have the bush. We here are the people of their increase. That is the story of Hauhunaari'i and Hauhunaaraha.

When Warioha had finished his narration, Casper Kaukeni, who was helping me to make an audio recording of the story, began to question him for more information regarding the exact nature of the relationship between Ha'atoibwari and the first couple. A dialogue ensued in which images of biological reproduction and manipulative placement were both suggested to describe this relationship.

CK: Who gave birth (ha'ahuta) to the two of them?
WW: Ha'atoibwari placed (nugaa) Hauhunaari'i and Hauhunaaraha. That's the spirit they had.
CK: They are its children?
WW: Children of Ha'atoibwari: Hauhunaari'i and Hauhunaaraha.

Prior to this exchange, however, Casper had become even more exercised by Warioha's account of how the children of the primal couple were instructed to "marry beyond the second village." He interrupted with questions that revealed that Warioha's narrative is in conflict with Arosi poly-ontology and lineage exogamy. "Who were they going to marry there?" he asked. "Were they going to marry their brothers and sisters?" Warioha tried to deflect these questions by reiterating: "That's why I said they had to go beyond two villages." But Casper was not satisfied and further queried, "Did these villages already exist on the island?" Casper found the spatial distance that Warioha introduced to be an inadequate degree of separation among groups that, according to the myth, belonged to one lineage. For Casper—like most Arosi—one lineage, regardless of the location of its members, cannot marry endogamously. If all Arosi were descended from one couple, as this myth envisions, no one could marry. In response to this problem, Warioha could only fall back on the statement, "I'm telling about the beginning of people!" Recall that it was Casper who had said that if everyone on Makira were of the same lineage "it would be the end," because no one would be able to marry. Thus, Warioha's vision of human origins is equivalent to Casper's doomsday scenario. Later, when I summarized Warioha's story to another friend who had directed me to Warioha as someone particularly knowledgeable in Arosi custom, he looked to have a fit of depression. "That is not *kastom!*" he said, "I'm saddened that we have different *kastom*."[2]

Between the 1850s and 1924 when Fox published his ethnography of Arosi, *The Threshold of the Pacific*, Anglican missionaries on Makira collected a variety of myths and traditions concerning generative spirit-snakes. As documented and interpreted by the missionaries, these myths and traditions preserved Makiran beliefs in a supreme creator snake who made everything on the island, including a primordial couple from whom all people are descended. On the basis of these earlier recorded traditions and Warioha's narrative, it would appear, therefore, that in Arosi there are two different representations of human origins: one poly-genetic, depicting multiple disparate human origins, and the other mono-genetic, positing a single origin. Side by side, these two models of human origins seem to exemplify what Gregory Schrempp (1992: 90) terms a "dual formulation," that is, "the coexistence of two different theories of ancestry and identity accounting for the origin and nature of major entities" in the cosmos. A dual formulation, in other words, is a double ontology providing two competing answers to the question: What is the number and nature of things in the universe?

This apparent contradiction between the majority of Arosi representations that imply "there are many types of people," and a minority of representations that imply "people are one" raises difficult historical questions. Are the minority representations of human unity best understood as evidence of European missionary interpretive biases and teachings? Or are they evidence of a continuous indigenous dual formulation involving an alternative or esoteric understanding of Arosi ontology? Or does Warioha's narrative point to both elements?

The historical sources and ethnographic data I examine in this chapter suggest that the dual formulation in Arosi today is the result of an ongoing dialogue about origins initiated in the mid nineteenth century between Anglican missionaries and Makirans. Persistent missionary attempts to instill the first article of the Christian creeds—belief in one creator God—by inquiring into indigenous accounts of origins elicited diverse Makiran testimonies about extraordinary snakes associated with the origin and increase of cultigens and animals on the island and sometimes credited with having given birth to or fash-

---

2. Burt distinguishes between a "contemporary movement to unite the Kwara'ae as the descendants of the first ancestor" (1982: 392) and "the autonomous local groups of precolonial times" (1982: 378). He documents no objections, however, to the "universally accepted" view among these north Malaitans that they are "a single descent group" originating with an apical ancestor (Burt 1982: 396; cf. 1983: 344).

ioned human beings. Comparative contextualization of these Makiran snake traditions reveals, however, that they belong to a wider regional complex of myths that share a capacity to index origins on more than one scale: global, insular, and most importantly, lineal. Evidence presented in this chapter favors the inference that European missionaries misconstrued Arosi and other Makiran snake myths pertaining to the formation and powers of the island of Makira and the origins of particular matrilineages as myths of global origins and ascribed to Makirans a "primitive" intuition of a supreme deity who was, in one way or another, responsible for the inception of a unified humanity. But the idea of a Makiran creator serpent has not been conceived by European missionaries alone, nor does the dual formulation of which it has become a part reflect the gradual unilateral displacement of Arosi cosmology by Christianity. Rather, it took shape and continues to serve as an image through which Arosi themselves seek to reconcile aspects of their poly-genetic models of coming into being with the biblical creation story. In the process of rapprochement between these two fundamentally incompatible visions of origins and their embedded ontologies, both European missionaries and some Arosi themselves have invoked myths of a generative snake, most often known by a variant of the name Ha'atoibwari, as the locus of *praeparatio evangelica*, that is, as a prefiguration of Christian truth planted by God among all people to enable them to accept the gospel when it arrives.

Ha'atoibwari is readily adaptable to this hermeneutical role, I suggest, because this generative snake indexes the fundamental and lasting unity of both the island of Makira and of each individual Arosi matrilineage as an ontological entity. Represented in every variant save Warioha's as the severed snake who remains whole, she is the wholeness of the island that is compromised by an indeterminate external agent prior to the appearance of spatially defined matrilineages, and the purity of each matrilineage that is similarly compromised by the necessity of exogamy. The severed snake is analogous, in other words to the umbilical cord that must be cut in order to reproduce lineage continuity. Concerned with the problem of an originary transition from unity to internal differentiation on two related scales—the island of Makira and each unique matrilineage—the myths of Ha'atoibwari display the logic of a mono-ontology operative within a deep poly-ontology. Appropriately, therefore, just as some European missionaries fastened on Ha'atoibwari as a kernel of genuine faith within Arosi "superstition," some Arosi have fastened on Ha'atoibwari as an indigenous figure of unity and creativity amenable to comparison and even harmonization with the biblical portrayal of the one creator God.

But even if the image of the serpent Ha'atoibwari as a high god who created a unified human race had no clear Makiran antecedent at this universal scale, the myths out of which Europeans and Arosi constructed this new global variant show by what logic Arosi cosmology may entail a potential for either indigenous dual formulation or ongoing transformation between poly- and mono-ontology. The Arosi versions of the Ha'atoibwari myth presented in this chapter may be interpreted as attempts to address a fundamental ambiguity in Arosi cosmology. On the one hand, Arosi cosmology represents all matrilineages that are truly *auhenua* as equally of the island. On the other hand, the multiple lineage origin narratives portray such matrilineages as inherently distinct and essentially unrelated. Yet, Makira, on which all lineages claim to have arisen, is a perceptibly finite whole—it is Hanuato'o, "The Strong Island." How, then, can the many matrilineages be of the one strong island without also being, in some way, its children and thus siblings to one another? As previously described, some Arosi overcome this conceptual problem simply by stating that divisions in the island already existed before the matrilineages originated. The idea of such a priori divisions expresses the ontological uniqueness of each matrilineage just as the distinct "rooms" in I'abwari mark the original speciation of marine animals. The myths of I'abwari's terrestrial analogue, Ha'atoibwari, constitute another medium for the expression of this model of an entity that, although a whole, gives rise to categories of being that are thereby in no way related to one another. As analyzed below, these myths strive to assert that the unity of the island, represented by a spirit-snake with fabulous generative powers, has been dismembered and banished as a precursor to the advent of separately engendered matrilineages. In the context of Arosi interaction with European missionaries, however, it appears that these myths have become revalorized by a few Arosi—such as Warioha—who have come to understand the Ha'atoibwari tradition as an expression of the common descent of all Makirans through the mediation of a single creative island spirit. These Arosi have realized the possibility of mono-ontology, available as an alternative interpretation of Arosi visions of origins, as a means of constructing both a pre-Christian Arosi tradition that contained truth and a truly Arosi Christianity. Theoretically, therefore, the ultimate conclusion must be that similar alternative interpretations of the island as the mother of all Arosi matrilineages could always have coexisted with the currently more evident poly-ontological interpretations and could have once even been dominant in the past. With or without Arosi engagement with Christianity, Arosi cosmology entails its own possibilities for mono-ontology.

It should be acknowledged at this point that one component of the following analysis—namely the assertion that some Arosi selected Ha'atoibwari for equation with the God of the Bible because this mythic snake was a figure of the unity of an Arosi matrilineage—bears a certain resemblance to

Durkheim's (1995: 288–299, 428) evolutionary model according to which totemic ancestors serve as the prototypes of higher-order deities in "inter-tribal" and "international" social contexts. Unlike Durkheim, however, I am not seeking to establish the evolutionary increments in a universal linear progression from one stage of religious life to another. Instead, I am analyzing a particular instance of cosmological transformation pertaining to a particular historical circumstance in which Arosi struggle to reconcile the inconsistencies between their poly-ontological structures and Judeo-Christian cosmology. In the context of this struggle, Ha'atoibwari does not evolve organically into a universal creator. Rather, in a historically contingent process, Europeans and Arosi alike have searched through Makiran concepts of ultimate generation for potential analogues to the God of the Bible. Moreover, instead of presenting Ha'atoibwari as a simple projection of a microcosm (an Arosi matrilineage) onto a macrocosmic plane (the universal biblical God), my analysis uncovers the ways in which an Arosi matrilineage resembles an absolute monad, making it, not an exact, but a productive indigenous parallel to the biblical models of one God and one humanity.

"Feeling after God"

From its inception in the 1840s, the Anglican Melanesian Mission programmatically and consistently sought to evangelize by finding and connecting with what missionary theologians understood to be the rudiments of truth, or expressions of the capacity for faith, in Melanesian belief and practice.[3] The leaders of the mission formulated a missiology of accommodation to indigenous custom. This approach was rooted in the twin theological presuppositions that humanity everywhere is driven by the same aspiration to apprehend God, and that God has left no people without some inkling of the true nature of divinity. Guided by these principles, the Anglican missionaries looked for what was consonant with Christian teaching in indigenous religion, such as belief in spiritual beings, belief in the human soul and in a form of afterlife, and basic ideas about right and wrong. Regarding such "points of contact" as

---

3. For detailed historical accounts of the Melanesian Mission, see Davidson 2000; Fox 1958; Hilliard 1966, 1978; Tippett 1967; Whiteman 1983. Sayes (1976) provides a comprehensive narrative history of the Anglican mission's activities on Makira up to 1918. The Melanesian Mission was a diocese in the Anglican Province of New Zealand until 1975 when the Province of Melanesia was established and the present Church of Melanesia inaugurated (Whiteman 1983: 294–302).

confirmation of a common humanity between Melanesians and Europeans, the missionaries also identified them as points of entrée for the implantation of the Christian message (Hilliard 1978: 191). At the same time, with a view to avoiding the unnecessary destruction of unobjectionable indigenous practices by imposing European tastes in the name of Christianity, they attempted to discern what was essential to Christianity and what was merely European cultural accretion. The following analytical review of the thought and work of the European Anglican missionaries involved in the evangelization of Makira discovers the process through which missionaries and their Makiran converts together constructed and then promulgated the idea that Makirans had once been the devotees of an ancient island-wide cult of a supreme creator god worshipped in the form of a snake.[4]

It is, of course, important to recognize that the missiological writings and directives of mission leaders do not constitute evidence of actual mission practices in the field and that there may often have been considerable discrepancies between the ideals of mission theory and the realities of evangelization on the ground. Different mission priests, for example, pursued different policies regarding whether or not to desecrate or perform exorcisms at pre-Christian sacred sites (see chapter 5), and there was definite Christian opposition—both European and indigenous—to practices such as cannibalism, warfare, infanticide, and disciplines aimed at acquiring powers through relationships with spirits other than the Holy Spirit recognized by the Church. Yet, as will emerge in this and the following chapter, there is considerable evidence that Anglican Christians on Makira have, with an exceptional degree of consistency, maintained both a theory and a practice of finding and building on points of contact between indigenous culture and Christianity and seeking to preserve the memory, and even in some cases the practice, of theologically unobjectionable aspects of Makiran culture (cf. Hilliard 2005). This approach has been more than a missionary initiative; it has been taken up and carried on by indigenous Anglican clergy and appears, furthermore, to be a common and productive part of the everyday outlook of laypeople. To take a recent case in point: during his 1992 diocesan tour in the context of the Church's official "Decade of Evangelism and Renewal," Bishop James Mason (Bishop of Hanuato'o, 1991–2004), a man of Santa Isabel, instructed a gathering of Arosi at 'Ubuna village that he wanted Christian renewal on Makira to include the revival of Makiran customs and traditions. He then likened the Church of

---

4. Jeudy-Ballini (1998) traces a similar process of the production of a supreme being in a Catholic mission context in East New Britain (Papua New Guinea).

Melanesia to a canoe with six anchors: "personal, cultural, sacrament, litur-
gical, doctrine, and history," thus putting indigenous culture on a par with the
content of Christianity. Although clearly engaged in a postcolonial project of
promoting local history and cultural pride within the contexts of global Christianity and the nation-state of Solomon Islands, Bishop Mason's theology of
culture owes much to the history of the European and indigenous co-pro-
duction of Solomon Islands Anglicanism reviewed here.

"I Believe in Kauraha the Father"

John Coleridge Patteson, the first bishop of the missionary diocese of
Melanesia (1861–71), provided the intellectual foundation for the Anglican
missiology of accommodation and appears to have been the first European to
experiment with identifying a Makiran snake spirit with the biblical God. In
1865, Patteson articulated a central tenet of his mission strategy when he
wrote: "There is an element of faith in superstition; we must fasten on that,
and not rudely destroy the superstition, lest with it we destroy the principle
of faith in things and beings unseen" (in Yonge 1874, 2: 151). For Patteson,
the element of faith found in superstition was a manifestation of universal
human longing for self-improvement, goodness, and truth. Christianity, he
believed, was the universally appropriable answer to this longing (Yonge 1874,
1: 298). As Sarah H. Sohmer (1994) has shown, Patteson drew inspiration and
confirmation for his views from the work of two earlier orthodox Anglican
theologians, Richard Hooker (1554–1600) and Joseph Butler (1692–1752).
From Hooker, Patteson appropriated the idea that natural religion and general revelation work together to draw humanity everywhere closer to God,
priming all people for acceptance of the special revelation of Christianity.
From Butler, he adapted the idea that Christian theological concepts can be
made intelligible to the common Christian only by analogy to what is already
experientially familiar. The synthesis he made of these ideas was a mission
methodology that called for building Christian understanding on the foundation of indigenous beliefs that could be evaluated as expressions of imper-
fect but innate inclinations toward truth.[5]

Desiring to comprehend the "state of the heathen mind," Patteson put his
mission methodology into practice by promoting the use of Melanesian languages in the mission school and striving to translate Christian theological

---

5. For fuller accounts of Patteson's missiology and its sustained influence on the
Melanesian Mission's methodology through the early decades of the twentieth century, see
Hilliard 1970, 2005; Sohmer 1988: 206–245; Whiteman 1983: 116–124.

Figure 8.1. John Coleridge Patteson (from an engraving by C. H. Jeens, 1873).

concepts into island vocabularies (in Yonge 1874, 2: 145; cf. Hilliard 1978: 15, 31, 34, 49). In the late 1850s, Patteson followed this procedure in his earliest efforts to produce Arosi translations of biblical narratives, Christian prayers, and catechisms. Published by the Melanesian Press at St. John's College in New

Zealand, these translations gloss "God" using the name Kauraha, the name of a mythic serpent that in later missionary writings is often equated or associated with Hatoibwari. The texts he produced include accounts of Adam and Eve and the expulsion from the Garden of Eden, the stories of Cain and Abel, Noah and the flood, the Tower of Babel, and the call of Abraham, as well as basic instruction concerning the atoning death of Christ (Church of England in New Zealand 1858a, 1858?b; Gabelentz 1861: 235–243; cf. Yonge 1874, 1: 294-296).[6] In rendering Christian ideas about God into Arosi, Patteson simply lets the name Kauraha stand for God. Thus, in the words of the Apostles' Creed, the Arosi Christian was to confess "I believe in Kauraha the Father, strong, maker of the sky and earth" (*Inau hinihinia Kauraha ni Ama, wetewete, haua ni aro mana ano*). Repeatedly throughout simple teachings and exhortations, prayers, and creeds alike, Kauraha is located "in the sky" where the believer is destined to join him (Church of England in New Zealand 1858a).

It is not clear why Patteson adopted the name Kauraha as an equivalent for God. He gives no account of any Makiran myth or tradition that would explain his willingness to regard Kauraha as an appropriate representation of the biblical God in Arosi terms. The writings of two subsequent Anglican missionaries, Cecil Wilson (Bishop of Melanesia, 1894–1911) and Charles E. Fox, indicate that Kauraha was a spirit-snake. According to Wilson (1932: 159), this spirit-snake was an object of veneration throughout Makira and was known by three different names: Kaaraha, Kahuahuarii, and Kahasubwari. Like Patteson before him, Wilson pursued his mission work with a conviction that Melanesians were "men who had been feeling after GOD, and had not found Him, but had satisfied the religious instincts GOD had given them with ... gods" that bore a crude resemblance to the creator deity of the Bible (in Hilliard 1978: 192). Also like Patteson (Hilliard 2005: 202, quoting Sarawia n.d.: 10–11), Wilson deliberately set out to collect and make catechetical use of indigenous ideas about origins. He gathered information regarding Makiran spirit-snakes by pointedly asking converts "who they formerly believed created the world" (Wilson *D*: June 22, 1909; July 4, 1909; and "Anthropology" 1909). His inquiries elicited two variants of a myth about the dismemberment, reconstitution, and self-imposed exile of a snake-grandparent figure. Responding to Wilson's query, do "the people ever speak of a creating spirit?" James Faiato, a mission-educated teacher at Naoneone (in Kahua, Makira), recounted:

---

6. The mission referred to the Arosi language, and to the island of Makira as a whole, as "Bauro" until the 1880s.

they only spoke of Kahasubwari a snake, who one day came to a woman who had borne a child and asked her to let it have it. It coiled itself round on the ground with the child in the center. The woman went to her husband in the garden who rebuked her for leaving the child alone. She said a snake was taking care of it. The man was angry and went with an adze [to] cut up the snake, but as fast as he threw the pieces away, they joined together again. The snake had been a man and was the child's grandfather, and he left the island because of this treatment. [He] went to Mala[ita] but could still see S. Christoval [i.e., Makira], so [he] went to the high mountains in Guadalcanar, where he could no longer see them. (Wilson D: "Anthropology" 1909; cf. Codrington 1880/81: 298–299; 1891: 150–151)

At Ngorangora (in Bauro, about two kilometers west of what is now Kirakira), an "old chief" made a clearer connection between a snake-grandparent and human origins. He said:

the old belief was that a man who had become a snake gave birth [to] the first woman. The first male came from a coconut. It changed into one [i.e., a man]. The 2 blind eyes of the coconut became his eyes, the one you pierce became his mouth. Kahuahuarii (the snake) coiled itself around the child, and was chopped to pieces by the man, and constantly rejoined itself, but proving tired of its treatment it retired to Gela [in the central Solomons]. (Wilson D: "Anthropology" 1909; cf. Coombe 1911: 234–235; MM SCL, November 10, 1909: 91; Wilson 1932: 159)

Wilson also attests that the people of the nearby village of Mwanihuki equated the snake-grandparent who had deserted Makira with a snake who was said at the same time to dwell and receive sacrifice at Haununu on the south coast of the island. The cult at Haununu consisted of sacrifices offered at the onset of the nutting season in July. "Every year when the nuts ripen word is sent from Haununu that sacrifices to [a snake] are to be offered. Earth brought from Haununu is kept in every canoe house on a shelf under the roof, and a piece of pudding is burnt under it by one who knows the right words to use" (Wilson 1932: 159–160).

After Wilson, Fox too continued to seek after and collect information about the pre-Christian worship of spirit-snakes. Concerning a snake known variously as Kauraha, Ka'auraha, Kaweraha, or Kagauraha, Fox preserves four narratives. In one tale, collected from west Arosi, Ka'auraha is a woman who takes the form of a snake after her death and receives sacrifice at Wainaou, Haununu (Fox T: "Kagauraha"; Fox 1978: 266); in another tale of unspecified provenance, Kagauraha is the subject of the snake-grandparent episode, this time in the more common form of a snake-grandmother (Fox 1924: 82–83). In two unpublished transcriptions of Arosi tales, Ka'auraha, or Kaweraha, works in partnership with another snake called Haitoibwari, or Kahausipwari, to create, in one instance, the first man and woman and, in another, simply "the world" (Fox *T*: "Hatoibwari" and "Kahausipwari"). Additionally, Fox reports that a mother snake named Kauraha, along with her brood, was the focus of sacrifice and divination on Santa Ana where "[t]hey believe these snakes made them and all things." On the authority of a young Makiran who had visited Santa Ana, Fox describes the cult center there as a house built over a cavern where the snakes lived, receiving first-fruit offerings and providing oracular responses to local inquiries (MM *SCL*, February 5, 1910: 138–139; cf. Coombe 1911: 236–237).[7]

On the basis of these later clues provided by Wilson and Fox, it is possible to conjecture that Patteson learned about a creating spirit-snake named Kauraha, whose cult was connected with snakes, from a group of young men from Arosi whom he recruited for the mission school at St. John's College, Auckland.[8] By his own account, while on tour in mid 1856 as missionary chaplain to George Augustus Selwyn (Bishop of New Zealand, 1841–69), Patteson (1857: 656) recruited five youths—Hiriha, Kariri, Kereaurua, Sumaro, and Remania—from the village of Mwata on the west coast of Arosi. After two months of interaction with these recruits back in New Zealand, Patteson wrote to a correspondent: "Is it not a significant fact that the God worshipped in Gera [i.e., Marau Sound, Guadalcanal], and in one village of Bauro [i.e., Makira], is the Serpent, the very type of evil?" (in Yonge 1874, 1: 293; cf. Fox 1924: 85). The village in question must be Mwata, as no other Makirans were under Patteson's tutelage at the time.[9] Twenty years later, Bishop Selwyn's son,

---

7. Curiously, Fox (1924: 89; Fox and Drew 1915: 144) later published a nearly identical account, but in this later discussion, he asserts that the cult described is located not on Santa Ana but at Haununu.

8. Each year, the missionaries brought Melanesian boys and young men to the College where they remained for about six months of instruction. After this period of instruction, the Melanesian "scholars" were returned to their villages where it was hoped they would disseminate what they had learned of Christianity. St. John's College was the site of mission instruction 1849–59 until the mission established a separate school for Melanesians at Kohimarama near Auckland. In 1867 the mission transferred the education of Melanesians to a new school at Norfolk Island, which operated until 1919 (Fox 1958: 215–217).

9. Seventy years later, Ivens (1930–32: 965) suggested that Stephen Taroaniara of Tawatana village had introduced Patteson to the idea of Kauraha. This seems unlikely, however, as a source from 1858 indicates that Taroaniara had not yet been brought to New Zealand by 1856–57 when the first translations were published (MM *AR*, 1858: 8–9). A

John Richardson Selwyn (Bishop of Melanesia, 1877–91), recorded that when he visited this same village, the chief, Irihaa, who had also received his father and Patteson, informed him about a cult involving sacred snakes.

> He told me of a place down the coast where dwells the spirit which they allege is the author of everything, especially earthquakes. There is a rock there in which the inhabitants say they hear the earthquakes but never feel them. They have a temple in his honour, with sacred snakes—to which they offer yams, but only very small ones. I should like to see this place, as I have never come across anything of the kind yet. (MM *IV*, 1877: 18)[10]

While this evidence is fragmentary, it points to the Mwata recruits as the source for Patteson's use of Kauraha as an indigenous approximation to the biblical creator God. Whatever the origin of the idea, Patteson appears to have found the technique unsatisfactory, and eventually desisted in his use of Kauraha as a translation for God.[11] Patteson's change in practice was so complete that in 1891 Robert H. Codrington could attribute the, by then, long normative use of the English word "God" in mission translations and discourse to the initiative of Patteson.

> The Melanesian Mission, under the guidance of Bishop Patteson, has used in all the islands the English word God. He considered the enormous difficulty, if not impossibility, of finding an adequate native expression in any one language, and further the very narrow limits within which such a word if it could be found must be used, since the languages are at least as many as the islands. It is difficult to convey

---

later source, the mission journal *Southern Cross Log* (MM *SCL*, July 15, 1898: 1), erroneously lists Taroaniara among the Mwata recruits of 1856 (cf. Fox 1958: 159; Hilliard 1970: 192–193).

10. The "place down the coast" may have been located at Haununu approximately fifty kilometers southeast from Mwata along the south coast of Makira. Compare this description of a snake cult with those located by Wilson (1932: 159) and Fox (1924: 80–85, 89, 324–334) at Haununu.

11. Edridge (1985: 135) attributes a brief Bauro (i.e., Arosi) catechism, entitled "Scripture questions," to Patteson in which the English word "God" stands untranslated ([Patteson] 1866?b). Her attribution is credible on the grounds that no other missionary is known to have had sufficient proficiency in Arosi to have produced such a document during this period. Although the document is undated, Edridge dates it to 1866, perhaps on the basis of the fact that one other Arosi language document also attributed to Patteson ("Vocabulary of Melanesian Languages: Bauro, San Christoval Island, Solomon Islands") was printed in that year ([Patteson] 1866a).

by description the ideas which ought to attach to the new word, but at least nothing erroneous is connoted by it. (Codrington 1891: 121–122 n. 1; cf. Ivens 1918: 165–166)

The Spirit-snake As Creator

Although Kauraha quickly fell out of favor with Patteson as a representation of God, Wilson and Fox carried on the search for an indigenous precursor to monotheistic belief. Their resulting writings represent Kauraha either as equivalent to or as a companion of another spirit-snake, variously known as Kahasubwari, Kahausibwari, Kahausipwari, Hatuibwari, Haudibwari, Hasibwari, Hatipwari, and Hatoibwari, about whom the dismembered snake-grandparent myth was also told (Fox 1924; 1978: 204; Wilson 1932: 159).[12] The first missionary to publish a Makiran version of this myth had been Codrington (1880/81: 298–299; 1891: 150–151). In his account, Kahausibware is a spirit who manifests itself as a female snake and is "in some way" the progenitor of a female human. Additionally, it is said of the snake that it was she "who made men, pigs, and other animals, cocoa-nuts, fruit-trees, and all the food with which the island is now furnished" (1891: 150). As in the narratives later collected by Wilson and Fox, the snake is left in charge of her grandchild only to be chopped into pieces (in this case by her own daughter) that spontaneously reassemble. Offended, she takes refuge on Guadalcanal. Codrington's summary stresses that before these events "all the fruits of the earth grew without labour and all was of the best," but "since her departure all things in San Cristoval have deteriorated" (1891: 150–151). Unlike Wilson and Fox, however, Codrington does not associate Kahausibware with any cult center or practice at Haununu or elsewhere. On the contrary, he asserts that "[n]o prayers or sacrifices are offered to Kahausibware; she is nothing but the subject of stories" (1880/81: 299).

---

12. At points, Fox writes as though he recognizes a distinction between Kauraha and Hatoibwari (1924: 326; *T*: "Hatoibwari"; cf. *T*: "Kahausipwari") and, furthermore, indicates his awareness that Kauraha—not Hatoibwari—was the name Patteson used to gloss God (1978: 266; Fox to Rivers, May 28, 1919, Perry Papers, B2). But at other points, Fox also writes as though he has arrived at an interpretive conflation of these two beings as versions of the same "great winged serpent" who is, ultimately, one with or an aspect of the overarching figure he calls Agunua (e.g., 1924: 79 n. 4; 1985: 85, 89). Thus, in the annotated bibliography to his unpublished Arosi grammar, he describes one of Patteson's earlier Arosi translations in the following terms: "Some prayers & simple instruction, in the Bauro language Bp Patteson 1865. Interesting as the name of Hatoibwari (Winged Serpent Deity) is used for God" (*BG*: A3). I find no evidence, however, that Patteson ever used any indigenous name other than Kauraha in his translations. See chapter 9, note 6.

In 1924, Fox published a composite Arosi portrait of a winged serpent labeled "Hatoibwari." Based, he implies, on the testimony of at least two informants, this portrait depicts a figure with a long undulating serpentine tale,
a human head and torso, two pairs of eyes, four teeth, two sets of female
breasts, and a pair of wings sprouting at the shoulders. This being, whom Fox
takes to be hermaphroditic, is said to dwell on mountaintops or to descend
from the sky to mountaintops. Fox, who consistently prefers the spelling Hatuibwari, presents knowledge about this being as quasi-esoteric, remarking:
"[I]t is only certain men who know anything about him at all, beyond his
name, and they are very unwilling to speak of him; but as I learnt more, and
they found I had some knowledge of him, they spoke more freely" (1924: 237;
cf. Fox to Rivers, May 28, 1919, Perry Papers, B2). Among the traditions
about Hatuibwari that Fox recorded is what he terms "a purely native myth"
according to which Hatuibwari created humanity.

> He came down to the mountain Hoto (in one legend) and here he
> created men. It is curious that in almost all the tales the woman is
> created first. He took hard red clay and rolled this in his hands till it
> became plastic, he breathed on it and rolled it again, and then he
> formed a clay image, forming the head, legs, and arms. This red clay
> image he then placed in the sun, and by and by the heat of the sun
> caused it to live. It was a woman. Later, when the woman slept, Ha-
> tuibwari took a rib from her side, he added more red clay and
> moulded this also, and from this he made a man. This first woman
> and man had children and increased. (Fox 1924: 238)[13]

Despite acknowledging that Christianity had been present on Makira for half
a century by the time he encountered this narrative, Fox (1924: 238) accepts
it as genuine indigenous tradition on the grounds that he discovered it in a
remote bush village but not on the coast. He furthermore implies that his data
lend support to Andrew Lang's theory that belief in a "supreme God," "Sky-
god," or "Creator" among "savage" peoples need not be the result of "borrowing" from European missionaries, but often coexists with the worship of
"ghosts" and animal spirits (Lang 1913, 1: 320–339).

Fox goes beyond presenting Hatuibwari as an uncanny indigenous parallel
to the biblical creator God and incorporates Hatuibwari into a larger project

---

13. I know of only one extant version of such a biblical-style creation transcribed by
Fox (T: "Hatoibwari"). According to this Arosi language text, Hatoibwari and Ka'auraha
together perform the creation of human beings from a lump of earth. In this version, collected in east Arosi, the man is created first and the woman is molded from his rib.

Figure 8.2. Hatoibwari (from, Fox, *Threshold of the Pacific*, 1924: facing 236). Used with permission of Kegan Paul.

of interpreting all snake symbolism and ritual involving snakes as aspects of a pervasive pre-Christian Makiran monism. The core datum in this reconstruction appears to be testimony he collected regarding the afterlife destiny of the *aunga*, one of two spirit entities that make up the human person according to Arosi. The *aunga*, Fox was told, must enter a rock and travel a road to reach an otherworldly river in which it must bathe (1924: 234–235; 1985: 85, 86, 89; *AMM*: 86–87). If the deceased person had been good, immersion in the river transforms the *aunga* into *'unua*, a pervading "immortal essence." This "vital essence" is the beginning and end of all life, so that the transformation of the *aunga* is understood to be a return to its source. Fox notes, however, that this return does not entail loss of discrete "personality" (1924: 236; 1985: 85, 89; MM *SCL*, October 1, 1920: 3). Furthermore, Fox claims that, conceived of as a transcendent unity, this "immortal essence" is known as A'unua (or Agunua in Bauro; Fox 1924: 79; 1978: 32; cf. 1962: 62–63; 1985: 85–89). Asserting that this A'unua, "whose cult was once widespread," was the true object of an annual nearly island-wide first-fruits sacrifice centered on a shrine in Haunnunu, Fox constructs a three-tiered hierarchy of fundamentally consubstantial spiritual beings. While Kagauraha, Kahausibwari, and Kahuahuarii rank among a multiplicity of "local representatives of Agunua" (Fox 1924: 82; cf. Codrington 1891: 151, 179), a human *aunga* that rejoins the "immortal essence" becomes "a sort of vice-regent for Hatuibwari, one of the serpent spirits henceforth" (Fox 1924: 235; cf. 1985: 85–89). If such spirits "return to the world of the living, they will have a serpent incarnation" (Fox 1924: 235). Thus, Fox (1924: 80) confidently concludes that all spirit-snakes are representations of A'unua, for A'unua, "as one native said, is 'all of them.'"

Taken together, these missionary sources suggest that in the mid 1850s Bishop Patteson heard reports from his Arosi pupils of a spirit-snake named Kauraha who gave birth to a female child and who was also associated with the fertility of the land. A shrine dedicated to this spirit-snake may have existed at that time in Haunnunu. Owing to Patteson's early tentative appropriation of Kauraha as an indigenous gloss on the Christian God, however, it is extremely difficult, if not impossible, to discern in later missionary accounts of spirit-snakes the difference between indigenous Arosi ideas and Arosi appropriations of early mission instruction. Additionally, it is possible that feedback from an even earlier mission enterprise has been a factor in the ongoing construction of a once island-wide cult of a creator snake.

A decade before Patteson, the Marist missionaries had spent twenty months attempting to convert the Islanders in the region of Makira Harbour.[14] As documented by Father Léopold Verguet, a member of the mission party, this Roman Catholic evangelical incursion also encountered snake symbolism and cult activity to which the brothers responded by introducing Makirans to the biblical account of creation.

> On this occasion I met face to face with idolatry of the worst kind: the adoration of the infernal serpent! I directed all my efforts to explaining to these fallen men the first page of the catechism: a creator God. I puzzled them by asking them who had given them the coconut, the *ngari* nut tree, and the breadfruit tree; they answered me pleasantly that they had always had these things. Although savages, they had enough sense to understand that it was necessary to arrive at a distant beginning when nothing existed on earth, and I returned continually to my much vexing question: "Who is the one who first planted the coconut on your island?" "We do not know." "Very well, I have come from Europe expressly to teach you: it is Jehovah."
>
> I explained to them then to the best of my ability the creation of man, the existence of a future life, heaven and hell. My discourse was filled more with gestures than with words. Not knowing in their language most of the abstract words, such as: to believe, to hope, to suffer, to be happy, it was necessary to supply these through the eloquence of action. In speaking of God the creator I kneaded a doll from clay and I blew on it as if to animate it; then I made a child lie down on the ground who, at my breath, rose up as if he had received life. I compared these two actions and said to them, "It is thus that Jehovah made the first man." (Verguet 1854: 159–160, author's translation)

Verguet's account, together with those of later Anglican missionaries, shows that over time Christian missionaries on Makira consistently inquired after indigenous beliefs about origins as a prelude to teaching the story of Genesis, thereby fostering a context of mutual translation and appropriation. Thus, Fox's position that the Arosi who told him of Hatoibwari's Adam's rib-style creation were naive to biblical narrative appears questionable. In fact, other evidence as well illustrates that Islanders could retain apparently fragmentary elements of Christian teaching, interpreting and recontextualizing them in

---

14. For detailed accounts of the Marist's residence at Makira Harbour (1845–47), see Laracy 1976; O'Brien 1995; Raucaz 1928; Sayes 1976; Verguet 1854; Wiltgen 1981.

ways unanticipated by the missionaries. Ironically, Fox himself traces the petitions offered to a spirit called Sukarito to the influence of the Marist missionaries. Concerning Sukarito, in whose name he recognizes an Arosi pronunciation of Jesus Christ, Fox writes that he was a spirit "who once came down to the world from the sky.... Only a few people know Sukarito, and have power with him" (ABM *R*, June 1, 1918: 39). In this case, the fact that the Roman Catholic mission had spent less than two years on the island did not deter Fox from finding their legacy in Sukarito, "the most powerful and feared of the spirits worshipped by the heathen in Arosi and the western end of San Cristoval" (ABM *R*, June 1, 1918: 39).

The Melanesian Mission's practice of removing young men from their villages for indoctrination at school in New Zealand and then returning them to live and teach among their neighbors ensured that the process of appropriation was mediated by indigenous interpretation and debate. After only a year of this practice, the Report of the Melanesian Mission for the 1857 tour of Makira describes the process of exchange of ideas that the mission promoted in Mwata and its neighboring villages.

> In each place the people who were not at work in the distant yam grounds came together into the largest building in the village, generally a boat-shed; and hours were spent in conversation and a desultory kind of teaching, sometimes carried on by question and answer, sometimes by merely stating the simplest and most elementary truths of Christianity. Mr. Patteson said, he thought he could detect evident signs of a good effect having been produced by the statements made to their own countrymen by the lads who had been in New Zealand, however imperfect and erroneous in some respects may have been their account of what they had been taught. He knew from them that they had talked on these subjects to their own friends as well as they were able.... (MM *AR*, 1858: n.p.; cf. Hilliard 1978: 19)

Names and concepts received and processed in this manner, even those that later fell out of use by the missionaries, could still be remembered. Around 1857, Patteson published a short prayer book in the language of Marau Sound, Guadalcanal (Church of England in New Zealand 1857?; cf. Gabelentz 1861: 243–251). Because this language appeared to him to be closely related to Arosi, Patteson translated God as Kauraha as he had done in his earliest Arosi translations. Seventy years later, the name Kauraha was still identified by Islanders in Marau Sound as the name of a "school ghost," that is, a spirit introduced through mission education (Ivens 1930–32: 965).

The Christian mission project as a whole initiated a dialogue between Europeans and Makirans regarding the nature of origins. In the following section I explore the possibility that some Arosi brought indigenous ideas and stories about spirit-snakes into this dialogue because these ideas and stories index two distinct scales of origin: the origin of the island and the origin of a matrilineage. For some Arosi, the snake represented the island of Makira as a whole and its productivity. At the same time, for a limited number of Arosi the snake was understood to be their lineage ancestress. Finally, for many Arosi, it was a form in which their ancestors might appear to them, making the snake a figure of matrilineal unity and continuity readily understood by all Arosi. These accounts—myths of the spirit-snake of the island, lineage origin narratives, and explanations of ancestral snakes—that Makirans presented to the missionaries became the building blocks for the cooperative construction of mythic variants of a pan-Makiran universal creator snake. Today only a small number of Arosi know and continue to use this myth as a means of thinking about origins. Of these, most appear still to be struggling to reconcile this myth with Arosi poly-ontology and its strict insistence on multiple absolutely distinct exogamous matrilineages. Like Warioha, however, a few appear to be ready to embrace the myth's implication that all Arosi belong ultimately to one lineage in which they ought to be united by love through the Christian God.

Hatoibwari: The One among the Many

I began this chapter with Wilsman Warioha's version of the Ha'atoibwari myth. Warioha stated that a snake, Ha'atoibwari, who was the image of the island, either gave birth to, or placed, or somehow gave rise to a lithomorphic male and female on Makira who became the progenitors of all subsequent inhabitants of the island. The following is a summary of another version that I recorded in which the theme of unified human origins is absent. This is the version of Hauni of 'Ubuna at the western end of Arosi. Hauni storied that,

> Hatoibwari[15] and her mate, the snake Ka'uraha, first lived at Haunnunu. The two cultivated a coconut on a cliff top. It bore so many nuts that they built a fence around it to keep the nuts from rolling

---

15. During the course of his narration, Hauni switched back and forth between the names Hatoibwari and Hausubwari.

down into the sea. The people who fished in the sea below saw the coconuts and asked if they might have some. Hatoibwari said: "I don't allow it yet. When they are dry and sprouting I will give them to you all; you won't buy it, I will just give it to you." But the fishermen climbed up the cliff and cut the fence, letting the coconuts fall down into the sea. When Hatoibwari saw that, she said, "So be it!" and pronounced a curse so that if the coconuts drifted ashore on other islands the people there could plant them and they would grow, but if they drifted back to Makira, the people might plant them but they would never grow. Then she said: "Therefore, in the custom law (*ringeringe auhenua*) of the island they've driven me away, that's what they've done, and I will not dwell here." So Hatoibwari was angry and went away into the bush, leaving her husband behind.

Now, Hatoibwari was pregnant when she went up into the bush to Gohumwaningari and she gave birth to a daughter. An old woman and her granddaughter from the village of Hoto discovered Hatoibwari and her child, and Hatoibwari allowed them to adopt her baby. They fed the snake's child, and she grew quickly until soon she was ready to marry. A man from the village desired to marry her and she also desired the man. When the man asked the old woman for the girl, the old woman consulted Hatoibwari, who said: "So be it! Whatever she wants. But my child is making a mistake for me. They will kill me. She will do something, and they will kill me for it." After the marriage, Hatoibwari instructed the old woman and her granddaughter to take a baby pig and a small basket of food to the man's house. When they arrived, they threw the basket of food and the pig into the house. Because of the power of the snake these small items multiplied to fill the house completely.

Eventually the newlyweds had a child of their own. When they would go off to work in their garden, the woman, without her husband's knowledge, would leave her baby in Hatoibwari's care. One day the man came home and smelled a foul odor on his child. He said, "My word, what's with this child? It smells like dirt!" "My goodness, I don't know," replied his wife, "Her grandmother looked after her all day." But the man was suspicious, and on another day he pretended to leave the house but returned after his wife had gone out. He looked in and saw the child lying in the coils of the snake. That evening he accused his wife of leaving his child with a snake, whereupon the snake appeared, and the man cut off its head with his ax. Hatoibwari said: "So be it! It has happened as I said it would." Then the movement of the snake's head caused a landslide that buried the village, but the snake's child survived with her baby and rejoined the snake's head to its body. Hatoibwari instructed her daughter to place one yam tuber inside a basket, then she swallowed her daughter and grandchild and departed from that place.

Hatoibwari swam out to sea through a river mouth and headed toward Guadalcanal. There were two young brothers living on Guadalcanal who were orphans. One day they went out to fish in their canoe and they met Hatoibwari, who asked to be taken home with them. The snake came ashore with them and used her power to fill the boys' house with cooked food. Thereafter the boys and the snake lived happily together and the snake helped the two of them to prosper. Every task that they began she completed for them by her power. In this way she taught them every step of how to make a yam garden and how to gather and store nuts. They had so much food that they made a feast to feed all of the neighboring people. Finally, Hatoibwari asked if she could trade places with the shark who inhabited the shrine at which the boys' dead father used to sacrifice. The shark conceded his place at the top of the hill, and Hatoibwari took up residence in the shrine at the top of the hill called Tatuve. That's what they call the hill today, but the old name was Bwari.

When he had finished narrating, Hauni said: "That's the story I know of the snake. Hatoibwari's husband Ka'uraha didn't leave Makira. Only Hatoibwari went out, but sometimes she would come back, and if she came back the food of the island would be good again and when she left the food would be bad. That was the way of Hatoibwari."[16]

---

16. An obvious parallel between Hatoibwari and the God of Genesis is that both plant a tree whose fruit is withheld from others. The forbidden fruit is stolen, resulting in alienation between people and a being who controls the generative power of the earth. In Genesis, the transgression of Adam and Eve causes God to curse them so that they must cultivate food by hard labor; in Hauni's account, the theft of the coconuts causes Hatoibwari to curse the island so that coconuts will not grow there. When the snake departs in anger she takes the productivity of the land away with her. Hauni's version is the only snake myth I know involving the particular detail of the plundered coconut tree; yet, in every version the theme of the snake's departure, and most often hostile alienation, from her original dwelling place is central. To my knowledge neither the Anglican missionaries nor Arosi themselves make the obvious comparison between the alienation of Hatoibwari and the Christian concept of the Fall. Nevertheless, it is difficult to doubt that this comparison was made, and the similarity perhaps elaborated, in dialogue between Arosi and missionaries seeking points of contact between pre-Christian Arosi religion and Christianity.

I take Hauni's telling of the Hatoibwari myth as an exemplar for analysis because, unlike Warioha's, it shares two elements in common with the majority of variants of a spirit-snake myth recorded by European missionaries. First, these myths agree that the snake is a primordial inhabitant of the island who exercises a wonderful generative power. By all accounts, however, she is driven from her place of original habitation, often taking with her the fertility of the land (e.g., Codrington 1880/81: 298–299; 1891: 150–151; Fox 1924: 82–83; *T:* "Hatoibwari"). Second, these myths almost always include the narrative unit of the dismembered snake-grandmother (cf. Wilson 1932: 159). This unit frequently stands for the explanation of the snake's alienation from Makira and journey to Guadalcanal where she imparts her knowledge of agriculture and powers of increase to those who adopt her and offer sacrifice to her. In the following analysis, I suggest that these two elements—the dismemberment of the snake-grandmother and her alienation from Makira—are mythic figurations of the problem of introducing internal differentiation within a bounded unity. In the myths, this problem is being negotiated at two distinct but analogous scales: the island as a whole and a matrilineage as an independent category of being.

Hatoibwari As True Auhenua

The thesis that Hatoibwari is a spirit who represents Makira and its vital forces draws support not only from Warioha's clear assertions that the snake is the image of the island, but also from those variants of the myth that explicitly state that her departure leaves the fecundity of the island depleted. In addition to the versions already cited that express this idea, a few of my consultants, who did not know a snake myth that they could recite in full, simply asserted that "all the power has gone from Makira" because of the snake's migration to Guadalcanal, and that, conversely, "today, gardening is easy on Guadalcanal—all different types of fruits are growing wild everywhere." Although Fox (1924: 237, 297, 363; 1978: 118) tentatively glosses the word *bwari* as "summit," the only definition that I elicited for this word was "spider." This meaning prompted two attempts to explain the significance of the name Hatoibwari, one that corroborates Warioha's view of the snake as the image of the island, and one that corroborates its association with fertility. Father Abel Ta'aimaesiburu of Tawatana explained to me that "from Marau Sound [Guadalcanal], Makira looks like a spider (*bwari*) with Hoto [a hill] in the center; that's why they call it Hotoibwari in some places."[17] The presence of

---

17. Hauni's account, which states that Hatoibwari took up residence on a hill in Guadalcanal named Bwari, and Father Abel's etymology both link Hatoibwari with hills.

the word *bwari* in both I'abwari and Hatoibwari caused Casper Kaukeni to speculate that, like spiders that he said he had found to contain numerous small spiders, both I'abwari and Hatoibwari were highly productive and life-giving beings.

As mentioned above, the missionaries Wilson and Fox both locate the center of Makiran snake worship at Haunanu Bay, which they say was the site of annual first-fruits sacrifices at yam harvesting time and when the canarium nuts ripen (Fox 1924: 85–86, 325; 1962: 58–60; *AMM*: 84–85; Fox to Rivers, March 14, 1918, Perry Papers, B2; Wilson 1932: 159–160). Fox asserts that at one time the yam harvest festival, called Ho'asia or Hogasia, had encompassed most of Makira—with the notable exception of most of Arosi—and inferred that it had even extended to the island of Ulawa and parts of Guadalcanal. The sacrifices and feasts that marked these seasonal celebrations were performed in a staggered sequence beginning at the shrine at Haununu Bay and spreading from village to village. Both missionaries observe, however, that already by the second decade of the twentieth century these rituals were impoverished and on the wane at Haununu and had fallen into desuetude throughout the rest of the island.[18] For Wilson and Fox these rituals were evidence that Makirans were united in their devotion to a single supreme spirit-snake who was the creator of the world and everything in it. Recognizing that the known versions of the Hatoibwari myth and the testimonies of my own Arosi interlocutors may be informed by this missionary interpretation of ritual practices concerned with organic growth cycles, it nevertheless emerges that some Arosi did

It is not clear, however, whether these cases support Fox's definition, or whether they both attest an Arosi perception that hills in some way resemble spiders.

18. In the mid 1960s on neighboring Santa Catalina, William Davenport observed an annual "renewal rite"—the *wogosia*—that marked the beginning of the new year and included "the last of a series of smaller first-fruits ceremonies" (Davenport 1996: 24; see also the film *Wogasia* [Chase and Aihunu 1982]; for brief accounts of this rite on Santa Ana, see Byer 1996: 336–337; Mead 1977: 136–137). Davenport writes that "[i]n earlier times … the ceremony commenced in the community of Haununu on the south coast of San Cristobal Island from where it traveled to other communities in the eastern Solomons, each some distance removed in a generally easterly direction" (1996: 25). Davenport's (1996: 25) consultants told him that—as part of this progressive celebration—"[t]raditionally, Santa Catalina received Wogosia from Makorukoru, a community (no longer extant) located on the southeastern coast of San Cristobal." But, by the time of Davenport's (1996: 25) field research, the people of Santa Catalina were "the only ones to continue the Wogosia tradition." Notably, Davenport makes no reference to a snake in his detailed account. David Akin (personal communication, June 10, 1999) informs me that, prior to 1927, the Kwaio of Malaita performed a similarly regionally staggered yam/canarium nut ritual complex involving snake divination (cf. Keesing 1982a: 121).

formerly, and do still today, understand Hatoibwari to be the spirit of the island and the ultimate source of the forms of life it supports.

Hauni's version of the Hatoibwari story furthermore foregrounds the idea that, as the very form and essence of the island, Hatoibwari is, in Arosi terms, the true *auhenua* of Makira. This idea, I suggest, governs the nature of her interactions with the fishermen who disobey her and prompt her initial departure from Haunanu. Recall that Hatoibwari promises that when her coconuts are ripe she will freely give them to the fishermen. But when they rob her, Hatoibwari's response is to declare that: "Therefore, in the custom law (*ringeringe auhenua*) of the island they've driven me away, that's what they've done, and I will not dwell here." Similarly, in the one Arosi language text collected by Fox that includes an Adam's rib-style creation of humanity, a further narrative unit immediately follows the creation scenario in which it is explained that Hatoibwari—whose gender is not specified—abandons Hoto for Guadalcanal after unidentified persons "make a stranger" (*haha'atawa*) of Hatoibwari.

> First Hatoibwari dwelled at Hoto, and they made [Hatoibwari] a stranger at Hoto, and therefore [Hatoibwari] went from there, and went west through the open sea, and drifted ashore at Guadalcanal. And [there were] two young men who were hunting pigs, and their dogs barked, and they went forth to look, and they asked, "Who are you?" and [Hatoibwari] answered, "I am Hatoibwari. They made a stranger of me at Hoto, it is I." (Fox *T*: "Hatoibwari")

The versions of Hauni and Fox both imply that, in her original dwelling, Hatoibwari represents the *auhenua* of that place, and her displacement occurs when interlopers usurp her rights to the land by treating her as though she were the outsider.[19] The departure of Hatoibwari, the true *auhenua*, entails the diminishment of the fruitfulness of the land and its exportation abroad. A clear correlation between Hatoibwari and the things of the island that are *auhenua* surfaced in the casual commentary that Hauni added to the recitation of his narrative. After he had remarked that whenever Hatoibwari returned to the island the food of the island would be good again and when she left the food would be bad, he went on to say that, "today they don't know [when Hatoibwari visits] because they make food from sweet potato, tapioca, and whiteman's taro—a different type of food, food of a different island; because in olden times

---

19. In his study of origin structures and precedence in Tana Wai Brama, Flores (Indonesia), Lewis identifies a similar pattern of foundational "act[s] of usurpation—of land, power over animals and ritual potency—of the aboriginal spirits of the domain" (1996: 166; cf. 1988: 270–274).

they didn't eat that food." In other words, the movements of Hatoibwari influence only those things that, like she herself, are *auhenua* in the island.

If Hatoibwari is the true *auhenua*, why do people treat her as though she were a stranger? These myths confront a peculiar dilemma that the existence of a primordial spirit of the island appears to pose for Arosi. If Hatoibwari is the *auhenua* spirit of Makira, inevitably, this implies that human beings, unless they are her matrilineal descendants, must be *sae boboi*—people who have come—in relation to her. Thus, in order to be *auhenua*, a matrilineage must understand itself as enjoying a direct substantial link to Hatoibwari, yet in order for the *auhenua* matrilineages to avoid the conclusion that they are siblings, they must assert that the particular portions of the island to which they are linked are distinct, and therefore distinguishing, portions of the island qua snake. To do this they must deny the *auhenua* quality that would grant the spirit of the island precedence over the individual matrilineages as an encompassing whole, while simultaneously granting the *auhenua* quality of their own particular matrilineal territories. That is to say, they must conceptualize Hatoibwari as having encountered an outside agent who challenged her *auhenua* status and broke the unity and power of the island, thereby enabling it to produce multiple unrelated matrilineal categories of being. The myth of the island's transition from wholeness to internal differentiation, therefore, follows precisely the same logic as the internal differentiation of a matrilineage through exogamous reproduction. At both scales of origin, contact with a representative of a separate category of being is required to effect the transition from oneness to internal multiplicity. In the narratives depicting individual lineage origins described previously, such representatives appear consistently in the form of a man of unspecified origin who marries the lineage ancestress; in the Hatoibwari myth, they similarly appear from no where to offend or assault the snake, driving her, and likewise the unity of the island, away.[20]

The Severed Snake As Lineage Origin Myth

Here it is crucial to recognize that the episode of the dismembered snake-grandmother constitutes a narrative unit that is often found on its own, not only on Makira but also in other parts of Solomon Islands, as a lineage origin narrative (e.g., Byer 1996: 41–43; Hogbin 1964: 79, cf. 94; Köngäs Maranda 1973; 1977: 104–108; O'Connor 1973: 66–67; Roga 1989: 10–13; Scheffler

---

20. For Peter Itamwaeraha this external agent was clearly the God of the Bible. Recall his assertion that, "The spirit of God placed the lineages on the land; it split the land for us. These divisions in the land already existed."

1965: 241; White 1991: 249 n. 6).[21] The same narrative was told to me as the origin of a particular, but now extinct, "snake-lineage" (*burunga i mwaa*). The fact that so many versions of the dismembered snake-grandparent myth are told explicitly as lineage origin stories points to the possibility that the early missionaries' investigations into indigenous ideas about origins prompted some Makirans to respond by telling this story as their theory of how they had come to be. What Makirans offered as accounts of origin at a matrilineal scale the missionaries assimilated to origin at a universal scale. This reconstruction would also account for the fact, doubtless puzzling to the missionaries, that most versions of the myth depict the snake and its offspring interacting and intermarrying with human beings whose pre-existence is taken for granted but whose origins are left unexplained.

Other interpreters have recognized that myths of the severed snake, variants of which are attested from Papua New Guinea and Vanuatu as well as Solomon Islands, constitute transformative perspectives on the themes of the establishment, nature, or subversion of either matrilineality or patrilineality as a cultural norm (Köngäs Maranda 1973, 1977; Young 1987). It has also been recognized that these myths simultaneously pertain to the origin and nature of a set of semantically related phenomena, including cultigens, shell valuables, death, sex, exogamy, and the opening of bodily orifices for purposes of eating and defecating. These themes further show the myths of the severed snake to be structurally related to an even wider set of Melanesian narratives that appear to trace the origins of sexual reproduction and/or death to a rupture within a once unified category of being. The rupture occurs when a snake-like originary grandmother figure attempts to shed or otherwise rejuvenate her skin but is no longer recognized by one of her descendants (e.g., Codrington 1891: 265; Fortune 1932: 186; Foster 1995: 141–142; Ivens 1927: 15; 1930: 206; Malinowski 1948: 127–128; Thune 1989: 156).

For the most part, commentators have tended to represent such myths as indigenous accounts of the single universal origin of a particular social institution or natural phenomenon. Thus, for example, when analyzing a myth that clearly describes the descent of two Lau (Malaita) clans from the daughter of a female snake cut to pieces by her son-in-law, Elli Köngäs Maranda takes the local scale of this variant to be a distortive diminution of its larger import: "The myth is of a weakened form; the universal role of Serpent is here

---

21. Published versions—from other parts of Melanesia as well as Solomon Islands—that are not explicitly framed as lineage origin narratives include, Fox 1924: 82–83, 86–88; Hogbin 1970: 34–35; Keevil 1972: 31–34; Köngäs Maranda 1977; Róheim 1950: 202; Young 1987.

denied: she becomes only the dispenser of agricultural *mana* for two clans (Fuusai and Langane). The issue is not the origin of cultigens, it is about the beginning of a localized cult" (1977: 104, author's translation; cf. Scheffler 1965: 241–242). Carl Thune (1989: 156), however, draws attention to the capacity of these myths to index multiple microcosmic scales of origin. Thune's northeast Normanby Island (Papua New Guinea) consultant, Lasaro, told him the story of Kekewageihi, a grandmother figure who, before she died, tried to secure the possibility for rejuvenation by instructing her daughter and grandchildren that she would return from the grave and would be able to go on living if they bathed the decay away from her body with hot water. When she returned from the dead, however, her grandchildren did not know her because of her putrefied state and failed to follow her instructions. Consequently, death became final and Kekewageihi went to dwell in the land of the dead where she sat with her back to her children. When he had finished his narration, Lasaro went on to explain that there are multiple lands of the dead, each with its own Kekewageihi. Kekewageihi is thus, according to Thune (1989: 156), "both a proper and a generic name" that refers to a multiplicity of parallel ancestral figures now thought to reside at a multiplicity of parallel lands of the dead, each corresponding to "a relatively unified cultural and ethnic group" (1989: 175 n. 7; cf. Fortune 1932: 186). It appears, then, that for the people of northeast Normanby Island the global origin of death is the sum of many local origins of death.

Thune analyzes this myth as an account of how each individual matrilineage loses its radical autonomy and integrity by achieving the internal distinctions and external connections with other matrilineages necessary for its reproduction. Excavating the implicit synonymy between the origin of death and the origin of exogamous reproduction, Thune sees in the failure of the grandchildren to recognize their grandmother and participate in her self-regeneration the exercise of what northeast Normanby Islanders value as "a self-assertive 'mind' and a 'body' that can only reproduce itself through an alliance with other matrilineages" (1989: 156; cf. Foster 1995: 141–142). The story of the origin of death is, in other words, the story of the transition of a proto-human matrilineal category from monadic isolation to fully human inter-lineal sociality told from the internal point of view of the originally pure category ruptured by its own self-sacrificial turn away from singular identity toward relations with others.

Fox (1924: 81–82) reports a Makiran version of this myth in which an old woman sloughs her skin but, "looking young and lovely once more," is unrecognized and rejected by her daughter until she resumes her old skin. As in Lasaro's version collected by Thune, there is no explicit reference to exogamy or any external agent impinging on the relationship between mother and daughter; there is only the internal rupture of non-recognition. Yet the figure of the old woman emerging young again from her cast-off skin is comparable, I suggest, to the *pwapwaronga* of the Amaeo origin myth who, as a category, had to cut their children from their mothers until one of them married a *masi* and succeeded in reproducing rather than merely self-replicating. Before they entered into exogamy-like relations with another category of being, the *pwapwaronga* were similarly snake-like beings who effectively shed their outer layers to rejuvenate themselves. Fox's myth of the origin of death finds its clearest complement, however, in Makiran versions of the myth of the severed snake. Recall that in Codrington's (1880/81: 298–299; 1891: 150–151) version of this myth, it is the daughter herself who cuts her serpent mother into pieces—a variation that parallels the internal perspective of the origin of death myths. But in most versions, as in Hauni's, the story of the loss of matrilineal autonomy and integrity is told with emphasis on the causal role of the impact of an external category. The causal role of the snake's daughter, who chooses to marry despite her mother's warning that "my child is making a mistake for me," is evident; but, as Michael Young (1987: 237) observes with respect to a northeast Normanby Island variant in which the severed snake is named Mwatakeiwa, the focus is on "an intrusive husband."

In variants like Hauni's, in which the internal and external agents of division are both present as two aspects of one rupture, it becomes clear that—like the northeast Normanby Island myth of the origin of death—the myth of the severed snake can index origins at multiple interdependent microcosmic scales without implying any global scale other than the sum of these analogous parts. There is no globally encompassing scale at which category distinctions arise wholly by internal processes. This is not to say that indigenous Arosi cosmology lacked a global-scale perspective; rather, although the parts may be envisioned as formally and functionally isomorphic, the relationship of parts to whole is metonymic rather than synecdochic. In other words, such variants of the myth of the severed snake can, as representatives of multiple microcosmic origins, imply a poly-genetic macrocosm.[22]

---

22. Foster's (1995: 141–142) analysis of a myth of the origin of death and sex from the Tangan Islands leaves the nature of the relationship between parts and whole ambiguous. In this variant, the grandmother figure attempts to auto-reproduce by changing skins. But the failure of her grandchildren, who are male, to recognize her in her rejuvenated form involves desire to engage in sexual relations with her in ways suggestive of incest within a matrilineage. Foster (1995: 142) asserts that this inappropriate desire (which is not fulfilled, but compels the grandmother to retrieve her old skin and make death permanent) "trans-

The Many within the One

Most versions of the myth of the severed snake collapse into a single narrative unit the parallelism between the displacement of a generative spirit of the land and the paradoxical fact that an originary proto-human category must be divided in order to reproduce. Hauni's version, however, distributes treatment of the two analogous components over two distinct narrative sequences, making their symmetrical relationship especially apparent. After her initial encounter with the fishermen who deny her *auhenua* status, Hatoibwari withdraws to the bush where she gives birth to a baby girl whom she permits to be adopted by an old woman and her granddaughter. When the snake's child is grown, she marries a man of unspecified, but independent origin, leading to the attempted murder and second displacement of Hatoibwari. This second movement of Hauni's narrative presents Hatoibwari, the true but now spatially contracted *auhenua* of Makira, attempting to engender a human matrilineage by producing an autochthonous female to be the ancestress of a people who will become the *auhenua* in a particular place. It appears that in Hauni's account this attempt proves unsuccessful, as the snake swallows her offspring, carrying them away never to be mentioned again. This conclusion is symbolically consonant with variants in which the snake takes her offspring away with her (e.g., Byer 1996: 42; Keevil 1972: 31–34; Róheim 1950: 202; Young 1987: 237); such endings refer to the snake's retraction and withholding of her productive powers. In other variants, however—even those not explicitly framed as lineage origin accounts—it is most often the case that the snake departs alone, apparently leaving her offspring to carry on a new lineage (e.g., Codrington 1880/81: 298–299; 1891: 150–151; Fox 1924: 82–83; Wilson D: "Anthropology" 1909). These two possible outcomes refer to two aspects of the same reality; they point separately to the single fact that the process of internal differentiation simultaneously entails both an ending and a new beginning, the demise of the old unity and the rise of a multiplicity. Although Hauni's narrative emphasizes only the former aspect, the latter aspect

---

forms an enate into an affine," and thus marks a transition from a state of "asexual regeneration" to one of "sexual intercourse between socially differentiated people." It is unclear, however, whether Foster means that now the grandsons must look beyond their originary category for proper sexual partners from other analogous categories, or that Tangans understand this myth as the story of how all their matriclans and matrilineages came into being through processes of internal differentiation inaugurated by a primordial incestuous desire within a single original proto-lineage. If the latter is the case, then the relationship of Tangan matrilineages to this original proto-lineage would be synecdochic and the Tangan model of human ontology would be monistic (but see Foster 1995: 68).

is clearly articulated in the variants that make this a lineage origin narrative, and it is even recognizable in the details of Hauni's rendition.

In Hauni's version, the possibility that there is a purposeful end to the violence of the son-in-law is suggested by the fact that Hatoibwari herself predicts that her daughter's marriage will lead to her death at the hands of her in-laws. The snake accepts her injury as inevitable because it represents, in the form of a literal cut, the discontinuity that exogamy interjects into the continuity of a matrilineal essence but which is necessary for its reproduction. In order for such an essence to become embedded in and reproduced as a fully constituted matrilineage, its absolute integrity must be sacrificed. Although severed in two, Hatoibwari does not die, but has the power to reconstitute herself as a whole. That is to say, that no matter how often the blood of a matrilineage is mixed with the blood of a man from another matrilineage in order to produce children, the matrilineage remains "one blood." Thus even while, as a figure of a single category of being, Hatoibwari is an image of the one among the many, she is also an image of the many within the one. As analyzed in chapter 4, congress between categories of being signals a transition from sterile isolated solidarity to reproductive internal differentiation within each category of being. Ironically, at the same time that the snake's act of swallowing her offspring appears to represent only a curtailing of her generative power, it may also make her a symbol of a now fully constituted matrilineage that, while still a continuous unity, literally contains internal differentiation through its children.

The concept of *auhenua* unites the first and second movements of Hauni's narrative and highlights the thematic parallelism between them. Hatoibwari is the bearer of this concept at two scales of origin, representing both the island itself as the only true *auhenua* and the progenitor of a matrilineage that is *auhenua* at a specific place. At both scales, the original unity of the *auhenua* is impinged on by confrontation with an outside category of being, resulting in a loss. The initial interaction between Hatoibwari and the fishermen entails the departure of Hatoibwari and the loss of productivity. Likewise, the subsequent altercation between Hatoibwari and her son-in-law entails another departure of Hatoibwari and another loss of productivity in the form of the daughter and child she takes away with her. Both departures and losses give rise to two analogous desires for reversal. Here, it is crucial to bear in mind that Arosi patterns of residence are patri-virilocal. Because of this practice, the daughters of the *auhenua* will often leave their land to raise their children elsewhere. Thus, just as Hauni's concluding remarks report a past expectation that, periodically, Hatoibwari might return and restore the goodness of food, lineages that understand themselves to be *auhenua* strive to bring the children of their daughters back to the land of their mothers to replenish the matrilineage.

Less obvious is a further parallel between the two phases of Hauni's story. In both sequences the loss of productive potential is accompanied, paradoxically, by successful reproduction or a generative transformation. This reality is most evident in the second phase of the story in the simple fact of human reproduction. Referencing exogamous reproduction, this episode highlights the contradiction that the purity of matrilineal essence must be compromised in order to achieve new births that will constitute and preserve the matrilineage. In chapter 4 I argued that a similar contradiction is negotiated at parturition via the actions of the midwife who cuts the umbilical cord. An act of cutting coincides with the propagation of a whole; loss coincides with gain. The gain that attends the first departure of Hatoibwari is nothing less than the establishment of the necessary preconditions for Arosi poly-genesis, leading to the formation of human society on the island. If Hatoibwari may be understood as a figure of the island as quintessentially autochthonous, her displacement introduces and ramifies a discontinuity within the unity of the island. This discontinuity is requisite to the foundation of human society as the aggregate of diverse categories of being brought into productive relationship with one another. Whole, the island provides no means of fixing and maintaining the distinctions between multiple categories of being. Divided, it becomes a medium of differentiation across which relationship may be achieved. The loss of the power that inheres in the island as a whole is, I contend, a foundational sacrifice. Unlike mythic representations of the cosmogonic sacrifice of a primordial unity that express the idea that all things in the universe are one, however, this sacrifice of unity claims that origin from the fragments does not communicate consubstantiality.

The paradigm of cutting the whole is explicitly enacted in these stories only at what I am interpreting as the scale of the individual matrilineage. Yet the story of the severed snake points to a similar dynamic of division at the scale of the island as a whole. Although the fact of the island's partition is not narrated in any variant of the Hatoibwari myth, it is, I submit, evident in peoples' ideas about local ancestral snakes. The majority of Arosi know nothing of Hatoibwari, but many of them nevertheless state that their ancestral spirits frequently appear in the form of snakes. They say, for example, that if a stranger violates one of their tabu places, or appropriates the resources of their land without their permission, their *auhenua* ancestors will take the form of snakes to frighten these intruders. It is commonly thought that ancestral snakes visit their descendants when someone dies. People repeatedly told me, however, that these ancestral snakes are not whole, but are distinctively truncated. "It was only the head and stomach of a snake without a tail," they would report of these ancestral sightings. "It was only a piece of a snake without a tail!" "It was part of snake; its tail was cut short," they said. In fact, when I in-quired how he could tell when a snake is an ancestor and when it is just a snake, one friend answered: "You can recognize them because they are short; if they weren't we'd confuse them." Another remarked that if a stranger cuts your ancestral snake in two it will mend itself. This general consensus that lin-eages are linked to their land through ancestors who manifest themselves as severed snakes, suggests that these demi-snakes represent individual lineage territories as fragments of a larger whole. In relation to the island as a whole these demi-snakes are microcosms resulting from a segmentation process. The island is no longer the image of a single snake; it is a collection of many snakes who bear the mark of their abbreviation.

In everyday thought and practice, many Arosi, especially members of Adaro, Amaeo, and Mwara lineages, assume that their ancestors may visit them in the form of snakes. These snakes represent, not Hatoibwari, the spirit of the island as a whole, but the unique spirit entities of their respective ma-trilineages. As discussed in chapter 5, Arosi assert that the seemingly different snakes reputed to inhabit the different shrines or burial sites associated with a particular matrilineage are manifestations of one and the same spirit entity. The unity ascribed to these ancestral spirit-snakes corresponds to the collec-tivity of ancestral spirits understood as extending matrilineal consubstantial-ity after death. No one but Warioha ever intimated to me that these spirit-snakes were somehow projections of Hatoibwari, or any other spiritual being, whose mono-ontology might encompass the poly-ontology of the many Arosi matrilineages.[23]

---

23. I add here a highly speculative note regarding the form and possible meanings of the Ho'asia/Hogasia festival. Fox (1924: 325) notes that the festival "reached as far as One-hatare in the south and Onetere on the north coast" and thus was not observed in Arosi, except in a small area of east Arosi. Intriguingly, he reported to Rivers that while "on the South Coast" he observed "the deep foot-like imprints in the rock of the great *adaro* spir-itual being Wamarea, where he stood to *withstand* the Hogasia, which now goes no fur-ther. Wamarea is the *koa* or fellow of the great creator of the west-end, whom I now beg to introduce, Hatoibwari" (Fox to Rivers, March 14, 1918, Perry Papers, B2, emphasis in original). Fox (1924: 282) makes only a passing reference to Wamarea in his published works to note that he is associated with a *du'a*, a sacred stone wall that "no one could cross over," that runs out into the sea at Onehatare on the south coast (about one and a half kilo-meters west of Tarahura'a village). These fragments of information suggest a tradition ac-cording to which the figure of Wamarea actively blocked the Hogasia festival from enter-ing Arosi. If this first-fruits festival marked the periodic return of a spirit identified with the generative power of the island, such a moment would have been fraught with the pos-sibility that the resurgence of the island's original integrity would assert the ultimate relat-edness of all Makiran matrilineages through the spirit of the island as apical ancestress. Ac-

From Poly-ontology to Mono-ontology

On the basis of the foregoing analysis of the Hatoibwari tradition and the testimony of my own consultants, I am inclined to infer that Fox's construction of an all-encompassing Arosi monism is the result of a reading of Makiran snake data that not only assimilates origins at the lineal and insular scales to origins at the universal scale, but also conflates the mythology of Hatoibwari and other spirit-snakes with Arosi explanations of what Fox (1924: 236) termed beliefs about "the final destiny of the soul." This reading amounts to a systematic snake theology that asserts the very proposition that I have said most myths of Hatoibwari seek to circumvent, that is, the proposition that everything is one.

Fox's project of systematizing and harmonizing all Makiran snake data was deeply informed by the theories of population migration and culture diffusion developed by W. H. R. Rivers (1914), Grafton Elliot Smith (1915), and W. J. Perry (1918, 1923).[24] So enthusiastic was he for these theories that, as he wrote to Rivers in 1918, he was prepared to subordinate his ethnographic data to experimentation with model-driven interpretations, even at the risk of making many errors:

> It is really absurd of me to write at all when I have read so little, unless I merely give facts, but that is not possible for me, I am so made that I *must* have an explanation, be it only a working explanation and cannot keep silence about it, for it is the explanation, not the facts that I care about, and so I must make all sorts of mistakes. (Fox to Rivers, April 30, 1918, Perry Papers, B2, emphasis in original)

---

cordingly, Arosi may have mythologized a purposive rejection of this festival and its implications from their end of the island. The staggered nature of the festival elsewhere might itself reflect a similar concern to prevent such a spirit from returning everywhere at once. Relayed from village to village, its power is repartitioned even as it progressively replenishes the fecundity of the island. That said, however, despite what may have been strategies to avoid such interpretations, there may have been some Makirans who held an esoteric teaching about Hatoibwari—or some other entity—as an originary being who encompassed all Makirans within a single category of being.

24. Ian Langham (1981: especially, Chapters IV and V; cf. Stocking 1995: Chapter 5) provides a detailed analysis of the intellectual relations among Rivers, Elliot Smith, Perry, and Fox. He also documents how Malinowski (1925) used the cover of an anonymous review of Fox's *Threshold of the Pacific* to mount a "savage attack on Rivers, Elliot Smith and Perry, who had all contributed towards getting Fox's material into print" (Langham 1981: 168).

One of his foundational "mistakes," I suggest, was to interpret Arosi matrilineages that happened to share a single clan name as branches of discrete ethnic groups with consistent elements of culture and religious practice and belief. Because he regarded all people who identified themselves using a particular clan name as representatives of a single island-wide culture, he regarded the testimony of each such representative as applicable to all as part of a shared ethnic heritage. Consequently, if a member of a lineage with a particular clan name told him the origin narrative of his or her lineage, he took that narrative to be the common belief about human origins held by all Makirans with that clan name. Fox furthermore attempted to determine a chronological sequence for the separate arrivals to the island of each of the discrete peoples that this method led him to discover.[25] In particular, he became convinced that after a succession of earlier population migrations to Makira, a relatively late wave of newcomers brought elements of Egyptian civilization to the island. These elements included "embalming," interment in "pyramidal stone burial mounds," a sun cult, and the worship of "a great Winged Serpent" (1924: 361).[26] Attributing this Egyptian-influ-

---

25. It is possible that this project of constructing a chronology of waves of immigrant groups was, in part, fostered by Arosi discourse concerning the relationship between "original people" or "former people" (i.e., *auhenua*) in a particular territory and immigrants (i.e., *sae boboi*). See also, Allan 1990: 126.

26. Malinowski (1925: 394) suggests that Elliot Smith and Perry—who had jointly prepared Fox's book from a manuscript sent by Fox to Rivers (Smith 1924)—may have been "busy altering parts of the manuscript" prior to publication so as "to yield the Egyptogenic climax." Langham (1981: 171) shows that A. C. Haddon likewise believed that "Smith and Perry 'tampered' with Fox's book." In fact, in his review of the book, Haddon (1925: 59–60) indicates that the explanatory text beneath the "Diagram of a stone *heo*" on page 219 introduces terms—"mummified" and "mastaba"—that are not found elsewhere in the book. Langham writes that Fox, in an unpublished response to Malinowski's review, was

> quick to declare the genuineness of his agreement with Rivers, Elliot Smith and Perry, that many San Cristoval phenomena are best explained on the hypothesis that Egyptian influences had penetrated the Solomon Islands. However, with regard to particular problems relating to the "preparation" of his material, Fox's account does little to exonerate the diffusionist trio. Specifically, a diagram of a San Cristoval "*heo*" or burial mound had appeared in the published book, presumably on the initiative of Perry, bearing an inscription which might have been taken to imply that "mastaba," the usual term for an Egyptian burial mound, was synonymous with "*heo*." "It is five years since I sent [Rivers] the manuscript," writes Fox, "and I am unable to be sure with that interval between." "And yet," he continues, "I feel sure I did not write the description of the *heo*, or write *mastaba*, which would seem to me begging the question, or say the bodies interred were mummified, since I have always known that they were not." "That," Fox states

enced culture to all lineages bearing the Araha name throughout the island, he credited this people with having promulgated a comprehensive serpent-focused monism (Fox 1924: 360–361, 364). Sadly, in Fox's estimation (1924: 368), a still later wave of immigrants bearing "a civilization inferior" to that of "the Araha" largely displaced the worship of "the great serpent spirits" in Arosi with "normal totemism." This eclipse of serpent worship by totemism explained the "clouding [of] older stories and beliefs, especially as regards the serpent" (Fox 1924: 368).

In Fox's defense, his perception that although "[p]eople have neglected snake worship, it *underlies* everywhere" was clearly based on observation of an actual plethora of ideas and practices on Makira that referenced snakes (Fox to Rivers, November 16, 1916, Perry Papers, B2, emphasis in original). Driven, no doubt as much by a biblically informed bias in favor of single global-scale origins as by diffusionist theories, he constructed out of this plethora a once dominant religion of serpent-centered monism by generalizing a multiplicity of lineage-scale ideas about origins and death to the level of an ethnos-specific cult that had been widely appropriated around Makira. In so doing, he divorced these ideas from their specific emplaced matrilineal referents, effectively disregarding the practical, conceptual, and narrative means by which Arosi avert the conclusion that all Makirans are genealogically related to one another through the spirit-snake of the island. His theory that the Egyptianized religion of "the Araha" had formerly penetrated the whole of the island allowed Fox (1924: 361) to find evidence for reconstructing the nature of the "chief serpent deity" and its "cult" in all manner of Makiran snake lore and ritual. Specifically, he took disparate versions of spirit-snake myths, some of them doubtless understood by their narrators as accounts of unique lineage origins, and brought them together as pieces of a larger shared whole. By this method, he was able to assert that "the Araha," and through them the whole of Makira, had once "believed in a great Winged Serpent with the face of a man…, that there are other great female serpent spirits, Hatuibwari's daughters, and from these men took their origin" (Fox 1924: 361–362; cf. 271).

The testimony of my own Arosi interlocutors leads me to conclude that Fox (1924: 30, 234–235) developed his notion of A'unua as a universal "immortal essence" from which human souls (*aunga*) emerge and return as *'unua* by similarly conflating the testimonies of diverse Arosi concerning the essential

---

with as much confidence as he could muster after a five-year interval, "was another's description." (Langham 1981: 170)

In contrast, the passage I am citing here appears to have been written by Fox and is representative of the position articulated in the book as a whole. Nevertheless, Fox later came to regret having been "influenced so much by Rivers and the 'English School of Diffusionism'" (Whiteman 1983: 243 n. 164; cf. Langham 1981: 355 n. 35).

Figure 8.3. Charles Elliot Fox (1878–1977), c. 1960. Used with permission of the Melanesian Mission UK.

oneness of their matrilineal ancestral spirits. Because many Arosi pay respect to snakes as manifestations of these ancestral spirits, Fox (1924: 79–80, 236) put all of this snake data together into one coherent snake ontology. He takes as confirmation of this snake monism one man's comment that A'unua is "all of them." To this comment I cannot help but juxtapose the words of my consultant who explained to me that all of his matrilineal ancestral snakes are "just one snake" (see chapter 5).

Although predicated on a basic misreading of Arosi socio-cosmic order, Fox's construction of Arosi snake monism is instructive because it illustrates a mechanism whereby Arosi poly-ontology may be transformed into mono-ontology. This mechanism is the conceptual separation of an *auhenua* matrilineage from its ancestral territory. By generalizing lineage-specific origin myths, along with ideas and practices relating to snakes, to the scale of an island-wide universal creation story with associated ritual complex disseminated by a supposed ethnic group, Fox severs matrilineal ontologies from matrilineal territories and raises them to the level of a total insular ontology. This analytical move functions to eliminate the distinctions among matrilineages, first spatially, and consequently, mythically. First, this move constructs Arosi, not as members of matrilineages who understand themselves to be inalienably connected to particular territories in the island, but as representatives of non-territorially specific culture-bearing peoples whose locus is simply the island as a whole. Once this step is taken, a second easily follows: the myth of Hatoibwari is no longer interpreted as asserting that an original partitioning of the island preceded the generation of multiple geographically speciated lineages, but is taken instead to affirm, as does Warioha's version, that all Makirans are genealogically related through common descent from the spirit of the island. In Arosi today, this same mechanism may be found at work in the proposal, championed by Ishmael Taroiara, that Arosi should adopt their de facto father to son land inheritance as normative. Although motivated by very different facts and goals than those that motivated Fox, Taroiara advocates acceptance of a similar conceptual separation of matrilineal essences from specific matrilineal territories, thereby promoting a similar possibility for the collapse of matrilineal ontologies—understood as discrete units of love—into one all-inclusive human ontology of shared love "in the likeness of God."

CHAPTER 9

AROSI ETHNO-THEOLOGIES

How do Arosi, most of whom have never understood themselves to be anything but Christians, negotiate the difference between the human mono-ontology inscribed in the Bible and the poly-ontology inscribed in the socio-spatial order they idealize and aspire to as customary? In this final chapter I examine several disparate examples of what I term ethno-theologies—that is, local schemes of original constructive Christian theology—each of which presents a different approach to this problem with a different outcome. Some of these ethno-theologies appear decidedly to prefer either mono-ontology or poly-ontology; others suggest that Arosi Christianity has the capacity to contain both in a dual formulation for an indefinite time to come.

The category of ethno-theology that I develop here is analogous to the category of ethnohistory, but at the meta-level of what Raymond Fogelson (1974: 106; 1989: 134–135) and Terence Turner (1988: 241–242) have called ethno-ethnohistory, by which they mean the historical consciousnesses and perspectives of ethnographic subjects. In like fashion, by ethno-theology I mean the indigenous theological speculations and projects, not only of trained clergy and intellectuals, but also of laypersons and even whole congregations or local communities (e.g., Beckett 1993; Lattas 1998; McDonald 2001: Chapter 4; Trompf 1987; Tuwere 2002). The ethno-theologies examined in this chapter happen to take the form of mythic and other discursive elaborations; but, theoretically, ethno-theologies may be evident in a variety of local forms of Christian expression. Beyond the often minor but meaningful types of amendings and paraphrasings of Bible passages evident in my consultants' discourses, these forms might also include local vernacular or regionally-specific European language versions of liturgies, hymns, choruses, prayers, sermons, church-related dramatic performances, Sunday School lessons, Bible studies—in short, any medium though which indigenous Christians reproduce the content of Christianity from their own points of view and in their own voices. By grouping these forms under the rubric of ethno-theology, I do not pretend to be the first or only anthropologist to study these types of data (on Melanesia see, for example, Burridge 1960; Burt 1983; Errington and Gewertz

1994; Lawrence 1964; Stritecky 2001; Toren 2004; Thune 1990). Rather, my aim is to contribute useful vocabulary for the ongoing intentional take-up of John Barker's foundational challenges to the anthropology of Christianity to study "the minutiae of Christian ideas and institutions in community settings" (1990: 10) and to look at "the actions or interpretations of individuals" in order to learn "how indigenous clergy and lay people understand and attempt to live out Christian beliefs" (1992: 155).

The Arosi discourses examined below, as well as reflecting the internal pluralism of Arosi Christianity on the issue of ontology, furthermore constitute instructive examples of the historically and geographically widespread theme of reflexivity in ethno-theologies. In theorizing the category of ethno-ethno-history, Turner (1988: 241–242) argues that a frequent, though not constant or necessary, theme of this genre of expression is the reflexive production of self-representation through representation of encounter with the Other, especially Western Others. Exhibiting a similar tendency toward reflexivity, Arosi ethno-theologies often take as their focus, or explicitly include at some point, interpretive representations of pre-Christian Arosi religious thought and practice vis-à-vis Christianity and the Bible.

Recent studies of Christianity in postcolonial contexts, especially ethnographic accounts of Pentecostal churches, have drawn attention to instances in which Christianity appears to impose what might be described as past-renouncing reflexive ethno-theologies: narratives of radical rupture with the past in which previous moral and religious regimes—including, sometimes, other forms of Christianity—must be rejected as wrong or even demonic (e.g., Austin-Broos 1997; Knauft 2002: 167–168; LiPuma 2000: 229–232; Robbins 2003; Rose 1988). Joel Robbins (2004: 319–320) goes so far as to suggest that the Pauline theology of the supercession of the ancient Hebrew law codes writes such a narrative of disjuncture into all forms of Christianity. In Arosi Anglicanism, it must be acknowledged, there remains a legacy of mission discourses that stigmatized the pre-Christian past as the "time of darkness" ('oha kuhi), "pagans" as ahurodo (dark stomach/mind; cf. White 1991: 9, 138), and the ancestors as "devils" (Pijin: devol) (cf. Dureau 2001; Keesing 1989). But this linguistically embedded pejorative view of the past notwithstanding, the reflexive representations in Arosi ethno-theologies are predominantly past-affirming, claiming essential continuity between indigenous Arosi traditions and Christianity—sometimes to the point of virtually denying the exogenous character of biblical religion.

Perhaps proving Robbins's point that Christianity is "equipped with a set of arguments for why people need to throw over an inadequate traditional moral system" (2004: 319), the production of past-affirming reflexive ethno-theologies in Arosi could be seen as the responsive formulation of a set of vigorous antitheses that imply the existence of the theses they negate. But in rejecting an interpretation of biblical religion that would rate their ancestors and ancestral mores as benighted or evil in the eyes of a God preoccupied until lately with human history elsewhere, Arosi are hardly alone among Christians past and present. Rather, like a whole variety of analogous ancient and contemporary ethno-theological projects, past-affirming reflexive Arosi ethno-theologies show that the Bible and Christian theology are equipped with as many arguments for elevating indigenous traditions as God-given as for throwing them away (e.g., Burt 1983; Carey 1999; Ferguson 1998; Jacka 2002; Kidd 1999; Otero 2003; A. Smith 2003). If anything is written into Christianity at a general level it is, in fact, a debate about the value of the past. Past-renouncing and past-affirming reflexive ethno-theologies are thus not mutually exclusive, but are likely to coexist in the same Christian context and even as different aspects of the same ethno-theology. In Arosi, past-affirming voices have a decided majority in this internal Christian debate. Refusing to have been left unchosen or to have deserved divine neglect, Arosi are prying wide the opening Pauline theology itself leaves for gentiles to have had some knowledge of God's law before the arrival of the gospel (Romans 1–2).[1]

This is not to say that the acceptance of Christianity has not contributed significantly to processes of far-reaching cultural change in Arosi, or that European missionaries and Arosi Christians themselves have never demanded the renunciation of some indigenous practices. It is only to point out that Arosi ethno-theologies evince a strong will to deny radical difference between Christianity and objectified formulations of custom. While Arosi freely accept, and indigenous clergy occasionally articulate, a familiar narrative according to which the Church brought peace by ending cannibalism and warfare, they value the Church's self-proclaimed victory over such practices more as a reformation than a displacement of ancestral custom—a calling of Arosi back to the true core of their ancestral ways, which like all God-given mandates for living, were subject to human error and deformation.

---

1. The neo-Israelite ethno-theologies on Malaita go further in claiming actual identity with Israel (Brown 2005; Burt 1983). This hermeneutical move makes Malaitan neo-Israelites the theological cousins of many gentile Christians elsewhere who have claimed descent or mystical priestly succession from the Patriarchs, the so-called lost tribes of Israel, or even antediluvian biblical figures. In these ethno-theologies it might be said that past-renouncing and past-affirming reflexivity are two sides of the same coin if one takes self-redefinition as Israel as a way of simultaneously rejecting and aggrandizing one's culture and history.

In these ethno-theological endeavors, Arosi have been encouraged by, and are themselves now continuing, the Anglican mission theology that "taught of a God who was a fulfilment rather than a denial of existing Melanesian beliefs" (Hilliard 2005: 211). Recall that Patteson, as the first bishop of the diocese of Melanesia, instructed his mission priests and teachers to "fasten on" the "element of faith in superstition" and promoted a pedagogy informed by Joseph Butler's method of explaining the unfamiliar tenets of Christianity to converts and cat-echumens through reference to what is already experientially familiar. Describ-ing Butler's approach as a "hallowed Anglican intellectual position," Sohmer (1994: 187) has shown that the Melanesian Mission was, from its inception, committed to inviting prospective and new believers to reason by analogy from what was known to what was unknown as the only way to make sense of Chris-tianity. Fifty years after Patteson, Fox was still teaching indigenous mission teach-ers to show other Makirans how their own ideas and practices were, not simply pedagogically useful analogues to, but prefigurations of Christian truths.

> I hope to go to Bellona shortly to start Ben Mononai [sic, read Mononga'i] there: but I think he will find out a lot there as he is now as keen as I am and keeps a note book and draws all sorts of things and talks to all the old men, as do several of my teachers since I have taught them what a splendid foundation the old ideas of the people are on which to build our new ones, e.g. the identity of men and animals after death and even in life, and similar Christian teachings as to God; the heathen baptisms and ours; the *marauhu* seclusions and our schools, and so on and so on; the teachers are finding by experience what vivid-ness and strength the knowledge of the people's ideas gives them, and how it makes the new teaching live. They had the idea that the Jewish passover etc. were preparation for Christianity, but I teach them that the customs and thoughts of these people were *their* preparation and intended to be so. (Fox to Rivers, May 24, 1918, Perry Papers, B2, em-phasis in original.)[2]

In a posthumously published memoir intended for a Solomon Islands read-ership, Fox continued to proclaim this pastoral message, adopting a self-in-

---

2. Here it is relevant to note that Fox was one of the last European missionaries to serve as District Priest on Makira. Paul Marita, a man of Ulawa, assisted Fox and Joseph Gilvelte as deacon from 1921 and succeeded both men as District Priest for Arosi and Bauro in 1924 (MM *SCL*, February 1, 1922; January 1, 1931: 9). Since that time, with a few exceptions such as Ralph de Voil (c. 1933–34), the Anglican clergy serving on Makira have been Solomon Islanders (MM *SCL*, October 2, 1933: 12–15; October 1, 1934: 4).

clusive first person plural: "We must not belittle our old religion before white men came to us, nor call it 'of the devil' or 'rubbish' as some white men do. Christ did not come to destroy but to fulfil ..." (1985: 86; cf. 93–94).

In an important contribution to the literature on the indigenization of Christianity, Robbins (2004) analyzes the recent conversion of the Urapmin of Papua New Guinea to Pentecostalism chiefly in terms of a model of cultural change he labels adoption. Cast as a development of Sahlins's approach to modernization, Robbins's model of adoption theorizes a scenario in which people appropriate a whole new cultural form or system "in its own terms" without necessarily either attempting to understand it in terms they already know or letting it impinge on their indigenous ways of knowing and being. In cases of adoption, Robbins argues, "people live with two largely distinct and, in important respects, contradictory cultures at the same time" (2004: 10). If such a theoretically conceivable situation is cognitively possible in practice, Anglican missiology and ongoing Arosi ethno-theological constructions have rendered such a way of being Christian, even as a temporary phase of indigenization, historically impossible in this context.

Interestingly, Robbins suggests that the immediate cause of a situation of adoption can be a sense of humiliation experienced in terms of the values and categories of the indigenous cultural order, and only sometimes but not necessarily brought on by encounter with the exogenous cultural order about to be adopted. Thus, according to Robbins (2004: 15–27), Christianity's arguments for why Urapmin should throw over their indigenous moral system did not shame them into despising their traditions and opting for Christianity; rather, Urapmin took up Christianity as a novel prestige item in order to overcome their sense of humiliating marginalization within a regional ritual system, little realizing they were bringing home an additional source of shaming. It may be the case that it takes time—perhaps at least a generation from conversion—for people to entitle themselves to be critical Christians, Christians who actively discard or develop different possible readings of a tradition they are confident in as fully their own. For their part, however, many Arosi talk about "the Church" as though they have always understood the potentially humiliating message of Christianity and questioned it. "So, when they [the Church] said all *adaro* were of Satan, that was a little confusing," one man explained to me. "We said, 'They are our ancestors who look after us!' The spirits of our ancestors are still helpful to us." Variations on this sentiment have moved Arosi to engage consistently—and by means of deliberate original hermeneutical constructions—with the new religion precisely where it displays an equal potential to subvert its own potentially humiliating message from within.

Anthropologists have long recognized such interpretive engagement with Christianity as the counter-hegemonic resistance strategies or cultural politics of colonized and formerly colonized people. And undeniably, many Arosi ethno-theologies—such as Ishmael Taroiara's Christian idealization of a matrilineage as a landless but sacred embodiment of unity and love—are inextricably linked to material and political interests. But they are also equally religious forms—projects of Christian reflection on ontology and moral order, some of which remain personal ruminations with little circulation or potential for social influence (cf. Scott 2005b: 119–120). Like the Australian Aboriginal narratives that Heather McDonald (2001) presents as examples of "colonial" and "post-colonial theologising," they constitute faithful attempts to formulate satisfactory answers to some of the existential questions biblical religion can pose to those who take it up. If God is a universal sovereign, why did it take him so long to help us? Or did it? Were our ancestors not God's children as much as the people in the Bible? In this respect, the ethno-theologies that follow are comparable to the many seemingly self-deprecating claims of Pacific people to inhabit "the last island" or "the last place," the remotest corner of the world into which the effects of colonization, development, and the gospel have finally come (cf. Foster 2002: 132–133; McDougall 2004: 130–143). For as Abel Tawai of Tawatana noted, quoting to me the enigmatic promise of the New Testament: "The first will be last and the last will be first. We're last and we'll be first!" (cf. Matthew 19:30, 20:16; Mark 10:31; Luke 13:30).

Hatoibwari in Arosi Ethno-theologies

Today, more than three quarters of a century after the first publication of Fox's synthesis of Makiran snake traditions into a spirit-snake monism, a few Arosi still employ the figure and myths of Hatoibwari to bridge the conceptual gap between Arosi poly-ontology and the biblical depiction of one God and one humanity. In so doing, these Arosi—sometimes in conflicting and sometimes in overlapping ways—are formulating their own ethno-theologies that attempt to locate Arosi in a universal divine plan according to which pre-Christian Arosi religious ideas and practices served the purpose of *praeparatio evangelica*. The role of Hatoibwari in this process is, I have suggested, not merely a construct thrust on the Arosi by foreign missionaries. Rather, Hatoibwari has been the precise element within Arosi narrative tradition that some Arosi themselves have logically foregrounded when seeking connection with the Christian view of monotheism and human mono-ontology. The selection of the figure of a generative spirit-snake as a gloss on Christian themes of oneness is not just the invention of Bishop Patteson, but makes sense in terms of the structures of Arosi cosmology. As an icon of microcosmic mono-ontology within a macrocosmic poly-ontology, Hatoibwari indexes two analogous scales of origin and unity: the island of Makira, and an Arosi matrilineage. This double representation of unity has made Hatoibwari a productive symbol in the Arosi project of appropriating Christianity.[3]

Wilsman Warioha, the narrator of the myth of the unified descent of all Makirans with which the previous chapter opened, is one example of someone for whom Hatoibwari is an important element in the work of reconciling Christianity with Arosi custom. As well as understanding Hatoibwari to be a spirit-snake who is the island, Warioha also asserts that "we know that God placed Ha'atoibwari, but the people before didn't know this; they only knew Ha'atoibwari." In his exegesis of pre-Christian Arosi custom, Warioha analyzes the relationships among God, Hatoibwari, and other spirits in terms of the relationship among God, Jesus, and Jesus' apostles. In the parallelism between these two sets of relationships he sees a commendation of the former as a locus of recognizable, if incomplete, truth. Thus, in Warioha's ethno-theology, God placed Hatoibwari who, in turn, placed, or in some way mediated the origin of, the first male and female, the stone-beings Hauhunaaraha and Hauhunaari'i. In this scheme, the analogy between Hatoibwari and Jesus as mediators between God and Makirans is only implicit; yet, when explaining the nature of Hatoibwari's link with other subordinate spirits, Warioha draws a clear comparison between Hatoibwari and Jesus. In addition to describing the multitude of spiritual beings to whom Arosi formerly directed charms and prayers—birds, sharks, pigs, snakes, stones, etc.—as small projections of Hatoibwari, Warioha also describes them as messengers, or apostles (*ha'ataari*),

---

3. In the examples that follow it is evident that my consultants' ideas and stories about Hatoibwari have been informed by Fox's ideas. As one man acknowledged, "Only a few people knew about Hatoibwari before. Only after Fox have a large number of people heard the story." Copies of *The Threshold of the Pacific* are held at the National Library in Honiara and the offices of the Diocese of Hanuato'o at Kirakira. To my knowledge, however, there are no copies in the Tawatana village library or in circulation in Arosi. My inquiries on this subject suggest that only a few people, other than Father Abel Ta'aimaesiburu (see note 8 below), have seen the book; others have heard—not always accurate—reports of its contents. Despite its relatively more recent date of publication (1985), no one indicated having possession or knowledge of Fox's *My Solomon Islands*. Significantly, none of the Arosi who shared their ideas about Hatoibwari with me simply replicated either a version of a snake myth as published by Fox or Fox's synthetic snake monism; rather, each is continuing a collaborative bricolage.

likening them to the priests, deacons, teachers, and apostles whom "Jesus placed ... to do his work."[4] Acknowledging that there were also "bad spirits" that made themselves known through the actions of wicked people, Warioha attributes to Hatoibwari the cautionary words: "Look carefully, some in my name will trick and some in my name will be true." Intrigued that he would attribute to Hatoibwari this paraphrase of words attributed to Jesus (Matthew 24:5; Mark 13:6; Luke 12:8), I asked: "Ha'atoibwari said this?" He replied:

> Yes, in thought. That's how they know those who were bad and those who were good. The spirit showed it out; Ha'atoibwari revealed it. Those [who are] good are good, and those [who are] bad are bad, and these come out in thought. "If you don't believe the thing I say you will die, if you love what I say you'll live"[5] — that's the news (*taroha*) he [i.e., Ha'atoibwari] revealed. That's what we see in the world: death and life. The pagan (*ahurodo*) thought this too.

In this way Warioha expresses his understanding that, before the arrival of the missionaries, pre-Christian Arosi had received from Hatoibwari a message tantamount to the gospel, or good news (*taroha goro*): those who are wicked will perish, but those who follow the way of Hatoibwari will live.

Of the few Arosi who continue to draw on the idea and stories of Hatoibwari, Warioha is the only one I encountered who says that Hatoibwari gave rise to Makirans by starting with only two beings who became the ancestors of all subsequent Islanders. As already indicated, this model of human origins provoked a strong response from Casper Kaukeni who interrogated Warioha on two specific points. He asked whether Hatoibwari had given birth to the first couple and with whom their children were going to intermarry. These questions, I suggest, correlate with the two questions posed by the majority of the Hatoibwari myths such as Hauni's version: how can all people be connected to the island as to an ancestor without being incestuously connected to one another, and how can an ontologically distinct matrilineage reproduce itself? Casper seeks to ascertain the precise nature of the relationship between Hatoibwari and the first couple by demanding: "Who gave birth to the two of

---

4. The word *ha'ataari* is used to translate "apostle" in Fox's Arosi translation of the gospels and Acts of the Apostles (British and Foreign Bible Society 1921) and in the Arosi prayer book (Church of Melanesia 1982). The new Arosi language New Testament follows this long-established usage (Bible Society of the South Pacific 2004).

5. This saying, with its emphasis on the contrasting fates of those who do and do not "believe," echoes sayings about and attributed to Jesus in the Gospel of John. See John 4:18; 5:24; 8:24.

them?" Just as he also quizzes, "Were they going to marry their brothers and sisters?" Casper formulates his question by suggesting the possibility he finds most troubling. If Hatoibwari gave birth to Hauhunaaraha and Hauhunaari'i then the island itself is the true parent of all human beings, and the union of the primordial couple is an incestuous one. In other words, Casper is concerned to follow the ontological implications of the story. For his part, Warioha is especially unclear on this point and runs through a series of possible construals of this crucial relationship: the first couple variously originate from (*hasubu mai*), dwell (*awa*), rise up (*suruta'e*), or are placed (*nugaa*). Finally, at Casper's own prompting, he confirms Casper's suspicions and states that they are Hatoibwari's children who marry incestuously.

Even if Warioha had settled on a non-genealogical model of relationship between Hatoibwari and the primordial couple, the implication of lineage endogamy among their descendants would still have remained to perplex Casper. In Warioha's narration the descendants of the initial pair disseminate, cutting pathways from bush to coast and establishing a series of villages, the residents of which may intermarry at a distance of three villages. For Casper, however, this depiction of a partitioning of the island by human beings themselves cannot render people sufficiently distinct to be appropriate marriage partners for one another. Nevertheless, despite his misgivings with respect to this particular version of a Hatoibwari myth, Casper characterizes Hatoibwari as something into which only a few pre-Christian Arosi had gained insight as part of a progressive movement toward discovery of the Christian God. "We knew that something, a [lineage] spirit, placed power and that's as far as we got, but some people found Ha'atoibwari."

Another person who draws Hatoibwari into his appropriation of Christianity is Father Abel Ta'aimaesiburu, the Anglican priest from Tawatana who teaches at the Provincial Secondary School and who is renowned for his interest in collecting Makiran custom. Perhaps on the basis of a somewhat cryptic and imprecise passage from Fox's *My Solomon Islands* (1985: 88–89), Father Abel told me (erroneously) that Bishop Patteson had used the name A'unua to stand for God in his earliest Arosi translations.[6] A'unua is, for Father Abel (as

---

6. The passage from *My Solomon Islands* to which I refer reads:

But I do not think village people knew much about Agunua. They thought the Creator of their islands was one of the great beings who had never been men. In Arosi he took the form, when he wished, of a great Winged Serpent and it was to him they would pray. Bishop Patteson even used his name for God in the first Arosi prayers he wrote. What I learnt about Agunua was from old men who conducted the sacrifices who were called "caves of wisdom." (Fox 1985: 88–89)

Fox clearly knew that the name Patteson had used was Kauraha (Fox 1978: 266; Fox to

he was for Fox), equivalent to the universal biblical God. Thus, like Warioha, he regards Hatoibwari as having been the generative agent of God.

> Hatoibwari is variously called Hotoibwari—at Ha'ani—Hadibwari, Hausibwari, Hagasubwari—in Bauro. It is also called Mwaaroto. It can live in water, the sea, or on dry land. It is both male and female. From a distance, from Marau Sound [Guadalcanal], Makira looks like a spider (*bwari*) with Hoto [a hill] in the center; that's why they call it Hotoibwari in some places. At first, only a snake lived on the island; there were no people. A'unua or Aawa gave power to Hatoibwari. When Bishop Patteson did not use "God" but used A'unua as God's name, it was considered so holy you couldn't say it. In fact, when I was young I didn't say it, but now I say A'unua all the time explaining it to people. A'unua gave power to Hatoibwari to reproduce. First, it produced the *kakamora* [i.e., *pwapwaronga*] male and then female and they multiplied. Later it produced *masi* and they multiplied throughout the island. Then it produced *bao nai Roiraha* and finally *kuru nai Waiane*. These four groups lived together on the island. But the *masi*, *bao*, and *kuru* all died out.[7]

In this depiction of first events, Hatoibwari, the original spirit of the island, gives life to primordial beings, not mono-genetically but serially, generating four essentially different types of proto-human primordial people. Thus, Father Abel creatively adapts the biblical view of a single creative agent so as to meet the Arosi demand for multiple unrelated categories of being. Father Abel is evangelical about his own synthesis of Arosi and Christian tradition; as he admits, however, since few people know of A'unua and Hatoibwari, he must first teach them what is ostensibly their own custom before he can demonstrate the affinity between indigenous Arosi belief and Christianity. The result

---

Rivers, May 28, 1919, Perry Papers, B2) and did not, I think, mean to suggest here that Patteson had used the name Agunua. It seems possible, nevertheless, that one could mistakenly take Agunua to be the antecedent to which the pronouns in this passage refer, rather than the nameless "Creator"—i.e., Kauraha. Note also, however, that a few pages earlier Fox (1985: 85) describes "Hatoibwani" (*sic*) in precisely the same terms used to describe this "Creator," suggesting that he may have come to regard Kauraha and Hatoibwari as different, perhaps local, names for a particular type of Makiran spiritual being (cf. Fox 1924: 80, 82; *BG*: A3). See chapter 8, note 12.

7. Arosi narratives depict the *bao* of Roiraha village as a horde of short but strong people and the *kuru* as a group of blind people without noses (cf. Fox 1924: 335; *T*: "Iraau na Masi").

Figure 9.1. Father Abel Ta'aimaesiburu, Tawatana.

of Father Abel's teaching is evident in the fact that most of the Tawatana people who know anything of Hatoibwari point to Father Abel as the source of their knowledge.[8]

Since the time of Fox's active missionary work in Arosi, Father Abel has not been the only clergyman whose teaching methods include the supposed re-education of Makirans with respect to their snake traditions. Father John Espagne, a Roman Catholic missionary who worked throughout Makira—apart from Arosi—from 1946 to 1958, became persuaded by Fox's serpent monism thesis and endeavored to add to its supportive database. Espagne worked with

---

8. Although Father Abel never indicated to me that he had consulted Fox's publications, his innovative interpretations clearly draw on Fox's (1924: 79–86; 1978: 80; 1985: 84–89) ideas and constitute a theological enterprise, informed by that of the mission tradition, of uncovering points of contact between Christianity and Makiran custom. Rev. Brian Macdonald-Milne, who was one of Father Abel's teachers at theological college in the 1960s, informs me that he taught Pacific Studies "inductively," relating aspects of indigenous culture to themes in Christian theology, and that, like Fox before him, he viewed aspects of indigenous religions as gospel preparation. Macdonald-Milne reports that he did not have his students read Fox's work (Macdonald-Milne, personal communications, June 24, 2005; September 20, 2005), but it seems likely that Father Abel has studied both *The Threshold of the Pacific* and *My Solomon Islands* as part of his personal research into Arosi custom.

an explicitly theological agenda of demonstrating that the Makiran snake tradition was a corrupted memory of God's primordial self-disclosure in Eden and the tragedy of the Fall. In a 1992 interview, Father Espagne explained to me that it had been his practice to instruct Makirans about the "Makiran creator snake" as a way of showing the Islanders that their own beliefs were elements of a dimly remembered truth. After teaching Makirans their own former beliefs he would then draw out the similarities between Makiran and biblical stories. He adopted this approach, he said, in response to a comment by a school-educated youth who had said of the story of the snake: "Perhaps it's true, perhaps it's not." Concerned that this type of skepticism might come to be applied equally to Christian teachings, Espagne set out to give both traditions greater authority by showing how they are mutually corroborative. Ironically, however, he found himself in the position of being sought out by Makirans who regarded him as an expert in their custom, causing him to be cautious lest he provoke a resurgence of interest in and return to pre-Christian belief and practice.

In his unpublished manuscript "Witless Trust," Espagne (1953) acknowledges that the story of one humanity descended from a single set of parents as told in Genesis and in the version of the snake myth he promulgated was anathema to the Makirans to whom he ministered. Turning this fact to advantage, he suggested to them that the snake myth must represent the distorted recollection of a "primitive revelation" to all of humanity, for clearly they themselves would never have invented such a narrative of their origin that violates all of their current social norms.

> The idea of incest is so repugnant to the native mind, whatever their other moral shortcomings were, that the whole clan system was based on the complete desire to avoid it, and that ... marriage within the one clan was opposed and carried with it heavy penalties, even when there was no question of close relationship by blood. The native is reminded of this, and shown how foreign it would be to the mind of his people to imagine out of their own heads a story of the origin of the race which meant such a thing at the very beginning. Their incorporating it into their memory of the origin of the race was due to their firm recalling that our first parents were in some way the children of the Creator. (Espagne 1953: 39)

Here Espagne anticipates and seeks to capitalize on the same resistance to human mono-ontology that I encountered in Arosi. But Espagne's theology asserts what much of Arosi ethno-theology seeks to deny, namely that there was a sharp divide within pre-Christian Arosi custom between what was of

God and what was merely of human devising. Rather than using Arosi custom regarding the distinctiveness of matrilineages and the necessity of exogamy as anti-models against which to prove the kernel of truth in the mythology of the snake, Arosi today live with an unresolved tension between these indigenous assumptions and the Christian view of humanity as one kindred. This tension constitutes a historically conditioned dual formulation in the context of which the obscure figure of Hatoibwari has become, for a small number, a symbol with which to negotiate between conflicting models of origins. Rather than confronting Arosi with a stark choice between the ways of God and the ways of humanity, Hatoibwari facilitates this negotiation because she is an indigenous image of the one among the many and the icon of two life-giving entities. Symbolizing both the generative power of the island as a whole and the reproduction of an integral matrilineage, she is selected by some as a pre-Christian intimation of the biblical creator God.

"True God, That is *Auhenua*"

Arosi ethno-theological projects are not limited to those that engage with the figure of Hatoibwari; in fact, the majority of Arosi hold to versions of an ethno-theological project that involves no reference to Hatoibwari. For this majority, the appropriation of Christianity as a cosmology that affirms, rather than challenges, Arosi custom is achieved by understanding the universal biblical God in terms of the concept of *auhenua* in all its aspects. This means that most Arosi assume that the power of God has always been in the island even when people did not realize that the power came from the Christian God. God is the true *auhenua* who established the *ringeringe*, custom law, of the island as a whole; his power transcends and is the source and guarantor of all localized power and authority. As the ultimate *auhenua*, it was God who, before the coming of Christianity, had placed the *auhenua* matrilineages and entrusted them with the maintenance of his custom in their territories. Thus, the concept of *auhenua* provides a means toward understanding Christianity that, like the myths of Hatoibwari, highlights the two levels of unity within Arosi poly-ontology, namely, the inherent quality of the island and the nature and role of a matrilineage in its territory. Unlike the myths of Hatoibwari, however, the concept of *auhenua* allows Arosi to appropriate Christianity by focusing on commonalities between customary and Christian ethics rather than on conflicting narratives of ultimate origins. That is to say, the concept of *auhenua* shifts interpretive energies away from abstract ontology and toward praxis, enabling Arosi to connect with Christianity where its practical demands and norms correspond with those of Arosi poly-ontology.

Arosi express the idea that God is the one true *auhenua* throughout the island most clearly in statements and practices that attribute to God a general power over the qualities and function of all things in the island, both living and inanimate. Contemporary gardening and other agricultural practices, especially, constitute a site at which it is clear that Arosi look directly to God as the controlling influence over the success or failure of their efforts. Routinely, Arosi seek to secure plenty by incorporating elements of Christian worship into their planting activities. One man, for example, demonstrated for me how he had managed to cultivate high-yielding coconut palms on land that was very poor and stoney by offering—"in the name of the Father, Son, and the Holy Spirit"—the following prayer as he worked: "'I don't have good land, I plant this coconut in a rocky place, you love me, you make this coconut bear well.'" "I also pray when I plant sweet potatoes," he added, "but I don't do so on good land, because this good land was provided by God." Another man described the ritual he employs to "bless" his garden and ensure that it will be fruitful. "I say the 'Our Father' inwardly in each corner [of the garden] and then in the center of the garden to dedicate the garden. If I do this, even if there is a lot of sun my sweet potato will not die." In addition to these personal planting ceremonies, Arosi also observe an annual "day of asking" as part of their church calendar. Each village as a congregation participates in a procession of prayer that encompasses the village cemetery, the local reef passage, and someone's garden. "We pray at the cemetery, but I'm not sure why we do so. Perhaps we do this so that a lot of souls will be saved. We pray at the passage so that there will be lots of fish, and we all go to a nearby garden to pray so that food will be plentiful."

Arosi understand God's control over the productivity of the land to be one way in which he, as the true *auhenua* of the island, exercises his moral will. They stress that their custom has always been consonant with the biblical Ten Commandments and that God had placed this law in the island, correlating it with organic processes so that those who obeyed God's *ringeringe* enjoyed good crops and many children, while those who neglected or violated this guideline for living found the earth and their own bodies barren. At the same time, Arosi say that God also uses the living things and other natural phenomena of the island to reward and punish. If someone's garden is spoiled by wild pigs, for example, it may be said that the person or a relative must have been guilty of some moral lapse. Alternatively, it may be said that divisions in the village have brought this trouble to chasten the entire village. As one man from Tawatana reasoned after a domestic pig from a neighboring village was found routing through the gardening area: "Pigs come and eat gardens because some things are amiss in the village. Why did the pig come from Maranuʻu to eat the gardens here and not eat the gardens at Maranuʻu? The pigs don't just wander following the food." Similarly, Arosi are inclined to interpret outcomes, such as whether a cyclone does or does not strike the coast near their village, as reflections of whether the village is divided by conflict and desultory in its worship, or united in communal work and faithful in church attendance.

Although it is a question always open to interpretation whether a particular mishap or misfortune is the retribution of God, an ancestral spirit, or God working through an ancestral spirit, Arosi nevertheless appear to assign different provinces of power to God and the ancestors. Ancestors can be understood to protect the land, material goods, and the persons of their descendants; God, however, enjoys a sphere of influence that encompasses this protective function and also includes power over increase of life and the ability to endow the things of the island, with their own different properties and effects. Thus, it is by the power of God and not by ancestors that, as I was instructed for my own benefit, the *darao*, a type of nettle, causes itching, and the *hiroadaro* is the tree to cancel out the itching caused by contact with the *darao*. Similarly, the *weri*, a small millipede, has power to burn, but the earth has power to cancel the pain. "If you get the liquid of a *weri* in your eye," I was advised, "dig a hole in the earth and look into the hole."

This general, if not absolute, division of labor between God and the ancestors may map a pre-Christian distinction between ancestral powers that were the objects of sacrifices offered locally by their descendants and powers associated with the productivity of the island that were the objects of sacrifices, such as those described by Wilson (1932: 159–160) and Fox (1924: 84–85, 325), that involved the inhabitants of large portions of the island.[9] Like Hatoibwari, or other powers associated with the productivity of the island,

---

9. Davenport (1986: 103–104; cf. 1997: 317) reports a similar division between "deities of the land" and "deities from humans" on Santa Catalina. Of the former, Davenport (1986: 104) writes, "They were present in and around the community before humans arrived; they made the environment usable, productive, and fertile." While deities from humans are the focus of most religious practices on Santa Catalina, the deities of the land are honored separately in the complex new year ritual, *wogosia*. Amplifying his ethnography in a more recent account, Davenport (1996: 26) calls the deities of the land "the Supernaturals of the Inhabited Land" and notes that they "are not seen as actual supernatural beings, gods, or deities. They are more like unseen mystical forces." These forces "transformed the bareness [of the physical island] by endowing soils with fertility for gardens and orchards, infusing the dwelling areas with life-sustaining power for the humans to live and reproduce, and

who received the first-fruits of the season's yield, God today is the power to whom Arosi offer thanks in return for the bounty of their gardens. Because Makirans no longer cultivate indigenous tubers in a structured and regular rhythm of planting and harvesting, such sacrifices are no longer made on a semi-island-wide synchronized seasonal basis; rather, each gardener remembers God when his or her garden begins to bear. Accordingly, when I went to harvest my first crop of sweet potatoes in the garden that my friends had helped me to plant, Nesta Nunu'au told me that I should take a basket of tubers down to the church as a first-fruits offering to be blessed at the following Sunday service. Later, I asked Nesta's young daughter, June, why it was necessary to do this, and she responded: "So that the remaining tubers will grow large, of course!"

Arosi recognize God to be the *auhenua* of the island and the source of its diffuse order and vitality, but are more likely to stress that, prior to the advent of the Christian Church as an institution in their land, God had mediated his *ringeringe* to the people of Makira through the *auhenua* matrilineages in their territories. Arosi tend, in fact, to speak of the *auhenua* matrilineages as though they had been God's representatives all along, drawing people together to live in their lands and promoting what one man referred to in English as "righteous living pleasing to the devils [i.e., the ancestral spirits] and now [pleasing] to God." Rosemary Magewa elaborated this idea to indicate that the relationship between God and an *auhenua* matrilineage was one of mutual representation:

> I say that the Holy Spirit was already here [before Christianity came], it is *auhenua* too because the person who is speaking true things, she really has [the spirit and] is true.... It was the spirit that placed this lineage of people here [and as a consequence] they have efficacious power (*mena*); they have the Holy Spirit, the big spirit. So when they speak it is efficacious, their mouths are *mena*, because the spirit follows those things that are straight and true and *auhenua*. To those that came, that lied, that stole, that were jealous, [the spirit] will not be *mena* with them.

For those Arosi who understand themselves to be representatives of the true *auhenua* matrilineages where they live, this special role and relationship with God is seen still to be operative. They say that because God has given them

---

stocking the fringing reefs and adjacent ocean areas with an abundance of marine life" (Davenport 1996: 26).

special responsibility as upholders of his law in their land, they are obligated to live up to that law themselves by humbly and generously making the use of their land available to those who acknowledge their precedence. When others take advantage, however, or when those who see themselves as the *auhenua* think that their position is being disregarded, the latter are confident that God will "place a sign so that people will know that they are true." In their capacity as the agents of God's power and moral will, the *auhenua* lineages were the forerunners of the Christian Church in Arosi. The *ringeringe* of the *auhenua* was, some Arosi contend, tantamount to the institution of the Church: "In olden times people made Church with the custom (*ringe*), the *ringe auhenua*, the *kastom lo*, that was their Church."

If the *auhenua* matrilineages in their territories served as precursors to the institution of the Church as God's representatives, then the institution of the Church today is, for Arosi, the functional successor to the supposedly defunct *auhenua* and their anointed chiefs. Beyond teaching and encouraging people to uphold the law of God, however, from the Arosi point of view, the principal way in which the Church carries on the work of the *auhenua* is as a force for peace that calls people from different locales with different lineage identities to live together in stable and cohesive village polities. The Church not only continues the unifying function of the *auhenua* and their representative chiefs; Arosi say it was mediated to them by their chiefs. To express and support their understanding that the Church is a positive influence that works in accordance with Arosi custom, people credit the former reigning chiefs—such as Takihorota'imae of Wango and Bo'orauaniara of Heuru—with having been the first to invite the missionaries or the Islanders they had trained as teachers to come and preach their message. Like pre-Christian chiefship before it, the Church is seen as a binding social institution in which persons of disparate lineages can find their nexus. The Arosi word for the Church emphasizes this community-building function; *haisoi* (also *heisoi*), a word coined expressly to refer to the new institution, means "a mutual calling" and was probably intended by missionaries to be a literal translation of the Greek word *ekklesia* (cf. Ivens 1918: 167). More than a scholarly nicety, however, the sense of this coinage epitomizes what the Church, since its first missionary successes, has represented for Arosi—a strong voice summoning people to a way of harmonious interaction free from feuding and violence. As elsewhere in the Solomons and throughout Melanesia, in Arosi, people welcomed the Church, in part, because of its reputation for successfully ending reciprocal murders and establishing peace (Hilliard 1978: 41, 51, 170; MM *SCL*, November 18, 1912: 99–103; June 1, 1915: 525–526; Tippett 1967: Chapter 13; White 1983, 1991: Chapter 6, 171–176; Whiteman 1983: 191–192; Wilson *D*: September

12–14, 1903). The Church, in other words, first coordinated with, and then inherited, the role of the peace-chief of the *auhenua*.[10]

The Arosi interpretation and appropriation of the biblical God and the Christian Church in terms of the role of the *auhenua* matrilineages and their chiefs would be insufficiently explained, however, simply as a means of promoting peace. An ontology-based analysis shows that, by thinking about God and the Church through the concept of *auhenua*, Arosi have successfully coordinated the first-order burden on praxis suggested by Arosi poly-ontology with the equivalent of a second-order burden on praxis suggested by Christian theology. Because Arosi poly-ontology posits the original autonomy of Arosi proto-lineages conceived of as independently arising categories of being, the primary and never definitely achieved *telos* of human activity is to bring these categories into an orchestration of productive relations that constitutes a socio-cosmic totality. In contrast, Christian interpretations of Genesis agree that, in the beginning there was an original communion between God and humanity that has been broken by sin. Likewise because of sin, the original unity and mutual understanding among human beings has been lost, and all human relationships are prone to fragmentation. Consequently, the *telos* of Christian belief, worship, and social practice is reconciliation between God and humanity and within humanity itself.

The present fallen condition of humanity described in ecumenical Christian theology, in which human beings are alienated from God and each other is, I suggest, formally analogous to the original primordial condition envisioned by Arosi poly-ontology. In both states the perceived paramount need is for human action capable of uniting people of otherwise separate and mutually alien backgrounds into a balanced life-sustaining order. Thus, in identifying God and the Church with the *auhenua*, Arosi connect their model of poly-ontological cosmogenesis with the Christian model of world redemption. They make this connection, not abstractly in terms of Christian theological concepts such as sin, Fall, and redemption, but concretely in terms of the *ringeringe* that is equally of God and of their island. This *ringeringe* exhorts

---

10. It has already been noted that Arosi regard the physical church building as a source of power analogous to pre-Christian shrines and burial sites. Additionally, although Arosi themselves do not make this connection, the church structure is equally a successor and analogue to pre-Christian structures, such as canoe houses and chiefly residences, that served as focal points for collective activity, and on which the cooperative efforts of the village were inscribed. Father Léopold Verguet describes such a structure from the village of Oné (Makira Harbour) as he saw it in the mid 1840s that, like the building of the new church at Tawatana in the early 1990s, required and elicited an intensive application of constructive care and skill (1885: 222–226; cf. Fox 1958: 70–71; Webster 1863?: 81–82).

them to embrace "love, peace, and unity," as the key to the good way of living together that they see as always having been the goal of their polity-building practices.[11] This focus on ethical exhortation and the identification of God, the Church, and the *auhenua* as three powers capable of calling the disparate things of the world to live together allows Arosi to embrace Christianity as a continuation of Arosi custom without raising the disconcerting conflicts between Arosi and Christian conceptions of deep human ontology. Instead, Arosi deep ontology intersects with Christian human ontology, not at its primary but at its secondary stratum—after the Fall—at which it depicts humanity as fragmented. By matching these essentially non-corresponding but semantically compatible levels of ontology, Arosi achieve a satisfactory interpretation of Christianity as positing a prevailing social atomism with a familiar attendant onto-praxis of promoting cooperative relationships.

Nevertheless, even while deflecting attention away from questions of deepest ontology, the Arosi emphasis on the *ringeringe auhenua* as the *ringeringe* of the true God also has the potential to erode matrilineal identities and even promote a shift toward the conceptualization of Arosi as one undifferentiated people. This can occur when *auhenua* comes to be defined more as a disposition of being loving, fostering togetherness, sharing with others, protecting peace, and being truthful, and less as the result of having become anchored in a territory through topogonic ancestral activities. In other words, emphasis on behavior that embodies the *ringeringe auhenua* as the criterion for being *auhenua* may begin to diminish the importance of physical markers that demonstrate a history of ancestral habitation as the criteria for becoming *auhenua* in a particular place. If defined strictly as a moral disposition in harmony with the will of God, *auhenua* could come to signify only a diffuse non-lineage and non-territory-specific moral quality. No one who follows the *ringeringe* would be more *auhenua* anywhere than anyone else who follows the *ringeringe*. Consequently, anyone could become *auhenua* anywhere simply by following the *ringeringe*. In fact, this seems to be a logical implication of identifying the concept of *auhenua* first and foremost with God and only secondarily with the matrilineages as God's representatives on Makira. The net effect of this revalorization of *auhenua* is similar to that of Ishmael Taroiara's assertion that a matrilineage is a landless unity of shared love. Like Taroiara's landless love, the concept of *auhenua* as a purely moral condition unrelated to matrilineages in their territories can become a category that, instead of

---

11. See White (1991: 125–129) for an analysis of the themes of "peace," "unity," and "love" in Christian rhetoric on Santa Isabel.

differentiating among Arosi, has the potential to unite them, not only with one another as one *auhenua* people on the coast, but also with peaceful, loving, and good people everywhere.

One senior man with whom I discussed the meaning of *auhenua* on several different occasions seemed at points in our conversations to reach this very conclusion, only to retreat from the full implications of this position in order to protect his commitment to the idea that his lineage is the one true *auhenua* lineage in his village. Repeatedly, he spoke of *auhenua* as an intangible internal orientation toward a quality he referred to in Arosi as *goroha*. Based on the root *goro* meaning "good," this term in general usage means "the goodness of things and of people," "good favor," and "a good way of living"; in this man's ethno-theology, *goroha* encompasses the constant triad of "love, peace, and unity" construed as an attribute of God and as the distinguishing characteristic of his particular lineage, the Araha lineage. This characteristic, rather than the ability to point to ancestral shrines and burial sites in the land, seems to be what he values as the clearest manifestation and proof of being *auhenua*.

> *Auhenua* is inside the [person's] spirit.... Today people say land means you are *auhenua*, but that's not true. Nowadays *auhenua* we call God. The Araha lineage was the chief in olden times; it was they who fought for *goroha*—they fight at the edge of *goroha* so that it will stand. The other lineages are supports [points to the cross beams supporting the roof of the house in which we were sitting], and they support the Araha lineage, that's how it looks. True God, that is *auhenua*. To talk about *hera* and *birubiru* is to use an argument based on the dark time that doesn't recognize God. Snakes and birds aren't *auhenua*, because *auhenua* is the thought in the life of people. But you can talk about them in court and the court can ask you about them.... In contrast, it is the ideas in Araha that come out into the light.

This man's ethno-theology combines past-renouncing and past-affirming aspects in ways that construct his matrilineage as an analogue to ancient Israel while casting other Arosi matrilineages as analogues to the gentiles of the Bible (cf. Scott 2005b). He does not deny that, relative to the present "time of light" inaugurated by the Church, all Arosi matrilineages were in the "dark time" before they became Christian. But relative to the Araha, who were already the special champions of *goroha* before the arrival of the Church, the other Arosi matrilineages were, and continue to be, even further from insight into God's ways.

To this man, it is extremely significant that the name of his matrilineage—Araha—also means "chief" and that Arosi have been using this word to gloss the title "Lord" with reference to both God and Jesus since Fox translated portions of the New Testament and the Book of Common Prayer into Arosi (British and Foreign Bible Society 1921; Church of England in New Zealand 1923; cf. Ray 1921: 154). As its name indicates, the Araha lineage, according to this man, was not only first among others in terms of political strength, it was first in godliness as well. Even though "knowing *goroha* was a little difficult" in the time of darkness, the Araha lineage had a unique grasp of and guardianship over the *goroha* of the heavenly Araha that set them apart from other lineages as a vehicle of divine light. "I am talking about the blood inside my lineage," he told me. "You'll see the light in it." Because they already had this light inside them, the Araha were quick to receive Christianity.

> So it was easy for us to grasp Christianity because it was nearly one with the ruling before. This [points to trees and other vegetation around] is the *goroha* that came down from heaven; they also held [*goroha*] in their lives that came from that place.

Although he does not make the comparison explicit, this man seems to understand the Araha lineage as having been an elect lineage vis-à-vis the other Arosi matrilineages, just as the Bible represents Israel as having been elect among the nations. But likewise, just as the Bible grants some natural knowledge of God's law to the gentiles, he allows that the other Arosi matrilineages had some inklings of *goroha* by virtue of their own *araha*, their chiefs of old.

> All lineages have Araha [i.e., chiefs] who want to keep love, peace, and unity. This *goroha* is then the first thing called Araha. Araha is the power of *goroha*. Other lineages have this in their life because every Araha holds them.... Other lineages come into the word Araha—this Araha also rules over every last one of them. Araha doesn't choose. No! Doesn't choose lineages. Other lineages have their own *goroha*, love, and unity.

Thus it appears that, in this man's mind, there is a spiritual hierarchy among Arosi matrilineages: "Other lineages look a little bit into the *goroha*; they are the supporters and witnesses.... These other lineages are the supports of Araha [lineage], of the chief, just as the bishop and priests are supports of Christ." The Lordly Araha lineage is, for him, essentially one with the spirit of God and the quality of being *auhenua*, all defined as *goroha*.

> You don't hear about the strength of other lineages, but you do hear of the strength of the Araha: it is *goroha* in life. The thing I call Araha, is the Spirit. You call him God; we call him *Hi'ona*. Our

> *Hi'ona* is *goroha*. The *Hi'ona* is only an *adaro*. *Adaro* are *auhenua* be-
> cause they stay in the island, so the *Hi'ona* is *auhenua*, is an *adaro*,
> is *goroha*.

But even as this series of equations serves to link the spirit of God that
makes the Araha lineage especially strong in *goroha* with the *auhenua* quality of the island, this man's identification of *goroha* as the hallmark of all of
these things opens the door to the possibility that other people and groups
beyond the island may also be of his lineage if they follow and maintain
goroha.

> *Araha* is *goroha*. Michael, you were brought here by *goroha*, and so I
> believe you are Araha too. Araha are for what? They are for people to
> live in peace, love, and unity. If I'm right in believing that the U.N.
> keeps *goroha*, then I think they are Araha. God is in *goroha*.

At one point, he even said: "I believe Queen Elizabeth is Araha because she
looks after *goroha*."

By completely ethicizing the quality of being *auhenua*, this man's system of
thought attenuates the connection between *auhenua* and the island. Anyone
who, according to his interpretation, exhibits and builds peaceful goodness
qualifies as a member of his *auhenua* lineage wherever they may have originated or be located. This conceptual move eliminates the possibility of differentiating between the *auhenua* and the non-*auhenua* either in terms of a
distinction between those who are of the island and those who have arrived
from offshore, or a distinction between Makirans who have become *auhenua*
in a particular place in Arosi and Makirans who are *auhenua* elsewhere on the
island. *Auhenua* is no longer strictly a function of place but a mode of moral
action. Accordingly, this man reproduces the lost place-based distinction between *auhenua* and *sae boboi* by transforming it into an action-based distinction between people who show forth the peaceful goodness that is the way of
his lineage and selfish people who do not work together with others but try to
grasp and hold the land for themselves. The latter show the error of their ways
by threatening to take others to court and trusting in the things of the pre-
Christian past to vindicate their claims to be *auhenua*.

> When people seek to verify that they are *auhenua* in the land they
> often talk about spirit-snakes, but they don't recognize the creation.
> They use arguments from the darkness; they verify from the darkness
> while we are in a time of light. Yes, some people win court on the basis
> of saying: "There's our burial site, there's our shrine, we worship
> spirit-snakes." But look, in doing this they stay inside the darkness.

They can, in fact, be in the Church but still believe only in the world. In doing this they are selfish and are claiming things as their own.

Unlike the ontological distinction between *auhenua* and *sae boboi*, however, such a distinction between those who follow the peaceful goodness of the spirit of God and those who follow selfishness and the things of the past, entails no grounds for resistance to the human mono-ontology of biblical narrative and ethics. This distinction, based only on truth versus error as displayed through action, ultimately collapses, even for this man who is concerned to preserve the privileged *auhenua* identity of his lineage. Invoking the biblical idea that God created human beings in God's own image, this man concludes: "Everyone must be Araha because man was created in God's image." The true difference between the good and the selfish is not a matrilineal or ontological distinction, it is only a difference between actions that reveal greater or lesser degrees of insight into truth. "Everyone is Araha and needs *goroha*, but they don't see it." Concerning the tense relations between his lineage and another lineage in his village that also understands itself to be *auhenua*, he says: "The Amaeo lineage is just Araha because they also have *goroha* with them. They want to live well and quietly, but their name is different. While this is so, all of our blood is the same color. We all only see one blood—red. We're all people of the Spirit, the true Spirit who created *goroha*."

With this thought, this man appears to adopt a nominalist stance regarding the nature of Arosi matrilineages according to which their plurality of names labels only superficial differences among people who are fundamentally of one blood because they are creatures of the same creating spirit. In other words, he appears to have embraced the Christian model of human mono-ontology. Of the many people with whom I frequently discussed the concept of *auhenua*, this elderly man was the only one who had drawn these particular abstract conclusions. As he said of himself: "Before, I used to work hard, but my body is weak, so I think." In his thinking he has explored the logical implications of appropriating God in terms of the Arosi concept of *auhenua* and emphasizing the ethical dimension of *auhenua* at the expense of the spatio-temporal dimension. In other interviews, however, this same man employed the image of blood, as did several of my other consultants, to describe the distinctiveness of each matrilineage as "one blood." Likewise, in keeping with the testimonies of other Arosi who think of their matrilineages as *auhenua* where they reside, he too acknowledged that he would have to story about the local shrines if called on to do so in a land dispute. Moreover, other people suspect him of wanting to put his lineage forward as the *auhenua* in the village. Despite his thoughts, therefore, he is also quietly, if not always imperceptibly, engaged—like most other Arosi—in the type of topogonic activity that today produces an Arosi coast that is a heterotopic lamination of diverse lineage identities.

Topogonic Farewells

In this and the previous chapter I have identified a number of phenomena, all associated with the appropriation of Christianity, that seem to have the potential to deterritorialize matrilineal particularity and move Arosi models of humanity toward mono-ontology. These phenomena—collective labor in the name of Christian unity, Taroiara's plan to institute father to son inheritance, myths of the spirit-snake Hatoibwari as interpreted by Europeans and Makirans, and other Arosi ethno-theologies that identify God as the true *auhenua* and privilege the ethical dimension of *auhenua*—all entail an inherent, if sometimes unexplored, possibility for reconceptualizing the Arosi people as one consubstantial *auhenua* lineage. In all of its forms, this possibility coexists in Arosi today in a historically conditioned dual formulation in tension with the dominant Arosi poly-ontological cosmology.

While the phenomena examined here and in the preceding chapter are instructive for what they reveal about how a poly-ontological cosmology such as that of Arosi might transform into a mono-ontology, the likelihood that this transformation will occur throughout Arosi in the near future seems small given the present prevalence of topogonic activity that is reproducing Arosi poly-ontology in the form of heterotopia. Compared to the number of people committed to the topogonic reformation of their matrilineages as the coastal *auhenua*, the number of people who tell a myth of unified human origins, advocate a reinterpretation of Arosi land tenure that could promote mono-ontology, or espouse an ethno-theology that implies mono-ontology is small. Furthermore, the strong objections of other Arosi to the representations and policy suggestions of such people demonstrate that most Arosi operate with poly-ontological assumptions immediately and intensely resistant to ideas that lead in the direction of mono-ontological models of human relations. If Arosi exhibits a historically conditioned dual formulation, it is decidedly a dual formulation of the many over against the few who embrace the one.

But the issue is not one of current statistics in a yet-to-be-decided contest between pressures exerted by Christianity and resistance mounted by Arosi poly-ontology. To the contrary, the situation in Arosi does not warrant the supposition that Christianity is inherently "a religion of placelessness" (McDonald 2001: 80, 201) that must necessarily undermine people's local emplaced identities in favor of global or otherworldly-oriented identities. In reproducing their emplaced matrilineal identities, Arosi are not operating in a world, governed solely by the cultural practices of the ancestral past, that is separate from their life and thought as Christians. It is as Christians that they are constructing ethno-theologies in which the land and the ancestral customs—the *ringeringe auhenua*—that they understand to be particular to their matrilineages in their territories were, and remain, valid and important instruments of divine revelation. They are developing ethno-theologies of place—theologies that attempt to reassert rather than supercede emplaced identities and to mediate between local and universal ways of being God's children (cf. Tuwere 2002). Demonstrating again that the Christian tradition is not univocal, Arosi are discovering and elaborating the resources within the tradition that can support their practical and spiritual needs to affirm their historical and territorial specificity—even their sense of chosenness.

Moreover, rather than compelling them to confront a problematic human mono-ontology, being Christian has, for most Arosi, actually facilitated the topogonic activities through which they are constructing their *auhenua* identities. As discussed in chapter 5, Arosi understandings of the presence of the Church and the power of Christian faith in their villages have rendered the nature of ancestral sites ambiguous and subject to a variety of positioned interpretations. At the same time, the identification of the *ringeringe auhenua* with "righteous living pleasing to the devils and now [pleasing] to God" has functioned in tandem with the overt consensus that the *auhenua* of the coast are dead to create an environment in which representatives of multiple matrilineages can develop their own self-understandings as *auhenua*. The sanction of the *ringeringe* against selfishness and the provocation of disputes enjoins a silence on the would-be *auhenua* that is paradoxically a boon rather than a restraint to their cause; through silence and modesty, many can freely articulate their mutually exclusive identities.

In fact, far from leading people to surmise that they must all belong to one great *auhenua* lineage, the Arosi appropriation of the Christian God as the true *auhenua* and author of the *ringeringe* has made the fulfillment of the ethical dimension of *auhenua* a primary component of topogonic activity. Now, in addition to being able to narrate an autochthonous history of ancestral territory formation, to become *auhenua* in the coastal land today, one must also be the unobtrusive force for stability and peace that is the true anchor on which village life is centered. As I was preparing to depart from the field, I became the occasion for a brief intensification of this form of topogonic activity. In final interviews and casual good-byes, members of some of the different matrilineages in Tawatana sought to imply that it had been through their lineages that I had been welcomed into the village, and that it had been chiefly the people of their lineages who had helped and lovingly provided for me. With warm smiles and knowing nods they posed the rhetorical question: "When you look who welcomed you, then you know who is *auhenua* here, don't you?"

GLOSSARY

adaro: a spirit; a corpse; the name of a deceased person; the name of several matrilineages.

ahui: the growing core or base of a tree; used figuratively to refer to an *auhenua* matrilineage in its territory.

ahurodo: literally, "dark stomach/mind," used to refer to people of the pre-Christian past.

araha: a traditionally anointed chief; a highly respected person; the name of several matrilineages; used to gloss "Lord" in Arosi translations of the Bible and the Book of Common Prayer.

auhenua: autochthonous; used to refer to matrilineages, people, animals, natural features, objects, and intrinsic qualities that are essentially and irrevocably of a place.

'awataa: a person or persons who are not members of the autochthonous matrilineage of the place (*auhenua*) where they reside—frequently, but not exclusively, people who have married members of the autochthonous matrilineage of a place.

bao: a mythic group of short, strong, human-like beings, now said to be extinct, but formerly located at Roiraha, thus sometimes referred to as *bao nai Roiraha*.

birubiru: a shrine dedicated to spirit-shark worship.

burunga: a matrilineage; a clan; a group of people.
  burunga i auhenua: the autochthonous matrilineage of a place.

dora anai suho'asi: a place for burned sacrifice.

dora maea: a shrine or burial site said to have been shaped by the powers placed in it by ancestors.

goroha: peaceful goodness.

ha'amaeaa: to invest with powers, to bless, to sanctify.

haia'ia'i: entangled, entwined.

haikawikawi: entangled, entwined.

haisoi: literally, "mutual calling," used to refer to the Church or Christianity.

haito'oranga'i: to be related to and therefore not permitted to marry; such a relationship.

hau ba'ewa: a shark stone said to be the image of the shark formerly honored in association with it; moveable stone elements of shark shrines (*birubiru*).

hera: a hole, cave, or built structure in which human bones were placed in pre-Christian practice; also, a Christian graveyard.

hi'ona: an ancestral spirit or island spirit; the Christian God.
　hi'ona maea: the Holy Spirit.

ho'asi: to offer sacrifice.

kolonia: a future era anticipated by followers of Maasina Rule in which individualistic capitalism and extreme commodification will prevail.

kuru: a mythic group of blind and noseless beings said to have lived at Waiane, thus sometimes referred to as *kuru nai Waiane.*

maea: holy, respected, set apart, invested with powers dedicated to the ancestors or to the Christian God.

mahuara: a visiting stranger.

mamaani: a narrative, story, history.
　mamaani suri waipo: to narrate a genealogy along matrilineal links.

marewana: the world of everyday experience (contrasted with *rodomana*).

masi: a category of human-like beings described in popular southeast Solomons folklore as having exterminated themselves through comic exploits of suicidal stupidity.

mena: efficacious power.

mwaa: a snake; the name of several matrilineages.

mwaeraha: a traditionally anointed chief.

ngari: the canarium nut tree; the nuts from this species of tree.

ngau: to eat.
　ngau suri ama: to eat through the father, i.e., to enjoy the privilege of residing in and taking sustenance from land previously held and worked by one's patrikin.
　ngau suri ina: to eat through the mother, i.e., to enjoy the privilege of residing in and taking sustenance from land where one is a member of the *auhenua* matrilineage of the land.

odo: a straight swathe of gardening land that stretches inland from the coast.

pwapwaronga: small autochthonous people described in custom stories and said still to live in caves on Makira; sometimes called *pwapwaangora* or *kakamora.*

raaraa: branch of a tree; used figuratively to refer to the *sae boboi* relative to the *auhenua* matrilineage as the *ahui* in its territory.

ramo: a warrior.

ringeringe: custom, law, rules.
  ringeringe auhenua: the traditional custom law of the land.

rodomana: the usually unseen realm of the spirits that can be visited during sleep (contrasted with *marewana*).

ruruha: a group of people or animals; an assembly.

ruruunga: trees (excluding coconut palms) from which people regularly collect nuts or fruit during the appropriate season; the nuts or fruits of such trees.

sae aidangi: an instructed or knowledgeable person.

sae boboi: a person or persons who are not members of the autochthonous matrilineage of a place (*auhenua*), i.e., the *'awataa* and *mahuara* taken together.

sae bwani: the people of old.

suho'asi: a burnt offering.

ta'a: bad.

taumwa: a type of pudding unique to Makira made with grated and pounded yam, banana, taro, cassava, or breadfruit, and coconut cream/oil; also known as "six-month pudding."

wa'animae: a warrior.

waipo: umbilical cord; navel; matrilineage.

BIBLIOGRAPHY

Abramson, Allen. 2000. Bounding the Unbounded: Ancestral Land and Jural Relations in the Interior of Eastern Fiji. In *Land, Law and Environment: Mythical Land, Legal Boundaries*, ed. Allen Abramson and Dimitrios Theodossopoulos, 191–210. London: Pluto Press.

Akin, David. 1993. Negotiating Culture in East Kwaio, Malaita, Solomon Islands. Ph.D. dissertation, University of Hawai‘i.

_____. 1999. Compensation and the Melanesian State: Why the Kwaio Keep Claiming. *Contemporary Pacific* 11(1): 35–67.

_____. 2003. Concealment, Confession, and Innovation in Kwaio Women's Taboos. *American Ethnologist* 30(3): 381–400.

_____. 2004. Ancestral Vigilance and the Corrective Conscience: Kastom as Culture in a Melanesian Society. *Anthropological Theory* 4(3): 299–324.

_____. 2005. Kastom as Hegemony: A Response to Babadzan. *Anthropological Theory* 5(1): 75–83.

Alasia, Sam. 1989. Politics. In *Ples Blong Iumi: Solomon Islands, The Past Four Thousand Years*, ed. Hugh Laracy, 137–151. Suva, Fiji: University of the South Pacific.

Allan, Colin H. 1950. The Marching Rule Movement in the British Solomon Islands Protectorate: An Analytical Survey. Master's thesis, Cambridge University.

_____. 1951. Marching Rule: A Nativistic Cult of the British Solomon Islands. *South Pacific* 5: 79–85.

_____. 1957. *Customary Land Tenure in the British Solomon Islands Protectorate: Report of the Special Lands Commission*. Honiara: Western Pacific High Commission.

_____. 1990. *Solomons Safari, 1953–58*. Part II. Christchurch, New Zealand: Nag's Head Press.

Amherst of Hackney, Lord, and Basil Thomson, eds. 1901. *The Discovery of the Solomon Islands by Alvaro de Mendaña in 1568*. London: Hakluyt Society.

Appadurai, Arjun. 1996. *Modernity at Large: Cultural Dimensions of Globalization*. Minneapolis: University of Minnesota Press.

Austin-Broos, Diane J. 1997. *Jamaica Genesis: Religion and the Politics of Moral Orders*. Chicago: University of Chicago Press.

Australian Board of Missions. [R] 1910–42. *A.B.M. Review*. Sydney.

Babadzan, Alain. 1983. Une perspective pour deux passages. Notes sur la représentation traditionnelle de la naissance et de la mort en Polynésie. *L'Homme* 23(3): 81–99.

Bakhtin, Mikhail M./Pavel N. Medvedev. 1985. *The Formal Method in Literary Scholarship: A Critical Introduction to Sociological Poetics*. Trans. Albert J. Wehrle. Cambridge: Harvard University Press.

Bamford, Sandra. 1998. Humanized Landscapes, Embodied Worlds: Land and the Construction of Intergenerational Continuity among the Kamea of Papua New Guinea. *Social Analysis* 43(3): 28–54.

Barker, John. 1990. Introduction: Ethnographic Perspectives on Christianity in Oceanic Societies. In *Christianity in Oceania: Ethnographic Perspectives*, ed. John Barker, 1–24. New York: University Press of America.

_____. 1992. Christianity in Western Melanesian Ethnography. In *History and Tradition in Melanesian Anthropology*, ed. James G. Carrier, 144–173. Berkeley: University of California Press.

Barnes, J. A. 1962. African Models in the New Guinea Highlands. *Man* 62: 5–6.

Barraud, Cécile, Daniel de Coppet, André Iteanu, and Raymond Jamous. 1994. *Of Relations and the Dead: Four Societies Viewed from the Angle of their Exchanges*. Trans. Stephen J. Suffern. Providence, RI: Berg.

Barrow, Lennox. N.d. Outlying Interlude: An Account of Life in the BSIP, 1942–47. PMB 517.

Barth, Fredrik. 1975. *Ritual and Knowledge among the Baktaman of New Guinea*. New Haven: Yale University Press.

_____. 1987. *Cosmologies in the Making: A Generative Approach to Cultural Variation in Inner New Guinea*. New York: Cambridge University Press.

Bathgate, Murray A. 1975. Bihu Matena Golo: A Study of the Ndi-Nggai of West Guadalcanal and their Involvement in the Solomon Islands Cash Economy. Ph.D. dissertation, Victoria University of Wellington.

_____. 1985. Movement Processes from Precontact to Contemporary Times: The Ndi-Nggai, West Guadalcanal, Solomon Islands. In *Circulation in Population Movement: Substance and Concepts from the Melanesian Case*, ed. Murray Chapman and R. Mansell Prothero, 83–118. Boston: Routledge and Kegan Paul.

Battaglia, Debbora. 1990. *On the Bones of the Serpent: Person, Memory, and Mortality in Sabarl Island Society*. Chicago: University of Chicago Press.

Beckett, Jeremy. 1993. Walter Newton's History of the World—or Australia. *American Ethnologist* 20(4): 675–695.

Bedford, Richard D. 1970. Population in the British Solomon Islands Protectorate, 1920–1952: Extracts from Archival Material held in the Central Archives for the Western Pacific High Commission, Suva. Canberra: Australian National University.

Bellwood, Peter. 1996. Hierarchy, Founder Ideology and Austronesian Expansion. In *Origins, Ancestry and Alliance: Explorations in Austronesian Ethnography*, ed. James J. Fox and Clifford Sather, 18–40. Canberra: Department of Anthropology, Research School of Pacific and Asian Studies, Australian National University.

Bennett, Judith A. 1974. Population Distribution and Village Relocation, 1870–1950. In *Tasi Mauri: A Report on Population and Resources of the Guadalcanal Weather Coast*, ed. Murray Chapman and Peter Pirie, 2.1–2.69. Honolulu: East-West Population Institute.

———. 1987. *Wealth of the Solomons: A History of a Pacific Archipelago, 1800–1978*. Honolulu: University of Hawai'i Press.

———. 2000. *Pacific Forest: A History of Resource Control and Contest in Solomon Islands, c. 1800–1997*. Boston: Brill.

Bernatzik, Hugo A. 1935. *South Seas*. Trans. Vivian Ogilvie. New York: Henry Holt.

———. 1936. *Owa Raha*. Vienna: Bernina Verlag.

Bhaskar, Roy. 1994. *Plato Etc.: The Problems of Philosophy and their Resolution*. New York: Verso.

Bible Society of the South Pacific. 2004. *Taroha Goro mana Usuusu Maea*. N.p.: Wycliffe Bible Translators.

Bird-David, Nurit. 1999. "Animism" Revisited: Personhood, Environment, and Relational Epistemology. *Current Anthropology* 40(Supplement): S67–S91.

Bonnemaison, Joël. 1994. *The Tree and the Canoe: History and Ethnogeography of Tanna*. Trans. Josée Pénot-Demetry. Honolulu: University of Hawai'i Press.

Bourdieu, Pierre. 1977. *Outline of a Theory of Practice*. Trans. Richard Nice. New York: Cambridge University Press.

Boutilier, James A. 1983. The Government is the District Officer: An Historical Analysis of District Officers as Middlemen in the British Solomon Islands Protectorate, 1893–1943. In *Middlemen and Brokers in Oceania*, ed. William L. Rodman and Dorothy Ayers Counts, 35–67. New York: University Press of America.

Breton, Stéphane. 1999. Social Body and Icon of the Person: A Symbolic Analysis of Shell Money Among the Wodani, Western Highlands of Irian Jaya. *American Ethnologist* 26(3): 558–582.

British and Foreign Bible Society. 1921. *Na Taroha Goro ma na Tauaro adaau i Ha'ataari*. Canberra: British and Foreign Bible Society in Australia.

334 THE SEVERED SNAKE

334 THE SEVERED SNAKE

British Solomon Islands Protectorate. [AR] 1897–1972. *Annual Reports* [Title varies]. London: Her Majesty's Stationery Office/Honiara: BSIP.

British Solomon Islands Protectorate (Western Pacific Archives). BSIP 1: Office of the Resident Commissioner (Secretariat). Registers, Indexes, General Correspondence, Dispatches and Telegrams, c. 1935–52. Solomon Islands National Archives, Honiara.

_____. BSIP 4: Office of the Resident Commissioner. Classified Correspondence, S+C Series, 1943–52 (1943–53). Solomon Islands National Archives, Honiara.

_____. BSIP 8: Central Office. General Correspondence, Files, Court Records, etc., 1925–74. Solomon Islands National Archives, Honiara.

_____. BSIP 9: District Office, Eastern District. General Correspondence, District Reports, Registers, and Miscellaneous Records, 1918–65. Solomon Islands National Archives, Honiara. Microfilm copy of BSIP 9/III/4 (Eastern District Monthly and Quarterly Reports, 1919–59) at the Auckland Institute and Museum Library (Microfilm No. 131).

Brown, Terry. 2005. Christian Contextual Theology: A Pacific Example. *Pacific Journal of Theology*, Series II 33: 4–35.

Burridge, Kenelm. 1960. *Mambu: A Study of Melanesian Cargo Movements and their Ideological Background*. New York: Harper and Row.

Burt, Ben. 1982. Kastom, Christianity and the First Ancestor of the Kwara'ae of Malaita. *Mankind* 13(4): 374–399.

_____. 1983. The Remnant Church: A Christian Sect of the Solomon Islands. *Oceania* 53(4): 334–346.

_____. 1994a. *Tradition and Christianity: The Colonial Transformation of a Solomon Islands Society*. New York: Harwood Academic Publishers.

_____. 1994b. Land in Kwara'ae and Development in Solomon Islands. *Oceania* 64(4): 317–335.

_____. 1998. Writing Local History in Solomon Islands. In *Pacific Answers to Western Hegemony: Cultural Practices of Identity Construction*, ed. Jürg Wassmann, 97–118. New York: Berg.

_____. 2001. Introduction to *A Solomon Islands Chronicle as told by Samuel Alasa'a*, ed. Ben Burt and Michael Kwa'ioloa, 1–9. London: British Museum Press.

Burt, Ben, and Michael Kwa'ioloa. 1992. *Falafala ana Ano 'i Kwara'ae: The Tradition of Land in Kwara'ae*. Suva, Fiji: University of the South Pacific.

Burt, Ben, and Michael Kwa'ioloa, eds. 2001. *A Solomon Islands Chronicle as told by Samuel Alasa'a*. London: British Museum Press.

Byer, Doris. 1996. *Die Große Insel: Südpazifische Lebensgeschichten. Autobiographische Berichte aus dem südöstlichen Salomon-Archipel seit 1914*. Vienna: Böhlau Verlag.

_____. 1997. Der erste Mordprozeß: Ein „zivilisatorisches Ereignis" auf den südöstlichen Salomon-Inseln zur Zeit der britischen Intervention 1915. *Historische Anthropologie* 5(1): 115–138.

Capell, Arthur. 1971. *Arosi Grammar*. Pacific Linguistics, Series B. No. 20. Canberra: Department of Linguistics, Research School of Pacific Studies, Australian National University.

Carey, John. 1999. *A Single Ray of the Sun: Religious Speculation in Early Ireland*. Aberystwyth: Celtic Studies Publications.

Carrier, Achsah H., and James G. Carrier. 1991. *Structure and Process in a Melanesian Society: Ponam's Progress in the Twentieth Century*. Philadelphia: Harwood Academic Publishers.

Chapman, Murray. 1987. Population Movement Studied at Microscale: Experience and Extrapolation. *GeoJournal* 15: 347–365.

Chase, Graham, and Alfred Aihunu. 1982. *Wogasia*. Lindfield, NSW: Produced for Solomon Islands with Australian Development Assistance Bureau by Film Australia.

Chowning, Ann. 1989. Death and Kinship in Molima. In *Death Rituals and Life in the Societies of the Kula Ring*, ed. Frederick H. Damon and Roy Wagner, 97–129. DeKalb, IL: Northern Illinois University Press.

Church of England in New Zealand. 1857? [Language of Guadalcanar. Prayer Book; untitled, begins: Amma me eru ...]. Auckland: Melanesian Mission Press.

_____. 1858a. *Hate hasuri ra ni inoni, do re mataia ni rihunga inia Kauraha*. Auckland: Melanesian Mission Press.

_____. 1858?b. [Scripture History; untitled, begins: Ia Kauraha bessi hura ...]. Auckland: Melanesian Mission Press.

_____. 1923. *Na buka ni rihunai*. Guadalcanal: Melanesian Mission Press.

Church of Melanesia. 1982. *Na Book ni Rihunai. Book of Common Prayer in the Language of Arosi, San Cristoval, Solomon Islands*. Honiara: Provincial Press.

Clammer, John, Sylvie Poirier, and Eric Schwimmer. 2004. Introduction: The Relevance of Ontologies in Anthropology—Reflections on a New Anthropological Field. In *Figured Worlds: Ontological Obstacles in Intercultural Relations*, ed. John Clammer, Sylvie Poirier, and Eric Schwimmer, 3–22. Toronto: University of Toronto Press.

Clark, Jeffrey. 1997. Imagining the State, or Tribalism and the Arts of Memory in the Highlands of Papua New Guinea. In *Narratives of Nation in the South Pacific*, ed. Ton Otto and Nicholas Thomas, 65–90. Amsterdam: Harwood Academic Publishers.

Clay, Brenda J. 1977. *Pinikindu: Maternal Nurture, Paternal Substance*. Chicago: University of Chicago Press.

_____. 1986. *Mandak Realities: Person and Power in Central New Ireland.* New Brunswick, NJ: Rutgers University Press.

Clemens, Martin. 1998. *Alone on Guadalcanal: A Coastwatcher's Story.* Annapolis, MD: Naval Institute Press.

Cochrane, D. Glynn. 1967. Power, Status and the "Vailala Madness." Ph.D. dissertation, University of Oxford.

_____. 1969. Choice of Residence in the Solomons and a Focal Land Model. *Journal of the Polynesian Society* 78(3): 330–343.

_____. 1970. *Big Men and Cargo Cults.* New York: Oxford University Press.

Codrington, Robert H. 1880/81. Religious Beliefs and Practices in Melanesia. *Journal of the Royal Anthropological Institute of Great Britain and Ireland* 10: 261–316.

_____. 1891. *The Melanesians: Studies in their Anthropology and Folk-lore.* Oxford: Clarendon Press.

Coombe, Florence. 1911. *Islands of Enchantment: Many Sided Melanesia.* London: MacMillian.

Coppet, Daniel de. 1968. Pour une étude des échanges cérémoniels en Mélanésie. *L'Homme* 8(4): 45–57.

_____. 1973. Premier troc, double illusion. *L'Homme* 13 (1–2): 10–22.

_____. 1976. Jardins de vie, jardins de mort en Mélanésie. *Traverses* 5–6: 166–177.

_____. 1981. The Life-Giving Death. In *Mortality and Immorality: The Anthropology and Archaeology of Death*, ed. S. C. Humphreys and Helen Kind, 175–203. New York: Academic Press.

_____. 1985. … Land Owns People. In *Contexts and Levels: Anthropological Essays on Hierarchy*, ed. R. H. Barnes, Daniel de Coppet, and R. J. Parkin, 78–90. Oxford: Anthropological Society.

_____. 1995. 'Are'are Society: A Melanesian Socio-Cosmic Point of View. How are Bigmen the Servants of Society and Cosmos? In *Cosmos and Society in Oceania*, ed. Daniel de Coppet and André Iteanu, 235–274. Washington, DC: Berg.

_____. 1998. Une monnaie pour une communauté mélanésienne comparée à la nôtre pour l'individu des sociétés européennes. In *La Monnaie Souveraine*, ed. Michel Aglietta and André Orléan, 159–211. Paris: Odile Jacob.

Coppet, Daniel de, and André Iteanu. 1995. Introduction to *Cosmos and Society in Oceania*, ed. Daniel de Coppet and André Iteanu, 1–19. Washington, DC: Berg.

Coppet, Daniel de, and Hugo Zemp. 1978. *'Aré'aré, un peuple mélanésien et sa musique.* Paris: Seuil.

Corban, Brian P. N. 1972. Law and Order in Melanesia. A Case Study: The Pacification of the British Solomon Islands, 1893–1900 and 1913–1930. Master's thesis, University of Auckland.

Corris, Peter R. 1973a. *Passage, Port and Plantation: A History of Solomon Islands Labour Migration, 1870–1914.* Melbourne: Melbourne University Press.

_____. 1973b. The Man Who Lived Before His Time. *Pacific Islands Monthly* 44(10): 49, 51.

Davenport, William H. 1986. Two Kinds of Value in the Eastern Solomon Islands. In *The Social Life of Things: Commodities in Cultural Perspective*, ed. Arjun Appadurai, 95–109. New York: Cambridge University Press.

_____. 1996. Wogosia: An Annual Renewal Rite in the Eastern Solomon Islands. *Expedition* 38(3): 24–40.

_____. 1997. Ritual Bowls of the Eastern Solomon Islands. *Baessler–Archiv* (n.s.) 45: 315–331.

Davidson, Allan K., ed. 2000. *The Church of Melanesia, 1849–1999.* Auckland: College of St. John the Evangelist.

Davies, Roy. N.d. Marching Rule: A Personal Memoir. PMB 1076.

Descola, Philippe. 1996. Constructing Natures: Symbolic Ecology and Social Practice. In *Nature and Society: Anthropological Perspectives*, ed. Philippe Descola and Gísli Pálsson, 82–102. New York: Routledge.

_____. 2005. *Par-delà nature et culture.* Paris: Gallimard.

Dinnen, Sinclair. 2002. Winners and Losers: Politics and Disorder in the Solomon Islands, 2000–2002. *Journal of Pacific History* 37(3): 285–298.

Dureau, Christine. 2001. Recounting and Remembering "First Contact" on Simbo. In *Cultural Memory: Reconfiguring History and Identity in the Postcolonial Pacific*, ed. Jeannette Marie Mageo, 130–162. Honolulu: University of Hawai'i Press.

Durkheim, Emile. 1995. *The Elementary Forms of Religious Life.* Trans. Karen E. Fields. New York: Free Press.

Durrad, W. J. 1922. The Depopulation of Melanesia. In *Essays on the Depopulation of Melanesia*, ed. W. H. R. Rivers, 62–66. Cambridge: Cambridge University Press.

_____. N.d. Introduction to A Missionary in Melanesia, by Charles E. Fox. Durrad Papers (Ms. Papers No. 1171), Papers and Letters Relating to C. E. Fox, 1950–1955, Folder 2. Alexander Turnbull Library, Wellington.

Edridge, Sally. 1985. *Solomon Islands Bibliography to 1980.* Wellington: Alexander Turnbull Library.

Eliade, Mircea. 1965. *The Two and the One.* Trans. J. M. Cohen. New York: Harper and Row.

Epstein, A. L. 1969. *Matupit: Land, Politics, and Change Among the Tolai of New Britain*. Berkeley: University of California Press.

Epstein, T. S. 1968. *Capitalism, Primitive and Modern: Some Aspects of Tolai Economic Growth*. East Lansing, MI: Michigan State University Press.

Ernst, Thomas M. 1999. Land, Stories, and Resources: Discourse and Entification in Onabasulu Modernity. *American Anthropologist* 101(1): 88–97.

Errington, Frederick K., and Deborah B. Gewertz. 1994. From Darkness to Light in the George Brown Jubilee: The Invention of Nontradition and the Inscription of a National History in East New Britain. *American Ethnologist* 21(1): 104–122.

Espagne, John. 1953. Witless Trust: Primitive Religion, Pagan Mythology and the Catholic Church in the Eastern Islands of the Vicariate Apostolic of the South Solomons' Mission. Unpublished manuscript. Photocopy of typescript in author's possession.

Feil, D. K. 1984. *Ways of Exchange: The Enga Tee of Papua New Guinea*. St. Lucia: University of Queensland Press.

Ferguson, William. 1998. *The Identity of the Scottish Nation: An Historic Quest*. Edinburgh: Edinburgh University Press.

Fienup–Riordan, Ann. 1994. *Boundaries and Passages: Rule and Ritual in Yup'ik Eskimo Oral Tradition*. Norman, OK: University of Oklahoma Press.

Fifi'i, Jonathan. 1989. *From Pig-Theft to Parliament: My Life Between Two Worlds*. Suva, Fiji: Institute of Pacific Studies, University of the South Pacific.

Fiji, (Colony of). 1896. *Report of the Commission Appointed to Inquire into the Decrease of the Native Population with Appendices*. Suva, Fiji: Edward John March, Government Printer.

Foale, Simon, and Martha Macintyre. 2000. Dynamic and Flexible Aspects of Land and Marine Tenure at West Nggela: Implications for Marine Resource Management. *Oceania* 71(1): 30–45.

Fogelson, Raymond D. 1974. On the Varieties of Indian History: Sequoyah and Traveller Bird. *Journal of Ethnic Studies* 2(1): 105–112.

_____. 1989. The Ethnohistory of Events and Nonevents. *Ethnohistory* 36(2): 133–147.

Forge, Anthony. 1972. The Golden Fleece. *Man* (n.s.) 7(4): 527–540.

Fortune, R. F. 1932. *Sorcerers of Dobu: The Social Anthropology of the Dobu Islanders of the Western Pacific*. New York: E. P. Dutton.

Foster, Robert J. 1990. Nurture and Force-Feeding: Mortuary Feasting and the Construction of Collective Individuals in a New Ireland Society. *American Ethnologist* 17(3): 431–448.

_____. 1995. *Social Reproduction and History in Melanesia: Mortuary Ritual, Gift Exchange, and Custom in the Tanga Islands.* New York: Cambridge University Press.

_____. 2002. *Materializing the Nation: Commodities, Consumption, and Media in Papua New Guinea.* Bloomington: Indiana University Press.

Foucault, Michel. 1986. Of Other Spaces. *Diacritics* 16(1): 22–27.

Fox, Charles E. 1919a. Social Organization in San Cristoval, Solomon Islands. *Journal of the Royal Anthropological Institute of Great Britain and Ireland* 49: 94–179.

_____. 1919b. The San Cristoval Heo. *Journal of the Polynesian Society* 28: 39–41.

_____. 1919c. Further Notes on the Heo of the Solomon Islands. *Journal of the Polynesian Society* 28: 103–105.

_____. 1924. *The Threshold of the Pacific: An Account of the Social Organization, Magic and Religion of the People of San Cristoval in the Solomon Islands.* London: Kegan Paul, Trench, and Trubner.

_____. 1958. *Lord of the Southern Isles: Being the Story of the Anglican Mission in Melanesia, 1849–1949.* London: A. R. Mowbray.

_____. 1962. *Kakamora.* London: Hodder and Stoughton.

_____. 1967. *The Story of the Solomon Islands.* Taroaniara, British Solomon Islands: Diocese of Melanesia Press.

_____. 1978. *Arosi Dictionary.* Pacific Linguistics, Series C. No. 57. Canberra: Department of Linguistics, Research School of Pacific Studies, Australian National University.

_____. 1985. *My Solomon Islands.* Honiara: Provincial Press.

_____. [AMM] A Missionary in Melanesia. Durrad Papers (Ms. Papers No. 1171), Papers and Letters Relating to C. E. Fox, 1950–1955, Folder 3. Alexander Turnbull Library, Wellington.

_____. [BG] Bibliography and Grammar. Charles Elliot Fox Papers (Mss. 18), A Dictionary of the Language of Arosi, ca. 1925, Box 1, Folder 1. Photostatic copy in Mandeville Department of Special Collections, University of California, San Diego.

_____. [D] Diaries Kept in the Solomon Islands, 1942–49. Originals held by the Department of Pacific and South-East Asian History, Research School of Pacific Studies, Australian National University, Canberra. PMB 550.

_____. [T] Tales. Church of Melanesia Archives, Item no. 32, Manuscript of Dr. Charles Fox's Arosi Dictionary. Solomon Islands National Archives, Honiara. Photostatic copy in Charles Elliot Fox Papers (Mss. 18), Box 2, Folder 1. Mandeville Department of Special Collections, University of California, San Diego.

Fox, Charles E., and F. H. Drew. 1915. Beliefs and Tales of San Cristoval (Solomon Islands). *Journal of the Royal Anthropological Institute of Great Britain and Ireland* 45: 131–228.

Fox, James J. 1988. Origin, Descent and Precedence in the Study of Austronesian Societies. (Public Lecture in connection with De Wisselleerstoel Indonesische Studie, 17 March 1988). Leiden: Leiden University.

_____. 1994. Reflections on "Hierarchy" and "Precedence." *History and Anthropology* 7: 87–108.

_____. 1995. Origin Structures and Systems of Precedence in the Comparative Study of Austronesian Societies. In *Austronesian Studies Relating to Taiwan*, ed. P. Jen-kuei Li, Cheng-hwa Tsang, Ying-kuei Huang, Dah-an Ho, and Chiu-yu Tseng, 27–57. Taipei: Symposium Series of the Institute of History and Philology, Academia Sinica No. 3.

_____. 1996. Introduction to *Origins, Ancestry and Alliance: Explorations in Austronesian Ethnography*, ed. James J. Fox and Clifford Sather, 1–17. Canberra: Department of Anthropology, Research School of Pacific and Asian Studies, Australian National University.

_____. 1997. Place and Landscape in Comparative Austronesian Perspective. In *The Poetic Power of Place: Comparative Perspectives on Austronesian Ideas of Locality*, ed. James J. Fox, 1–21. Canberra: Department of Anthropology, Research School of Pacific and Asian Studies, Australian National University.

Fraenkel, Jon. 2004. *The Manipulation of Custom: From Uprising to Intervention in the Solomon Islands*. Canberra: Pandanus Books, Research School of Pacific and Asian Studies, Australian National University.

Frazer, Ian L. 1973. *To'ambaita Report: A Study of Socio-Economic Change in North-West Malaita*. Wellington: Department of Geography, Victoria University.

_____. 1981. Man Long Taon: Migration and Differentiation Amongst the To'ambaita, Solomon Islands. Ph.D. dissertation, Australian National University.

Gabelentz, Hans C. von der. 1861. Die Melanesischen Sprachen nach ihrem grammatischen Bau und ihrer Verwandtschaft unter sich und mit den Malaisch-Polynesischen Sprachen. *Abhandlungen der Philologisch-Historischen Classe der Königlich Sächsischen Gesellschaft der Wissenschaften* 3: 1–266.

Geirnaert-Martin, Danielle. 1992. *The Woven Land of Laboya: Socio-Cosmic Ideas and Values in West Sumba, Eastern Indonesia*. Leiden: Centre for Non-Western Studies, University of Leiden.

Gell, Alfred. 1975. *Metamorphosis of the Cassowaries: Umeda Society, Language and Ritual*. London: Athlone Press.

_____. 1998. *Art and Agency: An Anthropological Theory*. Oxford: Clarendon Press.

Golden, Graeme. 1993. *The Early European Settlers of the Solomon Islands.* Melbourne: privately published for private distribution.

Goldman, L. R., J. Duffield, and C. Ballard. 1998. Fire and Water: Fluid Ontologies in Melanesian Myth. In *Fluid Ontologies: Myth, Ritual and Philosophy in the Highlands of Papua New Guinea,* ed. L. R. Goldman and C. Ballard, 1–13. Westport, CT: Bergin and Garvey.

Green, Kaye C. 1974. Historical Outline of European Contacts and Bibliography for use of Project Collaborators and Researchers in the Eastern District, British Solomon Islands. *Working Papers in Anthropology, Archaeology, Linguistics, Maori Studies* No. 34. Auckland: Department of Anthropology, University of Auckland.

_____. 1976. The History of Post-Spanish European Contact in the Eastern District Before 1939. In *Southeast Solomon Islands Cultural History: A Preliminary Survey,* ed. Roger C. Green, 31–46. Wellington: Royal Society of New Zealand, Bulletin 11.

Green, Roger C. 1970. Green Notebook II [Makira]. Unpublished archaeological field survey notebook. Solomon Islands National Museum, Honiara.

_____. 1974. South East Solomon Islands Culture History Programme: A Preliminary Report. *Journal of the Solomon Islands Museum Association* 2: 53–60.

Groenewegen, K. 1972. *Report on the Census of the Population, 1970.* Honiara: Western Pacific High Commission, British Solomon Islands Protectorate.

Grover, J. C. 1958. *The Solomon Islands: Geological Exploration and Research, 1953–1956.* London: C. F. Hodgson.

_____. 1962. A Brief History of Geological and Geophysical Investigations in the British Solomon Islands, 1881–1961. In *Geology and Social Earth Geophysics of the Pacific Basin,* ed. G. A. MacDonald, 171–180. Honolulu: University of Hawai'i Press.

Guidieri, Remo. 1972. La route des morts. Introduction à la vie cérémonielle Fataleka. *Journal de la Société des Océanistes* 28(37): 323–335.

_____. 1975. Enclos et Clôtures. Remarques sur les discontinuités et les segmentations océaniennes. *Journal de la Société des Océanistes* 31: 123–141.

_____. 1980. *La route des morts.* Paris: Seuil.

_____. 1988. Two Millenaristic Responses in Oceania. In *Ethnicities and Nations: Processes of Interethnic Relations in Latin America, Southeast Asia, and the Pacific,* ed. Remo Guidieri, Franceso Pellizzi, and Stanley J. Tambiah, 172–198. Austin, TX: University of Texas Press.

Guppy, Henry B. 1887. *The Solomon Islands and Their Natives.* London: Swan Sonneschein and Lowrey.

Gupta, Akhil, and James Ferguson. 1997. Beyond "Culture": Space, Identity, and the Politics of Difference. In *Culture, Power, Place: Explorations in Crit-*

ical Anthropology, ed. Akhil Gupta and James Ferguson, 33–51. Durham, NC: Duke University Press.

Haddon, Alfred C. 1925. Review of *The Threshold of the Pacific*, by Charles E. Fox. *Man* 25: 59–61.

Hanks, William F. 1996. *Language and Communicative Practices*. Boulder, CO: Westview Press.

Harrison, Simon J. 1987. Cultural Efflorescence and Political Evolution on the Sepik River. *American Ethnologist* 14(3): 491–507.

_____. 1988. Magical Exchange of the Preconditions of Production in a Sepik River Village. *Man* (n.s.) 23(2): 319–333.

_____. 1989. Magical and Material Polities in Melanesia. *Man* (n.s.) 24(1): 1–20.

_____. 1990. *Stealing People's Names: History and Politics in a Sepik River Cosmology*. New York: Cambridge University Press.

_____. 1993. *The Mask of War: Violence, Ritual and the Self in Melanesia*. New York: Manchester University Press.

_____. 2001. Smoke Rising from the Villages of the Dead: Seasonal Patterns of Mood in a Papua New Guinea Society. *Journal of the Royal Anthropological Institute* 7(2): 257–274.

Harvey, David. 1989. *The Condition of Postmodernity: An Enquiry into the Origins of Cultural Change*. Cambridge: Basil Blackwell.

Hauʻofa, Epeli. 1994. Our Sea of Islands. *Contemporary Pacific* 6(1): 148–161.

_____. 2000. Epilogue: Pasts to Remember. In *Remembrance of Pacific Pasts: An Invitation to Remake History*, ed. Robert Borosky, 453–471. Honolulu: University of Hawaiʻi Press.

Healey, Christopher J. 1988. Culture as Transformed Disorder: Cosmological Evocations among the Maring. *Oceania* 59: 106–122.

Heath, Ian. 1981. Solomon Islands: Land Policy and Independence. *Kabar Seberang Sulating Maphilindo* 8–9: 62–77.

Herlihy, Joan M. 1981. Always We Are Last: A Study of Planning, Development, and Disadvantage in Melanesia. Ph.D. dissertation, Australian National University.

_____. 2003. Marching Rule Revisited: When the Cargo Comes. *New Pacific Review* 2(1): 185–205.

Hilliard, David L. 1966. Protestant Missions in the Solomon Islands, 1849–1942. Ph.D. dissertation, Australian National University.

_____. 1969. The South Sea Evangelical Mission in the Solomon Islands: The Foundation Years. *Journal of Pacific History* 4: 41–64.

_____. 1970. John Coleridge Patteson: Missionary Bishop of Melanesia. In *Pacific Islands Portraits*, ed. J. W. Davidson and Deryck Scarr, 177–200. Canberra: Australian National University Press.

_____. 1978. *God's Gentlemen: A History of the Melanesian Mission, 1849–1942.* St. Lucia: University of Queensland Press.

_____. 2005. The God of the Melanesian Mission. In *Vision and Reality in Pacific Religion: Essays in Honour of Niel Gunson*, ed. Phyllis Herda, Michael Reilly, and David Hilliard, 195–215. Canberra: Pandanus Books, Research School of Pacific and Asian Studies, Australian National University.

Hirsch, Eric. 1995. Landscape: Between Place and Space. Introduction to *The Anthropology of Landscape: Perspectives on Place and Space*, ed. Eric Hirsch and Michael O'Hanlon, 1–30. New York: Oxford University Press.

_____. 2001. Making up People in Papua. *Journal of the Royal Anthropological Institute* 7(2): 241–256.

Hogbin, H. Ian. 1939. *Experiments in Civilization: The Effects of Culture on a Native Community of the Solomon Islands.* London: Routledge and Kegan Paul.

_____. 1964. *A Guadalcanal Society: The Kaoka Speakers.* Chicago: Holt, Rinehart and Winston.

_____. 1970. *The Island of Menstruating Men: Religion in Wogeo, New Guinea.* Scranton, PA: Chandler Publishing.

Hopkins, Arthur I. 1922. Depopulation in the Solomon Islands. In *Essays on the Depopulation of Melanesia*, ed. W. H. R. Rivers, 62–66. Cambridge: Cambridge University Press.

Hoskins, Janet, ed. 2002. *Blood Mysteries: Beyond Menstruation as Pollution.* Special issue. *Ethnology* 41(4).

Hutchins, Edwin. 1980. *Culture and Inference: A Trobriand Case Study.* Cambridge: Harvard University Press.

_____. 1990. Getting it Straight in Trobriand Island Land Litigation. In *Disentangling: Conflict Discourse in Pacific Societies*, ed. Karen A. Watson-Gegeo and Geoffrey M. White, 412–458. Stanford: Stanford University Press.

Hviding, Edvard. 1996. *Guardians of Marovo Lagoon.* Honolulu: University of Hawai'i Press.

Ivens, Walter G. 1911–12. Folk Tales from Ulawa. *Zeitschrift für Kolonialsprachen* 2: 137–154.

_____. 1918. *Dictionary and Grammar of the Language of Sa'a and Ulawa, Solomon Islands, with Appendices.* Washington, DC: Carnegie Institution of Washington.

_____. 1927. *Melanesians of the South-East Solomon Islands.* London: Kegan Paul, Trench, and Trubner.

_____. 1929. *A Dictionary of the Language of Saʻa (Mala) and Ulawa South-East Solomon Islands*. London: Oxford University Press.

_____. 1930. *The Island Builders of the Pacific*. London: Seeley, Service and Company.

_____. 1930–32. A Vocabulary of the Language of Marau Sound, Guadalcanal, Solomon Islands. *Bulletin of the School of Oriental Studies* 6: 963–1002.

Jacka, Jerry. 2002. Cults and Christianity among the Enga and Ipili. *Oceania* 72(3): 196–214.

Jeudy-Ballini, Monique. 1998. Appropriating the Other: A Case Study from New Britain. In *Common Worlds and Single Lives: Constituting Knowledge in Pacific Societies*, ed. Verena Keck, 207–227. New York: Berg.

Jones, Rhys. 1985. Ordering the Landscape. In *Seeing the First Australians*, ed. Ian Donaldson and Tamsin Donaldson, 181–209. London: George Allen and Unwin.

Kaberry, Phyllis M. 1967. The Plasticity of New Guinea Kinship. In *Social Organization: Essays Presented to Raymond Firth*, ed. Maurice Freedman, 105–123. London: Frank Cass.

Kapferer, Bruce. 1988. *Legends of People, Myths of State: Violence, Intolerance, and Political Culture in Sri Lanka and Australia*. Washington, DC: Smithsonian Institution Press.

_____. 2003. Sorcery and the Shapes of Globalization Disjunctions and Continuities: The Case of Sri Lanka. In *Globalization, the State, and Violence*, ed. Jonathan Friedman, 249–278. Walnut Creek, CA: Altamira Press.

Keesing, Roger M. 1971. Descent, Residence and Cultural Codes. In *Anthropology in Oceania: Essays Presented to Ian Hogbin*, ed. L. R. Hiatt and C. Jayawardena, 121–138. Sydney: Angus and Robertson.

_____. 1978. Politico-Religious Movements and Anti-Colonialism on Malaita: Maasina Rule in Historical Perspective. *Oceania* 48(4): 241–261; 49(1): 46–73.

_____. 1982a. *Kwaio Religion: The Living and the Dead in a Solomon Island Society*. New York: Columbia University Press.

_____. 1982b. Kastom and Anticolonialism on Malaita: "Culture" as Political Symbol. *Mankind* 13(4): 357–373.

_____. 1983. *'Elota's Story: The Life and Times of a Solomon Islands Big Man*. Chicago: Holt, Rinehart and Winston.

_____. 1984. Rethinking Mana. *Journal of Anthropological Research* 40: 137–156.

_____. 1985. Killers, Big Men, and Priests on Malaita: Reflections on a Melanesian Troika System. *Ethnology* 24(4): 237–252.

_____. 1989. Creating the Past: Custom and Identity in the Contemporary Pacific. *Contemporary Pacific* 1(1): 19–42.

_____. 1992. *Custom and Confrontation: The Kwaio Struggle for Cultural Autonomy*. Chicago: University of Chicago Press.

_____. 1993. "Earth" and "Path" as Complex Categories: Semantics and Symbolism in Kwaio Culture. In *Cognitive Aspects of Religious Symbolism*, ed. P. Boyer, 93–110. Cambridge: Cambridge University Press.

Keesing, Roger M., and Peter R. Corris. 1980. *Lightning Meets the West Wind: The Malaita Massacre*. New York: Oxford University Press.

Keesing, Roger M., and Jonathan Fifi'i. 1969. Kwaio Word Tabooing in its Cultural Context. *Journal of the Polynesian Society* 78(2): 154–177.

Keevil, Dick, ed. 1972. *Custom Stories of the Solomon Islands*. Vol. 2. 'Are'are Folklore Stories. Honiara: Solomon Islands Museum Association.

Kidd, Colin. 1999. *British Identities before Nationalism: Ethnicity and Nationhood in the Atlantic World, 1600–1800*. New York: Cambridge University Press.

Knauft, Bruce M. 2002. *Exchanging the Past: A Rainforest World of Before and After*. Chicago: University of Chicago Press.

Knibbs, Stanley George C. 1929. *The Savage Solomons as they Were and Are*. Philadelphia: J. B. Lippincott.

Köngäs Maranda, Elli. 1970. Les femmes Lau (Malaita, îles Salomon) dans l'espace socialisé. Notes de topographie sociale. *Journal de la Société des Océanistes* 26: 155–162.

_____. 1973. Five Interpretations of a Melanesian Myth. *Journal of American Folklore* 86(339): 3–13.

_____. 1974. Lau, Malaita: "A Woman is an Alien Spirit." In *Many Sisters: Women in Cross-Cultural Perspective*, ed. Carolyn J. Matthiasson, 177–202. New York: Free Press.

_____. 1977. La fille du Serpent: surnature et agriculture dans la mythologie mélanésienne. *Anthropologie et Sociétés* 1(3): 99–117.

Lang, Andrew. 1913. *Myth, Ritual and Religion*. 2 vols. London: Longmans and Green.

Langham, Ian. 1981. *The Building of British Social Anthropology*. Boston: D. Reidel.

Langness, L. L. 1964. Some Problems in the Conceptualization of Highlands Social Structure. In *New Guinea: The Central Highlands*, ed. James B. Watson. Special issue. *American Anthropologist* 66(4, part 2): 162–182.

Laracy, Hugh M. 1976. *Marists and Melanesians: A History of Catholic Missions in the Solomon Islands*. Honolulu: University of Hawai'i Press.

_____. 1983. Introduction to *Pacific Protest: The Maasina Rule Movement, Solomon Islands, 1944–1952*, ed. Hugh M. Laracy, 1–38. Suva, Fiji: University of the South Pacific.

Laracy, Hugh M., ed. 1983. *Pacific Protest: The Maasina Rule Movement, Solomon Islands, 1944–1952*. Suva, Fiji: University of the South Pacific.

_____. 1989. *Ples Blong Iumi: Solomon Islands, The Past Four Thousand Years*. Suva, Fiji: University of the South Pacific.

Laracy, Hugh M., and Geoffrey M. White, eds. 1988. *Taem Blong Faet: World War II in Melanesia*. Special issue. *'O'o: A Journal of Solomon Islands Studies* No. 4.

Lattas, Andrew. 1998. *Cultures of Secrecy: Reinventing Race in Bush Kaliai Cargo Cults*. Madison, WI: University of Wisconsin Press.

Lawrence, Peter. 1964. *Road Belong Cargo: A Study of the Cargo Movement in the Southern Madang District, New Guinea*. Manchester: Manchester University Press.

Leach, James. 2003. *Creative Land: Place and Procreation on the Rai Coast of Papua New Guinea*. New York: Berghahn Books.

Lederman, Rena. 1986. *What Gifts Engender: Social Relations and Politics in Mendi, Highland Papua New Guinea*. New York: Cambridge University Press.

Lepervanche, Marie de. 1967–68. Descent, Residence and Leadership in the New Guinea Highlands. *Oceania* 38(2–3): 134–158, 163–189.

Lévi-Strauss, Claude. 1963. *Totemism*. Trans. Rodney Needham. Boston: Beacon Press.

_____. 1983. *Structural Anthropology*. Vol. 2. Trans. Monique Layton. Chicago: University of Chicago Press.

Lewis, E. D. 1988. *People of the Source: The Social and Ceremonial Order of Tana Wai Brama on Flores*. Verhandelingen van het Koninklijk Instituut voor Taal-, Land- en Volkenkunde 135. Dordrecht, Holland: Foris.

_____. 1996. Origin Structures and Precedence in the Social Orders of Tana 'Ai and Sikka. In *Origins, Ancestry and Alliance: Explorations in Austronesian Ethnography*, ed. James J. Fox and Clifford Sather, 154–174. Canberra: Department of Anthropology, Research School of Pacific and Asian Studies, Australian National University.

Lichtenberk, Frantisek. 1985. Possessive Constructions in Oceanic Languages and in Proto-Oceanic. In *Austronesian Linguistics at the 15th Pacific Science Congress*, ed. Andrew K. Pawley and Lois Carrington, 93–140. Pacific Linguistics, Series C. No. 88. Canberra: Department of Linguistics, Research School of Pacific Studies, Australian National University.

Lincoln, Bruce. 1986. *Myth, Cosmos, and Society: Indo-European Themes of Creation and Destruction*. Cambridge: Harvard University Press.

_____. 1991. *Death, War, and Sacrifice: Studies in Ideology and Practice*. Chicago: University of Chicago Press.

Lindstrom, Lamont. 1990a. *Knowledge and Power in a South Pacific Society.* Washington, DC: Smithsonian Institution Press.

_____. 1990b. Straight Talk on Tanna. In *Disentangling: Conflict Discourse in Pacific Societies,* ed. Karen A. Watson-Gegeo and Geoffrey M. White, 373–411. Stanford: Stanford University Press.

LiPuma, Edward. 2000. *Encompassing Others: The Magic of Modernity in Melanesia.* Ann Arbor: University of Michigan Press.

Lomas, Christopher J. 1972. *A Study of the Present Resettlement Schemes in the British Solomon Islands Protectorate and their Relevance to Projected Programmes of Block Development, Further Resettlement and Modern Sector Small-Holder Farming.* Honiara: Government Printer.

Lynch, John. 1973. Verbal Aspects of Possession in Melanesian Languages. *Oceanic Linguistics* 12: 69–102.

_____. 1982. Towards a Theory of the Origin of the Oceanic Possessive Constructions. In *Papers from the Third International Conference on Austronesian Linguistics,* Vol. 1, *Currents in Oceanic,* ed. A. Halim, Lois Carrington, and S. A. Wurm, 243–268. Pacific Linguistics, Series C. No. 74. Canberra: Department of Linguistics, Research School of Pacific Studies, Australian National University.

Macdonald-Milne, Brian. 2003. *The True Way of Service: The Pacific Story of the Melanesian Brotherhood, 1925–2000.* Leicester: Christians Aware.

Macintyre, Martha. 1987. Flying Witches and Leaping Warriors: Supernatural Origins of Power and Matrilineal Authority in Tubetube Society. In *Dealing With Inequality: Analysing Gender Relations in Melanesia and Beyond,* ed. Marilyn Strathern, 207–228. New York: Cambridge University Press.

_____. 1989. The Triumph of the Susu: Mortuary Exchanges on Tubetube. In *Death Rituals and Life in the Societies of the Kula Ring,* ed. Frederick H. Damon and Roy Wagner, 133–152. DeKalb, IL: Northern Illinois University Press.

Maenu'u, Leonard P. 1981. *Bib-Kami na Ano: Land and Land Problems in Kwara'ae.* Honiara: University of the South Pacific.

_____. 1992. Our Mother Earth: Land Tenure Effects. In *Independence, Dependence, Interdependence: The First 10 Years of Solomon Islands Independence,* ed. Ron Crocombe and Esau Tuza, 67–70. Honiara: Government Printing Press.

Malinowski, Bronislaw. 1948. *Magic, Science and Religion and Other Essays.* Garden City, NY: Doubleday.

[Malinowski, Bronislaw]. 1925. The Anthropology of San Cristoval. Review of *The Threshold of the Pacific,* by Charles E. Fox. *The Times Literary Supplement,* June 11, No. 1221: 394.

Mallett, Shelley. 2003. *Conceiving Cultures: Reproducing People and Places on Nuakata, Papua New Guinea*. Ann Arbor: University of Michigan Press.

Maranda, Pierre. 2001. Mapping Cultural Transformation through the Canonical Formula: The Pagan versus Christian Ontological Status of Women among the Lau People of Malaita, Solomon Islands. In *The Double Twist: From Ethnography to Morphodynamics*, ed. Pierre Maranda, 97–120. Toronto: University of Toronto Press.

Maranda, Pierre, and Elli Köngäs Maranda. 1970. Le crâne et l'utérus: deux théorèmes Nord-Malaitains. In *Echanges et Communications*, ed. Jean Pouillon and Pierre Maranda, 829–861. The Hague: Mouton.

Marriott, McKim. 1976. Hindu Transactions: Diversity without Dualism. In *Transaction and Meaning*, ed. Bruce Kapferer, 109–142. Philadelphia: Institute for the Study of Human Issues.

McArthur, Norma. 1967. *Island Populations of the Pacific*. Canberra: Australian National University Press.

McDonald, Heather. 2001. *Blood, Bones and Spirit: Aboriginal Christianity in an East Kimberley Town*. Melbourne: Melbourne University Press.

McDougall, Debra. 2000. Paths of Pinauzu: Captivity and Social Reproduction in Ranongga. *Journal of the Polynesian Society* 109(1): 99–113.

_____. 2004. The Shifting Ground of Moral Community: Christianity, Property, and Place in Ranongga. Ph.D. dissertation, University of Chicago.

_____. 2005. The Unintended Consequences of Clarification: Development, Disputing, and the Dynamics of Community in Ranongga, Solomon Islands. *Ethnohistory* 52(1): 81–109.

Mead, Sidney M. 1973a. *Material Culture and Art in the Star Harbour Region, Eastern Solomon Islands*. Toronto: Royal Ontario Museum.

_____. 1973b. Folklore and Place Names in Santa Ana, Solomon Islands. *Oceania* 43(3): 215–237.

_____. 1977. Bodrogi's Art-Area Concept: The Case of the Eastern Solomons and Star Harbour. *Acta Ethnographica Academiae Scientiarum Hungaricae* 26 (1–2): 129–162.

Meigs, Anna S. 1984. *Food, Sex, and Pollution: A New Guinea Religion*. New Brunswick, NJ: Rutgers University Press.

Melanesian Mission. 1886. *Wano: Mani Rihunai*. Norkfolk Island: Melanesian Mission Press.

_____. [AR] 1852–1942. *Annual Reports*. Auckland or Sydney.

_____. [IV] 1874–1903. *The Island Voyage*. Ludlow.

_____. [*SCL*] 1895–1972? *Southern Cross Log.* New Zealand and Australian edition, Auckland and Sydney.

_____. [*SXL*] 1901–72? *Southern Cross Log.* English edition, London.

Meltzoff, Sarah Keene, and Edward LiPuma. 1986. Hunting for Tuna and Cash in the Solomons: A Rebirth of Artisanal Fishing in Malaita. *Human Organization* 45(1): 53–62.

Merlan, Francesca. 1998. *Caging the Rainbow: Places, Politics, and Aborigines in a North Australian Town.* Honolulu: University of Hawai‘i Press.

Merrett-Balkos, Leanne. 1998. Just Add Water: Remaking Women through Childbirth, Anganen, Southern Highlands, Papua New Guinea. In *Maternities and Modernities: Colonial and Postcolonial Experiences in Asia and the Pacific,* ed. Kalpana Ram and Margaret Jolly, 213–238. New York: Cambridge University Press.

Miller, Daniel. 1977. Notebook II, Makira, November 1977. Unpublished archaeological field survey notebook. Solomon Islands National Museum, Honiara.

_____. 1979. *National Sites Survey Summary Report.* Honiara: National Museum.

Mimica, Jadran. 1981. Omalyce: An Ethnography of the Ikwaye View of the Cosmos. Ph.D. dissertation, Australian National University.

_____. 1988. *Intimations of Infinity: The Cultural Meanings of the Iqwaye Counting and Number System.* New York: Berg.

Ministry of Provincial Government and Rural Development, Rural Development Division. 2001. *Makira/Ulawa Province Development Profile, August 2001.* Honiara.

Monnerie, Denis. 1996. *Nitu: les vivants, les morts et le cosmos selon la société de Mono-Alu (Iles Salomon).* Leiden: Research School CNWS.

_____. 1998. Oceanian Comparison Reconsidered: The Mono-Alu Problem. *Social Anthropology* 6(1): 91–107.

Moore, Clive R. 1985. *Kanaka: A History of Melanesian Mackay.* Port Moresby, Papua New Guinea: Institute of Papua New Guinea Studies.

_____. 2004. *Happy Isles in Crisis: The Historical Causes for a Failing State in Solomon Islands,* 1998–2004. Canberra: Asia Pacific Press.

Mosko, Mark S. 1983. Conception, De-conception and Social Structure in Bush Mekeo Culture. *Mankind* 14(1): 24–32.

_____. 1985. *Quadripartite Structures: Categories, Relations and Homologies in Bush Mekeo Culture.* New York: Cambridge University Press.

_____. 1992. Motherless Sons: "Divine Kings" and "Partible Persons" in Melanesia and Polynesia. *Man* (n.s.) 27(4): 693–717.

_____. 2000. Inalienable Ethnography: Keeping-While-Giving and the Trobriand Case. *Journal of the Royal Anthropological Institute* (n.s.) 6(3): 377–396.

Munn, Nancy D. 1983. Gawan Kula: Spatiotemporal Control and the Symbolism of Influence. In *The Kula: New Perspectives on Massim Exchange*, ed. J. W. Leach and E. Leach, 272–308. New York: Cambridge University Press.

_____. 1986. *The Fame of Gawa: A Symbolic Study of Value Transformation in a Massim (Papua New Guinea) Society*. New York: Cambridge University Press.

Naitoro, John. 1993. The Politics of Development in 'Are'are, Malaita. Master's thesis, University of Otago, New Zealand.

Nash, Jill. 1974. *Matriliny and Modernisation: The Nagovisi of South Bougainville*. New Guinea Research Bulletin No. 55. Canberra: Australian National University.

Neumann, Klaus. 1992. *Not the Way it Really Was: Constructing the Tolai Past*. Honolulu: University of Hawai'i Press.

Noyes, John. 1992. *Colonial Space: Spatiality in the Discourse of German South West Africa, 1884–1915*. Philadelphia: Harwood Academic Publishers.

O'Brien, Claire. 1995. *A Greater Than Solomon Here: A Story of Catholic Church in Solomon Islands, 1567–1967*. Honiara: Catholic Church Solomon Islands.

O'Connor, Gulbun C. 1973. The Moro Movement of Guadalcanal. Ph.D. dissertation, University of Pennsylvania.

Oliver, Douglas L. 1989. *Oceania: The Native Cultures of Australia and the Pacific Islands*. Vol. 2. Honolulu: University of Hawai'i Press.

Otero, Rodolfo A. 2003. The Transformation of Identity through Possession Rituals in Popular Religion. *Religion* 33: 249–262.

Ouou, Emulio-Ree. 1980. *History of South Malaita, Origin of Livings, Centre and Diameter of the Universe*. Honiara: Government Printer.

Pacific Islands Monthly. 1947–53. Sydney.

[Patteson, John Coleridge]. 1857. Notes of a Voyage Amongst the Pacific Islands (by this Bishop of New Zealand's Missionary Chaplain). *The Monthly Packet* 14: 553–560, 655–662.

_____. 1866a. *Vocabulary of Melanesian Languages: Bauro, San Christoval Island, Solomon Islands*. [Kohimarama, Auckland: Melanesian Mission Press.]

_____. 1866?b. *Scripture questions. (Bauro)*. [Kohimarama, Auckland: Melanesian Mission Press.]

Pawley, Andrew K. 1973. Some Problems in Proto-Oceanic Grammar. *Oceanic Linguistics* 12: 103–188.

Pawley, Andrew K., and Timoci Sayaba. 1990. Possessive-Marking in Wayan, A Western Fijian Language: Noun Class or Relational System? In *Pacific Island*

Languages: Essays in Honour of G. B. Milner, ed. Jeremy H. C. S. Davidson, 147–171. Honolulu: University of Hawai'i Press.

Pedersen, Morten A. 2001. Totemism, Animism and North Asian Indigenous Ontologies. *Journal of the Royal Anthropological Institute* (n.s.) 7(3): 411–427.

Perry Papers (MS ADD 279). B2: Papers re Fox and Solomon Islands. Special Collections, UCL Library Services, University College London.

Perry, William J. 1918. *The Megalithic Culture of Indonesia*. Manchester: Manchester University Press.

———. 1923. *The Children of the Sun: A Study in the Early History of Civilization*. London: Methuen.

Philp, John Ernest. 1978. *A Solomon Sojourn: J. E. Philp's Log of the* Makira, *1912–1913*, ed. R. A. Herr and E. A. Rood. Hobart, Australia: Tasmanian Historical Research Association.

Piot, Charles. 1999. *Remotely Global: Village Modernity in West Africa*. Chicago: University of Chicago Press.

Pitt-Rivers, George Henry Lane-Fox. 1927. *The Clash of Culture and the Contact of Races*. London: George Routledge.

Poirier, Sylvie. 2005. *A World of Relationships: Itineraries, Dreams, and Events in the Australian Western Desert*. Toronto: University of Toronto Press.

Pouwer, J. 1960. Loosely Structured Societies in Netherlands New Guinea. *Bijdragen tot de Taal-, Land-, en Volkenkunde* 116: 109–118.

Povinelli, Elizabeth A. 2002. *The Cunning of Recognition: Indigenous Alterities and the Making of Australian Multiculturalism*. Durham, NC: Duke University Press.

Provincial Planning Office. 1988. *Makira Ulawa Province Development Plan, 1988–1992*. Kirakira, Makira.

Raucaz, Louis M. 1928. *In the Savage South Solomons: The Story of a Mission*. Lyons: Society for the Propagation of the Faith.

Ravuvu, Asesela. 1983. *Vaka i Taukei: The Fijian Way of Life*. Suva, Fiji: University of the South Pacific.

Ray, Sidney H. 1921. San Cristoval and the Scriptures. *Bible in the World* 17: 153–156.

Reed, Adam. 2003. *Papua New Guinea's Last Place: Experiences of Constraint in a Postcolonial Prison*. New York: Berghahn Books.

Richards, A. I. 1950. Some Types of Family Structure Amongst the Central Bantu. In *African Systems of Kinship and Marriage*, ed. A. R. Radcliffe-Brown and Daryll Forde, 207–251. London: Oxford University Press.

Riesenfeld, Alphonse. 1950. *The Megalithic Culture of Melanesia*. Leiden: Brill.

Rivers, W. H. R. 1914. *The History of Melanesian Society*. 2 vols. Cambridge: Cambridge University Press.

_____. 1922. The Psychological Factor. In *Essays on the Depopulation of Melanesia*, ed. W. H. R. Rivers, 84–113. Cambridge: Cambridge University Press.

Robbins, Joel. 2002. My Wife Can't Break off Part of her Belief and Give it to Me: Apocalyptic Interrogations of Christian Individualism among the Urapmin of Papua New Guinea. *Paideuma* 48: 189–206.

_____. 2003. On the Paradoxes of Global Pentecostalism and the Perils of Continuity Thinking. *Religion* 33: 221–231.

_____. 2004. *Becoming Sinners: Christianity and Moral Torment in a Papua New Guinea Society*. Berkeley: University of California Press.

Roberts, Stephen H. 1927. *Population Problems of the Pacific*. London: George Routledge.

Rodman, Margaret C. 1987. *Masters of Tradition: Consequences of Customary Land Tenure in Longana, Vanuatu*. Vancouver, BC: University of British Columbia Press.

_____. 1995. Breathing Spaces: Customary Land Tenure in Vanuatu. In *Land, Custom and Practice in the South Pacific*, ed. R. Gerard Ward and Elizabeth Kingdon, 65–108. New York: Cambridge University Press.

Roga, Kenneth, ed. 1989. *Na Tututi Moa pa Ghanogga: Historical Tales of Ranongga Island*. Gizo, Solomon Islands: Western Province Government.

Róheim, Géza. 1950. *Psychoanalysis and Anthropology: Culture, Personality and the Unconscious*. New York: International Universities Press.

Roman Catholic Church, North Solomon Islands. 1900–40. Miscellaneous Papers: Letters, Church Reports, Mission History, Journal. Archives of the Society of Mary (Marist Fathers), Rome. PMB 4.

Rose, Deborah B. 1986. Consciousness and Responsibility in an Aboriginal Religion. In *Traditional Aboriginal Society, A Reader*, ed. W. Edwards, 257–269. Melbourne: Macmillan.

_____. 1988. Jesus and the Dingo. In *Aboriginal Australians and Christian Missions: Ethnographic and Historical Studies*, ed. Tony Swain and Deborah Bird Rose, 362–375. Bedford Park, SA: Australian Association for the Study of Religions.

_____. 1992. *Dingo Makes Us Human: Life and Land in an Aboriginal Australian Culture*. New York: Cambridge University Press.

Ross, Harold M. 1973. *Baegu: Social and Ecological Organization in Malaita, Solomon Islands*. Chicago: University of Illinois Press.

Rumsey, Alan, and James Weiner, eds. 2001. *Mining and Indigenous Lifeworlds in Australia and Papua New Guinea*. Adelaide: Crawford House Publishing.

Sack, Robert. 1980. *Conceptions of Space in Social Thought: A Geographic Perspective*. Minneapolis: University of Minneapolis Press.

_____. 1986. *Human Territoriality: Its Theory and History*. New York: Cambridge University Press.

Saemala, Francis. 1983. Constitutional Development. In *Solomon Islands Politics*, ed. Sue Tarua, 1–8. Suva, Fiji: Institute of Pacific Studies, University of the South Pacific.

Sahlins, Marshall. 1963. Poor Man, Rich Man, Big Man, Chief: Political Types in Melanesia and Polynesia. *Comparative Studies in Society and History* 5(3): 285–303.

_____. 1981. *Historical Metaphors and Mythical Realities: Structure in the Early History of the Sandwich Islands Kingdom*. Ann Arbor: University of Michigan Press.

_____. 1985. *Islands of History*. Chicago: University of Chicago Press.

_____. 1995. *How "Natives" Think: About Captain Cook, For Example*. Chicago: University of Chicago Press.

Sarawia, George. N.d. *They Came to my Island: The Beginnings of the Mission in the Banks Islands*. Trans. D. A. Rawcliffe. Taroanaiara, Solomon Islands.

Saura, Bruno. 2002. Continuity of Bodies: The Infant's Placenta and the Island's Navel in Eastern Polynesia. *Journal of the Polynesian Society* 111(2): 127–145.

Sayes, Shelley A. 1976. The Ethnohistory of Arosi, San Cristobal. Master's thesis, University of Auckland.

Scheffler, Harold W. 1965. *Choiseul Island Social Structure*. Berkeley: University of California Press.

_____. 1971. The Solomon Islands: Seeking a New Land Custom. In *Land Tenure in the Pacific*, ed. Ron Crocombe, 273–291. New York: Oxford University Press.

Schieffelin, Edward L. 1976. *The Sorrow of the Lonely and the Burning of the Dancers*. New York: St. Martin's Press.

Schneider, David M. 1965. Some Muddles in the Models: Or, How the System Really Works. In *The Relevance of Models for Social Anthropology*, ed. Michael Banton, 25–85. New York: Tavistock.

Schneider, Gerhard. 1998. Reinventing Identities: Redefining Cultural Concepts in the Struggle between Villagers in Munda, Roviana Lagoon, New Georgia Island, Solomon Islands, for the Control of Land. In *Pacific Answers to Western Hegemony: Cultural Practices of Identity Construction*, ed. Jürg Wassmann, 191–211. New York: Berg.

Schrempp, Gregory A. 1992. *Magical Arrows: The Maori, the Greeks, and the Folklore of the Universe*. Madison: University of Wisconsin Press.

Schwimmer, Erik. 1973. *Exchange in the Social Structure of the Orokaiva: Traditional and Emergent Ideologies in the Northern District of Papua*. New York: St. Martin's Press.

Scott, Michael W. 1990–91. Constitutions of Maasina Rule: Timothy George and the Iora. *Chicago Anthropology Exchange* 19: 41–65.

_____. 2000. Ignorance is Cosmos; Knowledge is Chaos: Articulating a Cosmological Polarity in the Solomon Islands. *Social Analysis* 44(2): 56–83.

_____. 2001. Auhenua: Land, Lineage, and Ontology in Arosi (Solomon Islands). Ph.D. dissertation, University of Chicago.

_____. 2005a. Hybridity, Vacuity, and Blockage: Visions of Chaos from Anthropological Theory, Island Melanesia, and Central Africa. *Comparative Studies in Society and History* 47(1): 190–216.

_____. 2005b. "I Was Like Abraham": Notes on the Anthropology of Christianity from the Solomon Islands. *Ethnos* 70(1): 101–125.

_____. 2007. Proto-People and Precedence: Encompassing Euroamericans through Narratives of "First Contact" in Solomon Islands. In *Exchange and Sacrifice*, ed. Pamela J. Stewart and Andrew Strathern. Durham, NC: Carolina Academic Press.

Sillitoe, Paul. 1998. *An Introduction to the Anthropology of Melanesia: Culture and Tradition*. New York: Cambridge University Press.

Silverman, Eric Kline. 1996. The Gender of the Cosmos: Totemism, Society and Embodiment in the Sepik River. *Oceania* 67: 30–49.

Silverstein, Michael. 1998. The Improvisational Performance of Culture in Real-time Discursive Practice. In *Creativity in Performance*, ed. R. Keith Sawyer, 265–312. Greenwich, CT: Ablex Publishing Corporation.

Smith, Anthony D. 2003. *Chosen Peoples*. New York: Oxford University Press.

Smith, Brian K. 1989. *Reflections on Resemblance, Ritual, and Religion*. New York: Oxford University Press.

Smith, Grafton Elliot. 1915. *The Migrations of Early Culture*. Manchester: Manchester University Press.

_____. 1924. Preface to *The Threshold of the Pacific*, by Charles E. Fox, v–ix. London: Kegan Paul, Trench, and Trubner.

Sohmer, Sara H. 1988. "A Selection of Fundamentals": The Intellectual Background of the Melanesian Mission of the Church of England, 1850–1914. Ph.D. dissertation, University of Hawai'i.

_____. 1994. Christianity Without Civilization: Anglican Sources for an Alternative Nineteenth-Century Mission Methodology. *Journal of Religious History* 18: 174–197.

South Sea Evangelical Mission (formerly Queensland Kanaka Mission). [*ND*] 1909–37? *South Sea Evangelical Mission* (A series of variously titled numbered letters written by Northcote Deck), Sydney.

_____. [*NIV*] 1895–? *Not in Vain* (Annual Reports and Quarterly Newsletters), Sydney.

Statistics Office. 1997. Report 2: Village Resources Survey 1995/96. *Statistical Bulletin* 10. Honiara: Ministry of Finance.

Stewart, Pamela J., and Andrew Strathern. 2001. Substance Transfer: Conception, Growth, and Nurturance in Highlands Papua New Guinea. In *Humors and Substances: Ideas of the Body in New Guinea*, ed. Pamela J. Stewart and Andrew Strathern, 83–97. Westport, CT: Bergin and Garvey.

_____. 2002a. *Remaking the World: Myth, Mining, and Ritual change among the Duna of Papua New Guinea*. Washington, DC: Smithsonian Institution Press.

_____. 2002b. Power and Placement in Blood Practices. *Ethnology* 41(4): 349–363.

Stocking, George W. 1995. *After Tylor: British Social Anthropology, 1888–1951*. Madison: University of Wisconsin Press.

Strathern, Andrew. 1972. *One Father, One Blood: Descent and Group Structure among the Melpa People*. London: Tavistock.

_____. 1973. Kinship, Descent and Locality: Some New Guinea Examples. In *The Character of Kinship*, ed. J. Goody, 21–33. Cambridge: Cambridge University Press.

_____. 1979. "We are all of one father here": Models of Descent in New Guinea Highlands Societies. In *Segmentary Lineage Systems Reconsidered* (Queen's University Papers in Social Anthropology 4), ed. Ladislav Holy, 145–155. Belfast: Department of Social Anthropology, Queen's University.

Strathern, Andrew, and Pamela J. Stewart. 2000. *The Python's Back: Pathways of Comparison Between Indonesia and Melanesia*. Westport, CT: Bergin and Garvey.

_____. 2004. *Empowering the Past, Confronting the Future: The Duna People of Papua New Guinea*. New York: Palgrave.

Strathern, Marilyn. 1988. *The Gender of the Gift: Problems with Women and Problems with Society in Melanesia*. Berkeley: University of California Press.

_____. 1992. *Reproducing the Future: Anthropology, Kinship and the New Reproductive Technologies*. New York: Routledge.

_____. 1999. *Property, Substance and Effect: Anthropological Essays on Persons and Things.* New Brunswick, NJ: Athlone Press.

Stritecky, Jolene Marie. 2001. Israel, America, and the Ancestors: Narratives of Spiritual Warfare in a Pentecostal Denomination in Solomon Islands. *Journal of Ritual Studies* 15(2): 62–78.

Swain, Tony. 1993. *A Place for Strangers: Towards a History of Australian Aboriginal Being.* New York: Cambridge University Press.

Tahiti British Consulate Papers. Vol. 5: In-Letters, 1857–1866. Mitchell Library, Sydney. Microfilm copy at the Hamilton Library, University of Hawai'i (Microfilm No. S01356).

Taro, Tarcisius K. 1990. A Socio-political Pressure Group: A Study of the Moro Movement of Guadalcanal. *'O'o: A Journal of Solomon Islands Studies* 2(2): 42–62.

Taylor, Christopher C. 1999. *Sacrifice as Terror: The Rwandan Genocide of 1994.* New York: Berg.

Thomas, Nicholas. 1990. Sanitation and Seeing: The Creation of State Power in Early Colonial Fiji. *Comparative Studies in Society and History* 32: 149–170.

_____. 1991. *Entangled Objects: Exchange, Material Culture, and Colonialism in the Pacific.* Cambridge: Harvard University Press.

_____. 1997. *In Oceania: Visions, Artifacts, Histories.* Durham, NC: Duke University Press.

Thune, Carl E. 1983. Kula Traders and Lineage Members: The Structure of Village and Kula Exchange on Normanby Island. In *The Kula: New Perspectives on Massim Exchange,* ed. Jerry W. Leach and Edmund Leach, 345–368. New York: Cambridge University Press.

_____. 1989. Death and Matrilineal Reincorporation on Normanby Island. In *Death Rituals and Life in the Societies of the Kula Ring,* ed. Frederick H. Damon and Roy Wagner, 153–178. DeKalb, IL: Northern Illinois University Press.

_____. 1990. Fathers, Aliens, and Brothers: Building a Social World in Loboda Village Church Services. In *Christianity in Oceania: Ethnographic Perspectives,* ed. John Barker, 101–125. New York: University Press of America.

Tiffany, Sharon W. 1983. Customary Land Disputes, Courts, and African Models in the Solomon Islands. *Oceania* 53: 277–290.

Tippett, Alan R. 1967. *Solomon Islands Christianity: A Study of Growth and Obstruction.* London: Lutterworth Press.

Toren, Christina. 2004. Becoming a Christian in Fiji: An Ethnographic Study of Ontogeny. *Journal of the Royal Anthropological Institute* 10(1): 221–240.

Traube, Elizabeth G. 1986. *Cosmology and Social Life: Ritual Exchange among the Mambai of East Timor.* Chicago: University of Chicago Press.

Trompf, Garry W., ed. 1987. *The Gospel is Not Western: Black Theologies from the Southwest Pacific*. Maryknoll, NY: Orbis Books.

Tryon, Darrell T., and Brian D. Hackman. 1983. *Solomon Islands Languages: An Internal Classification*. Pacific Linguistics, Series C. No. 72. Canberra: Department of Linguistics, Research School of Pacific Studies, Australian National University.

Turner, James West. 1997. Continuity and Constraint: Reconstructing the Concept of Tradition from a Pacific Perspective. *Contemporary Pacific* 9(2): 345–381.

Turner, Terence. 1988. Ethno-Ethnohistory: Myth and History in Native South American Representations of Contact with Western Society. In *Rethinking History and Myth: Indigenous South American Perspectives on the Past*, ed. Jonathan D. Hill, 235–281. Chicago: University of Illinois Press.

Tuwere, I. S. 2002. *Vanua: Towards a Fijian Theology of Place*. Suva, Fiji: Institute of Pacific Studies, University of the South Pacific.

Valeri, Valerio. 1982. The Transformation of a Transformation: A Structural Essay on an Aspect of Hawaiian History (1809–1819). *Social Analysis* 10 (May): 3–41.

_____. 1985. *Kingship and Sacrifice: Ritual and Society in Ancient Hawaii*. Trans. Paula Wissing. Chicago: University of Chicago Press.

_____. 1989. Death in Heaven: Myth and Rites of Kinship in Tongan Kingship. *History and Anthropology* 4: 209–247.

_____. 1990. Diarchy and History in Hawaii and Tonga. In *Culture and History in the Pacific*, ed. J. Siikala, 45–79. Helsinki: Finish Anthropological Society.

_____. 1995. Miti Cosmogonici e Ordine. *Parole Chiave* 7/8: 93–110.

_____. 2001. *Fragments from Forests and Libraries: A Collection of Essays by Valerio Valeri*, ed. Janet Hoskins. Durham, NC: Carolina Academic Press.

Verguet, Léopold. 1848. Lettre du P. Verguet, Missionaire Apostolique de la Société de Marie, à son Père (Arossi, San-Christoval, le 24 juin 1846). *Annales de la Propagation de la Foi* 20: 434–446.

_____. 1854. *Histoire de la première mission catholique au Vicariat de Mélanésie, par C. M. Léopold Verguet, Missionnaire Apostolique, S.M. de 1844 à 1884*. Carcassonne: P. Labau.

_____. 1885. Arossi, ou, San Cristoval et ses habitants. *Revue d'Ethnographie* 4: 193–232.

Viveiros de Castro, Eduardo. 1999. Comments on Nurit Bird-David, "Animism" Revisited: Personhood, Environment, and Relational Epistemology. *Current Anthropology* 40(Supplement): S79–S80.

Wagner, Roy. 1967. *The Curse of Souw*. Chicago: University of Chicago Press.

_____. 1974. Are there Social Groups in the New Guinea Highlands? In *Frontiers of Anthropology*, ed. M. Leaf, 95–122. New York: Nostrand.

_____. 1977. Analogic Kinship: A Daribi Example. *American Ethnologist* 4(4): 623–642.

_____. 1986. *Asiwinarong: Ethos, Image, and Social Power among the Usen Barok of New Ireland*. Princeton: Princeton University Press.

_____. 1991. The Fractal Person. In *Big Men and Great Men: Personifications of Power in Melanesia*, ed. Maurice Godelier and Marilyn Strathern, 159–173. Cambridge: Cambridge University Press.

Watson, James B. 1965. Loose Structure Loosely Construed: Groupless Grouping in Gadsup. *Oceania* 35(4): 267–271.

Webster, John. 1863? *The Last Cruise of* The Wanderer. Sydney: F. Cunninghame.

Weiner, Annette B. 1976. *Women of Value, Men of Renown: New Perspectives in Trobriand Exchange*. Austin, TX: University of Texas Press.

_____. 1978. The Reproductive Model in Trobriand Society. *Mankind* 11: 175–186.

_____. 1980. Reproduction: A Replacement for Reciprocity. *American Ethnologist* 7(1): 71–85.

_____. 1988. *The Trobrianders of Papua New Guinea*. New York: Holt, Rinehart and Winston.

_____. 1992. *Inalienable Possessions: The Paradox of Keeping-While-Giving*. Berkeley: University of California Press.

Weiner, James F. 1988. *The Heart of the Pearl Shell: The Mythological Dimension of Foi Sociality*. Berkeley: University of California Press.

_____. 1995. *The Lost Drum: The Myth of Sexuality in Papua New Guinea and Beyond*. Madison: University of Wisconsin Press.

_____. 2001. Afterword. In *Emplaced Myth: Space, Narrative, and Knowledge in Aboriginal Australia and Papua New Guinea*, ed. Alan Rumsey and James F. Weiner, 233–245. Honolulu: University of Hawai‘i Press.

Westermark, George. 1997. Clan Claims: Land, Law and Violence in the Papua New Guinea Eastern Highlands. *Oceania* 67(3): 218–233.

Western Pacific High Commission. 1915–18. Records of the WPHC Secretariat. Inwards Correspondence General. Foreign and Commonwealth Office, London. Microfilm copies at Auckland University Library (Microfilm No. 576) and the Hamilton Library, University of Hawai‘i (Microfilm No. S00522).

_____. 1875–1914. Records of the WPHC Secretariat. Series 4. Inwards Correspondence General. Foreign and Commonwealth Office, London. Microfilm copies at Auckland University Library (Microfilm No. 576) and the Hamilton Library, University of Hawai'i (Microfilm No. S00522).

White, Geoffrey M. 1978. Big Men and Church Men: Social Images in Santa Isabel, Solomon Islands. Ph.D. dissertation, University of California, San Diego.

_____. 1983. War, Peace, and Piety in Santa Isabel, Solomon Islands. In *The Pacification of Melanesia*, ed. Margaret Rodman and Matthew Cooper, 109–139. New York: University Press of America.

_____. 1988. Symbols of Solidarity in the Christianization of Santa Isabel, Solomon Islands. In *Culture and Christianity: The Dialectics of Transformation*, ed. George R. Saunders, 11–31. New York: Greenwood Press.

_____. 1991. *Identity Through History: Living Stories in a Solomon Islands Society*. New York: Cambridge University Press.

_____. 1993. Three Discourses of Custom. *Anthropological Forum* 6(4): 475–494.

White, Geoffrey M., David Gegeo, David Akin, and Karen Watson-Gegeo, eds. 1988. *The Big Death: Solomon Islanders Remember World War II*. Suva: Institute of Pacific Studies.

Whiteman, Darrell L. 1983. *Melanesians and Missionaries: An Ethnohistorical Study of Social and Religious Change in the Southwest Pacific*. Pasadena, CA: William Carey Library.

Williams, Nancy. 1986. *The Yolngu and their Land: A System of Land Tenure and the Fight for its Recognition*. Stanford: Stanford University Press.

Williksen-Bakker, Solrun. 1990. Vanua: A Symbol with Many Ramifications in Fijian Culture. *Ethnos* 55(3–4): 232–247.

Wilson, Cecil. 1932. *The Wake of the Southern Cross: Work and Adventures in the South Seas*. London: John Murray.

_____. [D] Diaries of Bishop Cecil Wilson, 1894–1911. 6 vols. Church of Melanesia Archives, Item no. 45, Solomon Islands National Archives, Honiara. PMB 530.

Wiltgen, Ralph M. 1981. *The Founding of the Catholic Church in Oceania, 1825–1850*. Canberra: Australian National University Press.

Woodford, Charles M. 1922. The Solomon Islands. In *Essays on the Depopulation of Melanesia*, ed. W. H. R. Rivers, 69–77. Cambridge: Cambridge University Press.

Worsley, Peter. 1968. *The Trumpet Shall Sound: A Study of "Cargo" Cults in Melanesia*. New York: Schocken Books.

Yonge, Charlotte Mary. 1874. *Life of John Coleridge Patteson: Missionary Bishop of the Melanesian Islands*. 2 vols. London: Macmillian.

Young, Michael W. 1987. The Tusk, the Flute and the Serpent: Disguise and Revelation in Goodenough Mythology. In *Dealing with Inequality: Analysing Gender Relations in Melanesia and Beyond*, ed. Marilyn Strathern, 229–254. New York: Cambridge University Press.

_____. 1997. Commemorating Missionary Heroes: Local Christianity and Narratives of Nationalism. In *Narratives of Nation in the South Pacific*, ed. Ton Otto and Nicholas Thomas, 91–132. Amsterdam: Harwood Academic Publishers.

INDEX

Note: Some page numbers refer to footnoted text.

Aboriginal Australia, 12, 131, 229, 306

adaro, 327; spirits of the dead known as, xxx, 172–187, 220, 305, 315–316, 322; spirits other than those of the dead known as, 98–100, 159–161, 204, 295, 315–316; as term for name of a deceased person, 195–199, 220. *See also* ancestors; *hi'ona*; illness; names, personal; Satan.

Adaro lineage, 164, 195, 204, 295

adoption, 78, 146–148, 152, 154, 227, 283, 285, 292. *See also* buying people to lengthen a lineage.

afterbirth. *See* gendered powers and substances.

agency, 4, 18–24, 92–93, 163–164, 201, 216, 220, 240–242, 305, 318–319

Agunua. *See* A'unua.

Akin, David, 7, 286

Allan, Colin H., 16, 70, 101–102

Amaeo lineage, 125, 138, 139–141, 158, 159, 164, 195, 201, 203, 208–209, 291, 295, 323

Americans, 108–109, 112, 114–116, 118–119, 121–122, 126–128

ancestors; actions of as models for present practice, 241–243 [*see also* neo-topogonic activities]; as particular spirits or matrilineal essence, 194–199, 279, 298–300; as primordial or historical agents, xxvi, xxvii, xxviii, 7, 13, 14, 33, 34, 69, 70, 74, 91, 115, 127, 134, 138, 157, 159, 165, 166–168, 175–176, 189–199, 201–205, 207–209, 212–217, 219–221, 223, 225, 228, 231, 234, 235–238, 241–243, 249, 259, 282, 288–291, 292, 308, 319; as spirits, xxviii, xxxi, 7, 9, 34, 71, 74, 81, 142, 154, 163, 164, 172–187, 188, 193–199, 203, 216, 219–221, 222, 223, 226, 227, 230, 234, 249–250, 262, 282, 294–295, 299–300, 302–303, 305, 315, 316. *See also adaro*; shrines, pre-Christian.

Anglicanism, 9, 49, 50–51, 84, 100, 168, 172, 173, 179, 180, 268–270, 302, 304. *See also* Church of Melanesia; Melanesian Mission; missiology and mission methodology.

anthropogony, 139–155, 209, 221. *See also* childbirth; cosmogony.

Comparative Austronesian Project, 23–24, 70–71, 138, 191, 205. *See also* Austronesian language family; botanic metaphors; precedence.

congregational life, xxv, 39, 40, 46, 48–56, 57, 58, 184, 261, 314, 316, 318. *See also* church day feast; clergy, indigenous; lay leadership.

consensus that coastal *auhenua* are extinct, xxvii, xxix–xxxi, 61, 63–67, 69–70, 72, 74, 127, 231, 244–249, 251, 252, 257, 325

conversion, 79, 96, 97–100, 117, 120, 269, 272, 305. *See also* ethno-theology; missiology and mission methodology.

Coppet, Daniel de, 34, 77, 79, 127, 194, 203, 211, 218, 221

copra, 40, 42, 58, 61–65, 95, 102, 107, 129, 169, 171, 189, 197

cosmogony; and anthropogony, 139–155; and anti-cosmogony, 139, 155–161, 242, 245, 250; comparative data on, 4–5, 10–12, 13, 19–20, 23, 30, 35, 131, 148, 149, 242–243; mono-genetic, 10–12, 14–16, 23, 30, 133, 149, 242–243, 294; poly-genetic, 10, 12–13, 15–17, 34, 132–133, 207, 230, 234, 246, 249–250, 266, 291, 294; processual nature of, 10, 32–36, 133, 136, 202, 209, 218, 222, 228, 230, 234, 242, 250; and sacrifice, 148–149, 294. *See also* proto-people; topogonic primordiality; utopic primordiality.

cosmology, xxxi, 3–5, 10–13, 15, 18–22, 30–31, 33–34, 35–36, 40, 76, 148–149, 152, 220–221, 230, 242, 245, 265, 266–268, 291, 307, 313, 318, 324. *See also* cosmogony; ontology.

Councils of Elders, 120. *See also* Native Councils.

courts and court cases, 71, 73–74, 108, 232, 250, 253, 257–258, 320, 322. *See also* Native Courts.

creation. *See* cosmogony.

creator. *See* God, Christian; Hatoibwari; Kauraha; snakes.

cultural change, xxix–xxx, xxxii, 3, 20, 34–35, 36, 44, 45–46, 53–56, 70, 74–76, 79–82, 129, 199, 202, 227–228, 229–231, 240–243, 257–258, 259–260, 261–262, 265–268, 300, 301–306, 319, 322, 324–326. *See also* colonial reorganization projects; custom; development; ontology-centered methodology; onto-praxis.

custom (*ringeringe*; *kastom*), 6–10, 53–54, 75, 91, 105, 110, 111, 119–128, 182, 241, 248, 253, 254–260, 264–265, 301, 310–312, 313, 316–323, 325–326. *See also* cultural change; *kastom buk*; knowledgeable people; land tenure; original lineages of the land [ethic of]; tabu.

dark time, xxx, 173, 302, 320–322. *See also* pagans.

Davenport, William H., 6, 286, 315–316

Davies, Roy J., 118

death. *See adaro*; ancestors; *aunga*; Marapa; mortuary practices; origin of death, myths of.